© 2013 Abbott

Library of Congress Control Number: 2012901077

ISBN: 978-1-88277-133-2

Published by Abbott
100 Abbott Park Road
Abbott Park, IL 60064-6400, U.S.A.
847 937 6100
www.abbott.com

Abbott trademarks appear in italics.

Special Acknowledgment

The culture of an organization is kept alive and thriving by those people who care enough to work to preserve it and transmit it to others. And when a history is as long and full as Abbott's, that takes great commitment and considerable effort. At Abbott we do this through the careful maintenance of our corporate archives; through exhibits at Abbott House, our heritage center; through ongoing communications that draw on our 125-year tradition; and, now, through this commemorative book. As these pages make clear, many, many people have contributed to making this great history. And many have been involved in the creation of this book and our other efforts to carry our proud heritage forward. I would like to thank all of these friends and colleagues, who are named on the Acknowledgments page, for their dedicated stewardship; but I wish to call out here, for particular recognition, our company's devoted historians, Karmin Maritato and Rick Moser, for whom keeping our history alive is a true passion, and this book a labor of love.

Miles

Contents

A Message from our Chairman and Chief Executive Officer

Welcome to this celebration of Abbott's 125th anniversary. If you've received this book, you already know our company. But few know the full breadth and depth of the great story that began when Dr. Wallace Abbott began his business in 1888 — the story captured in these pages.

As the heft of this volume suggests, Abbott's history is not only long, but highly eventful. In these pages you'll learn about critical breakthroughs in the history of medical science: the early development of the scientific practice of pharmacy, as well as other major areas of modern medicine, such as intravenous solutions, immunodiagnostics, and scientifically formulated nutritional products. You'll read of breakthroughs in anesthesia, in anti-infectives, in biologics, in medical devices — innovations that changed the practice of medicine and the lives of countless beneficiaries.

For 125 years our company has carried forward Dr. Abbott's original vision of advancing the state of medical science to meet people's most fundamental need: their health. But, over the years, we've done this in more ways than the Doctor could ever have imagined — in fields that were unknown in his time, through technologies that were undreamt of; around the world; across the spectrum of health care, and at every stage of life.

As you read this proud history, one key theme becomes very clear: successful change, across successive eras. Abbott has thrived for a century and a quarter because it has continually adapted to the changing environment around it. Science, the practice of medicine, our markets, regulations, geopolitical conditions — all of these have been in constant flux throughout Abbott's long and productive history. We're here and strong today because we have succeeded in transforming our company with the times. That's why, today, our businesses are ready for their next 125 years — to keep delivering the future of health care for the sake of all the people we serve.

I hope you'll enjoy this story of a great company, of the people who've made it so, and of the good it's done for so many for so long — a legacy now carried forward by two leading companies: Abbott and AbbVie. We present it to you with tremendous pride in our past — and an equal commitment to making the future just as great.

Sincerely,

Miles D. White

Miles D. White
Chairman of the Board and Chief Executive Officer

The Abbott Promise

A Promise for Life
Turning Science into Caring

We are here for the people we serve in their pursuit of healthy lives. This has been the way of Abbott for more than a century — passionately and thoughtfully translating science into lasting contributions to health.

Our products encircle life, from newborns to aging adults, from nutrition and diagnostics through medical care and pharmaceutical therapy.

Caring is central to the work we do and defines our responsibility to those we serve:

We advance leading-edge science and technologies that hold the potential for significant improvements to health and to the practice of health care.

We value our diversity — that of our products, technologies, markets and people — and believe that diverse perspectives combined with shared goals inspire new ideas and better ways of addressing changing health needs.

We focus on exceptional performance — a hallmark of Abbott people worldwide — demanding of ourselves and each other because our work impacts people's lives.

We strive to earn the trust of those we serve — by committing to the highest standards of quality, excellence in personal relationships, and behavior characterized by honesty, fairness and integrity.

We sustain success — for our business and the people we serve — by staying true to key tenets upon which our company was founded over a century ago: innovative care and a desire to make a meaningful difference in all that we do.

The promise of our company is in the promise that our work holds for health and life.

Abbott at a Glance
1888–Today

1888–1900

1888
Dr. Wallace C. Abbott, a 30-year-old practicing physician in Chicago, begins making granules of "alkaloidal" medicine—remedies containing the active ingredients of plants and herbs—in the rear of his People's Drug Store. First-year total sales reach $2,000.

1890
The first non-family employee, Miss Jo Fletcher, is hired for $12 a week. Yearly sales climb to $8,000.

1891
Until now relying strictly on word of mouth, Dr. Abbott places his first ad, in the journal *Medical World*. Pitched at doctors, it costs 25 cents — and returns $8 in orders.

1894
The firm is christened The Abbott Alkaloidal Company. Dr. Abbott publishes the *Alkaloidal Clinic*, a 36-page journal founded by his friend, Dr. William T. Thackeray. It contains articles on averting and treating disease as well as eye-grabbing ads.

1896
Dr. Abbott is an early proponent of employee health. Workers can earn gold watches by giving up smoking, and by riding bicycles to work. Dr. Abbott's motto: "Think right, feel right, be right, live and let live: do the square thing, have a conscience and use it."

1897
Dr. William F. Waugh is hired to edit the *Alkaloidal Clinic*, and to co-write with Dr. Abbott a standard reference work, the *Text Book of Alkaloidal Therapeutics*.

1898
Sales exceed the $100,000 mark.

1900–1910

1900
Dr. Abbott's business is officially incorporated in Illinois as The Abbott Alkaloidal Company.

1901
With its business growing, the company builds a four-story brick building to house The Clinic Publishing Company.

1902
The Alkaloidal Clinic reaches almost 200 pages in length, and goes to 1 out of 4 physicians in the United States. Full-page ads cost $55, yearly subscriptions $1.

1904
The erudite Dr. Alfred S. Burdick, editor of the *Medical Standard*, joins the company, serving as an editor and high-level aide for $35 a week. He will eventually become company president.

Products and publications ▶ contain the company's first logo, a circle inscribed with the words "Purity, Accuracy Guaranteed," with Dr. Abbott's initials entwined in the center.

S. DeWitt Clough joins Abbott as a copywriter. He will rise to president and chairman of the board.

1905
A fire guts the 50,000-square-foot printing plant, though a lucky breeze saves the pharmaceutical production facility.

▼

1906
Construction of a new laboratory and manufacturing facility, complete with sprinklers and power plant, was supervised by future Chairman Edward H. Ravenscroft.

1910–1920

1910
The company has agencies and branches in London, Toronto, Bombay, New York, San Francisco and Seattle. The customer list totals 50,000 of the 130,000 physicians in the United States, as well as 1,000 in Europe and 500 in Latin America.

1911
The sales force expands to 35.

1912
Revenues decline for the first time as demand for alkaloidal products drops off.

1913
Future board chairman James F. "Sunny Jim" Stiles, Jr. joins the company.

1914
With Dr. Abbott's blessing, Dr. Burdick switches the company's focus from alkaloidal to synthetic medicines. The First World War breaks out, creating a pressing need for more effective antiseptics on battlefields and in field hospitals.

1915
The name of the firm is changed from The Abbott Alkaloidal Company to Abbott Laboratories.

1916
Abbott produces its first synthetic medicine, *Chlorazene*, a breakthrough antiseptic developed by British chemist Dr. Henry Dakin to treat wounded soldiers.

1917
Abbott manufactures another invention of Dakin's, *Halazone*, which makes contaminated water drinkable.

1918
Sales top $1 million for the first time.

Future president, chairman, and National Inventors Hall of Fame member Ernest H. Volwiler joins the company.

1919
Elmer B. Vliet, a former student of Ernest Volwiler, joins Abbott. He, too, will become company chairman.

1920–1930

1920
Abbott begins construction of a new headquarters located in the town of North Chicago.

1921
Dr. Abbott dies after 33 years as head of the company he founded, and Dr. Burdick succeeds him as president.

1922
Dr. Volwiler and Dr. Roger Adams develop *Butyn*, a fast-acting, non-habit-forming topical anesthetic.

1924
Dr. Abbott's widow, Clara, dies, and her will establishes the Clara Abbott Trust. The bequest will, in time, lead to the creation of the Clara Abbott Foundation.

1925
All facilities are moved to North Chicago, and the old plant is sold for $300,000 to G.D. Searle & Co.

1927
Abbott develops the antiseptic *Metaphen* and the antisyphilitic *Bismarsen*.

1928
Abbott acquires pharmaceutical manufacturer John T. Milliken and Company for $125,000, along with its 40 salesmen, technical experts, and list of 20,000 retail pharmacists.

1929
Abbott is listed on the Chicago Stock Exchange for $32 a share; the stock closes at $40.50 on the first day of trading.

1930–1940

1930
Dr. Volwiler and Dr. Donalee L. Tabern create the fast-acting anesthetic *Nembutal*, which rarely produces nausea or stupor in patients.

Abbott acquires medical products maker Swan-Myers. Its president, Rolly M. Cain, and his son, George R. Cain, both will become Abbott presidents.

1932
At the height of the Great Depression, Abbott manages to rapidly expand. "Few of the leading industrial organizations of the country," notes *Nation's Commerce*, "can show a sounder record for the past year than the Abbott Laboratories."

Abbott manufactures *Haliver Oil*, a vitamin product derived from the livers of halibut.

1933
Abbott offers its employees inexpensive health and accident insurance.

Edward H. Ravenscroft becomes chairman of the board.

1934
Under sales executives Manuel Doblado and Raymond E. Horn, Abbott greatly expands its sales presence in Mexico, paving the way for significant international expansion.

1935
Abbott begins to manufacture intravenous (IV) fluids. In time, Abbott will become the largest supplier of IV solutions in the United States.

1937
After six years of research by Drs. Volwiler and Tabern, Abbott introduces *Pentothal*. A fast-acting anesthetic injected directly into the bloodstream, *Pentothal* will become the world's most widely used anesthetic.

Abbott sets up subsidiaries in Buenos Aires, Argentina; Rio de Janeiro, Brazil; Havana, Cuba; and Manila, The Philippines; and a new manufacturing center is established near London, England.

1939
Sales reach the $10 million mark.

1940–1950

1940
The Clara Abbott Foundation, established by Dr. Abbott's widow, begins to distribute funds to aid Abbott employees in financial distress.

1942
At the behest of the U.S. Government, Abbott works with a consortium of pharmaceutical makers to ramp up production of penicillin for wartime use.

1943
Far-sighted President S. DeWitt Clough sets up planning committees to draw up the Abbott 1950 Plan, a blueprint for transitioning and expanding Abbott in the post-war world.

Abbott commissions popular artists to create paintings like this one for use in war-bond sales drives.

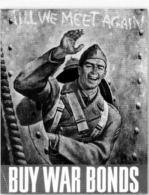

1945
For much of the decade, Abbott scientists, such as Dr. Marvin A. Spielman and Dr. Richard K. Richards, conduct research leading to the anti-epileptic drug *Tridione*, beginning Abbott's long leadership in treating this disease.

1948
Abbott becomes the first U.S. drug firm to make radiopharmaceuticals for medicine and research.

1949
Abbott puts out 74 new medical devices, pharmaceuticals, or drug reformulations, its biggest introduction of products to date. For the decade, there are 518 new Abbott products.

1950–1960

1950
Abbott introduces *Sucaryl*, an artificial sweetener, creating a new food category.

1951 ►
In a move into a mass consumer market, Abbott introduces *Selsun Suspension* shampoo for dandruff control.

1952
Abbott's nuclear lab for making radiomedicines begins shipping product to customers.

James F. Stiles is named chairman of the board.

1955
The U.S. Pharmacopoeia, the standard-setting authority for pharmaceuticals, formally lists its first atomic medicine: Abbott's radio-iodine.

Abbott installs its first digital computer.

1956
Abbott outfits a purchased dairy farm in Long Grove, Illinois, creating a new agricultural products division for the development of drugs for farm animals and improved crops.

1957
Sales reach $100 million.

1958
Ernest H. Volwiler is named chairman of the board.

1959
Abbott introduces 40 new products.

Elmer B. Vliet succeeds Ernest Volwiler as chairman of the board.

Abbott introduces a new logo, a stylized letter "A". It appears as part of a major new corporate identity initiative. A classic of industrial design and one of the industry's most recognizable marks, it is still in use today, the centerpiece of a rebranding effort almost 50 years later.

▼

1960–1970

1960 ►
Abbott's restructuring in the 1960s under President George Cain would be featured in the 2001 best-seller, *Good to Great: Why Some Companies Make the Leap … and Others Don't*. Author Jim Collins chose Abbott as one of 11 companies — out of 1,435 — that had the product, service, organizational, and people quality to engender truly great performance.

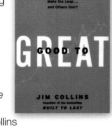

1962
George R. Cain is named chairman of the board.

1964 ►
The company acquires M&R Dietetics, the manufacturer of *Similac* and other infant formulas, the company's largest acquisition to that time.

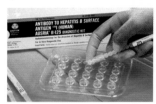

1967
Abbott's continuous international expansion is highlighted by construction of an antibiotics facility in Puerto Rico. This will grow to become one of the company's largest locations worldwide.

1969
Abbott buys Chicago's Murine Company, acquiring its *Murine* eye drops, *Lensine* solution for contact lenses, and *Clear Eyes* for dry, red, itchy eyes.

▼

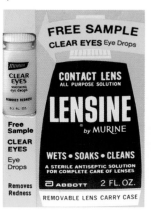

1970–1980

1970
The FDA bans the low-calorie sweetener *Sucaryl* in the United States. As a result, Abbott loses $19 million in annual profits.

After its removal from the market, *Sucaryl* is proven to be safe and harmless.

1972
The ABA-100 blood chemistry analyzer is introduced. Abbott also introduces *Ausria*, a breakthrough radioimmunoassay test for detecting serum hepatitis.

▼

1973
A new diagnostics division is formed that encompasses biologicals, radiopharmaceuticals, and clinical instrumentation. The aim is to devise automated diagnostic tests that are accurate, simple, and low in cost.

The company introduces ► *Ensure*, its first adult medical nutritional.

1976
Edward J. Ledder is named chairman of the board.

The antibiotic erythromycin, available since the 1940s, proves effective in fighting the deadly outbreak of Legionnaire's disease that is one of the year's top healthcare stories.

Abbott sales exceed one billion dollars.

1977
Abbott and Takeda Chemical Industries, Ltd. of Japan form TAP Pharmaceutical Products. It goes on to become one of the most successful joint-venture companies ever.

The VP clinical analyzer reaches the market; it can inexpensively and accurately test 400 blood samples per hour.

1980–1990

1981

The *TDx* therapeutic drug monitoring system is introduced, allowing physicians to adjust the doses of medicine in patients' bloodstreams, avoiding adverse reactions and expensive hospital stays.

Robert A. Schoellhorn is named chairman of the board.

1982

A pharmaceutical resurgence hits high gear: Seven new drugs are introduced that will account for 17 percent of sales by 1985.

1985

U.S. Health and Human Services Secretary Margaret Heckler, left, and FDA Commissioner Frank Young, right, call a press conference to hail approval of an Abbott breakthrough: the first licensed test to identify the HIV virus in blood.

1986

Abbott introduces 70 new diagnostics, including *TestPack*, a diagnostic tool for the doctor's office that can rapidly test for conditions such as strep throat, Chlamydia, and viral infection.

1987

The *IMx*, a blood chemistry analyzer for medium-sized laboratories, is introduced, along with tests for cancer, heart conditions, anemia, hepatitis, and other illnesses.

1990–2000

1990

Duane L. Burnham is named chairman of the board.

1991

Abbott develops the first automated test for monitoring prostate specific antigen, PSA, used to screen for prostate cancer.

1994

AxSYM, an immunoassay diagnostic system for hospitals and high-volume labs, is introduced. It can handle more than 85 different immunoassays.

1995

The anti-epileptic drug *Depakote* is approved for treatment of bipolar disorder, or manic depression, which becomes its primary use.

Total company sales reach the $10 billion mark.

1996

Abbott acquires MediSense Inc., an innovator in blood glucose monitoring.

The FDA approves *Norvir*, a protease inhibitor that is a major breakthrough in the treatment of HIV/AIDS. For this achievement, Abbott is later awarded the Prix Galien, the pharmaceutical industry's highest scientific honor.

1998

Abbott introduces *Glucerna*, a group of cereals, health shakes, and snack bars formulated specifically for diabetics and others with dietary restrictions.

1999

The company launches the ARCHITECT family of diagnostic instruments.

Miles D. White becomes chairman of the board.

2000–2013

2000

Abbott announces its intention to purchase the pharmaceutical business of German chemical giant BASF for $6.9 billion. With the acquisition, its largest ever, Abbott's international presence is immediately expanded by 40 percent and its scientific capability significantly enhanced.

2002 ▶

Humira, the first fully-human monoclonal antibody drug, is approved by the FDA. It will go on to become the company's most successful product to date.

2003

Abbott enters the healthy-living nutrition market when it adds ZonePerfect to its nutrition portfolio.

The acquisition of TheraSense, a leader in glucose monitoring technology that requires smaller blood samples, leads to the formation of Abbott Diabetes Care.

2004

The spin-off of Abbott's Hospital Products Division creates Hospira, today a strong, independent Fortune 600 company.

2006 ▶

The acquisition of Guidant's vascular business makes Abbott a leader in this market. The *Xience V* drug-eluting stent is launched. It goes on to become the market leader.

The purchase of Kos Pharmaceuticals, with its portfolio of lipid management therapies, builds Abbott's presence in the largest segment of the pharmaceutical market.

2009

In one of its most strategically active years ever, Abbott executes a series of acquisitions across its business base, including entry into a new business, vision care, creating Abbott Medical Optics.

2010

The acquisition of Solvay Pharmaceuticals and Piramal Healthcare Solutions expands Abbott's position in developing countries and leads to the creation of its Established Pharmaceuticals Division.

2013

Abbott separates into two leading healthcare companies: A diversified medical products company under the Abbott name and a research-based pharmaceutical company, named AbbVie.

Just to work, and to get, as I give, "the Square deal". Fraternally yours, [Wm.] A. Abbott. Univ. of Mich. '85

1888–1900
A Hustling Start to a Grand Medical Enterprise

The young physician was frustrated. As a freshly minted M.D. from the University of Michigan, he was eager to make a real impact for his new patients. But the tools available to him in 1888 weren't equal to the task. Medications of the day were, at best, unscientific and ineffective — at worst, pure quackery and detrimental to the patient. Since the accurate and efficacious medicines he needed did not yet exist, Dr. Wallace Calvin Abbott decided to make them himself. Thus was born a company that would improve countless millions of lives — of patients, physicians, investors, employees, and fellow citizens — for generations to come.

PREVIOUS SPREAD
Dr. Wallace Calvin Abbott was a man of considerable personal presence, despite standing just 5'4". On this photograph, he wrote his motto, "Just to work, and to get as I give, 'the square deal.'"

Dr. Abbott, the young entrepreneur, with some members of his early office staff.

Fresh from the University of Michigan, Dr. Abbott served briefly as a physician's assistant in his native Vermont before coming to Chicago to start his new practice and business.

A farm boy from Vermont, Wallace Abbott entered college late and finished it early. With his extraordinary energy and deep desire to make a difference in the world, he was very much a young man with a mission, determined to make absolutely the most possible of his time and talents. His medical school mentor, Dr. Victor C. Vaughn, understanding the young man's ambition and ability, urged him to, "Go anywhere, Abbott. You will succeed wherever you go."

A Young Doctor's Start

When the new Dr. Abbott graduated from the University of Michigan Medical School in 1885, he eagerly cast about for work, unaware he would soon lay the foundation of one of the world's great healthcare companies — and from his very own home. A family friend had told the ambitious young doctor about his brother, Dr. William C. Dodge, who wanted to sell his medical practice. It was located in Ravenswood, then a small village north of Chicago.

Abbott borrowed train fare from relatives and rushed out to see Dodge. The latter enthused about the nearby township of Lake View, foreseeing "a boom, more people … then one of these days Lake View will become part of Chicago." The Windy City was already a center of the medical and chemical industries. "And that," foretold Dodge, "is when things will really start to hum!"

Dodge's price for his practice seemed immense: $1,000. But Abbott immediately telegraphed Dr. Edward Putney, an official at his old preparatory school in Vermont, and asked for a loan. Back came two $500 checks. That summer, Abbott and his new bride, childhood sweetheart Clara A. Ingraham, moved to Ravenswood.

Abbott began visiting patients, often on a Beckley-Ralston bicycle, which he preferred to horse and buggy. He charged $2 per house call versus $1 for office visits.

He also established "The People's Drug Store," in a frame house where he and Clara Abbott resided. There he started to concoct medicinals like Dr. Abbott's Tooth Ache Drops. The drugstore offered other wares, such as French Dental Cream, Worm Medicine, and Anodyne Liniment.

From Mortar and Pestle to Doses and Pills

A frequent visitor to Dr. Abbott's pharmacy was an irrepressible doctor, one William T. Thackeray. A hospital corpsman in the American Civil War, he took part in a strife-torn attempt to establish Spain's first republic in the 1870s. Captured while heading up a medical unit, Thackeray was court-martialed and sentenced to be shot — then spared within an hour of the appointed execution. Fleeing to Paris, he became acquainted there with the novel theories of a Belgian-born physician, Dr. Adolphe Burggraeve.

Dr. Abbott took his innovative ideas on "dosimetric medicine" from Belgian physician Adolphe Burggraeve, shown here on the book plate of Abbott's company, which also signaled the importance of product quality, the company's founding principle.

Pharmacists of the day still prepared many medicines with mortar and pestle. They mashed plants or herbs, then poured in water or alcohol. The result was a sloppy, imprecise mix that yielded unpredictable medical results, but the near certainty of nausea for patients downing such noxious elixirs.

Burggraeve, chief surgeon of the teaching hospital in Ghent, Belgium, was appalled by these practices. A doctor plying a patient with fluid extracts, he noted, could not know the exact amount, or effect, of the medicine provided. And he saw the hallowed practice of letting a disease "run its natural course" as tantamount to abandonment of the patient.

Instead, Burggraeve preached that a physician should attack a disease from its start, by "closely, persistently assaulting it with specified alkaloidal doses." An "alkaloid" is a plant-derived active ingredient, such as morphine or atropine, which can be used in a specific dose of medicine.

In tests with typhoid patients, Burggraeve administered half-milligram doses of digitalin and other alkaloids at regular intervals, and cured the sufferers within two weeks. He insisted on "chemically pure and mathematically measured agents … which are always uniform as to quantity and quality."

Impressed by Burggraeve's theories, the adventurous Thackeray returned to the United States, where he served as an Army doctor on the western frontier. Then he obtained work as a Chicago-based sales representative for the Parke-Davis drug company.

Continues on page 8 ▶

Dr. William Thomas Thackeray, a medical corps veteran of the American Civil War, helped convert Dr. Abbott to modern, dosimetric medicine.

Dr. Wallace Calvin Abbott

Descended from Puritans who settled near Plymouth Rock, Wallace Calvin Abbott rushed through life as hardworking, idealistic, and intent on self-betterment as any Pilgrim.

Upon receiving his degree, the young Dr. Abbott came to Chicago, a rising city that matched his own immense energy. With a loan of $1,000 he purchased a medical practice and the People's Drug Store. His career was begun.

Born on October 12, 1857, Wallace Calvin Abbott grew up on his parents' farm near Bridgewater, Vermont. His father, Luther, frowned on formal education, so, from age 14, Wallace worked as a full-time farmhand, hauling sacks of feed and sawing logs. When he asked his father for a hunting gun, Luther told him to earn it through extra chores. So the husky young man cleared out a meadow of weeds. For good measure, and perhaps sensing a commercial opportunity, he planted the ground with potatoes. Such labors, noted future company head Dr. Alfred S. Burdick, "helped give him the tremendous physical endurance which later carried him through many a hard struggle."

Unlike her husband, the young man's mother, Weltha Barrows Abbott, was an advocate of formal education. When Wallace was 20 she convinced Luther to send their son to the State Normal School, a training ground for instructors. Within three years Abbott and boyhood friend Henry B. Shattuck had earned their teaching certificates. By then Abbott had decided to make medicine his career. He and Shattuck headed off to prep school at St. Johnsbury Academy in St. Johnsbury, Vermont.

Abbott told the school's assistant principal, Dr. Edward Putney, "I intend to finish the four-year course in two years, sir." He did so while working his way through school.

While reciting the conjugation of Greek verbs, Abbott and Shattuck chopped kindling from refuse dumps for 12 cents an hour. Sleeping little, Abbott served as founder, purchasing agent, and cook for a supper club, which charged students $1.25 a week. As a student "his ability as an organizer and counselor gave him a prominent place," remarked Professor W.F. Rochelieu, one of Abbott's teachers. "He was always at the front in all good works."

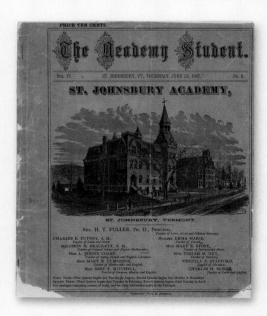

For the student newspaper of Vermont's St. Johnsbury Academy, pictured here, the young Abbott wrote — presciently, it would prove — on such subjects as the proper management of large institutions.

Dr. Abbott and wife Clara with
their daughter Eleanor.

Abbott was picked to write the graduating class motto:

*"Our course here is ended —
its tasks now are done.
New fields lie before us —
more laurels must be won."*

After a year of premedical studies at Dartmouth College, Abbott transferred to the University of Michigan's medical school. While tackling the arduous curriculum he also took on multiple jobs. He soldered plumbing lines and mopped floors at the school, and worked as a nurse at the university hospital, all the while running the Students Club and piling on extra courses.

He graduated in 1885. Abbott later said of his medical school regimen: "I do not recommend others to do it."

The young scholar drank up the lectures of Professor Victor C. Vaughan, the medical school's future dean, on the "active principles" contained in medicinal plants like digitalis. Abbott would later place Vaughan's active ingredients in actual medications, and help found the practice of modern pharmaceutical medicine. Burdick recalled he "often heard Doctor Abbott say those lectures were of more value to him than anything else in his entire medical course."

On graduation, Abbott asked Prof. Vaughan for career advice: "Go anywhere, Abbott," his mentor replied. "You will succeed wherever you go." Though only 5'4", Abbott was barrel-chested and a barrel of incessant, yet focused, energy.

Abbott made good on Professor Vaughan's prediction. His firm grew to become a major corporation during his lifetime, while enduring such challenges as occasional financial downturns, a disastrous fire that destroyed the greater part of the company's publishing facility, a switch from alkaloidal to synthetic medicines, and a world war.

When his company had become established, Dr. Abbott would, on arriving at his office, always follow the same routine. He'd slip off his shoes to relieve his fallen arches. He'd roll up his sleeves. The wall signs around read "DO IT NOW!" "EVERYBODY GET BUSY!" was a note frequently passed around the office. He then proceeded to follow his own advice, often working from early morning to well into the night.

Dr. Abbott "had the eyes of an eagle," recalled L.C. Beck, manager of the Seattle-based Northwest branch. "Energy exuded from every pore. He had secretaries constantly busy and dictated to them with machine-gun rapidity."

Still, Abbott would remember his student days. The University of Michigan's colors had a prominent place in his office. And he would fête the graduating classes of Chicago's medical schools on company grounds.

At these occasions the relentless entrepreneur recited a favorite poem, one that he exemplified:

*"Pluck wins: it always wins …
Pluck will win; its average is
sure; He gains the prize
who will most endure; Who
faces issues; he who never
shirks; Who waits and
watches, and who always
works."* ∎

Before the alkaloidal medicine of pills and precise dosage, pharmacists would laboriously, and inaccurately, make their products by grinding ingredients with mortar and pestle, then mixing them with liquids.

At an 1885 meeting of the American Medical Association, Thackeray came across an exhibit featuring machines for making "dosimetric" granules — Burggraeve-style pills and tablets. He bought the equipment on the spot. Meeting with Parke-Davis' general manager, Thackeray urged him to take the firm into the granule business. The fellow replied: "The idea would not be a success and, if it was, it would mean the ruin of the fluid extract business."

Undaunted, Thackeray, in 1887, set up his own Metric Granule Company. His Chicago firm put out an early periodical on dosimetrics, *The Alkaloidal Clinic*. Armed with company literature, Thackeray, dapper with a thick white mustache, led sales calls. At the People's Drug Store in Ravenswood, he made a convert of Dr. Abbott, who recalled lectures relating to alkaloids at medical school.

Dr. Abbott began purchasing pills and tablets from the Metric Granule Company. Each contained one to 10 percent of an active substance, such as atropine for whooping cough. Another sales item was cicutine, a sedative pitched as a means to "curb excessive sexual passions."

> "Think right, feel right, be right, live and let live: do the square thing, have a conscience and use it."
>
> — DR. WALLACE C. ABBOTT

Setting Up Shop

The perfectionist in Abbott found fault with the purchases. Many granules were not as soluble as claimed. Yet the pills of other manufacturers were few and costly. He decided, with characteristic directness, to make his own drugs.

He started by fashioning granules of medicine in the kitchen of his small apartment. In manufacturing pills Abbott relied on Dr. Burggraeve's *New Handbook of Dosimetric Therapeutics* as his guide. "I consider a handy case of active remedies in a convenient form far superior to the time-honored methods of bottles full of nauseous mixtures," noted Abbott, echoing Burggraeve. Abbott advocated using "the smallest possible quantity of the best obtainable means to produce a desired therapeutic result." To dispose of any bitter taste, he rolled pills in round-bottom pans or stuck them on pins to dip them in sugary liquid.

In 1888, his first year as a maker of pharmaceuticals, Dr. Abbott marked $2,000 in sales. The business became a family concern. By 1890, it had quadrupled, grossing $8,000. Dr. Abbott now had the means to bring his parents to Chicago; they lived with his sister Lucy, two blocks from the People's Drug Store. Their parlor was a storage room for the firm, their kitchen a spare lab. Everyone lent a hand. The role of Dr. Abbott's father, Luther, was to fill medicine bottles and paste shipping labels on boxes.

With his business flourishing, in 1891 Dr. Abbott built a grand, new three-story home at 4605 North Hermitage Avenue, Ravenswood, Illinois, with broad porches and an ornate cupola. More than a century later, the company that bears his name would construct a replica of the house at its world headquarters. The building, known as Abbott House, re-creates many original features, as a living symbol of all that Abbott stands for (see pages 330–331).

In 1894, Abbott christened his growing firm The Abbott Alkaloidal Company.

Energetic marketers from the start, Abbott Alkaloidal used coupons to promote its goods.

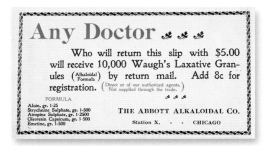

Any Doctor ✌ ✌ ✌

Who will return this slip with $5.00 will receive 10,000 Waugh's Laxative Granules (Alkaloidal Formula) by return mail. Add 8c for registration. (Direct or of our authorized agents. Not supplied through the trade.) ✌ ✌

FORMULA
Aloin, gr. 1-25
Strychnine Sulphate, gr. 1-500
Atropine Sulphate, gr. 1-2500
Oleoresin Capsicum, gr. 1-500
Emetine, gr. 1-500

THE ABBOTT ALKALOIDAL CO.

Station X. · · CHICAGO

This monthly statement from the first years of Abbott's business listed popular products like toothache drops and a blood purifier.

RELIABLE ARTICLES.

Dr. Abbott's Tooth Ache Drops.
Rock Candy Cough Syrup.
Anodyne Liniment (for internal and external pains).
Blackberry Balsam.
Tonic Laxative Pills.
Laxative Lozenges.
Worm Medicine (solid and liquid).
Spring Blood Purifier.
French Dental Cream.

TERMS:

STATEMENT RENDERED MONTHLY.

Ravenswood, Ill., _____ 188_

M _____

In Acc't with **DR. W. C. ABBOTT**

Physician and Surgeon,

PROPRIETOR PEOPLE'S DRUG STORE

All bills due at date of rendering. 8 per cent. interest after 30 days.

Staffing Up

His first outside hire was a Miss Jo Fletcher — the Doctor nicknamed the hardworking young lady his "whale" for her huge capacity and importance to his work. For the tidy sum of $12 a week, she swept floors and filled prescriptions.

Another prized early employee was Ida Richter, Dr. Abbott's private secretary, who resided at the Hermitage Avenue house. Abbott often dictated memos and articles to her until late into the night, then roused her again in the early morning to take still more dictation.

Continues on page 13 ▸

A Publishing House as Well as a Pharmaceutical Firm

With The Abbott Alkaloidal Company off the ground, and growing rapidly, Dr. Abbott began placing advertisements, rather than continuing to rely purely on word of mouth. A notice in the June 1891 *Medical World* was pitched at doctors interested in dosimetric granules. The ad cost 25 cents, and brought in $8 in orders. A catalog was clearly needed.

That year, Abbott put out a 14-page compendium of some 150 products, from acetanilid for lessening pain to zinc valerinate for nerve spasms. The price: 10 cents for each 100 granules, or 65 cents for 1,000.

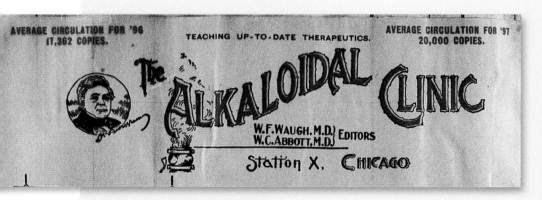

After taking over the periodical *The Alkaloidal Clinic* from Dr. William Thackeray, Dr. Abbott, with assistance from co-editor Dr. William F. Waugh, turned it into a widely read medical journal. To recognize his medical model, Abbott memorialized Dr. Burggraeve with a likeness in the publication's masthead.

Along with alkaloids, the catalog offered more traditional therapies, like effervescent salt. "Minor ailments often require nothing more," the catalog read, "as its use, clearing the alimentary canal of indigestible fermenting residues, freshens and purifies the blood."

Dr. Abbott inserted a personal pledge in each catalog that his granules were "accurate, the solubility rapid and perfect, and the keeping quality assured." He was also pleased to print letters from fervent converts to alkaloidal medicine. Wrote a Dr. Coleman from Houston: "Oh how my soul revolts when I recall the nauseous doses I prepared and poured down the throats of little innocent sufferers!"

In 1894, the United States suffered through a business depression, typical of the boom and bust cycle of the era. In what would become the norm, Abbott's firm prospered despite hard times, with sales that year reaching $29,000. However, the business of Dr. Abbott's acquaintance, Dr. Thackeray, floundered. One day Abbott ran into Thackeray, and asked him what would become of his publication, *The Alkaloidal Clinic*.

Thackeray replied that, "If [Abbott] wanted it and would publish it, it was his."

Abbott did, quickly tripling its size to 36 pages, crammed with letters from grateful doctors, articles on treating fevers and heart ailments, and colorful ads. It was also filled with Abbott's crusades against poor health habits.

Cigarette smoking, he wrote, "seems to have about the same demoralizing effect upon the general character that cocaine has." Makers of unscientific and unproven patent medicines were another target, compared to "the rum hole and the brothel which steal men's money and damn men's souls!"

The staff of Dr. Abbott's Clinic Publishing Company taking a break during the firm's early years.

Dr. Abbott and Dr. William F. Waugh co-wrote two standard texts on dosimetric medicine.

TWO PRE-EMINENT BOOKS

Later that year Dr. Abbott created his own Clinic Publishing Company. He bought a frame house next door to Abbott Alkaloidal, and filled it with printing presses, a composing room, a bindery, and editorial offices. Fifteen typesetters and press-room workers occupied the space, churning out editions of the journal *The Alkaloidal Clinic*, as well as booklets, catalogs, prescription pads, and other printed matter.

The Alkaloidal Clinic editorialized on the best ways to handle ailments minor and grave, from diphtheria to indigestion and carbuncles. It even advised on how long syphilitics should wait before marrying — estimates ranged from two years to six. The journal's busy co-editor was Dr. William F. Waugh, formerly head of Philadelphia's *Medical Times*.

Waugh and Abbott, churning out scores of articles, were nicknamed "the Alkaloidal Twins." They co-wrote two text books on alkaloidal therapeutics, which became the standard reference works on dosimetrics. Further, Waugh managed the production of two best-selling cathartics. One was the Waugh-Abbott Intestinal Antiseptic Tablet, an admixture of lime, soda, and zinc; and the other, Abbott's Saline Laxative.

An editorial standout was a cosmopolitan physician, Dr. Ephraim M. Epstein. A native of Belarus, Epstein practiced medicine in Istanbul and was a surgeon for the Austrian Navy. In America, he served as South Dakota University's founding president. Along the way, which included a stint in languages and theology at Andover, Massachusetts, the white-bearded scholar raised seven children, while learning Arabic, Latin, Greek, Hebrew, and the Romance languages, as well as several Slavic tongues.

While he was the erudite organizer of the company library, Epstein's prescriptions could smack of folk remedies. "A first-born child came into the world small, feeble, and exceedingly jaundiced," he wrote in *The Alkaloidal Clinic*. "A dough of finely sifted rye flour was wrapped [around the infant] from head to foot. It was also bathed daily in a strong decoction of bean, to which a liberal amount of beer was added. In about two weeks, the child regained strength and grew up well."

In 1897, *The Alkaloidal Clinic's* monthly circulation reached 20,000 copies. Its staff of editorial and production workers reached 62. It was among America's five most widely read medical journals. Yet Dr. Abbott was sympathetic to the financial challenges of its customers.

"If times are hard, Doctor, and dollars are hard to get, you can save one and help us by showing the *Clinic* to your friends. Send us three new subscribers and we will advance your subscription one year." ∎

Abbott leaders working in the original company library. Dr. Abbott, left, Dr. Ephraim M. Epstein, reading at a desk, editor and physician William F. Waugh, in front of book shelves, Dr. George H. Candler reading to secretary, and future company president Dr. Alfred S. Burdick, far right.

Dr. Abbott with some members of his early work-force. His sister Lucy was to his left, his workhorse aide, Jo Fletcher, bottom right.

Richter was unfazed. At a 1909 dinner in honor of her retirement — the company's first — she recalled: "I was having a small part in something that was for the uplift of mankind." Her boss set an impressive example: Even as the firm's size and demands grew, Dr. Abbott kept his medical practice, getting along on just five hours of sleep.

More relatives and friends were put to work. Clara Abbott's brother-in-law, James Ranson, filled orders. Dr. Abbott's middle-school friend, Henry Shattuck, kept the books — he went on to become company treasurer.

From the start, the Abbott firm was a pioneer in employee benefits, tied to their leader's far-sighted notions about good health. If workers rode bicycles to work, Abbott arranged for purchase of steeply discounted bikes from the Beckley-Ralston Company. If they quit smoking cigarettes, he gave them gold watches for Christmas.

Dr. Abbott's oft-repeated motto:

"Think right, feel right, be right, live and let live: do the square thing, have a conscience and use it."

Dr. Abbott's personal touch
was evident in all aspects of
his young company — as this
customer letter shows.

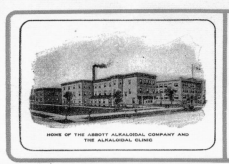

DR. W. C. ABBOTT,
PRES'T AND GEN'L MGR.

DR. W. F. WAUGH, VICE-PRES'T.
L. P. SCOVILLE, SEC'Y.

H. B. SHATTUCK, TREAS.
J. W. RANSON, ASS'T TREAS.

The Abbott Alkaloidal Co.
Manufacturing Chemists
RAVENSWOOD STATION

NEW YORK
50 WEST BROADWAY
J. W. RANSON, MANAGER

Chicago

SAN FRANCISCO
9-11 PHELAN BUILDING
S. J. PLATT, MANAGER

HOME OF THE ABBOTT ALKALOIDAL COMPANY AND
THE ALKALOIDAL CLINIC

Dr E G. Cummer
Mansfield Center, Conn.
Dear Doctor:-

CHICAGO,

Enclosed we hand you a special booklet on Waugh's Laxative--a scientific, successful treatment for Constipation. It has been painstakingly prepared and we hope you will read it carefully.

Desiring to have you try the treatment, we have included in the booklet a form for a special cut-price (introductory) order, which we ask you to accept on our suggestion. Order liberally, Doctor, and if you are not satisfied that it is a good thing by the time you have used one-third to one-half (enough for a liberal test), send back the balance by post, say so, and we will refund your money.

Orders for other goods may come at the same time, but the special "Waugh's Laxative Order Blank" must be used on this offer--won't you use yours now? There's satisfaction and dollars in it for you. One dollar invested will easily make you ten to twenty- medicines that are right (ours) plus brains that know how (yours), will do it. We await your pleasure.

Very truly yours,

A-10.

THE ABBOTT ALKALOIDAL CO.
Dr. W. C. Abbott.

P. S. The regular price of these granules is 55 cents per 1000, postpaid for cash with order. We propose to send you all you want (once only) up to $10.00 worth as follows: In "Bulk" at the rate of 3000 for $1.00; or in dispensing boxes of 20 prescription vials (wood) carrying 130 each-- an average one-week's treatment--at $1.00--either style or assorted. These prices are only good when order is made on or accompanied by the special blank which constitutes the last page of the enclosed booklet, and for cash with order! Money back if not satisfied.

Pocket medicine cases sold by The Abbott Alkaloidal Co. For $1.50, doctors could buy small leather cases holding 12 vials of medications that fit snugly in their upper vest pockets. For a premium, larger "crackerjack" cases could be had.

Eight years after its founding, the company met its first controversy, a precursor of future, industrywide disputes over generic drugs. The American Pharmaceutical Association criticized doctors who bought directly from Abbott instead of from drugstores, which were said to offer products of equal quality.

Dr. Abbott fought back hard to defend his company's honor: "It is a well-recognized fact that these products do differ," he stated. "The 'just as good' and 'so much cheaper' are accountable for much of professional failure and set up a bigger row of grave stones every year."

On its tenth anniversary, even as the United States suffered through an economic depression, The Abbott Alkaloidal Company was prospering. Sales in 1898 hit $100,000.

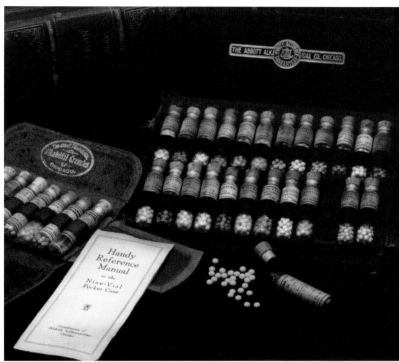

A shop for making dosimetric granules.

Soon the firm was supplying 349 different granulated tablets. Also offered were gelatin capsules, pill boxes, bandages, trusses, and gummed labels and letterheads. Further, Abbott made what proved a lasting move into medical devices by selling such items as syringes, thermometers, and surgical tools. It was the company's first step toward diversification.

As the new century approached, The Abbott Alkaloidal Company was established as a leading maker of dosimetric medicines. On his stationery for 1900, Dr. Abbott proudly printed the motto: "Watch Us Grow!"

Decade at a Glance

1888–1900

▲ 1888
Dr. Wallace C. Abbott, a 30-year-old practicing physician in Chicago, begins making granules of "alkaloidal" medicine — remedies containing active ingredients derived from plants and herbs — at his People's Drug Store.

First year revenues: $2,000.

1889
Dr. Abbott continues to make medical granules in the kitchen sink of the apartment where he and his wife, Clara, live. He more than doubles annual sales of his fledgling business to $4,500.

1890
Dr. Abbott's parents and sister begin working for the company; his father, Luther, packs boxes and fills medicine bottles. The first non-family employee, Miss Jo Fletcher, is hired for $12 a week.

▲ Dr. Abbott with some members of his early workforce. His sister Lucy is to his left, his workhorse aide, Jo Fletcher, bottom right.

Yearly sales reach $8,000.

1891
Until now, relying strictly on word of mouth, Dr. Abbott places his first ad in the journal *Medical World*. Pitched at doctors, it costs 25 cents — and returns $8 in orders.

Dr. Abbott, with profits from his business and private practice, builds a fine private home at 4605 North Hermitage Avenue, today a Chicago landmark.

▼

1892
The business is moved from the People's Drug Store to a house one block away. There, Dr. Abbott initially manages a staff of seven women.

1893
The company literally "sugar-coats" its pills by dipping them in a sweetened solution.

1894
Pocket medicine cases sold by The Abbott Alkaloidal Company. For $1.50, doctors could buy small leather cases holding 12 vials of drugs that fit snugly in an upper vest pocket. Larger "crackerjack" cases were had for a premium.

▼

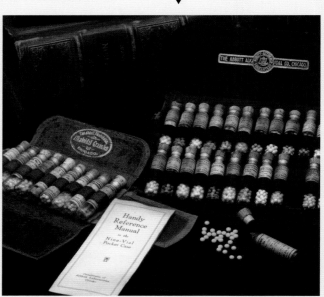

The firm is christened The Abbott Alkaloidal Company. Dr. Abbott publishes *The Alkaloidal Clinic*, a journal founded by his friend, Dr. William T. Thackeray. It contains articles on averting and treating disease, as well as eye-grabbing ads.

1896

A shop for making dosimetric granules. Abbott's high-tech production processes lay years ahead: Early manufacturing was labor-intensive and performed by hand.

1897 ▶

Dr. William F. Waugh is hired to edit *The Alkaloidal Clinic*, and to co-write with Dr. Abbott a standard reference work, the *Text Book of Alkaloidal Therapeutics*. Waugh will also supervise manufacture of the Waugh-Abbott Intestinal Antiseptic Tablet and of Abbott's Saline Laxative.

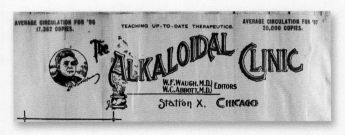

1899

The Clinic Publishing Company, the publishing side of the firm, launches *Helpful Hints for the Busy Doctor*. It is part medical journal, part product catalog, and includes endorsements and ads. Its first issue is mailed, with an order slip, to every doctor in the United States and Canada.

Dr. Abbott with staff in the company's library.

▼

Dr. Abbott is an early proponent of employee health. Workers can earn gold watches by giving up smoking, and by riding bicycles to work. Dr. Abbott's motto: "Think right, feel right, be right, live and let live: do the square thing, have a conscience and use it."

1898

The circulation of *The Alkaloidal Clinic* exceeds 20,000 copies a month, making it one of the top-five medical journals in the United States. Its production and editorial staff reaches 62 in number. On its 10th anniversary, The Abbott Alkaloidal Company attains sales of $100,000.

ABBOTT ALKALOIDAL CO.
UFACTURING CHEMISTS.
ING THE MEDICAL PROFESSION ONLY.

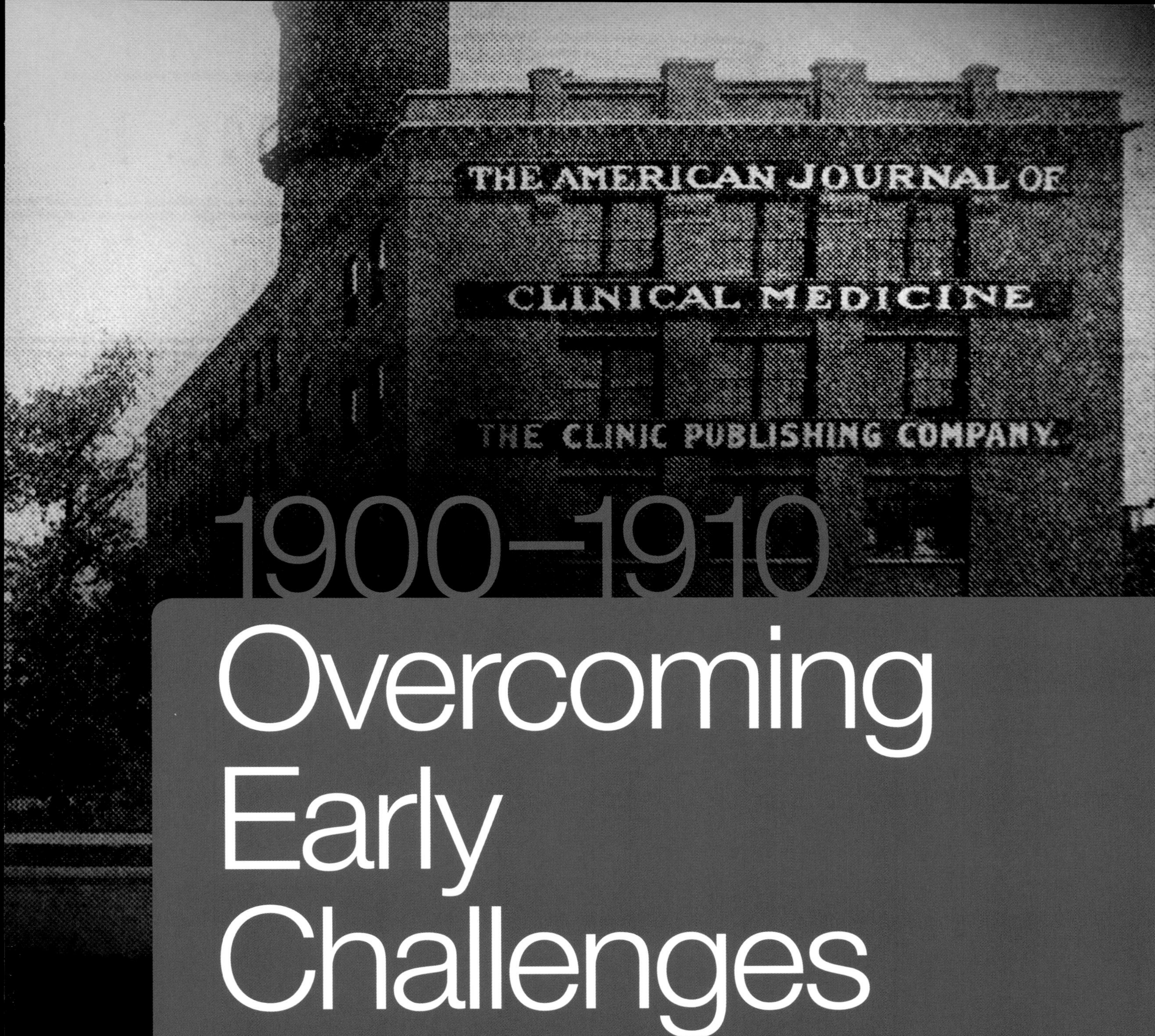

THE AMERICAN JOURNAL OF

CLINICAL MEDICINE

THE CLINIC PUBLISHING COMPANY.

1900–1910

Overcoming Early Challenges

As usual, Dr. Abbott was at his large oaken desk late into the night. During the day, he'd roam the manufacturing plant, supervising his production team. Later, he switched to managing the publishing business. He corresponded ceaselessly with doctors, wrote articles for *The Alkaloidal Clinic*, and personally composed dunning letters. His personal style was unmistakable:

"If you owed us a thousand dollars instead of this mere pittance," read one billing notice, "I shouldn't even have to ask for it, but 'we need the money,' hence this letter and the enclosed bill. Right now will suit us tip top!"

PREVIOUS SPREAD
Abbott's restored prosperity allowed construction in 1908 of a five-story research and manufacturing plant, shown on the left. The publishing facility is on the right.

His paper-stuffed desk as
backdrop, Dr. Abbott confers
with Ida Richter, his private
secretary.

Abbott Alkaloidal rang in the new century with its incorporation, signified by its first stock certificate. Abbott would become a publicly owned company in the 1920s.

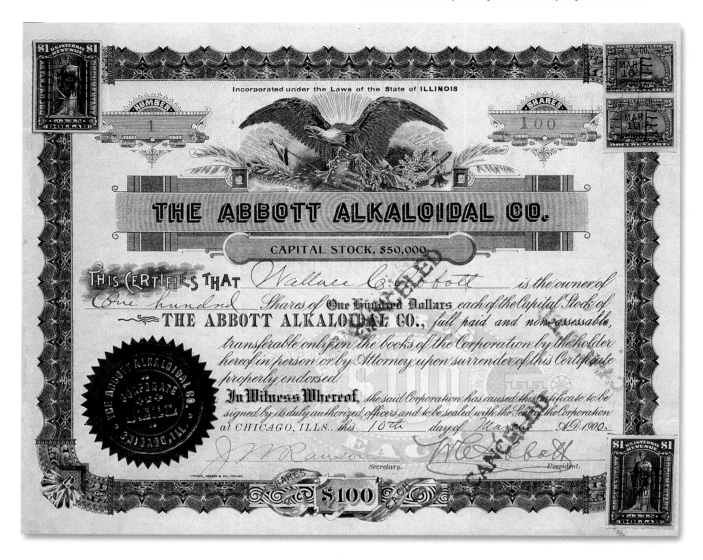

For years he had gotten by on just five hours of sleep. But, in 1907, Dr. Abbott had taken to working 24 hours at a time, grabbing naps on an office cot. He felt an overriding urgency. After 18 years of success, a fire had burned down his publishing plant. And a nationwide financial crisis had forced layoffs. Pulling out a sheet of paper, Dr. Abbott began writing an offer, a plea really, to subscribers, asking them to invest in company bonds to help it through the hard times. And things were about to get worse, as the nation's most prestigious medical journal was readying a pointed attack on his name.

A Growing Prosperity

At the dawn of the new century, Abbott had been on a roll. An array of new products was launched, and Abbott's place in alkaloidal medicine had become assured. Sales in 1900 of the newly incorporated company reached $125,000, and rose steadily higher. The firm even made its first corporate acquisition, as Dr. Abbott purchased the Tengwall File and Ledger Company, which made binders for keeping office records.

The most valuable asset acquired with Tengwall proved to be Simeon DeWitt Clough, a young ad man who would be Abbott's third president.

Swelling revenues enabled construction, on the site of the old cottage, of a four-story brick building for The Clinic Publishing Company. The size of the publications also grew. The November 1903 issue of *The Alkaloidal Clinic* was almost 200 pages long. One ad was for an Empire Umbilical Truss "with button inserted at the navel"; another was for a $650 Oldsmobile car.

The Clinic Publishing Company produced a periodical, *Helpful Hints for the Busy Doctor.* It was part medical journal, part medical catalog, and was to be published for decades.

In its early years, Abbott seemed almost as much a publishing firm as a pharmaceutical maker. Its growing prosperity permitted construction, in 1901, of an impressive new building to house The Clinic Publishing Company (far right).

Chief pharmacist Fred Hunsche (right) oversaw workers in the formulation room of the production plant, still located, in 1903, in an old wood-frame house.

With a year-long subscription costing only $1, *The Alkaloidal Clinic* reached a quarter of the doctors in America. The new building bustled with editorial, business, and advertising employees working on the publication, *Helpful Hints for the Busy Doctor*.

> ## "A good definition of a 'nobody' is a man without enthusiasm."
>
> — SIMEON DEWITT CLOUGH

This was a lively grab-bag of medical articles, a medical catalog, product endorsements, and ads. The first issue of *Helpful Hints* was mailed, with a pink order slip within each copy, to every physician in the United States and Canada.

The Clinic Publishing Company had brand-new facilities. In the laboratory, pulleys pushed by a gas-fired engine hauled material to workers operating tablet and coating machines.

Recalled supervisor Ernest Richter, "[It] had a very low ceiling, and a very unpleasant smell and noise." At the time, breathing masks weren't used in the industry. Employees sometimes swooned from the odors; neighborhood residents sometimes complained of the smell.

Finished material was sent up a rope elevator to the above floor, where 30 young women and managers Frank Rastell and Jennie Orum bottled the granules and pills for shipping. The floor above held barrels of saline solution. A runway outside went to a shed that stored the finished product.

New Talent, Future Leadership

The growing company attracted top talent. Two important new players, contrasts in style, joined in 1904.

Dr. Alfred S. Burdick, age 37, a soft-spoken son of a clergyman, was an editor at *The Medical Standard*. S. DeWitt Clough, 25, was a garrulous offspring of Chicago's hard-nosed West Side, a writer of florid, inspirational ads, who had worked his way up to become sales manager for the publications *BusinessWorld* and *Newspaperdom*. Both men in time would become chief executives of the company.

Dr. Abbott made Dr. Burdick editor of *The Alkaloidal Clinic*. As they shook hands on the $35-a-week-job, Abbott told him: "I want you to do more for us than write and edit. I'm going to count on you for advice on anything else."

Clough's starting pay was less impressive, $10 a week. But it was quickly raised to $12.50 after Clough pulled in a great many ads for *The Alkaloidal Clinic* and *Helpful Hints for the Busy Doctor*. Dr. Abbott found a kindred soul in the energetic Clough, who once wrote: "A good definition of a 'nobody' is a man without enthusiasm."

Clough composed most of the advertising copy, his colorful prose matched by eye-grabbing graphics. One ad, placed in normally staid medical periodicals, took aim at bogus patent-medicines for curing baldness and rheumatism, while touting Abbott's trustworthiness: "DOCTOR, WHO MAKES YOUR MEDICINE?… Are you one of the fifty thousand doctors who buy and prescribe the products of *this company* that *positively* makes 'no dope for quackery'?"

Two future CEOs joined the firm in 1904: Dr. Alfred S. Burdick (below) and S. DeWitt Clough (right). From the start Dr. Burdick served as a strategic adviser to Dr. Abbott, as well as chief editor of the firm's medical journal.

A product of tough Chicago streets, fast-talking S. DeWitt Clough headed up Abbott's colorful advertising efforts by age 25.

To promote itself, Abbott mass-mailed pamphlets and catalogs to doctors and druggists.

This Abbott ad for *Calcidin*,
iodized calcium, reflected
S. DeWitt Clough's arresting
communication style.

Ad from the early
1900s promoting Abbott's
specialty, alkaloidal
medicines.

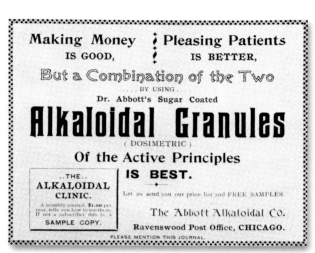

A popular product boosted by Clough was *Calcidin*, or tablets of iodized calcium, touted as a remedy for the grippe and croupe, otherwise known as the flu.

Another big seller was the H-M-C Tablet, as in Hyosine, Morphine, and Cactin, the latter derived from cactus, and serving separately as a heart drug. H-M-C, cried Abbott ads, was "the greatest advance in surgical anesthesia since the discovery of ether." Dr. Abbott himself wrote, "Men write us they are putting a stop to family quarrels" through the drug. A useful alkaloid was the anti-inflammatory Apocynin, to treat liver and heart ailments.

The company wasn't above offering prosaic yet profitable items. It sold hair removal powder, liquids to remove warts and moles, and an item called "Yohimbine Spiegel" to "stimulate dilation of the penile tissue" while acting as "no drug to aid the seducer."

Abbott's Sales "Missionaries"

Since its beginning, The Abbott Alkaloidal Company had promoted itself only through ads and mail-order catalogs, as well as agent-distributors in a few major cities. In *Helpful Hints*, Dr. Abbott had written: "We have no salesmen, therefore we cannot camp at your door with long-winded talk and a bag of samples. We haven't time to do it."

But now, with the growing firm facing boundless opportunity and increased competition, Clough and Dr. Burdick lobbied Dr. Abbott to set up a sales team. He agreed, and to run it brought in an old hand, the ubiquitous Dr. Thackeray, Abbott's old link to the theories of Dr. Burggraeve.

The first seven salesmen, mostly former pharmacy workers, were dubbed "Abbott Missionaries." Their fervor made an impact on the industry for decades. The initial crew received a three-day training course, featuring talks from Dr. Abbott, Dr. Burdick, Clough, and scholarly Dr. Epstein.

Dr. Abbott plied them with sales tips. "I would try to be a high-class, dignified salesman. Cultivate the acquaintance of everyone in the store," he said, "remembering that the clerks of today become the dealers of tomorrow."

Psychology and timing were vital. "I would learn the place to get enthusiastic, the place to get solemn, the place to bang my fists on the druggist's counter, and the place to shut my mouth," Abbott continued. And "I would defend my house to the last breath."

The salesmen were given price lists, product samples, and expense money. They were told to write down the names and personal interests of every druggist, veterinarian, and medico they met. Then they hit the road, evangelizing the occupants of pharmacies and doctors' offices throughout the land, traveling by buggy and railroad, by Model T, even by oxcart in Arkansas, by riverboat steamer in Washington state, and by stagecoach in Idaho.

Soon the salesforce was expanded. The senior sales representative was one John Charles Brown, his beat Missouri and southern Illinois. He wrote verses that attendees at company sales conventions would sing for years thereafter:

"Carry your grip with a smile,
Carry your grip with a smile,
You may doctors from old lines,
To our lines beguile,
If you carry your grip with a smile."

The first official Abbott logo appeared in 1904, in the 19th edition of the company's product catalog. The catalog cover had a circular icon with the phrase, "PURITY-ACCURACY GUARANTEED" around its outer edge. Entwined in its center were Dr. Abbott's initials, "WCA."

Salesman H.S. Jones took Dr. Abbott for a ride in Jones' state-of-the-art vehicle, proudly dubbed "The Alkaloid."

A tremendous 1905 fire gutted Abbott's publishing plant. The adjoining property, housing the pharmaceutical production facilities, was miraculously saved by prevailing winds.

In 1938, after 33 years in sales, Brown would reflect back: "I wasn't just selling pills and tablets. I was helping to relieve pain, to allay disease, to build better health for countless thousands of people whom I never saw."

The new sales strategy worked. In 1906, revenues rose to $240,000.

A Fiery Crisis

But with Abbott Alkaloidal booming, disaster struck. It came in succession on three separate fronts and tested the company's mettle.

On November 9, 1905, a tremendous fire gutted the 50,000-square-foot brick edifice housing Abbott's publishing company and power plant. "It was one of the fiercest fires ever seen in this part of the city," stated a leaflet published by Dr. Abbott. No one was hurt, but damages ran to $200,000, which insurance only partly covered. Abbott's critical printing operation lay in ashes and molten metal.

> "With the willing hands of the great city, we shall go on. Watch us grow!"
>
> — DR. WALLACE C. ABBOTT

In New York City at the time with Clough, Dr. Abbott turned in a textbook performance in crisis management. Telling Clough to find new printing plates and existing ad copy from New York advertisers, Abbott hurried back to Chicago to inspect the still-smoldering ruins. He reported, "The wind was in a lucky direction. Otherwise, we'd have lost our laboratories. Though our machinery plant is gone, our subscription records were saved." Upbeat in tragedy, he added, "With the willing hands of the great city, we shall go on. Watch us grow!"

Abbott paid local printers to publish a special edition of *The Alkaloidal Clinic*. And he told Peter Bartzen, the print facility's contractor, to meet him.

When Bartzen informed the Doctor that it would take six months to rebuild, Abbott responded that it needed to be done in three, and that he'd pay a bonus if it were.

The AMERICAN JOURNAL of CLINICAL MEDICINE

Vol. 15   JANUARY, 1908   No. 1

"THE MOVING FINGER WRITES"

A few words of holiday cheer and New Year's greeting to the readers and friends of Clinical Medicine, also introducing our "Special Progress Number"

WE have tried to make this number of CLINICAL MEDICINE, our "Progress number," better than any of its predecessors. We think we have succeeded, but we are content to leave the decision to our fellow-members of the great "CLINIC family" to whom we present it with all the good wishes of this season of joy and good cheer. May the "Happy New Year" upon which we are entering be as prosperous to all of us as the one that has just passed. In spite of the clouds that have overspread the financial horizon we believe that the future holds more of promise—for you of the medical profession and for us that cater to you—than has ever come to us in the past. Our united effort can bring all the good things to pass!

We are making history, you and I. The spirit of progress is at last breathing new life into Medicine, and especially into that most neglected, yet most important branch of it, Therapeutics. Nihilism has been the dominant note during the last decade. It was part of that "rationalism" which doubted everything—necessary, perhaps, to aid in casting off of the chrysalis of traditional errors and encumbering theories, but too destructive in its tendencies. The therapeutics of the future must be con-

structive; it must have definite aims; must not be wedded so closely to "pure science" as to lay aside the primal aid of medicine— the healing and relief of the sick. In other words, it must add to the scientific exactitude of modern science the more exalted motive of the altruist.

We are passing through a period of moral upheaval. It is a time of questioning, of ourselves and of others; of search for and passion for the truth; yet most of all for self-examination and self-justification. But instead of the despairing cry of the pessimist, "What's the use?" we are seeking to know "of what use" we can be in the world, and have come to realize that the greatest good comes in the giving of the greatest service. When that spirit has been breathed into our profession, medical science will cease to be a "valley of dry bones," but a warm, vitalized, living force. When we, as members of the profession, are actuated mainly by that spirit, placing the desire to help others above everything else, the medical millennium will be much nearer than it now is!

"The moving finger writes"—not, as the Persian poet would have it, something predestined and unchangeable, but under the impulse of forces of which we are a

Rising from the ashes of the fire, and from the new publishing house built on that site, was *The American Journal of Clinical Medicine*. Dr. Abbott's sophisticated new publication covered many medical matters other than alkaloidal care.

Dr. Abbott and Clough hustled to raise funds for rebuilding. They mailed every past and present subscriber a brochure with a picture of the burnt-out edifice. An enclosed note from Dr. Abbott pleaded: "Dear Doctor, from the ashes of our misfortune, a little late, but still in the ring, I hand you with my compliments a sample of *The Alkaloidal Clinic* for December."

Clough tossed in some plucky verses:

"'Spose you haven't got a cent, keep a'pullin'!"
"'Not a red [penny] to pay the rent, keep a'pullin'!"…
"Grit will make a man sublime, keep a'pullin'!"
"Can't fetch business with a whine, keep a'pullin'!"

Meanwhile Bartzen, spurred by Dr. Abbott's pledge of a bonus, haunted local bars to recruit construction workers.

By early 1906 Bartzen's crew had quickly erected a fireproof five-story building. The business offices were spacious, with tall windows allowing in much light. The editorial and print offices were crowned by spanking-new linotype presses. To match its new lodgings, *The Alkaloidal Clinic* was made over into *The American Journal of Clinical Medicine*.

The new name, which dropped the word "Alkaloidal," was significant. Dr. Burdick had persuaded Dr. Abbott to broaden the company's reach, and revenues, beyond dosimetrics. The subtitle to the new monthly journal said it all: "Devoted to Accuracy, Dependability and Honesty in Every Department of Medicine." *The American Journal of Clinical Medicine* was filled with learned articles from foreign sources, as well as medical anecdotes and commentaries.

A Financial Crisis

Clough, as business manager, took steps that reflected tightened finances from the fire. He slashed expenses while upping ad rates and annual subscriptions. It wasn't enough.

So Dr. Abbott tapped into his own savings. He also sold off, for about $15,000, his file and ledger company. Further, he offered takers $20 bonds in his company. Ads for these read: "Doctor, these are as sure as the sun, as safe or safer than a bank."

Few bonds sold. Physicians were offered $200,000 worth of preferred stock in Abbott; few bought in. Dr. Abbott even attached a 12-room "Abbott Alkaloidal Sanatorium" to the rear of his home. Patients there could receive personal attention from Dr. Abbott; fellow physicians could get some rest and relaxation.

The financial Panic of 1907 set off a run on banks, such as this one in New York.

All the belt-tightening and revenue-raising swam against the current of the Panic of 1907, a severe run on the banks. Financier J.P. Morgan eventually eased the distress by organizing a pool of funds from secure banks and the government to inject liquidity into the banking system.

The financial turmoil hit the nation, and Chicago, hard. Dr. Abbott, Clough, and the Abbott company secretary, L.P. Scoville, were ranking officers for the local Ravenswood Exchange Bank. The bank failed, its debt $400,000. The three pledged to pay back deposits, which they largely did over three months.

Their own company took longer to fix. The depression caused a sharp drop in customer receipts. With cash short to pay off daily expenses, some employees were laid off. Others took voluntary pay cuts, many put in longer hours. Still more put off raises in return for promises of company stock down the road. Some of these workers would, in later decades, thus become millionaires. Dr. Abbott permitted a few employees to invest in Little Mattie, a gold mine he owned in Colorado's Chicago Creek. The investments were a bust, but Dr. Abbott eventually paid back all the investors.

Jousting with the *Journal*

It was during this difficult period that Dr. Abbott took to all-nighters, catching naps on office bedding.

Then, even as the firm's fiscal fortunes started to pick up, another blow befell it. Editorial attacks were launched on Abbott's business practices from an unusual source: the *Journal of the American Medical Association*.

In 1907–1908, the *Journal of the American Medical Association* and Abbott Alkaloidal fought a very public battle over the proper role of science and commerce in medicine. A sample from one of the *Journal's* salvos.

The Journal of the American Medical Association

Published under the Auspices of the Board of Trustees

Vol. XLVIII.   CHICAGO, ILLINOIS, MAY 18, 1907.   No. 20.

Address

THE COMMERCIAL DOMINATION OF THERAPEUTICS AND THE MOVEMENT FOR REFORM.*

GEORGE H. SIMMONS, M.D.
CHICAGO.

PROPRIETARY MEDICINE A RECENT DEVELOPMENT.

The proprietary medicine business as we know it is a development of only a little over a generation. In 1875, Lawrence, of *Medical Brief* fame (?), and his junta of nostrum makers, whose output and that of their offshoots alone have run into the hundreds, were unknown. Thirty years ago the so-called German synthetic chemicals were unheard of as medicines; now, if we include the true and the false, there are thousands of them. Including the typical nostrums, the more or less legitimate proprietary mixtures and the synthetic compounds, the number of proprietary medicines has become so vast that no one is rash enough to attempt to estimate it. A few of these, we may admit, have a distinct value; they represent original work and are worthy of recognition as remedial agents. The vast majority, however, are but the simplest of mixtures or are well-known drugs put out under fanciful names, with no advantage whatever; or are absolute frauds and swindles. Some of these remedies are made by manufacturing pharmaceutical and chemical houses of greater or less repute; the majority by men —or "companies"—who know nothing about medicine, pharmacy or chemistry, and who have gone into the business as they might have gone into any other get-rich-quick enterprise.

This business has been growing more rapidly than ever during recent years, and the statement made here in Baltimore last December that the use of this class of preparations has doubled during the last decade is probably true. But worse than the increase in number is the development in the advertising literature of unblushing falsehood and palpable deception. Conditions in this regard had become so disgraceful—I put this in the past tense because there has been a change since the Council began its work—that there seemed to be no statement too silly, no claim too extravagant, and no falsehood too brazen for use by those who wrote the advertising literature that physicians were asked to read and to believe. It was, therefore, not only the character of the preparations, but the methods of exploitation that had become unbearable and a disgrace to the profession that tolerated it. In brief, this business, the annual profits of which run into the millions, has grown until the use of proprietary medicines by many physicians has almost displaced the use of the

*The Annual Oration before the Medical and Chirurgical Faculty of Maryland, April 24, 1907.

individual official drug. It has checked advance in scientific methods of treatment, inhibited intelligent clinical observation and developed an optimism that is unwarranted by facts—an optimism that is more fatal than the most radical therapeutic nihilism. But above and worse than all, this commercialized materia medica has blighted our literature by debauching our medical journals and even by tainting our text-books.

And whose is the fault? That the business has developed in this country to such extent, with scarcely a protest on the part of our profession, is a reflection on the common sense and intelligence of the physicians of the United States. We, as well as manufacturers, are at fault. We must assume the blame for becoming such easy dupes to their enterprise and sagacity.

But a change is taking place; a halt has been called, and our profession is awakening to the disgrace of it all. It is about the movement for ridding our profession of this disgrace that I want to speak to-night.

NO PROTECTION IN THE PAST.

We have long suffered from a want of governmental or other supervision over the manufacture of medicines. In no other country has the standard and quality of drugs been left entirely to the manufacturer's honor. From time to time the medical profession has made spasmodic, but weak, efforts to remedy the condition: we find records of this even as early as the beginning of the nineteenth century.

The agitation of those early days resulted in the adoption of a Pharmacopeia, the first issue of which was published in 1820. This standard, by the way, was the work of physicians and was gotten out by them for the guidance of pharmacists, who, however, had nothing to do with its preparation. It is to be regretted that conditions have changed, and that, while the physicians then were the ones interested, for the last fifty years they have left it practically to the pharmacists. While the Pharmacopeia furnishes standards which were accepted by a few as authoritative, it was, after all, but an advisory instrument, and was followed or ignored as suited the manufacturer.

The Pharmacopeia only partially improved matters, and society transactions continued to contain records of criticisms of the prevailing conditions. So it went on until the organization of the American Medical Association. At its first meeting resolutions were adopted indicating that the question was still a vital one. So, again, in 1849, 1850 and every year or two thereafter this subject was discussed. Then, however, the unreliability of drugs was the source of irritation, the proprietary medicine abuse not yet being so much in evidence. In 1879 we first find the Association recognizing that incipient evil which has since developed into the modern curse—proprietary medicines. In the Transactions for that year we find the following:

Magazines like *Collier's* crusaded against shoddily made patent medicines. Lurid illustrations like E.W. Kemble's "Death's Laboratory" satirized such quackery.

Radam's "Microbe Killer" claimed to be "a positive and certain cure for all diseases," despite being nothing more than water charged with gases. It was precisely to counter such quackery that Dr. Abbott founded his company — which made Simmons' accusations all the more infuriating.

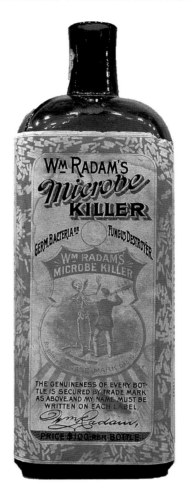

The assaults reflected the Progressive Era's concern over the substandard production of some foodstuffs and medicine. This was the time of Theodore Roosevelt's trust busting, and Upton Sinclair's muckraking exposés of the meatpacking industry. Some unethical manufacturers traded in cheaply made, even dangerous, patent medicines.

The patent medicine industry, which grossed more than $60 million a year, put dangerous ingredients like cocaine and opium in some products, while making wild claims about cures for cancer and obesity. The *Ladies Home Journal*, foreshadowing the food nutrition labels mandated decades later, campaigned for drug manufacturers to list out the chemicals in their medicines.

The outcry led to the federal Pure Food and Drug Act of January 1, 1907. In December of that year the medical *Journal*, which had supported the Act, turned its guns on Abbott Alkaloidal.

The target of its article was Abbott's Hyosine-Morphine-Cactin product, and its subtitle summed up the content: "An Interesting Example of the Subordination of Science to Commercialism." A full broadside followed in March 1908, while Dr. Abbott was suffering from meningitis. It called *The American Journal of Clinical Medicine* a "house organ devoted to the interests of the company and to the advertising of its products."

The article charged that "The company, though engaged in commercial lines, are members of medical societies and use this membership in medical meetings to advance the interests of their firm." Another Abbott officer was singled out for "effrontery" in offering preferred stock for the company during a financial depression. The *Journal* even chastised Dr. Abbott for his voluminous writing. Abbott officers and outside physicians were denounced as part of "The Alkaloidal Cult."

The instigator of the *Journal*'s attacks, chief editor Dr. George H. Simmons, began his career, ironically, as a medical crusader. Simmons began in hydropathy, which prescribed water baths and water binges as a cure-all for intestinal and rectal woes. He later converted to conventional, scientific medicine, serving as secretary and treasurer of the Western Surgical and Gynecological Association, before rising, in 1899, to editorship of the influential *Journal*. Simmons' targets were not always obvious ones.

They included Charles W. Post of Battle Creek, Michigan, maker of Postum and Grape Nuts cereals, and an advocate of healthy nutrition. And an early ally of his attacks against useless patent-medicine "nostrums" was none other than Dr. Abbott. In 1904–1905, Abbott had attacked "the Poison Trust" and "the secret nostrum evil, which is growing at such a dangerous pace."

Bloodied but unbowed, Dr. Abbott unleashed a ferocious rebuttal in July 1908 against "this campaign of persecution and vilification." With help from Clough and Burdick, his pen churned out a 48-page booklet, called "An Appeal for a Square Deal." The title was taken from a slogan of President Theodore Roosevelt.

DOCTORS' WAR GROWS BITTER

Lydston-Simmons Controversy Stirs Medical Profession.

CAREER OF ONE ATTACKED.

Editor Criticised for Advertising Old Medical Institute.

Newspapers savored the unusual battle royale among medical professionals.

"I have been sneered at, vilified, and abused," wrote Dr. Abbott. He asked why drug firms such as Merck and Parke-Davis, and their house organs, had escaped the *Journal*'s wrath. "Why am I and my Company singled out for persecution, when other men and other similar concerns enjoy complete immunity?"

"Has there been complaint on the part of honest professional men using our products?" wondered Abbott. "On the contrary, there is abundance of testimony from thousands of physicians all over the country that we have given them trustworthy goods and honest service."

The *Journal* wouldn't print Dr. Abbott's responses, so he went around it. He mailed the appeal directly to physicians and medical journals across the country. They found a publication crammed with arguments — and with impressive photos, figures, and physician testimonials on the company.

Dr. Abbott saw behind the attacks the vested interests of pharmacists seeking to retain their drug-making trade. "Gigantic and complete is this great scheme;" he wrote, "merciless is its application; and more far-reaching and deadly to therapeutic progress …" He also saw lurking the practitioners of "galenical" medicine — the crude mortar-and-pestle practices dating back to the ancient Greek physician Galen.

"Houses which have thousands of dollars invested in galenic medicines," Dr. Abbott inveighed, "see in the unstoppable growth of the active-principle movement … their ultimate Waterloo." He declared, "A clam-hunting tramp might as well attempt to sweep back the Atlantic with a broom."

Abbott defended the right of companies and doctors to pursue their trades without undue outside interference. "In the medical profession, as in religion or science, the perils of dominating influence cannot be escaped … intelligent thought and honest independent effort should be left *free*, untrammeled by the incubus of personal hatreds and the fixed and unvarying dicta of self-made authorities."

The *Journal*'s Simmons tried parrying the counterattack with personal invective. He chided the tactics of "astute but unprincipled demagogues … of a pathetic, lachrymose character … in which mock-heroics and anathemas were about evenly distributed." Meantime, newspapers covered the unusual mudslinging among medical professionals with relish. Headlines blared: "Going for a Medical Combat," and "Doctors' War Grows Bitter."

Physicians and medical publications around the country weighed in on one side or the other.

Dr. Abbott made a fierce and thorough rebuttal of the *Journal*'s charges against his company with a fact-filled booklet, "An Appeal for a Square Deal."

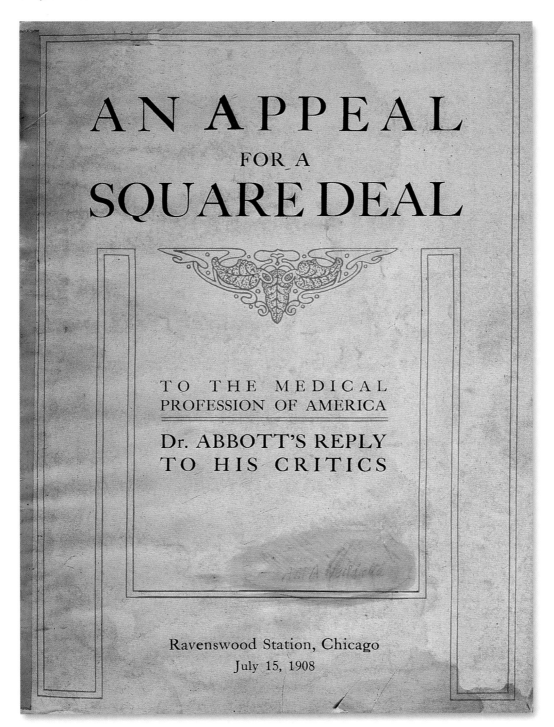

AN APPEAL
FOR A
SQUARE DEAL

TO THE MEDICAL
PROFESSION OF AMERICA

Dr. ABBOTT'S REPLY
TO HIS CRITICS

Ravenswood Station, Chicago
July 15, 1908

While the charges and countercharges flew, Abbott and the *Journal* — like two rival powers seeking to avoid all-out war — began to conduct back-channel diplomacy. Ad chief Clough met regularly with the *Journal*'s business manager, Will C. Braun. In time, a truce was reached. Negative words were silenced. The *Journal*'s ban on Abbott advertising was lifted.

Continues on page 41 ▶

Making Medical Products and Journals

The 1907–1908 attacks on Abbott by the *Journal of the American Medical Association* produced an unintended windfall for history, namely, the many period photographs of Abbott's production and print facilities prepared for Dr. Abbott's booklet, "An Appeal for a Square Deal." That work was Dr. Abbott's fierce, detailed rebuttal to the *Journal*'s charge of commercialism. It countered the charge by laying out, with pictures and carefully crafted text, the professionalism and state-of-the-art technology behind the company's manufacturing and publishing prowess.

Abbott's pharmaceutical endeavors began with intense laboratory research into new drugs, and carried through to manufacturing, packaging, and the dissemination of new medical knowledge.

A researcher dwarfed by shelves of chemicals in a room of the "physiologic" laboratory of the manufacturing and research building. The development of new medicines began through "chemical, pathological, and microscopic work."

Employees operated
vacuum dryers to remove
the moisture from "granula-
tions" to make the material
suitable for compression
into tablets and pills.

3

2

The workers turned out 500
tablets of medicine each
minute — 6 million tablets
a month.

4

A line of cylindrical coating
pans was used to apply a
glaze coating to granules
and tablets.

6

After receiving bulk goods from the labs, workers bottled the products, and sent them on to the shipping department.

5

The saline department mixed and dried salts, and turned them into granules for products like saline laxative.

7

From the shipping department, the goods of Abbott Alkaloidal were sent out to the world. Pictured here, Abbott employees Frank Rastell, Roy Thunberg, Patrick Carey, Myra Keppler, Edna Hurst.

8

Across from the research and manufacturing building stood the publishing plant. There employees set the type for assorted publications, such as *The American Journal of Clinical Medicine*.

9

The printing presses, including the smaller "pony" presses here, regularly rolled out thousands of copies of journals and pamphlets.

10

Once a publication was typeset, printed, and mailed out, employees in the circulation department kept track of subscribers old and new.

The Abbott Fleet, 1909

Although a high-tech company from the beginning, The Abbott Alkaloidal Company in 1909 still did not own a single automobile. Advertising director S. DeWitt Clough sought to remedy that. He suggested to Dr. Abbott that the company's founder might be able to trade in his bicycle for a new car. He had in mind the Waverley, an electrically powered vehicle made in Indianapolis. Clough thought he could cut a good deal for the auto, and the Doctor told him to try.

After a series of letters between Clough and the Waverly's maker, the canny ad man secured a brand-new automobile, plus several hundred dollars, in exchange for a year's worth of ads in *The American Journal of Clinical Medicine*.

A month later, a Chicago railroad concern informed Clough that the car had arrived at its terminal. He rushed over to pick it up. However, it was the first time Clough had been in a car, much less driven one. A "crash" course in driving ensued.

The freight men helped the Abbott official get the Waverley out on the street, and showed him how to move the steering lever back and forth. Still, recalled Clough, "It was only by a miracle and driving the car at three miles per hour that I finally arrived in front of Dr. Abbott's home."

Dr. Abbott happily accepted the new toy. But he was more accustomed to riding around on two wheels than four. One morning, while backing the Waverley out of the garage, he mucked up the gears. The car shot backward through a fence, and crashed into a tree. The Doctor wasn't badly hurt, but did sprain an arm.

He stayed mum about the incident, but tongues wagged when

MODEL NO. 29, PRICE $1,100

THE POPE *Waverley* PHYSICIAN'S ROAD WAGON

The above model is designed especially to meet the requirements of the physician. It is made roomy, with a broad and high back seat, fully upholstered, for comfort; the top is large and extends well forward for protection from the weather. An ideal runabout throughout.

POPE MOTOR CAR CO., Waverley Dept., INDIANAPOLIS, IND., U.S.A.
WRITE FOR COMPLETE CATALOGUE

The "clean and odorless" Waverley electric car. Advertising chief S. DeWitt Clough made a deal to obtain this "physician's road wagon" for Abbott. Clough and Dr. Abbott, although high-ranking officers in a technology-driven firm, had difficulty mastering the novel apparatus of the automobile.

he showed up at work with the arm in a sling. His secret revealed, Dr. Abbott returned to riding his bicycle.

In 2007, Abbott would become the first Fortune 500 company to commit to making its entire U.S. fleet — then more than 20,000 vehicles — carbon neutral. ∎

With crises behind it, Abbott relied on talented employees such as engineering and financial wizard Edward Hawks ("E.H.") Ravenscroft to raise it to new success.

Bouncing Back

When the dust cleared from the three major challenges it faced in just its second full decade of operation, Abbott Alkaloidal had not only survived, but prospered. Even during the depression year of 1907, while other drug companies faltered, its sales actually went up, to $290,000. They then soared, increasing by 50 percent in 1908 and by almost 25 percent in 1909.

A restored treasury led to construction, in 1908, of an overdue, five-story building for pharmaceutical production and research, next door to the new publishing plant. Built of fire-resistant brick and concrete, it featured a modern sprinkler system that turned on automatically in case of fire. It also had two large boilers to supply power, electric light, and heat. Construction was supervised by the nationally known railroad bridge engineer Edward Hawks (E.H.) Ravenscroft, the husband of Dr. Abbott's sister Lucy.

> ## "Just to work, and to get as I give, 'the square deal.'"
>
> — DR. WALLACE C. ABBOTT

When the American Medical Association, the parent organization of the *Journal*, met in Chicago in 1909 for its annual summer convention, the Abbott company crowed a little. Attending doctors were brought by newfangled automobile along Chicago's Lake Shore Drive, and then to the firm's new production plant. There they found literature marked by Dr. Abbott's unique style, celebrating "a huge establishment employing hundreds of conscientious workers. It's 'on the square' and we want to see you and get acquainted … Every doctor is invited. Come at any time!"

The young firm was decidedly back on its feet and ready for the future. And none too soon — Abbott would find its endurance and mettle tested again in the next decade, in the form of a world war.

In 1909 a retirement party was held for the company's first retiree, Dr. Abbott's personal secretary, Ida Richter. The invaluable aide left no detail undone concerning Dr. Abbott's demanding work schedule. This marked the beginning of a long and continuing tradition of caring for the people who built the company throughout their retirement from it.

Decade at a Glance

1900–1910

1900

Dr. Abbott's business is officially incorporated in Illinois as The Abbott Alkaloidal Company. The catalog features more than 350 granules, tablets, and medical devices such as syringes and abdominal belts.

Abbott stock certificate on the company's incorporation in 1900. ▶

Abbott makes its first acquisition, the Tengwall File and Ledger Company, which produces binders for office records.

Abbott's chief pharmacist and two employees in a small formulation room.

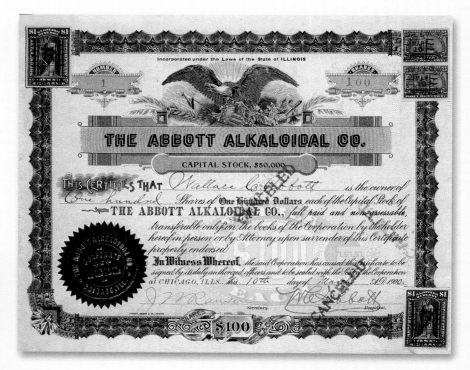

1901

With its business growing, the company builds a four-story brick building to house The Clinic Publishing Company.

1902

The Alkaloidal Clinic reaches almost 200 pages in length, and goes to 1 out of 4 physicians in the United States. Full-page ads cost $55, yearly subscriptions $1. Included with advertisements for medicines are ones for trusses and hair removal powder.

1903

Working 14 to 16 hours a day, Dr. Abbott wins over customers with a stream of letters, editorials, and advertising copy. He hardly has time to clean his desk: stacks of papers cover it, and fill the floor around his chair. He dictates into the night, and sometimes rouses his secretary during pre-dawn hours. Some 30 employees work to produce alkaloidal and other medicines. Sales of saline laxative are also brisk.

1904

The erudite Dr. Alfred S. Burdick, editor of the *Medical Standard*, joins the company, serving as an editor and high-level aide for $35 a week. He will eventually become company president.

Products and publications contain the company's first logo, a circle inscribed with the words "Purity, Accuracy Guaranteed," with Dr. Abbott's initials entwined in the center.

▼

Garrulous Simeon DeWitt Clough joins the company and soon writes much of the ad copy. He too will one day become company president, as well as board chairman. Clough's outlook on life: "A good definition of a 'nobody' is a man without enthusiasm."

▲

1905

A fire guts the 50,000-square-foot printing plant, though a lucky wind saves the production facility. Damages amount to $200,000. Dr. Abbott is unbowed, bidding the world to: "Watch us grow!" He quickly arranges for rebuilding funds. The company boasts of its product quality that it produces, "No dope for quackery!"

1906

Dr. Abbott has a five-story brick replacement building constructed for the printing plant. The fire-proof offices gleam with light from tall windows; the print offices sport new linotype presses. *The American Journal of Clinical Medicine* is launched, and includes learned articles by foreign writers. The company forms its first sales force of seven "Abbott missionaries," managed by Dr. Thackeray. Armed with expense money and product samples, they travel to prospective clients by horse-and-buggy, railroad, and riverboat.

1907

Company belt-tightening follows the nationwide Panic of 1907 financial crisis. Some employees defer pay for a promise of future stock, which later makes many millionaires. Bonds, preferred stock, and even stakes in a gold mine are offered to raise scarce funds. Dr. Abbott takes to working 24-hour shifts.

The company begins doing business in the United Kingdom, beginning growth outside the United States that is still accelerating today.

A salesman and Dr. Abbott in an early automobile.

▼

1908

◀ A feud breaks out with Dr. George Simmons, editor-in-chief of the *Journal of the American Medical Association*, who accuses Abbott's publications of commercialism. This culminates in Dr. Abbott's fierce response to critics, *An Appeal for a Square Deal*, which defends the firm's right to produce and publish as it sees fit. Despite it all, Abbott's sales soar to $360,000.

◀ A five-story building for manufacturing and research is constructed next to the printing plant. Construction of the new laboratory and manufacturing facility, complete with sprinklers and power plant, is supervised by future chairman Edward H. Ravenscroft.

1909

Dr. Abbott offers free automobile rides to take delegates from the Chicago convention of the American Medical Association, following the Square Deal episode, for tours of the company's new production facilities. Production workers are turning out 500 tablets of medicine a minute — 6 million tablets monthly.

▲

Workers at Abbott bottling and packing drugs.

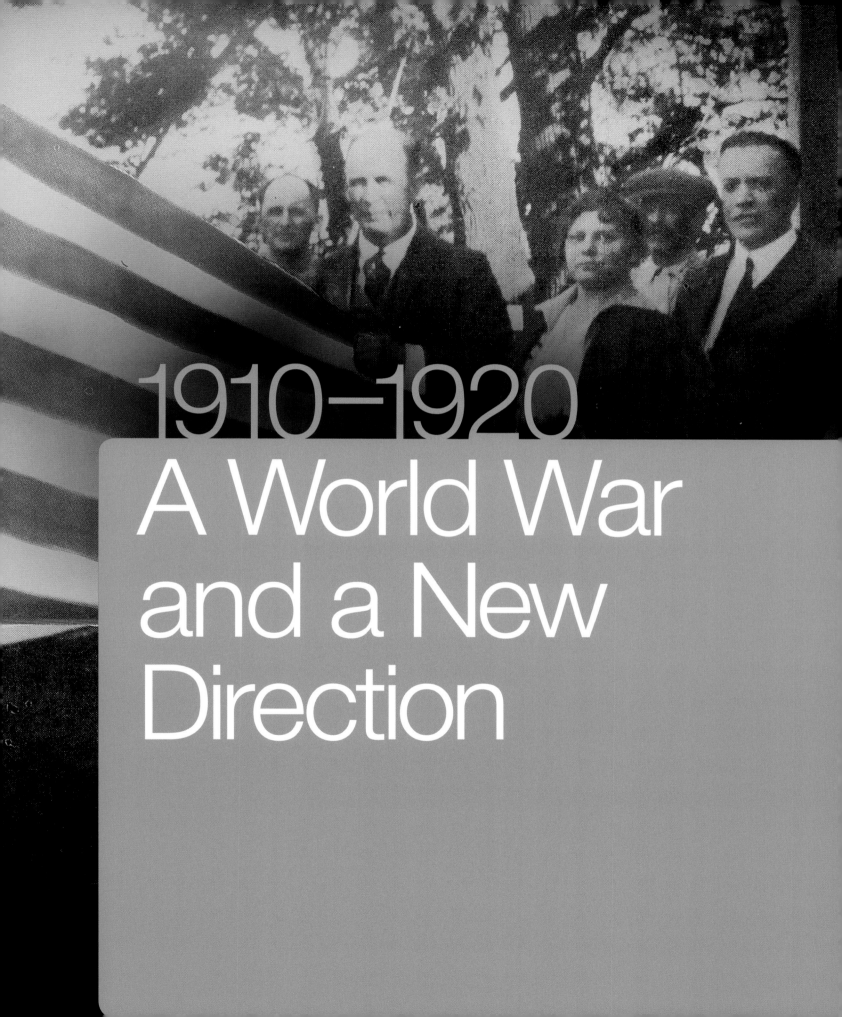

1910–1920
A World War and a New Direction

It was 1918, and his country was in the midst of the Great War. Ernest H. Volwiler was a young chemist finishing up his Ph.D. work at the University of Illinois, and wanted to serve his country and mankind.

He asked Dr. Roger Adams — a high-level consultant to Abbott in "synthetic" drugs made from chemical compounds in the laboratory — about an impressive offer by the wartime government. Uncle Sam wanted to make Volwiler a lieutenant, and assign him to chemical warfare work.

"The war may be over before you have a chance to get really settled," Adams replied. "Why don't you work for the Abbott people? They are engaging in research on barbiturates and other synthetic drugs. They have a contract with the Navy to furnish some and they'll need some good people."

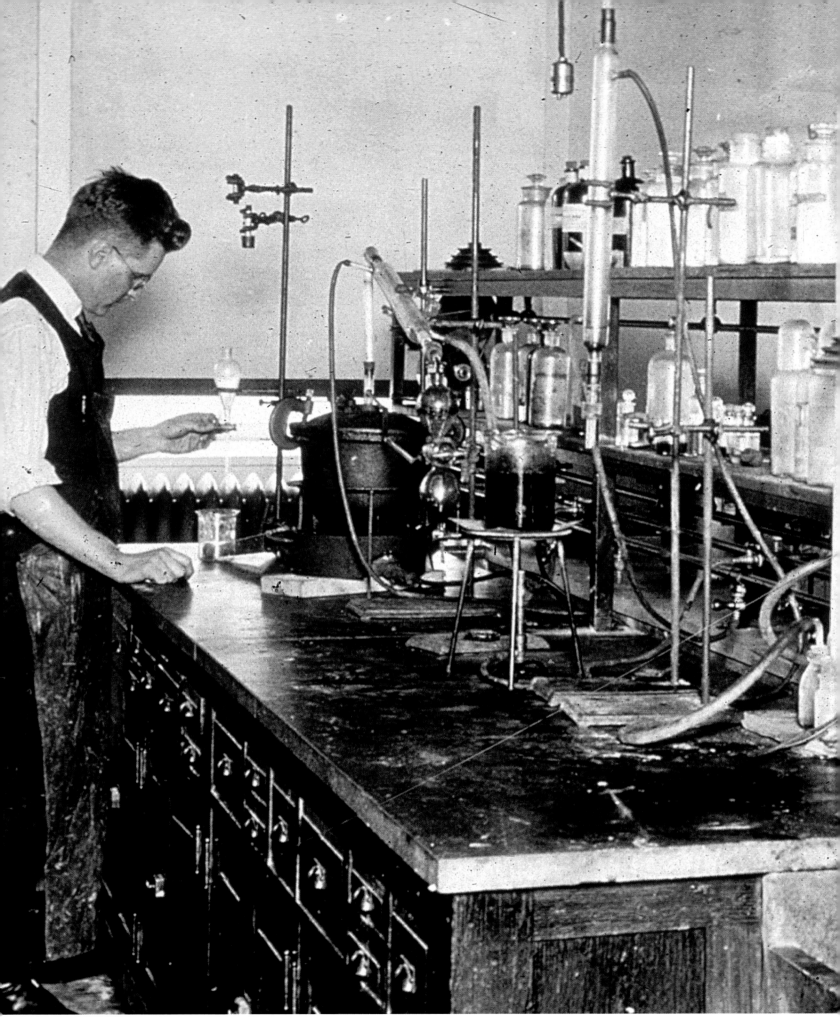

Dr. Ernest H. Volwiler conducted tests on alcohol-based pain killers in a lab built especially for his work. The discoloration on the lab bench attests to the long hours he spent in the lab. Over a storied 41-year Abbott career, he would rise to become the company's president and chairman.

Volwiler, like many clever, hard-working scientists and managers, signed up with Abbott's war effort. The company and the country's drug industry would be changed unalterably as a result.

Bringing in New Talent

After overcoming the crises of 1905–1908, Abbott Alkaloidal prospered again. In 1910, fully 50,000 doctors, of the 130,000 in the country, were on its mailing lists. Revenues crossed the half-million-dollar line. Its catalogs offered more than 700 items, including the mainstay alkaloidal medicines. Still, the product line had many somewhat prosaic items, including purgatives such as Saline Laxative, antacids, and cold remedies such as Calcidin.

A growing Abbott attracted outstanding new talent. This included manufacturing expert Ferdinand H. "Fred" Young, pictured circa 1935, who would later supervise major production efforts of drugs such as penicillin.

In addition to its facilities in Chicago, Abbott had opened branches in New York, San Francisco, Seattle, and London. From the early years it had attracted talent from, and sold its goods to, nations overseas. Reflecting this early focus on expansion, it opened branch offices and agencies across the United States and as far away as India.

Now a larger and established company, Abbott brought in another impressive group of new hires. Directing the recently built research labs was Dr. Joseph Favil Biehn, once an instructor in bacteriology at Northwestern University. Cronies of Chicago Mayor Fred Busse had made him resign as director of the city's Health Department labs when he tried to enforce the pure milk laws. Biehn, a stickler for strict quality control, went on to work extensively in pharmaceuticals and to head Abbott's medical department. He also helped establish a veterinary operation, for which Clough published *Helpful Hints for the Veterinarian*.

Rivaling Clough as a "boy wonder" was Ferdinand H. "Fred" Young. At age 20, he was deputy manager of an Indiana pharmaceutical maker. He was aggressive. He was hired after corralling Dr. Abbott in his office and demanding: "How would you like to make the finest concentrates in the world?" Young came cheap: Abbott hired him at 20 cents an hour for the alkaloid production shop. But he used his experiences to eventually lead Abbott's vast future manufacturing operations.

Executive Energy

Although back to a full five hours of nightly sleep, Dr. Abbott remained a very hands-on manager. He was forever dreaming up ways to improve the business, wherever he went. One time, Dr. Burdick caught him jotting down thoughts in his "memory rest" notebook during a choir performance at the Ravenswood Methodist Episcopal Church.

"Back up and try again!"

— DR. WALLACE C. ABBOTT

While roaming the offices and labs, Dr. Abbott remained intensely involved in colleagues' work and lives. When he learned of an employee who needed work on her teeth, he had a neighborhood dentist care for her. When he found another worker had a boil on his neck, he lanced it on the spot. Company parties and picnics were common.

Yet, perhaps mindful of the recent financial downturn, Abbott was also an advocate of "tough love." He'd admonish his charges: "Never get careless about your work, and imagine that you are indispensable." And: "If you have to earn a living you might just as well be happy as morose over it. You will not only enjoy yourself … but you will rise higher and faster."

Dr. Abbott, not one to waste words or actions, mastered the quick, motivating phrase. After a production line faltered, he'd shout, "Back up and try again!" When a worker or manager procrastinated on a task, he'd cry, "Do it now!"

"Everybody get busy—
the Doctor."

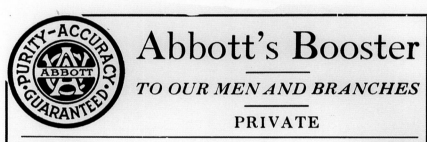

Abbott's Booster

TO OUR MEN AND BRANCHES

PRIVATE

Second Year	May-June, 1912	No. Two

I WANT MORE SMOKE

You men who are out on the road these days getting the orders, or trying to get them, are exactly the fellows who are supposed to keep the smoke coming out of the towering chimney of this plant. It is upon you that we depend.

The volume of smoke emitted by the chimney the last thirty days has been by no means inconsiderable; it has been sufficient to darken the landscape around here all right. But still I am not satisfied. Not quite!

I want more smoke.

Now, beginning next week, I am going to make it a point to watch my chimney every day at high tide, to see if I am getting it. So get busy, every one of you, and shoot in the orders—the fuel that makes the smoke that comes out of the towering chimney over the engine house.

I want smoke and plenty of it—the densest, the blackest smoke that ever wended its way skyward. And when the warm breezes commence to blow in I don't want to see the smoke line getting any smaller around or thinner or less black than it is right now—or will be in a week from now.

I want more smoke and I want it all spring and summer, without lull or intermission. If I do not get it I shall be very disappointed, I can tell you.

So please knuckle down—all—and keep the stream of orders coming in uninterruptedly. Let's all do our very best to make this year a record-breaking one. We can; we've got a good start; and the outlook is fine.

Keep pushing Calcidin hard—and harder yet. In these spring months, with their changeable weather, there is no end to the indications for it. Statistics show that there are more cases of pneumonia in the late spring than in mid-winter. And the crop of "colds" and catarrh is a bumper one.

All together now, for more smoke and a big year! You know me—"I want what I want when I want it."

A notable memo of spring 1912, in *Abbott's Booster*, was aimed at spurring the 35-member sales team. Titled "I WANT MORE SMOKE," it read in part:

"You men who are out on the roads these days getting the orders … are exactly the fellows who are supposed to keep the smoke coming out of the towering chimney of this plant … I want more smoke and I want it all spring and summer without lull or intermission. If I do not get it I shall be very disappointed I can tell you … You know me — 'I want what I want when I want it.'"

Dr. Abbott didn't only give constructive criticism; he was eager to receive it as well. He sent advance copies of ads to sales personnel, telling them:

"You need never feel you are obtrusive; our writers admit they know a lot but not quite all … we urge you to read them all carefully and to note particularly about arguments we use …

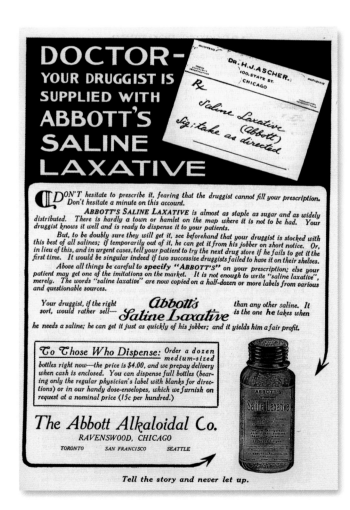

In the early 1910s, much of Abbott's revenues were from rather prosaic items such as salt-laden laxatives. It was time for a change in direction.

And if you find we have missed a good selling point — one that you have been using successfully — call our attention to the omission, so that we and your brothers on the road may benefit … Don't be selfish like the mongrel dog guarding his delectable bone!"

A Change in Direction

Such missives from Dr. Abbott were generated partly out of growing concern over slowing sales. In 1912, revenues dropped for the first time in company history, to $558,000 from $600,000. In *Abbott's Booster*, to spike sales of alkaloidal medicine, the Doctor urged: "Everybody hustle! … Don't forget to suggest them in bulk … and never write down any order for less than 1,000 unless the customer insists that you do so."

An alternative way to take in money was to sell stock, previously attempted during the 1907 depression. In 1911, Abbott sold 10–share blocks of 7 percent preferred stock for $100. The shares were offered to a list of physicians.

With sales of alkaloidal drugs slowing, the company turned to alternative money raisers, including stock offerings.

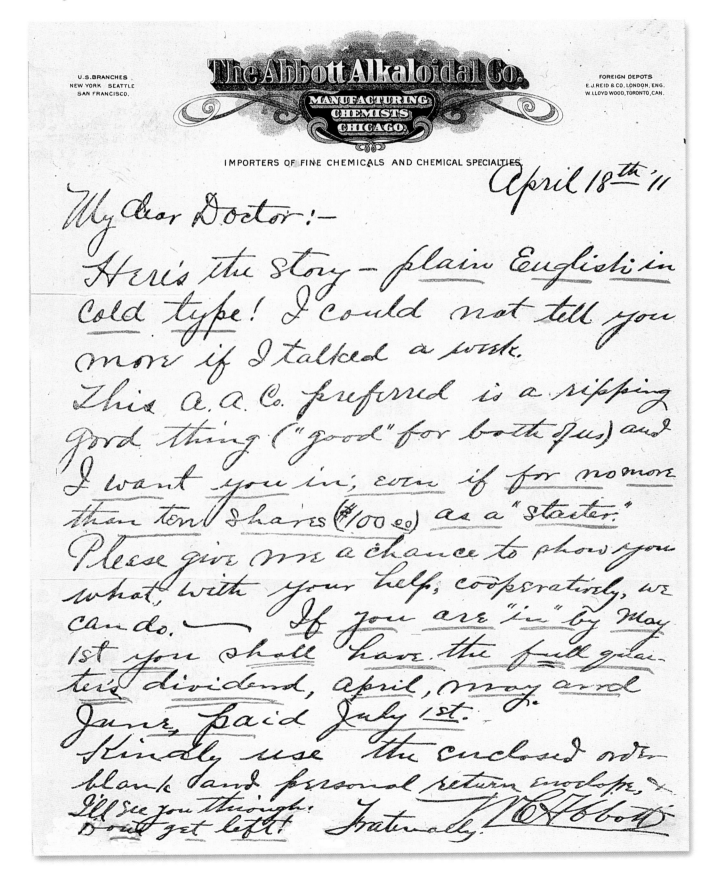

The Abbott Alkaloidal Co.
MANUFACTURING CHEMISTS CHICAGO.

U.S. BRANCHES
NEW YORK   SEATTLE
SAN FRANCISCO.

FOREIGN DEPOTS
E.J.REID & CO. LONDON, ENG.
W. LLOYD WOOD, TORONTO, CAN.

IMPORTERS OF FINE CHEMICALS AND CHEMICAL SPECIALTIES

April 18th '11

My Dear Doctor:—

Here's the story — plain English; in cold type! I could not tell you more if I talked a week.

This A.A. Co. preferred is a ripping good thing ("good" for both of us) and I want you in; even if for no more than ten Shares ($100 ea) as a "starter."

Please give me a chance to show you what, with your help, coöperatively, we can do. — If you are "in" by May 1st you shall have the full quarter's dividend, April, may and June, paid July 1st. —

Kindly use the enclosed order blank and personal return envelope, & I'll see you through! Don't get left!   Fraternally, W C Abbott

Abbott people have always balanced their hard work with social outlets of all kinds. Above, an Abbott picnic and below, left to right, circa 1912: employees Ralph, Harry, Katherine, and Hazel, of The Abbott Alkaloidal Orchestra.

Most who took the offer soon sold the stock off, despite a handwritten pitch from Dr. Abbott himself. His lively solicitation read:

"Here's the story — *plain English in cold type!* I could not tell you more if I talked a week. This A.A. company preferred is a ripping good thing ('good' for both of us) and I want you in: even if no more than ten shares ($100.00) as a 'starter.' If you are 'in' by May 1st, you shall have the full quarter's dividend, April, May, and June, paid July 1st … I'll see you through. Don't get left."

Despite these efforts, the next big thing in pharmaceuticals was not alkaloids derived from plants, but synthetic drugs, devised in the lab from mixing and matching various chemical compounds. Scientists like the brilliant German Dr. Paul Ehrlich had developed synthetic compounds to fight previously untreatable diseases like diphtheria and syphilis. Substances like saccharin, for more mundane concerns like weight loss, were also being made. Drug companies abroad had started to generate large revenues from these "chemical drugs."

Dr. Burdick had a great command of current medical literature, and saw which way the winds were blowing. He urged Dr. Abbott to shift the company's focus to the discovery and production of synthetic drugs. After long

consideration, Dr. Abbott agreed. Dr. Burdick expanded the chemistry staff, bringing aboard the likes of Harvard-trained Ph.D. Franklin P. Summers, and wide-ranging, Danish-born pharmacist Carl Nielsen, R.Ph. The latter had taken refuge in Abbott's Chicago office after the 1910 Mexican Revolution ended his work fermenting exotic plants for the Mexican government.

As part of this transition, in 1915 the company changed its name — from The Abbott Alkaloidal Company to Abbott Laboratories.

Yet a major obstacle blocked Abbott's chemical drug ambitions, as it did all United States firms. The worldwide industry in chemical drugs and their precursor chemicals was dominated by German companies. In the early 1900s, imperial Germany was the worldwide leader in pharmaceuticals and medicine. German firms had invented, and held the patents on, the blockbuster drugs of the time, like Novocaine, the local anesthetic, and Veronal, a much-used barbiturate.

And Germany played hardball to protect its leading position. If an American concern had the know-how to make and market a rival drug, the Germans had the deep pockets and market share to wage a price war, forcing the rival out of business.

The Impact of War

Then, in August 1914, the First World War erupted, changing the rules of the game. Britain's Royal Navy blockaded Germany, cutting off exports of its drugs and chemicals. This created shortages of both, as well as vast incentives for American firms to make their own synthetic drugs and chemical precursors. More immediately, trench warfare, with its millions of casualties, created a pressing need for more effective antiseptics on battlefields and in field hospitals.

Abbott, with its research and production teams bulked up by the war's outbreak, was primed to fill the emerging need.

Here Dr. Burdick's habit of scouring the medical literature came into play. He was struck by a report in the *British Medical Journal* of breakthrough work on a powerful new antiseptic by Dr. Henry H. Dakin. Dakin, a young Englishman attached to the French Army, was stationed at a hospital in Compiegne. There thousands of wounded soldiers were dying from sepsis, and from the irritating effects of existing antiseptics on wounds and healthy tissue. Frustrated doctors and nurses had taken to "antiseptic nihilism," relying on water, alcohol, and soap alone. A new kind of germicide was desperately needed.

As with so many of its drugs, Abbott chemists prepared variants of the original, in this case *Chlorazene*. In addition to tablets mixed in water, it took the form of *Chlorazene Surgical Powder* and *Chlorazene Surgical Cream.*

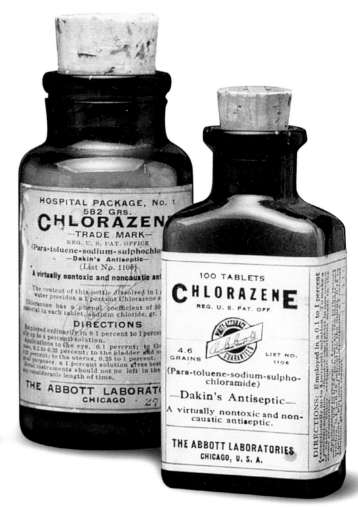

Dakin experimented with a vast array of chemical combinations, including 200 variants of chlorine. Finally he came up with the formula for para-toluene-sodium-sulfo chloramide, dubbed chloramine. A white crystal smelling faintly of chlorine and dissolvable in water, it cured infections far better than old standbys like carbolic acid. And the "precious fluid," as elated medical personnel called it, was non-toxic to wounds and healthy flesh. Recovery rates among the casualties of war skyrocketed.

Dr. Burdick, on learning of Dakin's innovation, fired off a memo to Dr. Abbott: "Somebody is going to take this up in the United States and pretty soon."

That someone was Abbott. Within half a year of the article's appearance, the company was manufacturing chloramine, which it marketed as *Chlorazene*. Hitting the market in summer 1917, *Chlorazene* worked 50 times more effectively against certain bacteria than carbolic acid. And it acted 80 times faster than preparations of mercury. Uses for *Chlorazene* extended far beyond surgery, to dental extractions, burns, even gonorrhea and athlete's foot.

The Abbott brain trust, in a jovial mood, 1913. Standing, left to right: S. DeWitt Clough, E.H. Ravenscroft, Franklin P. Summers, Dr. Abbott. Seated, left to right: W.R. Laughlin, C.O. Brown, Dr. Burdick.

Dr. Dakin's chlorine-based antiseptic, produced and marketed by Abbott as *Chlorazene*, greatly reduced fatalities among wounded patients undergoing surgery.

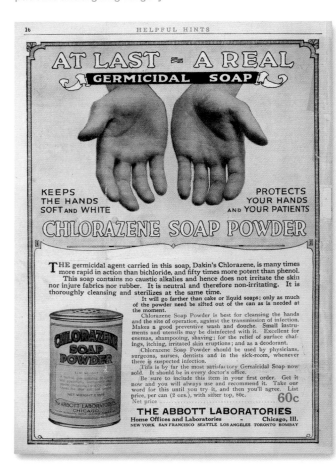

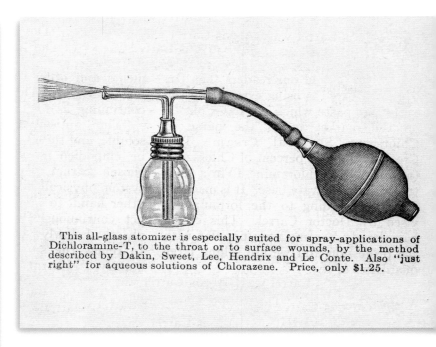

The device shown above was available from the Abbott catalog. It delivered *Dichloramine-T*, a substance related to *Chlorazene*, to the nasal passages.

A Proud Tradition of Anesthetics

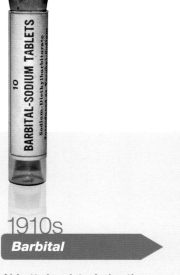

1910s
Barbital

Abbott chemists during the First World War synthesized the German anesthetic Veronal, renaming it *Barbital*.

1920s
Butyn

In the 1920s came inexpensive, non-addictive *Butyn*.

Soldiers stuck without drinkable water — or farmers with bad well water — found *Halazone* disinfectant tablets invaluable.

A chemically related product prepared in oil, called *Dichloramine-T*, was geared to nasal infections. It was administered through a hand-held "atomizer," or glass bottle with a squeeze spray.

Vital to soldiers in the field is potable water, and here Dr. Dakin scored another triumph in research with a U.S. Army Medical Corps officer, Major E.K. Dunham. They formulated tablets that made polluted water, even sewage, drinkable. Water so treated kept for months and "was not unpleasant to the taste." Abbott manufactured this substance too, calling it *Halazone*.

Helpful Hints for the Busy Doctor noted: "Tap water containing 5 percent sewage and bacillus coli is disinfected by *Halazone*, dilution 1:175,000 to 1:500,000, in 30 to 60 minutes … Not only are [these tablets] sure to be employed by soldiers in the field, but they will be extensively used by travelers, campers."

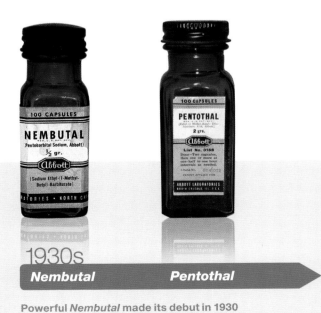

1930s
Nembutal   Pentothal

Powerful *Nembutal* made its debut in 1930 and, in 1937, *Pentothal* — in time the world's most used anesthetic.

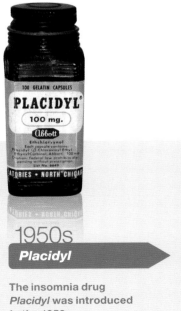

1950s
Placidyl

The insomnia drug *Placidyl* was introduced in the 1950s.

1990s
Ultane

Ultane, also known as sevorane, a universal anesthetic with very few side effects, was first marketed in 1995.

The spring 1917 cover of *Helpful Hints for the Busy Doctor* reflected a world at war, and a company's sense of duty.

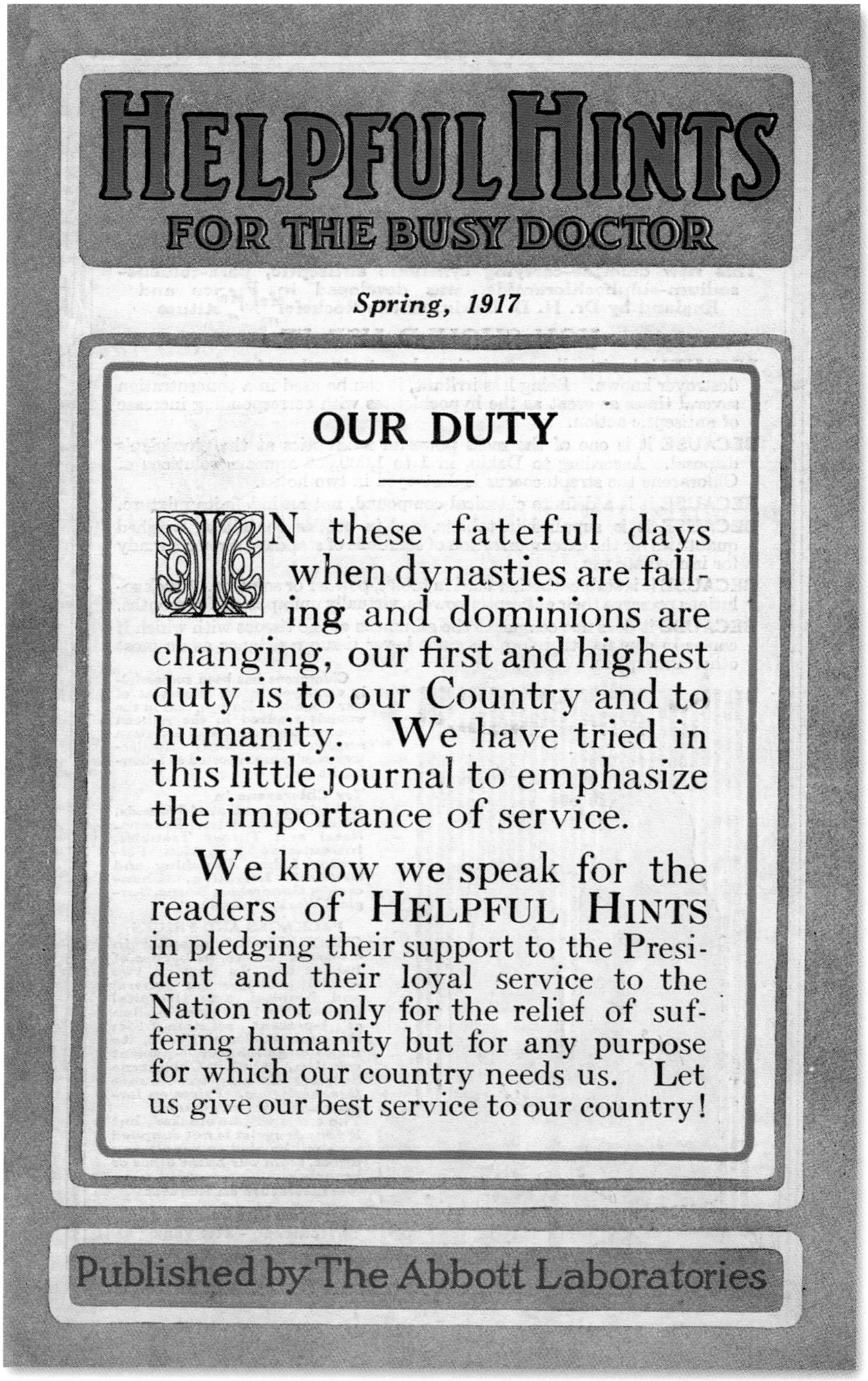

HELPFUL HINTS
FOR THE BUSY DOCTOR

Spring, 1917

OUR DUTY

———

IN these fateful days when dynasties are falling and dominions are changing, our first and highest duty is to our Country and to humanity. We have tried in this little journal to emphasize the importance of service.

We know we speak for the readers of HELPFUL HINTS in pledging their support to the President and their loyal service to the Nation not only for the relief of suffering humanity but for any purpose for which our country needs us. Let us give our best service to our country!

Published by The Abbott Laboratories

The Home Front

Other major products were developed in-house, spurred by the severe shortages of German drugs. In 1915, the British allowed through their blockade a German ship carrying Salvarsan, an effective remedy against syphilis. Distributed ashore, the price of the drug soared to $35 and, later, $100 a tube.

During a United States Senate hearing, Herman Metz, a representative of German drug giant Farbwerke Hoechst, assaulted a Johns Hopkins Hospital doctor for accusing his firm of price fixing. Thundered the *Journal of the American Medical Association*: "It is the duty of Congress to abrogate the patent … on all medical preparations of importance."

Eager to encourage American production, in October 1917 Congress passed the Trading with the Enemy Act.

It permitted U.S. firms to make some German drugs under different names. Such drugs had to meet the highest quality standards, approved by the Federal Trade Commission, on the advice of the National Research Council. The Council was filled with noted chemists such as Dr. Moses Gomberg of the University of Michigan and Dr. Julius Alfred Steiglitz of the University of Chicago.

A vital Abbott point of contact, as well as research *wunderkind*, was chemist Dr. Roger Adams, then 28. Descended from the famed Adams family of Boston, and Harvard-schooled, he had practical experience with the best in German pharmacology, having also studied at Kaiser Wilhelm Institute in Berlin, before moving on to Harvard to obtain his Ph.D.

There Adams set up a laboratory of 10 student chemists to make some 125 organic chemicals for companies, government laboratories, and colleges around the country. Adams "had an encyclopedic knowledge of synthetic and structural organic chemistry," according to a biography, "including recent developments that had not yet reached the scientific journals."

In 1916, Adams had been mulling over his job prospects when Dr. Burdick, on the prowl for chemists, asked one of Adams' chemistry professors, Dr. George Beal, if he knew of any good prospects. Beal approached Adams, who commented of Abbott, "It's a small firm. Do you think it will ever amount to much?"

Beal answered, "My father had often spoken his high regard for Drs. Abbott and Burdick."

Dr. Adams began work in the summer of 1917. Before year's end, his dynamic team of chemists had synthesized the German drugs Novocaine and Veronal. Abbott rechristened them *Procaine* and *Barbital*, and swiftly brought them to market. For this help Adams received a royalty of 2.5 percent on their sales, a considerable boost to his $50 dollar-a-month consulting fee. Another research team developed an equivalent of Atophan, a German remedy for arthritis and gout, redubbed *Cinchophen*.

Patriotic flags of the United States and its British and French allies, and stacks of company products, decorated Abbott's exhibit at the 1917 American Medical Association convention in New York City.

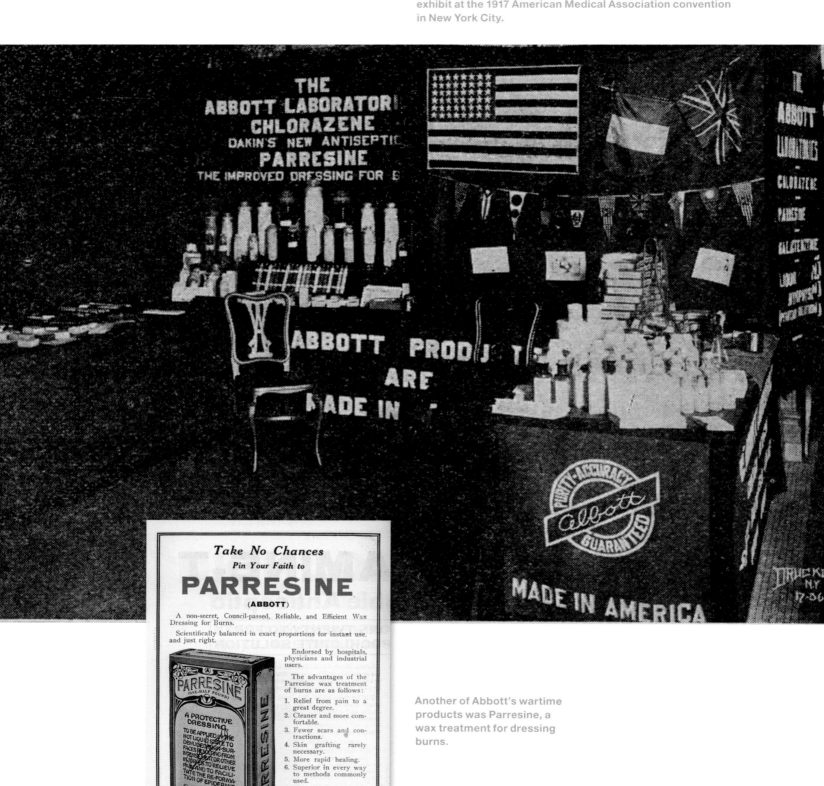

Another of Abbott's wartime products was Parresine, a wax treatment for dressing burns.

The war's demands and rising production drew much other talent to Abbott, while others who had joined earlier rose in the ranks. That year James F. Stiles, a future chairman of Abbott's board, whom Dr. Abbott had personally delivered to the world, started at the firm by packing boxes in the shipping department.

In April 1917, Elmer B. Vliet, later a vital researcher, quality control expert, and Abbott chairman, was a college junior attending an Abbott-sponsored dinner at a YMCA. There he first learned of the U.S. entry into the war from Dr. Burdick. Vliet joined Abbott in 1919 at age 22 after a research stint in the government's Chemical Warfare Service.

> "I'm convinced that those [Abbott] people are making remarkable progress in producing real American-made pharmaceuticals and chemicals."
>
> — DR. MORRIS FISHBEIN
> *Journal of the American Medical Association*

Ernest Henry Volwiler, another future top researcher — and also a future Abbott chairman — was, in 1918, a doctoral student at the University of Illinois. It was then that he asked Dr. Adams about a commission offered him from the Chemical Warfare Service. Adams convinced him instead to work for Abbott, which was engaged in research for the Navy on painkillers and other synthetic pharmaceuticals. That spring, Volwiler became the first of many of Dr. Adams' Ph.D. graduates. He began work at Abbott on *Barbital*. For many years to come, Volwiler would excel as a groundbreaking researcher and executive in the field of anesthetics.

Abbott's production efficiencies built on its personnel's smarts. The firm manufactured *Barbital* and *Procaine* at less than the pre-war cost of their German equivalents, charging one-third less for *Barbital*. Meanwhile, researchers assisted by Dr. George W. Raiziss, at The Dermatological Research Laboratories in Philadelphia, puzzled out the formula for Salvarsan. The drug, the antidote for "blood poison," as syphilis was called, was reformulated and named *Arsenobenzol*, and sold at one-third the pre-war price. Even when German companies returned to market at war's end, their monopoly had disappeared.

And Abbott's continuing profitability in the world of synthetic drugs was assured. Stoked by the addition of the new drugs, sales exploded from $664,000 in 1916 to

$1,259,000 in 1918. When the terrible, war-stoked flu pandemic of 1918–1919 emerged, Abbott also stressed the sale of medications for alleviating pain and fever.

Dr. Abbott must have savored the symbolism at the American Medical Association's 1919 convention. The Abbott exhibit at the Atlantic City event was patriotically festooned with U.S. flags highlighting *Halazone, Barbital, Procaine, Chlorazene, Dichloramine-T*, and other company products. Dr. Morris Fishbein was an adjutant to Dr. Simmons, Dr. Abbott's old "Square Deal" foe. In an Association booklet, he gushed, "I'm convinced that those [Abbott] people are making remarkable progress in producing real American-made pharmaceuticals and chemicals."

As the post-war era began, the company was poised for further, rapid expansion into new markets and new fields.

Decade at a Glance
1910–1920

1910

More than 700 products are listed in the Abbott catalog.

The customer list totals 50,000 of the 130,000 physicians in the United States, as well as 1,000 in Europe and 500 in Latin America.

In addition to existing agencies and branches in Toronto, New York, San Francisco, and Seattle, Abbott establishes an agency in Bombay, India.

1911

The salesforce expands to 35.

1912

Revenues drop for the first time as demand for alkaloidal products declines.

1913

A growing Abbott attracted outstanding new talent. They included manufacturing expert Ferdinand H. "Fred" Young and James F. "Sunny Jim" Stiles, Jr., who joins the firm as a shipping department packer. He will, over time, create the company's employee benefits programs, and become chairman of the board.

▲

Abbott's top managers in a jovial mood. Standing, left to right: S. DeWitt Clough, E.H. Ravenscroft, Franklin P. Summers, Dr. Abbott. Seated, left to right: W.R. Laughlin, C.O. Brown, Dr. Burdick.

1914

With Dr. Abbott's blessing, Dr. Burdick switches the company's focus from alkaloidal to synthetic medicines.

The First World War breaks out creating a pressing need for more effective antiseptics on battlefields and in field hospitals.

1915

The name of the firm is changed from The Abbott Alkaloidal Company to Abbott Laboratories.

▼

1916

Abbott produces its first synthetic medicine, *Chlorazene*, a breakthrough antiseptic developed by British chemist Dr. Henry Dakin to treat wounded soldiers.

▼

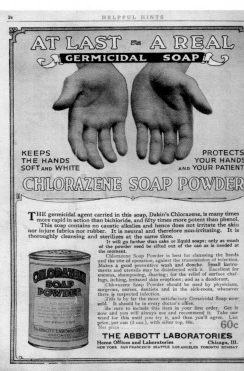

1917
Dr. Roger Adams begins work as a consultant for Abbott, and helps develop processes for producing the German anesthetics Veronal and Novocaine, renamed *Barbital* and *Procaine*.

▼

Abbott manufactures another invention of Dakin's, *Halazone*, which makes contaminated water drinkable.

▼

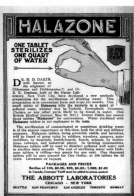

Unfurling of the American flag by Dr. Burdick and Dr. Abbott at a war-era company gathering at Dr. Abbott's summer home in Pistakee Bay, Illinois.

▼

▲

1918
Chemist Dr. Ernest H. Volwiler joins Abbott and works on the development of *Barbital* and *Procaine*. Volwiler will later serve as Abbott's president and chairman.

Sales almost double to $1,259,000.

Ads celebrated Abbott's production of many drugs for wounded soldiers.

▼

1919
Elmer B. Vliet, a former student of Dr. Volwiler, joins the firm after serving in the U.S. Chemical Warfare Service. Vliet will help establish Abbott's reputation for quality control and become board chairman.

▼

1920–1930

Soaring Growth in the Roaring Twenties

In the Ravenswood district containing its factory and printing house, Abbott erected an additional single-story manufacturing plant next to an apartment building. Yet the apartment's residents did not like the fumes emanating from the place, and the Chicago Fire Department was displeased at the many small fires breaking out inside of it.

Abbott began looking for something bigger, better — and more distant from the city, offering room to accommodate the company's dynamic growth in the years ahead.

Dr. Abbott's sprawling, cupola-capped home at 4605
N. Hermitage Avenue, which housed his family and offices.
The home, located on the corner of Wilson and Hermitage,
in the Ravenswood neighborhood of Chicago, was blocks
from the manufacturing plant.

Bolstered by rising revenues, Abbott began building a large, new manufacturing complex in North Chicago, 30 miles north of the company's original Chicago locale. This image of "Building M1" ("M" for Manufacturing) at the new North Chicago site dates from 1924.

Many firms were hurt by the recession and high unemployment that followed the First World War boom. In 1921, even Abbott's sales fell, from $1,663,000 to $1,453,000. Then, as the vast United States economic upsurge of the 1920s got underway, Abbott grew along with it. Yet, to feed more growth, production centers greater than its lone five-story building were needed.

North Chicago

Engineering chief E.H. Ravenscroft and manufacturing expert Fred Young were assigned to find a new location that could accommodate the booming company's long-term growth. They zeroed in on an empty 26-acre tract of land in the town of North Chicago, 30 miles north. The heavily industrial area was home to machine works, an electrical firm, and the American Steel and Wire Company. The land was strategically placed near switching yards of the Chicago and Northwestern Railroad.

"The name North Chicago has a commercial value, especially to those manufacturers who send out travelers or sell by advertising," noted a local realtor, seeming to describe Abbott itself. Another selling point: Business taxes in North Chicago were one-third those of the Windy City to the south.

A now gray-haired Dr. Abbott, in a car borrowed from "Sunny Jim" Stiles, the youthful aide at whose birth he had attended, drove out with Dr. Burdick to inspect the property. But their company's poor luck with the now-established technology of the automobile continued. On route to the sparsely populated place, they got a flat tire. The duo lacked a spare; no service station could be had for miles. Finally a passing motorist lent a hand. They completed their journey, to the lasting benefit of North Chicago.

Ravenscroft and Young, they found, had done their homework. Burdick gave the land a thumbs-up. Abbott snapped up the property, paying for it with $250,000 in bonds.

Dr. Abbott stands with his bicycle in front of his house with family, friends, relatives, and employees.

Ravenscroft drew up plans for the first buildings slated for chemical manufacturing. Dr. Abbott took a keen interest in the designs. "Why not just ask Merck and Co. for the blueprints of their plant at Rahway, New Jersey," he suggested. Not surprisingly, Merck declined.

Dr. Abbott told Ravenscroft and Elmer Vliet, the young researcher who had joined Abbott during the First World War, to get on a train to Rahway. From a railway platform there, they spent 20 minutes examining the nearby Merck plant, then left. Ravenscroft continued working on his blueprints. On June 9, 1920, Dr. Abbott literally led the ground-breaking, with horse, harness, and plow, at North Chicago. He then invited everyone with him to a celebratory picnic under a shade tree.

The Passing of Dr. Abbott

Dr. Abbott was now 63 years old. His health had been worn down by years of continual cares and long working hours. Along with a bout of typhoid fever, he suffered from rheumatism and kidney disease, maladies his firm would, in later times, address. Despite spurts of his old energy, and occasional rounds about the offices, he had turned supervision of the firm over to Dr. Burdick. On July 1, 1921, Dr. Abbott walked slowly home from work and took to bed, ill. On July 4, he passed away. His wife, Clara, and daughter, Eleanor, survived him.

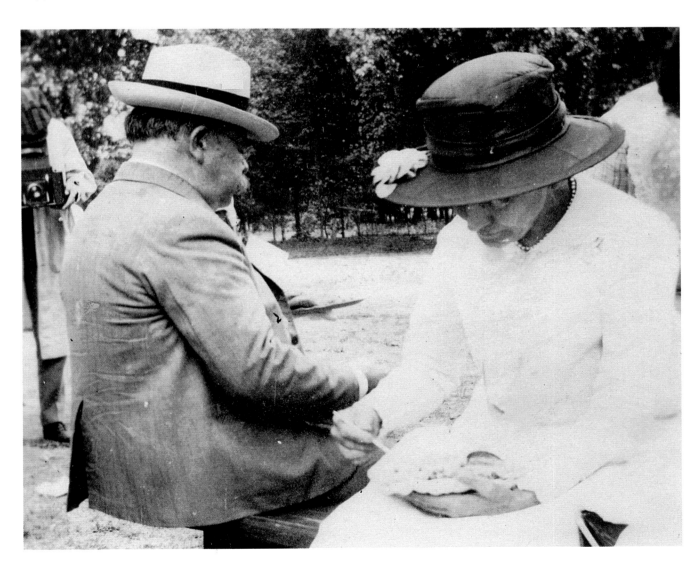

Dr. Abbott and Clara, his wife of 35 years, at a company picnic in 1921.

On his death, his many friends paid tribute. One of
the most venerable, Dr. William Thackeray, stated: "He
lived to realize our dream of the manufacture of the fine
alkaloids and synthetics." The Abbott Laboratories board
lauded its founder as "always an advocate in word and
deed of the great principle of the Square Deal." Over 33
years, Dr. Abbott had built a tiny business started in his
apartment into a significant concern prepared for greater
growth and pursuing ever loftier goals.

A New President Makes a New Acquisition

The cerebral, soft-spoken Dr. Burdick had been the
effective head of Abbott for several years. The company's
directors swiftly elected him the new chief. Although quiet
in manner, he was to prove a dynamic business and
scientific leader in fast-moving times.

As Burdick wrote in one of a series of reports to the
widowed Mrs. Clara Abbott in 1922, "I look forward to
very marked expansion during the next few years." In fact,
as construction continued at the North Chicago tract, he
made an important acquisition for the company.

In the summer of the following year, Burdick and
sales head Clough were playing golf in New York, during a
break in the pharmaceutical manufacturers' convention.
While on the links, Burdick heard disturbing news. A
chemical industry representative told him that The
Dermatological Research Laboratories, or DRL, which
Burdick had been eyeing for acquisition, was about to be
sold to another concern. Burdick, who had held several
meetings on a possible purchase with DRL's founder,
dermatologist Dr. Jay Frank Schamberg, was flabber-
gasted.

> ## "I like the way you operate and I like what I hear about Abbott Laboratories."
>
> — DR. JAY F. SCHAMBERG
> *The Dermatological Research Laboratories*

During the First World War, even before Abbott had
deciphered the formulas for German drugs like Novocaine,
DRL's first-rate research and production team had cracked
the formula for Salvarsan, the German remedy for syphilis.

One noted researcher was the erudite Dr. George
W. Raiziss, a Russian educated in Germany and
Switzerland. A rival suitor, Burdick knew, was none
other than Herman Metz, the man who had assaulted a
witness during Senate hearings on the high wartime
price of Salvarsan. The Philadelphia-based DRL was
too great a prize to lose. Burdick and Clough rushed
to Philadelphia to meet Schamberg.

"It's not true," the DRL head assured his worried
visitors. "I'm not interested in selling to Metz … Besides,
I like the way you operate and I like what I hear about
Abbott Laboratories."

Burdick's meeting with Schamberg was followed
by a series of negotiations. In November 1922, Abbott
acquired DRL's stock, manufacturing plant, and inventories.
A treasure house was gained for the bargain price of
$181,000. Abbott bolstered its product line with anti-
syphilitic drugs and with DRL's iodine-, silver-, and
bismuth-based formulations, used as germicides and for
stomach disorders. Soon Raiziss would devise *Metaphen*,
an organic mercury compound used as an antiseptic.

Abbott's Philadelphia-based Dermatological Research
Laboratories staff in 1928. Dr. George W. Raiziss is in the
front row, third from left.

The DRL acquisition also brought Abbott other vital
talent, including top-flight production staff, and a clutch of
salesmen headed by Raymond E. Horn, former top aide
to United States President William Howard Taft's Attorney
General. Horn would eventually become Abbott's
president.

Dr. Burdick informed Mrs. Abbott: "The purchase of
The Dermatological Research Laboratories was an
exceedingly fortunate venture. This business is not
seasonal, it runs throughout the year … I think it is perfectly
safe to say that we will make during the first year of
operation enough to pay for the entire plant."

Still, the aggressive Metz and other rival firms
attempted to thwart Burdick's prediction. They launched a
war, slashing prices by half. Abbott's new president coolly
instructed the salesforce to maintain its margins, and to
promote Salvarsan's alternate uses — a remedy for trench
foot and assorted tropical diseases. The price war ended
with Abbott victorious.

Burdick kept his pledge to Mrs. Abbott. In the year
following the DRL purchase, company sales went from
$1,651,000 to $2,154,000, an increase well over twice the
cost of the acquisition.

A year later, in 1924, Clara Abbott died. The generous
woman left a wealthy estate that, starting in 1940, according to the terms of her will, would endow major projects in
local universities and hospitals, and offer medical and
educational grants to Abbott employees (see page 148).

A force behind Abbott's pioneering work with vitamins was Danish-born scientist Carl Nielsen.

A Move into "Vita-Mines"

Burdick moved to acquire new products as well as firms. And one of the healthcare industry's great novelties of the time was vitamins.

Although vitamin supplements are common items today, the science behind them emerged only a century ago. In 1911, Polish scientist Casimir Funk, working at the Lister Institute in London, found he could cure laboratory pigeons of the crippling disease beri-beri by giving them vitamin B, which is found in non-polished rice husks. Researchers were learning a great lesson: Some illnesses were due not to germs, but to the absence of certain nutrients. Mistakenly thinking the life-giving substances were chemical amines, Funk named them "vita-mines."

In the United States, two teams of scientists, at Yale University and the University of Wisconsin, separately found that lab rats denied certain fats grew tissues over their eyeballs, rendering them blind. Feeding the animals food containing the fats cured the blindness. In 1914, the curative substance in the food, vitamin A, was identified; it was found to be plentiful in common foods like carrots. Munching on carrots, it was said, rather imprecisely, "helps your eyesight." An explosion in research and discovery about other vitamins ensued.

Keenly observing all this was Abbott's research chief, Carl Nielsen, a Dane whom Dr. Burdick had brought in to expand the synthetic medicine staff. At a medical conference Nielsen came into contact with one of the University of Wisconsin researchers, Dr. Harry Steenbock, a shy professor of biochemistry. Steenbock had discovered the close relationship of the sun's ultraviolet rays to the stimulation of vitamin D. His lab rats were cured of the bone disease rickets if exposed to sunlight, or if fed millet irradiated with ultraviolet rays. After many more experiments, he learned, in 1924, that the substance ergosterol, under ultraviolet light, was transmuted into vitamin D.

At the conference an eager Nielsen buttonholed Steenbock. He told him: "Our president, Dr. Burdick, is very interested in vitamins. He has been urging us to keep on the alert … to become involved with anyone who is making any real progress … Will you let us know when you intend to make your process available commercially?"

The good professor was happy to speak with the agent of a reputable company, for he had watched less savory businesses bastardize his findings. The window display of one Chicago pharmacy, touting a "Demonstration of Steenbock Vitamin Process," had shown an ordinary light bulb flickering on a dish of olive oil. In horror, Steenbock set up a research foundation of university alumni to properly commercialize his work.

Abbott applied Dr. Harry Steenbock's findings about the benefits of vitamin D in its product *Viosterol*, shown here on the packing line. It proved successful in the treatment of rickets.

In 1922, Abbott scientists created *Butyn*, a faster, more powerful anesthetic than Novocaine; and a safer one than another popular agent of the day — cocaine.

[PAGE FIVE]

At Last—A Substitute for Cocaine

The remarkable story of BUTYN, the new synthetic chemical which is now replacing Cocaine for anesthetizing mucous surfaces. Discovered after three years of intensive research work, and after discarding thirty-seven new synthetic bodies. A victory for American chemistry!

BUTYN (get this name fixed in your mind) is pronounced Bute-in, with the accent on the first syllable. This name is derived from butyl alcohol, but the chemical formula of the product is too long to remember or even pronounce. It contains just forty-seven letters. BUTYN is here to replace cocaine preceding operative work on the eye and other mucous surfaces. The outstanding feature of BUTYN is that is has been used in over 10,000 actual cases without a single recorded case of toxicity. This in addition to hundreds of pharmacological tests on animals. Think of what this means. And the clinical work has been done by the leading specialists, at the request of the Council on Pharmacy and Chemistry of the American Medical Association. Surely this must mean much to those who are now using co-

observation, use and clinical tests. The preliminary report appearing in the J. A. M. A. was very encouraging as far as BUTYN was concerned. The final report, which appeared in the J. A. M. A., of February 4, speaks for itself. Following are the conclusions of the committee exactly as reported:

"1. It is more powerful than cocaine, a smaller quantity being required.

"2. It acts more rapidly than cocaine.

"3. Its action is more prolonged than that of cocaine.

"4. According to our experience to date, Butyn in the quantity required is less toxic than cocaine.

"5. It produces no drying effect on tissues.

"6. It produces no change in the size of the pupil.

"7. It has no ischemic effect

The foundation rejected the requests of breweries and chewing gum companies to put Steenbock's nutrient into their wares. Instead, it engaged five pharmaceutical companies, Abbott among them, to make irradiated ergosterol.

In 1929, Abbott introduced its brand, calling it *Viosterol*. It was made by dissolving ergosterol in ether, then suspending the solution in quartz containers irradiated by ultra-violet lamps. After drawing out the ether, methanol was used to purify the ergosterol, which was then evaporated and dissolved in corn oil or sesame oil.

Viosterol turned into a major seller, with "around-the-clock" shifts producing it. In 1936, the *Bulletin of the Johns Hopkins Hospital* was to find that *Viosterol*, by building up calcium and phosphorus in the bones of infants and children, much aided recovery from rickets. Professor Steenbock, in the meantime, garnered about $1,000,000 in royalties from his discovery, and donated most of it to his university research.

Advancing Anesthesia

Abbott was also producing breakthroughs in its own labs, induced, in part, by a pressing deadline. The company had licenses to make the anesthetics *Procaine*, *Barbital*, and *Cinchophen*. These were versions of German drugs, such as Novocaine, developed in the First World War. Yet all the patents for the Abbott drugs were to expire by 1923. So, back in 1919, Dr. Burdick had directed two of his keen researchers from the University of Illinois, Dr. Roger Adams and protégé Dr. Ernest Volwiler, to try to find a substitute for Novocaine.

Novocaine, which was non-addictive and non-toxic, though slow to numb the affected area, was supplanting the anesthetic cocaine, which, although faster working, was highly addictive. Adams and Volwiler sought to find a related substance that had the advantages of both but the disadvantages of neither.

At first they were stymied by the lack of alcohols that could be used as chemical bases to make a substitute. A key to their solution came with butyl alcohol, a byproduct of acetone, employed during the war to make high explosives. Volwiler called this chain alcohol his "building stone."

Abbott came up with an array of *Butyn*-based products that worked as an anesthetic against skin irritation, and to treat burns.

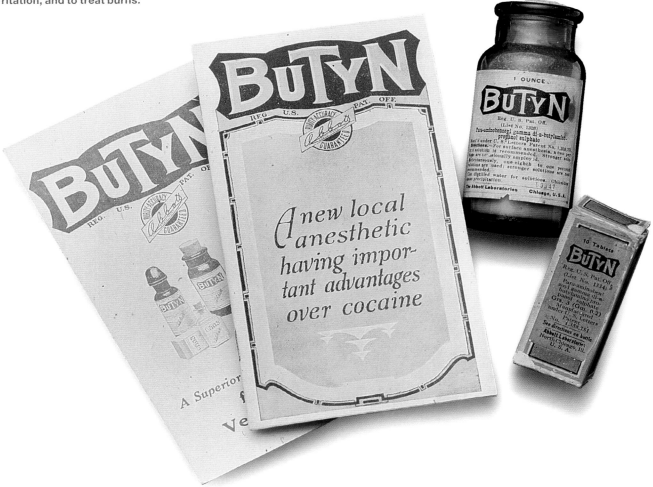

Working for more than two years with Professor Oliver Kamm, another leading scientist at the University of Illinois, Adams and Volwiler tried out 40 different compounds on laboratory animals. Carl Nielsen performed the pharmacological tests on how a drug affects the body. Clinical tests were conducted by hundreds of dentists, ophthalmologists, and doctors. In 1922, the Council on Pharmacy and Chemistry of the American Medical Associations approved the fruit of the research, a white powder called *Butyn*.

Butyn acted faster and more powerfully than cocaine, but without addicting the patient. Less expensive to produce than Novocaine, *Butyn* proved an effective anesthetic for surgery on the sensitive surface membranes of eyes, throats, and nasal passages.

Variants soon followed, such as *Butesin*, a powder for skin irritation that proved more potent than Abbott's synthetic drug *Anesthesin*. Floyd K. Thayer was another University of Illinois scientist, brought in by Adams and Vliet. Thayer combined *Butesin* with picric acid, a substance for treating burns. The resulting ointment, *Butesin*

Picrate, was tested by industrial surgeons at Indiana's Inland Steel Company and the American Steel and Wire Company in Illinois. It proved popular, both medically and commercially, to address eye lesions and burns suffered by factory workers.

In addition to advancing medicine, *Butyn* illustrated the financial and intellectual property risks of drug development. Creation of a drug like it cost up to $50,000 at the time. And the Société des Usines du Rhône, a French chemical maker, for a time fought Abbott's patent application for *Butyn*. "Few people realize," Dr. Burdick wrote in an article for the *Journal of the American Pharmaceutical Association*, "how expensive it is to 'discover' and put on the market a new synthetic chemical. At the present time, in the United States, the manufacturer who wishes to go into this field must take a gambler's chance." By the 21st century, that gamble would cost more than $1 billion for every new drug that actually made it through the development process to reach patients.

THE MANUFACTURE OF SYNTHETIC MEDICINAL CHEMICALS IN AMERICA.*

BY ALFRED S. BURDICK, M.D.

Before the Great War, this country cut a small, indeed, an almost contemptible figure in the manufacture of synthetic chemicals of all kinds, and particularly in the production of synthetic medicinals. It is not the province of this paper to discuss the tremendous progress which has been made in the manufacture of dyes, although, as a matter of fact, dye production and the production of medicinals are so closely interwoven as to be almost inseparable for a clear understanding of the subject. Sufficient to say that in spite of the fact that the United States had almost illimitable sources to draw on for raw materials through its coal mines, coke ovens and gas plants, its manufacture of medicinal synthetics prior to 1914 was virtually limited to the salicylates, including salicylic acid and its salts, acetylsalicylic acid and salol. These substances were made in this country entirely by German-owned corporations.

A few other synthetics of closely allied character were being produced in small quantities, the principal ones being saccharin (the invention of an American chemist) and phenolphthalein, the manufacture of both of which was begun, I believe, by the Monsanto Chemical Company prior to 1914. Argyrol, which was also introduced by an American chemist, was being manufactured, but, strictly speaking, this can hardly be called a synthetic. I believe that these are the only medicinals, or near-medicinals, which we produced in any considerable quantity prior to this time.

---

* Read before Chicago Branch A. Ph. A., January meeting, 1922.

Expense of Research.—Few people realize how expensive it is to "discover" and put on the market a new synthetic chemical. At the present time, in the United States, the manufacturer who wishes to go into this field must take a gambler's chance. The Abbott Laboratories has been willing to take this chance because it believed that the future of any pharmaceutical firm depends upon its ability to measure up to the spirit of the times and bring its business into accord with the changing and developing tendencies of the age. Thus far we have been satisfied with the result, but we are free to confess that we cannot plumb the future. Our own experience has been that to develop a purely synthetic medicinal chemical, involving what we may call an average degree of difficulty for one of the finer preparations of this class, means a cash outlay of from $25,000 to $50,000. I

Dr. Donalee L. Tabern began his extraordinarily productive Abbott career when Dr. Ernest H. Volwiler hired him in 1926.

"Research — and More Research"

Meanwhile Abbott's top management kept looking to expand and, at times, to consolidate. With the construction of the large, new North Chicago facilities done by 1925, Burdick sold the original manufacturing and printing plants in Ravenswood. The Chicago drug company G.D. Searle purchased the properties for $300,000. Destined for great success, the North Chicago site stumbled at the start: On day one, a fire destroyed the shipping room, causing almost $100,000 worth of lost goods and damaged structures.

"We regret to advise you," wrote Dr. Burdick to the company's sales branches, "that a fire in our pharmaceutical building at North Chicago has today destroyed a portion of our finished and unfinished stocks … Double shifts will be put on in production and finishing departments. We hope to be back to normal, or nearly so, within a week."

The following year, Abbott considered a merger with Frederick Stearns and Company of Michigan. Like Abbott, that company had been a leader in the "ethical drugs" movement, by which medicines were dispensed only through a doctor's prescription. Negotiations between the two firms took place, and a name for the merged concern was proposed — Allied Laboratories. Dr. Volwiler, who along with his research was engaged in work on product

trademarks, was directed to check on the originality of the name. At the same time, Dr. Burdick tossed and turned over the deal. After a sleepless night, he came down against the merger.

"We might lose our identity," he explained. "I hope we will always be known as Abbott long after we are all gone."

While searching for other acquisitions, Abbott kept developing its own ideas. Its progress was pushed by the scholarly Dr. Burdick's views on the importance of scientific inquiry.

"Research — and more research," he pronounced. "Research is fundamental and vital. Without it real progress is impossible." Medical inquiry, according to Abbott's chief, was akin to public utilities: "The supplying of medicine is as important a service to the public as a municipal, state, or federal franchise to furnish light, heat, or transportation — the very foundation stones of our civilization."

"We believe," Burdick stated, "that the future of this institution must rest upon sound scientific work." From 1925 to 1929, company spending on research and development, including new equipment, increased by $100,000 per year.

> "Research — and more research. Research is fundamental and vital. Without it real progress is impossible."
>
> — DR. ALFRED S. BURDICK

A critical research hire occurred in 1926. Dr. Donalee L. Tabern, after earning three degrees at the University of Michigan and an instructorship at Cornell University, joined Abbott as an organic chemist. Dr. Volwiler hired him on the recommendation of University of Michigan Professor Moses Gomberg, the discoverer of free radicals and the future president of the American Chemical Society. Building on Dr. Volwiler's work on the sedatives *Barbital* and *Neonal*, Tabern began more than a decade of investigation into barbiturates. His discoveries in that realm and, later still, in nuclear medicine, would lead to a number of breakthrough medicines as well as a new field for Abbott — diagnostics.

Continues on page 80 ▶

Mystery Break-In at North Chicago

The two night watchmen at the gate of the North Chicago complex didn't stand a chance. Eight masked men in dark suits, sporting machine guns and pistols, overpowered and gagged them, and tied them up with ropes. It was 1927, the height of Prohibition-era Chicago: The guards may have felt that Al Capone's boys had dropped in.

The two guards managed to free themselves the next morning, after being bound for seven hours. They were unhurt except for some rope burns. Police and Abbott officials were contacted.

Trails of cigarette butts marked the progress of the interlopers. They had proceeded methodically from building to building. One group ransacked desks and files, strewing the floors with papers and folders. The other looked through all the lockers. But a fortune in chemicals and narcotics they left untouched, as well as the expensive lab apparatus and all the office equipment. Two safes, however, were found blown open with nitroglycerin.

The newspapers speculated on motive. The bandits sought, it was surmised, a secret formula for a synthetic, non-addictive painkiller. The description exactly fit *Butyn* — Abbott's anesthetic drug created in the early 1920s.

"They took no money," commented an Abbott officer, "because there was none to take.

"They took no formulae, because none of our formulae are secret. They took no stamps, because our stamping is done by machine. But really, they did a perfect job." ■

Eight masked gunmen took over Abbott's North Chicago headquarters in June 1927. Apparently the gang that couldn't shoot straight, they sought the "secret" formula for a drug made public years before.

NEW DRUG LURED CHICAGO GUNMEN

Abbott Laboratories Had Secret Formulæ.

NON-HABIT-FORMING NARCOTIC

Police Believe It Was Sought for the 'Bootleg' Trade.

CHICAGO, June 13 (A. P.).—Secret formulæ, including one for a synthetic non-habit-forming narcotic of reputed pain killing potency, may have been the lures which drew eight masked robbers carrying machine guns and revolvers to the Abbott Laboratories in North Chicago early yesterday.

Such was the line along which police today were investigating the robbery which required seven hours in its execution and during which the robbers carefully barricaded themselves behind their machine guns against any possible surprise attack.

One of two watchmen who were overpowered quoted one of the raiders as saying: "We are set to resist all the police of North Chicago."

Officials of the $3,000,000 concern, who have posted rewards of $500 each for the capture of the robbers, inclined with the police toward the belief that formulæ were sought, inasmuch as cash and few stamps were kept in the plant. They expressed themselves, however, as confident no practical commercial use could be made of any formulæ that may have been taken, as all are protected under patent laws.

They were uncertain, too, whether any formulæ had been taken. A thorough check will be necessary before it can be determined the exact nature of the loot. It appeared, however that little else of value was missing, as the stock of alcohol and narcotics was untouched.

During their seven hours' stay in the plant the robbers broke open two safes and ten filing cabinets. The watchmen, who were left bound and gagged, believe the men got what they were after, for they said the robbers appeared highly pleased when they departed in two automobiles about 5:30 A. M.

One member of the band remained after his companions had gone, standing guard over the watchmen. It was thirty-five minutes before he, too, departed.

Investigators were told that scientists in the employ of the Abbott laboratories recently completed a formula for a synthetic narcotic of great efficiency in easing pain but lacking any habit-forming qualities. Police suggested that a paying bootleg traffic could be carried on if such a formula should have fallen into robber hands even though patent laws prevented its open sale.

Although the watchmen could offer no adequate descriptions of the robbers, both for the reason that they were masked and dressed alike, police noted certain characteristics of the "jobs" as resembling the handiwork of a well known "mob" leader for whom search is being made.

An Array of New Products

Important new products emerged from the research of Dr. Raiziss and his group at Abbott's Dermatological Research Laboratories in Philadelphia, Pennsylvania. One was a powerful topical antiseptic, derived from mercury, called *Metaphen*.

Doctors could apply it to fragile mucous membranes with less harmful impact than other medicines. "*Metaphen* is at least 500 times more powerful than phenol and its effect on bacteria is considerably higher than that of other known chemical compounds," stated a medical magazine ad from Clough.

In addition to disinfecting skin, surgeons used *Metaphen* to disinfect their instruments or to mark up a region of the body for surgery. The versatile substance was even employed as a mouthwash. Abbott priced a gallon of Tincture *Metaphen* at $25. In 1927, Raiziss and team created another anti-syphilitic, a mixture of bismuth and arsenic dubbed *Bismarsen*. It had fewer side effects, such as skin irritation, than other treatments.

Abbott's anti-infective *Metaphen* was used for a range of purposes, from sterilizing surgical instruments to mouthwash.

These products sold well. The marketing department emphasized their quality. Amateur poet Clough placed the following verses in a salesmen's bulletin:

"Don't try to buy a thing too cheap
From those with things to sell —
Because the goods you'll have to keep,
And time will always tell.
The price you paid you'll soon forget,
The goods you get will stay;
The price you will not long regret —
The quality you may."

Not all new products were commercial hits. Abbott sometimes looked for "volume sellers" — popular, less expensive items whose sales would underwrite rising expenses in research. Sunscreen was one such attempt. In 1920, Elmer B. Vliet synthesized a substance that absorbed ultraviolet light. Yet he determined that manufacture of the ointment was too costly. Nonetheless, the sunscreen was combined with cold creams and vanishing creams — which Vliet and Clough tried out themselves to see if they worked. Then another, less expensive substance derived from a dye was found. However, it proved unstable in ointment form, and Abbott lacked the pharmacists on staff to stabilize it.

Still, Clough avidly pushed ahead with the offering, dubbing it *Sunex*, "The Sunshade in a Tube." Ads pictured "*Sunex* Girls" who could, announced Clough's ad copy, evade freckles, tans, and burns while "enjoying the outdoors with absolute freedom." Unfortunately, *Sunex* looked bad on the skin, and a vanishing cream variant corroded the tube containers. *Sunex* vanished from the market.

Some products that failed commercially led to successes of a different sort. In 1922, Carl Nielsen had worked on another hoped-for volume seller, a baby food that much impressed Dr. Burdick. To make the nutritive, Abbott's president ordered the construction of a whole new building outfitted with a large spray-drying device. For a year in the North Chicago building, copious amounts of the food were produced and studied. Finally, Burdick concluded that high investment costs and competitors with more experience in food making rendered the project unprofitable.

Despite attractive advertising from Clough,
Sunex failed to make it in the sunscreen market.

The building seemed a white elephant, until 1926. At that time Norman A. Hansen, a production chemist from the University of Illinois, decided to leave Abbott after a disagreement with Fred Young over manufacturing processes.

Burdick, sorry to see the talented young fellow leave, asked him: "What would you like to do?"

"I've been thinking about developing a system," replied Hansen, "a laboratory where products can be made on a larger scale than in the research laboratory before they go into mass production."

Abbott's head told Hansen to try out his idea in a corner of one of the labs. It turned out so well that he was allowed to set up expanded facilities in the development lab of the baby-food building. In the coming years, the product development lab proved a big plus.

Abbott had come up with another infant product in 1925. The highly nutritious product was called *Lactigen*. To make it, milk was sterilized by steam, the fat removed, and the result packaged in ampoules. But here, too, Abbott's lack of experience in baby food manufacturing compelled Dr. Burdick to pull the product from the market. Abbott's interest in the infant formula business, however, remained. Thirty-nine years later, Abbott would acquire M&R Dietetic Laboratories, the makers of Similac, a popular infant formula developed in 1925, around the same time as Abbott's original efforts.

Continues on page 86 ▶

State of the Art, 1929: A Fine Chemical Plant

In 1929, James A. Lee, an editor with *Chemical & Metallurgical Engineering* magazine, visited Abbott's huge, newly completed North Chicago facilities. He left impressed.

"This plant is unique among fine chemical plants," wrote Lee, "… because of the unusually efficient arrangement of buildings and selection of equipment." As such, it set the standard for the state-of-the-art manufacturing facilities Abbott would build around the globe in years to come.

Just nine years after Dr. Abbott had personally broken ground, the complex had 18 buildings and 650 employees. The focus of the site was a group of three steel-and-concrete buildings for the making of synthetic drugs. In the center of these were storage houses for chemicals and crude pharmaceuticals.

The sprawling, yet carefully laid-out, North Chicago complex, photographed from the air after originally planned construction had been completed.

The production of *Barbital*, *Neonal*, and other "hypnotics" involved centrifugal and steam-jacketed kettles.

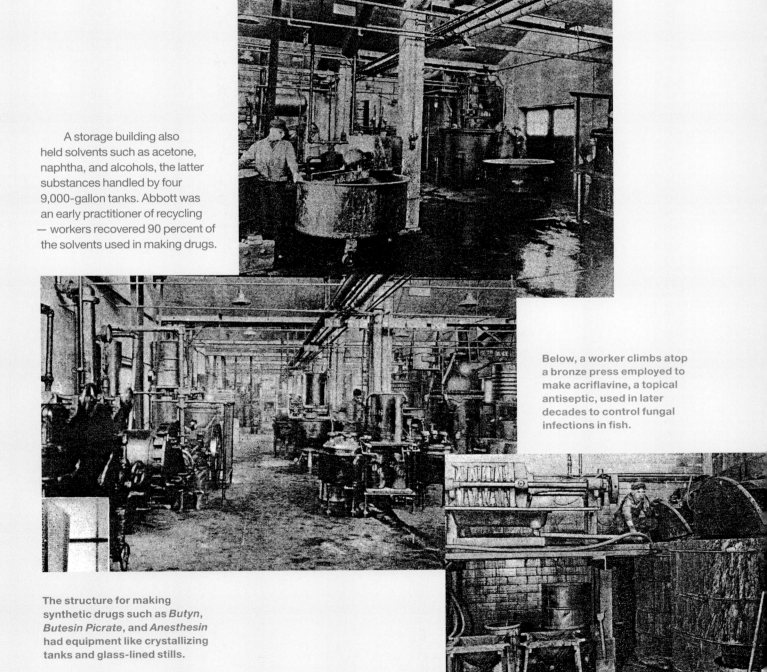

A storage building also held solvents such as acetone, naphtha, and alcohols, the latter substances handled by four 9,000-gallon tanks. Abbott was an early practitioner of recycling — workers recovered 90 percent of the solvents used in making drugs.

Below, a worker climbs atop a bronze press employed to make acriflavine, a topical antiseptic, used in later decades to control fungal infections in fish.

The structure for making synthetic drugs such as *Butyn*, *Butesin Picrate*, and *Anesthesin* had equipment like crystallizing tanks and glass-lined stills.

Different drug types demanded different structures. A four-story concrete building made drugs extracted from dense, bulky material, including plants, extracts, and resins.

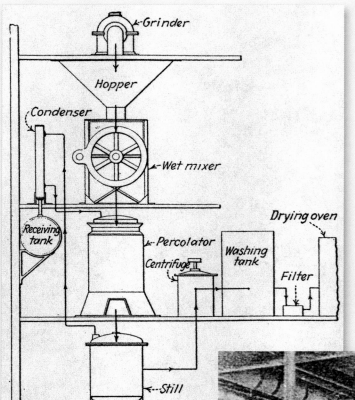

Gravity was employed to move raw materials from the higher to the lower floors of the drug extraction building. This made it easier to process heavier matter—like plants. Ground matter fell down a hopper to a mixer, then to a percolator, and further down to a still.

The second floor of the drug extraction building, below, contained, on the left, percolators and solvent recovery equipment and, on the right, cloth filters for resins.

The library in Building A1 ("A" for Administration) of North Chicago enabled scientists such as future chairman Elmer B. Vliet, on the right, to easily access medical literature.

Floor plan schematic of a building that housed capsule and pill finishing spaces, assorted supply areas, and the shipping and receiving rooms.

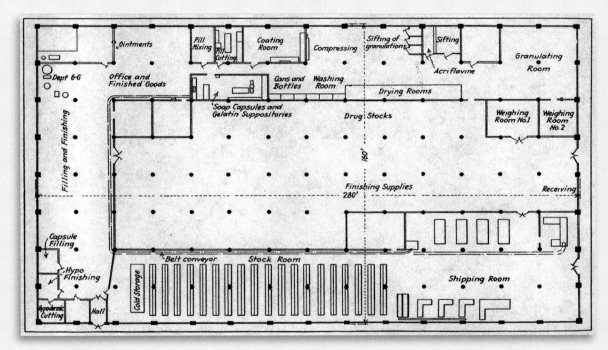

Hundreds of raw materials and chemicals constantly poured in from around the world, with production attendants ensuring they were immediately sent to tightly scheduled machine runs and production lines.

Still, the headquarters complex did much more than drug manufacturing. Other structures held the vital research laboratories, including centers for clinical research. In its labs, Abbott performed "bioassays" to test a drug's effectiveness.

The headquarters also had a printing plant for the company's many publications, a large cafeteria, the well-stocked research library, and offices for managers, administrators, and clerical workers. Another building made effervescent salts. And North Chicago contained chemist Norman Hansen's "baby food" facility, now a place for test runs of newly developed products.

"Much credit," wrote Lee, "is due E.H. Ravenscroft, general superintendent and engineer responsible for designing and laying out the plant."

"The visitor is certain of receiving," concluded the magazine, "a most courteous and hospitable reception by the entire personnel." ∎

Abbott's first public stock certificate, ironically issued
in 1929, the year of the stock market crash that marked
the beginning of the Great Depression. Abbott shares
rose sharply that first day and continued gaining over
good times and bad.

A Bargain Purchase

Commercial successes or no, Dr. Burdick kept on a constant
prowl for acquisitions to enhance Abbott's operations. In
1928, while on a regular visit to the Chicago sales office,
he met an investment banker who told him that financially
troubled drug maker John T. Milliken and Company might
be had for a bargain price.

Its founder had started up the St. Louis-based firm
due to a feud with the manufacturer of Listerine — Lambert
Pharmacal. Having made a fortune in railways and oil, Mr.
Milliken poured resources into the production of a rival
antiseptic, Pasteurine. Pasteurine flopped, but the eccen-
tric Milliken kept on with fluid extracts of the type Abbott
had superseded. The poor-selling product line encompassed Pava-Pepsin, for indigestion, and a "glandular
preparation for female diseases."

Yet, a treasure lay underneath the uninspiring surface.
Milliken had modern, well-outfitted labs and production
plants, 40 traveling salesmen, and a list of pharmacists that
exceeded 20,000. Volwiler and Vliet were sent over to
inspect the production lines and laboratories, while Clough
had a tête-à-tête with Milliken president John D. Gillis.
Negotiations led to a bargain purchase of $125,000.

Milliken's list of druggists brought on a big change for
the marketing department: a plan for direct retail distribution. And joining Abbott were skilled technicians like
Charles F. Lanwermeyer, who would prove instrumental
in making Abbott a leader in the world of vitamins.

Abbott's 1929 Annual Report, its first as a public company, ran all of eight pages; its core was a one-page Balance Sheet and a one-page Income and Surplus (Profit) Summary. The closing page was rather like an advertisement for the firm's leading products, along with a display of its new, well-designed research and manufacturing facilities.

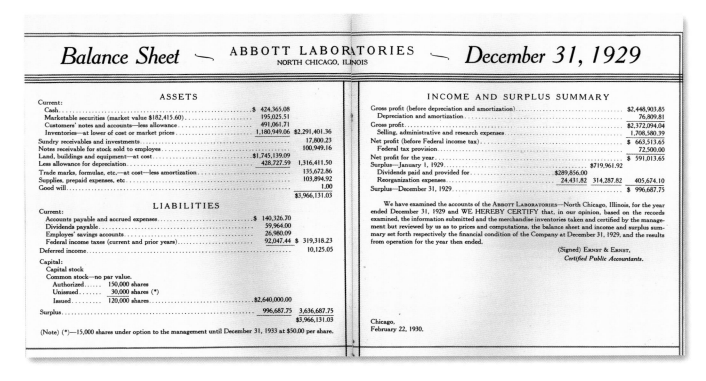

Going Public

As the Roaring Twenties and its booming stock market approached its end, Abbott — until then a closely held company — decided to go public. In March 1929, Abbott was listed on the Chicago Stock Exchange with a share price of $32. The price was high enough to make small fortunes for those who had received stock in place of salary during the 1907 panic. Over the years ahead the value of those shares would grow by a multiple of 10,000.

An observer in October 1929, after witnessing the great stock market crash of that month, would have concluded that Abbott blundered in going public just before the onset of the Great Depression. However, that observer would have been surprised to learn that, during the next 10 lean years for the national and world economies, Abbott would steadily grow its stock price, and triple its revenues — through a combination of brilliant research and highly innovative marketing.

Decade at a Glance
1920–1930

1920

Dr. Abbott turns over the first furrow of land on the new North Chicago site.

▼

Engineer Edward H. Ravenscroft and production expert Ferdinand H. "Fred" Young are commissioned to find a new location for the company's expanded facilities. They select a 26-acre site in North Chicago.

1921

Dr. Abbott dies after 33 years leading the company he founded, and Dr. Alfred S. Burdick succeeds him as president.

▼

1922 ▲

Dr. Volwiler and Dr. Adams develop *Butyn*, a fast-acting, non-habit-forming topical anesthetic.

Abbott acquires, for $181,000, The Dermatological Research Laboratories (DRL) of Philadelphia, which focuses on organic mercurial and arsenical compounds for the treatment of syphilis.

1923

Dr. Volwiler develops the sedative *Neonal*, leading to further advances in barbiturates.

1924

Dr. Abbott's widow, Clara, dies, and her will establishes the Clara Abbott Trust. It endows the medical sciences and, in time, aids Abbott employees and their family members in times of need.

▼

1925

Equipment for manufacturing synthetic chemicals. ▶

All facilities are moved to North Chicago, and the old plant is sold for $300,000 to G.D. Searle & Co.

1926

To preserve the Abbott name, Dr. Burdick vetoes a near-merger with Frederick Stearns and Company.

Dr. Donalee L. Tabern joins the firm. He will help develop breakthrough anesthetics and the radio-medicines that lead to Abbott's diagnostics business.

▼

Chemist Norman A. Hansen sets up a developmental laboratory that will prove important in testing products before large-scale production.

1927

The DRL division develops the antiseptic *Metaphen*, and the antisyphilitic *Bismarsen*.

▼

A worker climbs atop a bronze press employed to make acriflavine, a topical antiseptic, used in later decades to control fungal infections in fish.

▼

1928

Abbott acquires pharmaceutical manufacturer John T. Milliken and company for $125,000, along with its 40 salesmen, technical experts, and list of 20,000 retail pharmacists.

The library in Building A1 ("A" for Administration) of North Chicago enabled scientists, such as future Chairman Elmer Vliet, right, to easily access medical literature.

▼

1929

Abbott is listed on the Chicago Stock Exchange for $32 a share; the stock closes at $40.50 on the first day of trading.

▼

By decade's end the company has 18 buildings, strategically arranged for process efficiency, at its new North Chicago headquarters.

▼

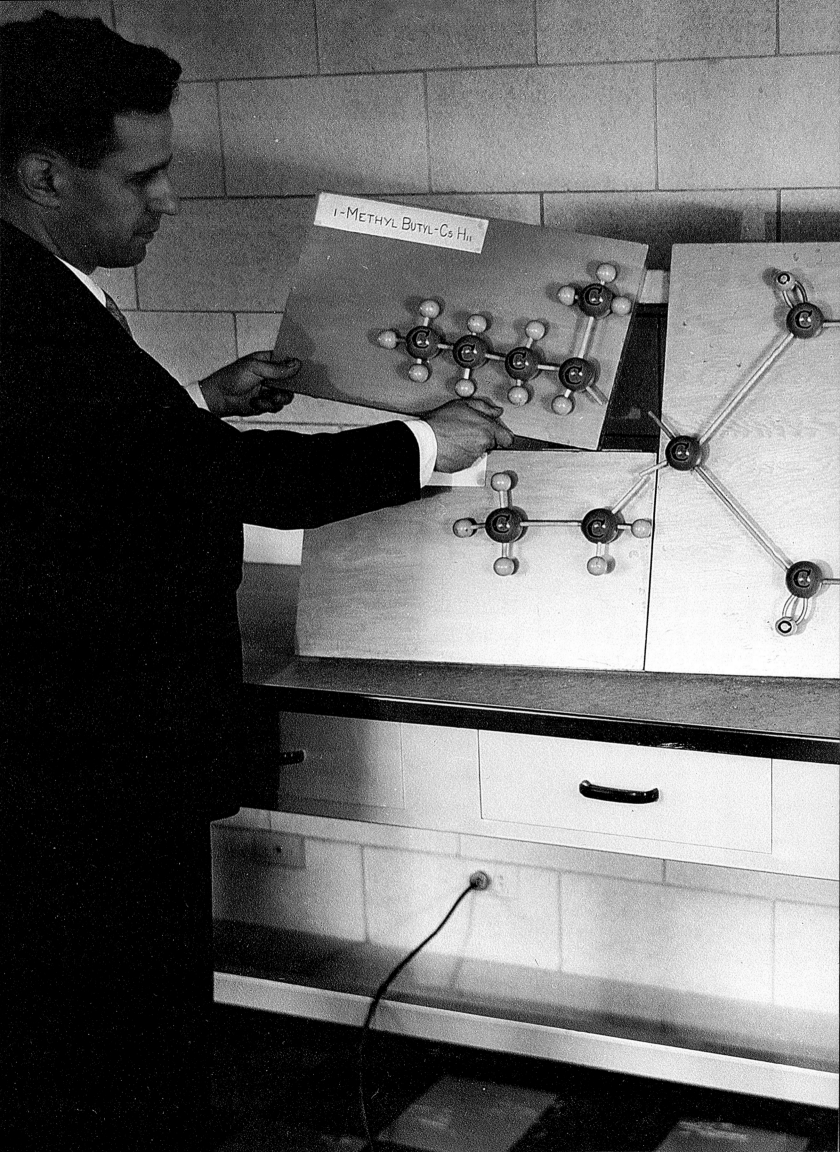

1930–1940

Growing Through the Great Depression

.

In 1930, at a fisherman's boarding house, a Royal Canadian Mounted Policeman confronted a thin, close-mouthed American.

"You're from the States," the Mountie demanded, "you have no visible means of support, you keep taking pictures and talking to fishermen. What is this all about?"

The interloper provided an outlandish alibi, and for three days was confined to his room while the police ran down his improbable tale. Finally, his story confirmed, the foreigner, Abbott's Charles F. Lanwermeyer, was let go.

The wide-ranging researcher continued his unlikely work of collecting samples of halibut. From them his firm would devise a new, vitamin-rich product that would supercharge Abbott's sales during a worldwide financial crisis.

PREVIOUS SPREAD
Following a common practice of Abbott scientists, Dr. Donalee L. Tabern put together models of the molecules on which he was working. Here he demonstrates the structure of Abbott's anesthetic, *Nembutal*. This breakthrough will lead to another of even greater importance: *Pentothal*.

Charles F. Lanwermeyer holds the source of one of the successes that saw Abbott through the Great Depression: halibut. Their livers were used to make Abbott's *Haliver Oil*.

In addition to surgical use,
Nembutal was also used
as a remedy for insomnia.

As the 1930s began, even as a great economic crisis gripped the United States and the world, Abbott continued to prosper and expand — sometimes through the most unusual means.

The Timely Dew of Sleep

The breakthrough product *Nembutal* was built on Abbott's long-standing work in anesthetics, and specifically on the work of Dr. Donalee L. Tabern, the relentless researcher who had joined up with Dr. Ernest H. Volwiler in 1926.

Volwiler had been looking into applying certain alcohols to barbituric acid. Tabern, in his lab, studied one of these substances, l-methyl-butyl-alcohol, and devised a new barbiturate, labeled "Abbott 844." A laborious series of tests followed.

First, Henry C. Spruth, Abbott's head of pharmacology, tried out the compound on animals. Then, University of Wisconsin Professor Arthur L. Tatum performed more extensive testing on the promising anesthetic. Next, Abbott medical director Dr. J.F. Biehn called in the heavy artillery.

He asked Dr. John Silas Lundy, chief of anesthesia at the Mayo Clinic in Rochester, Minnesota, to do the clinical tests. Lundy administered the drug to 700 patients, starting with ones closest to home. The first person to get Abbott 844 was Dr. Lundy's wife. The second was Dr. Charles H. Mayo, the clinic's co-founder. The third was former heavyweight boxing champ Jack Dempsey, visiting the clinic for minor surgery.

Lundy found the drug acted twice as powerfully as existing anesthetics. Just one-and-a-half grains of the drug knocked a patient out in less than 20 minutes. A standard dose would bring on two hours of unconsciousness. Abbott 844, when taken the night before and the morning prior to surgery, proved an excellent companion drug to longer-lasting anesthetics. Patients, wrote Volwiler and Tabern in a 1930 edition of the *Journal of the American Chemical Society*, were rendered unconscious in short order and woke up without nausea or stupor.

Dr. Lundy renamed the compound Embutal, after **e**thyl l-**m**ethyl-**b**utyl, plus "**al**," a suffix for barbiturates. Volwiler

and Tabern worked out a sodium salt formulation, which made the substance more quickly absorbed and easier to produce. They tagged on the chemical symbol for sodium, **N**a, and the Abbott trade name became *Nembutal*. The common chemical term for it: pentobarbital sodium.

Nembutal epitomized the dual devotion to painstaking research and zealous salesmanship that had become an Abbott hallmark. Once a month or more, Dr. Tabern, at his own expense, drove about the byways of the Midwest demonstrating the advantages of *Nembutal*. His marketing tool, along with many medical charts, was a movie of *Nembutal's* harmless effect on test puppies and rabbits.

Continues on page 98 ▶

The first product of the extraordinary scientific partnership of Drs. Ernest H. Volwiler and Donalee L. Tabern was *Nembutal*, a breakthrough anesthetic.

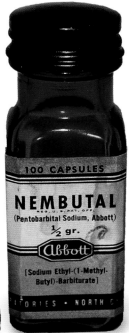
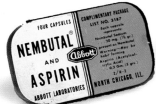

[Contribution from the Abbott Laboratories]

5,5-SUBSTITUTED BARBITURIC ACIDS[1]

By E. H. Volwiler and D. L. Tabern

Received December 26, 1929   Published April 7, 1930

Of the many types of chemical compounds which can produce sleep, the derivatives of barbituric acid continue to be by far the most important. During recent years, the availability of new alcohols has made possible the more systematic study of the homologs of the parent member of the series, barbital (diethylbarbituric acid), with the result that several new hypnotics of superior therapeutic merit have become available. More than a hundred barbituric acid derivatives have been synthesized and most of them have been pharmacologically tested; a number of them have found their way into clinical use.

Considerable variation in sleep-producing activity exists among the members of this series, ranging from none at all to over four times that of barbital. If this increase in efficiency over barbital were merely accompanied by a corresponding increase in toxicity, there would be little attained by the study of the newer barbituric acid derivatives. This is not neces-

[1] Presented before the Medicinal Products Division of the American Chemical Society at Minneapolis, Sept. 10, 1929.

Drs. Volwiler and Tabern published their findings on the valuable new anesthetic they had developed in the *Journal of the American Chemical Society*, in 1930.

Dr. Alfred S. Burdick

From the moment Dr. Abbott hired him to help edit *The Alkaloidal Clinic*, Dr. Alfred Stephen Burdick served as a senior counselor. It was an ideal way to prepare a future company president. When Dr. Abbott fell ill late in his career, Dr. Burdick was the natural choice to take on his duties.

Dr. Alfred S. Burdick, hired by Dr. Abbott himself and trained over a long apprenticeship, became the company's leader after its founder's death and led Abbott into a new era.

Born in 1867, the studious son of a New York clergyman, Alfred Burdick was a school teacher before getting his medical degree, then teaching again at Illinois Medical College. He was deeply intellectual, a Renaissance man. A physician, instructor, and accomplished corporate chief, he also loved languages and the arts. In his sixties, he learned German and practiced his Italian. Some work days, he took off from the North Chicago complex for downtown Chicago's Art Institute, and spent hours amidst the galleries. He also haunted used bookshops, buying up biographies and poetry collections. These he turned over to corporate librarian Edith Joannes, who set up a general-interest section in the company library.

Despite his broad range, he had the scientist's regard for the smallest item. "When we left school," he once stated, "we dreamed of the great things we would do … Yet nine-tenths of the failures in life are due to despising or overlooking detail … Woe to the one who doesn't think it necessary to his or her career to know, and knowing do the little things."

Though trained as a scientist, Burdick had superb business sense. It was he who negotiated the canny deal to acquire The Dermatological Research Laboratories, and who initiated the acquisition of the

The company presented Dr. Burdick with this life-size portrait on his 10th anniversary as company president, in 1931, along with a tribute signed by every employee.

Milliken company. And it was he who vetoed the proposed merger with Frederick Stearns and Company, for fear of diluting the Abbott brand.

As much as anyone, Burdick made ever-increasing research investment an Abbott hallmark. "Research — and more research," he wrote. "Research is fundamental and vital. Without it real progress is impossible."

Burdick was the critical force in, perhaps, Abbott's most important early change: its shift from alkaloidal to synthetic medicines. Dr. Burdick brought in the brilliant Dr. Roger Adams to lead this effort, which resulted in the anesthetics *Barbital* and *Procaine*. He also pushed Adams and Dr. Ernest H. Volwiler to develop the anesthetic *Butyn*, all critical early products for the firm.

Further, Dr. Burdick envisioned a large potential for vitamins at a time when that market scarcely existed. Upon his death, at the height of the Great Depression,

his successor S. DeWitt Clough inherited a profitable firm that was able to declare quarterly dividends and afford Christmas bonuses for its employees.

And Burdick solidified Abbott's intense focus on quality control. One of his favorite phrases was, "Let the seller beware."

Like his predecessor, President Burdick liked to range about the offices and workshops, engaging employees in conversation personal, technical, or commercial. He sometimes invited younger workers to his home, where, ever the strategic thinker, he would ply them with the critical question, "Where do we go from here?" He urged those invited to maintain a sense of priority: for mankind, for science, for Abbott, and then for themselves.

He corresponded continually with his charges, too. When the wife of Norman A. Hansen, the development lab head, died in 1930, Burdick penned the grieving man a five-page letter of commiseration.

When Dr. Burdick died in 1933, at 66 years of age, some of the mourners recalled his 10th anniversary as president of Abbott. At that surprise 1931 party in the company cafeteria, Burdick received the following resolution, signed by every worker:

"We are happy to congratulate him — and ourselves — For the gift of his leadership. For his affectionate and kindly interest in our people. For his scientific trend of mind. For his cheerfulness and enthusiasm. For his calm self-control … For his unfailing patience and courtesy. For his rare combination of a head and a heart. For his great understanding and sympathy." ■

The formal announcement of
Abbott's acquisition of
Swan-Myers.

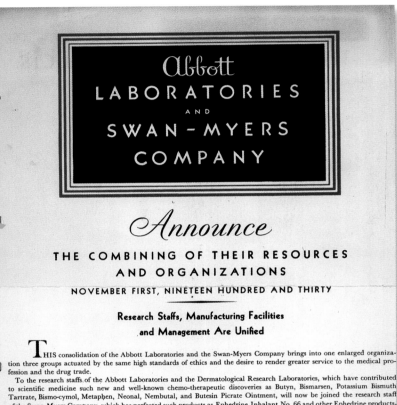

Abbott
LABORATORIES
AND
SWAN-MYERS
COMPANY

Announce

THE COMBINING OF THEIR RESOURCES
AND ORGANIZATIONS

NOVEMBER FIRST, NINETEEN HUNDRED AND THIRTY

Research Staffs, Manufacturing Facilities
and Management Are Unified

THIS consolidation of the Abbott Laboratories and the Swan-Myers Company brings into one enlarged organization three groups actuated by the same high standards of ethics and the desire to render greater service to the medical profession and the drug trade.

To the research staffs of the Abbott Laboratories and the Dermatological Research Laboratories, which have contributed to scientific medicine such new and well-known chemo-therapeutic discoveries as Butyn, Bismarsen, Potassium Bismuth Tartrate, Bismo-cymol, Metapḥen, Neonal, Nembutal, and Butesin Picrate Ointment, will now be joined the research staff of the Swan-Myers Company, which has perfected such products as Ephedrine Inhalant No. 66 and other Ephedrine products, Bacterial Vaccines, Pollens and Pollen Extracts, Bacteriophage, Ampoule Solutions for intravenous and subcutaneous use, Kerakote Glandular Products, Ophthalmic and Nasal Ointments, Para-Psyllia Emulsion and others.

All of these products will continue to be manufactured under the same rigid control and marketed under the same labels as heretofore, with the Abbott, D.R.L. and Swan-Myers guarantee of purity, accuracy and dependability.

With the enlarged and unified branch distributing facilities to physicians, through pharmacists and the wholesale drug trade, the research products of these three companies will now be more widely and conveniently accessible throughout this country and abroad and on the same terms as are now in effect.

The same officers and executives who have guided these companies in the past will manage and direct the combined organization. The laboratories of Swan-Myers Company will be operated for the present in Indianapolis.

It is with much pleasure we offer to you these combined resources and respectfully invite your attention to the new as well as the better-known fine pharmaceutical products illustrated and described on the following pages.

Abbott   Swan-Myers   **ABBOTT LABORATORIES**

ALFRED S. BURDICK, M.D., President
R. M. CAIN, Vice-President
(Former President, Swan-Myers Company)

Tabern and Abbott's purchasing agent Ray Ranson would fill the back seat of Tabern's car with film apparatus and animals, then head out in the pre-dawn hours to talk up groups of hospital officials, nurses, doctors, and medical students.

One time, while driving to Lansing, Michigan, the pair was pulled over by a motorcycle cop. Prohibition was still in effect, and authorities were on the alert. The policeman, eyeing the cloth-covered bundles in the rear, was convinced the two Chicagoans were bootleggers transporting a different kind of painkiller. The two Abbott men managed to reassure the peace officer.

Stoked by Tabern's promotional élan, *Nembutal* became a big seller. The North Chicago complex formulated it in capsule form, as a powder, and in solution. A widely used anesthetic, the drug was further applied as an antispasmodic and pain-killing analgesic, relieving childbirth pains, convulsions, and delirium tremens, as well as insomnia and seasickness.

The tireless Tabern, meantime, went back to the lab, where he broke ground on another anesthetic that, a half-dozen years later, would have an even greater impact on medicine, as well as on psychology and military affairs.

Acquiring a Wealth of Talent

In June 1930, Abbott's garrulous ad chief, Clough, was attending a convention of the American Pharmaceutical Manufacturers Association in Hot Springs, Virginia. He struck up a lengthy conversation with Rolly M. Cain, head of Swan-Myers, an Indianapolis maker of intravenous solutions and cold and hay-fever remedies. Cain was an impressive figure, a former pharmacist clerk who had grown his firm's revenues from $35,000 to more than $1,000,000 a year.

After chatting about the two companies' early years, Clough asked Cain: "Would Swan-Myers be interested in joining forces with a view of enhancing the growth of both companies?"

A stunned Cain replied: "Let me sleep on the idea and let you know later."

"If you're at all interested," continued Clough, "I suggest that Dr. Burdick be brought into further conversations. I don't know that he'd be interested for Abbott, but I'll speak with him when I arrive home."

Within a week Rolly Cain was touring the impressive, newly completed North Chicago complex. Cain came back several times for negotiations; a deal was struck in early November. The two companies merged, with Swan-Myers getting $1,000,000 of stock created during Abbott's public offering the previous year.

Swan-Myers provided a personnel roster that was outstanding. Adding to Abbott's already formidable research and production prowess was Edgar B. Carter, Swan-Myers' science and manufacturing chief. Among its prominent scientists were Dr. E.E. Moore and Marjorie B. Moore, his spouse; bacteriologist Dr. Hobart W. Cromwell; and botanist/allergist Oren C. Durham.

Continues on page 102 ▶

The Swan-Myers employees posing outside their Indianapolis headquarters include two future Abbott presidents, a father-son combination. Front row, second from right, was Swan-Myers president Rolly M. Cain. Directly behind him, to the left, was his son, George R. Cain.

Oren C. Durham, the Father of the Pollen Count

Today, every allergy sufferer takes pollen counts for granted. Yet, Abbott had a seminal role in their creation, through the painstaking research of Oren C. Durham.

Abbott researcher Oren C. Durham (below) performed landmark data collection on allergic reactions.

In 1916, when the self-taught Durham began his investigations into the science of allergic reactions, myths abounded. Roses were blamed for hay fever. Some believed allergies could be fought off by applying shellac to the nasal passages.

Born in 1889, Durham joined the Swan-Myers Company in 1925, serving as chief botanist, and came aboard in 1930, when Abbott acquired the firm. "Swan-Myers hired me," he recalled years later, "as a combination adviser, trouble-shooter, and pollen gatherer for the allergenic products line."

Eventually Durham compiled statistics and drew up charts on the

onset and amount of pollen in some 100 metropolitan areas across North America. In the 1930s, newspapers daily published his data on ragweed concentrations, giving sufferers strategic intelligence on the threat. Later, television and radio followed suit.

Much of the research was collected in the air over cities, courtesy of United Airlines. Durham

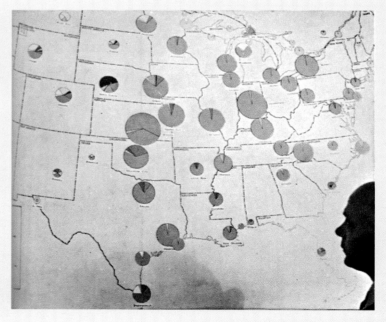

cleverly fashioned a "sky hook," a streamlined bracket attached to an airplane, which captured pollen on a greased microscope slide. Durham later added information on fungus spores to his piles of information.

Samples were carefully examined and cataloged by scientists in the lab.

Oren Durham (below left) collects a pollen sample.

Durham also worked with the United States Weather Bureau, and its sister agencies in Canada and Mexico, to collect tens of thousands of specimens at ground stations. Researchers changed the Vaseline-slicked slides every morning (below). Even the U.S. Navy was enlisted to check for pollen over bodies of water.

Later, Abbott would construct its own daily pollen count. Each day from the onset of allergy season until first frost, a technician mounted the roof of a North Chicago research building, and collected a pollen slide from a spinning box mounted on a metal post (lower left.) The results were announced in a recorded phone message, and also used by local radio stations to inform the public about daily pollen counts.

Abbott's researchers had become world-leading authorities on pollen. Their work fed into allergy medicines developed by Abbott, such as *Thenylene* for hay fever. More importantly, the work broke important new ground in a previously primitive field of research. ■

Another influential addition from Swan-Myers was copywriter Charles S. Downs. As the head of Abbott's advertising, Downs would coax higher sales during the Depression, manage a major new medical magazine, and spur the company's famous war bonds drive of the Second World War.

With the merger, Rolly M. Cain became Abbott's head of sales, while Clough was made vice president. Rolly's son George came on board later. Remarkably, both father and son were to become Abbott presidents. James "Sunny Jim" Stiles moved up to treasurer from his comptroller slot. The new personnel brought a true changing of the guard. Founders James W. Ranson, Clara Abbott's brother-in-law, and Henry B. Shattuck, Dr. Abbott's childhood friend, retired from the board.

Abbott took advantage of small acquisitions as well as large ones. Dr. Burdick moved to buy up a pharmaceutical products agency in Los Angeles run by an old acquaintance of Dr. Abbott's, Dr. John S. Miller. Abbott made the place its branch office for Southern California. Miller's son, John Jr., stayed on as manager, and increased its annual sales of $250,000 by tenfold.

New Leadership: Growing Abbott in Tough Economic Times

By the end of 1932, Abbott's prosperity stood out among the economic difficulty of the Depression.

"Few of the leading industrial organizations of the country," noted *Nation's Commerce* magazine, "can show a sounder record for the past year than the Abbott Laboratories."

> ## "We want fight and dash and pep from morning to night."
>
> — RAYMOND E. HORN

Then, on February 11, 1933, with the United States weeks from a nationwide bank closure, tragedy struck the firm. After attending a sales meeting at the New York branch office, Dr. Burdick caught pneumonia and died. He was 66 years old.

Simeon DeWitt Clough, who joined Abbott in 1904 for $10 per week, became the company's third chief executive, in 1933.

Kinetic sales chief Simeon DeWitt Clough was made Burdick's successor.

Taking over in the depths of an economic crisis, Clough showed himself to be, like the company's founder, an able crisis manager, and not one to shrink from a challenge. The Depression, he felt, put a premium on effective marketing.

"We are going to build up this company, depression or no depression!" the new president announced. When the new United States President, Franklin Roosevelt, declared a temporary bank "holiday," Clough sent every salesman a $100 postage money order to keep their solicitations going until the crisis' end. He was a good neighbor, too, steering $20,000 to North Chicago's financially strapped schools.

The marketing guru immediately launched a "Make Your Goal!" sales campaign, one Clough had spent years planning. To direct it, he gave his old job of sales manager to Raymond E. Horn, the ex-DRL sales standout, who was assisted by David D. Stiles, the brother of "Sunny Jim."

Horn seemed to inherit the zest for sales of both Clough and Dr. Abbott. "A CLARION CALL TO ARMS!" he wrote to his salesforce. "We want fight and dash and pep from morning to night."

His attitude was contagious. Responded Seattle Branch Manager Lewis C. Beck: "I believe enthusiasm is a salesman's greatest asset. I believe in the extrovert; he confides, confesses, consults … I believe the rut is the grave and that the end of effort is the end of progress. I believe no salesman need become a slave to habit, the lazy habit of the order-taker; that no man need content himself with what he is."

Buttressing the high morale were concrete moves to make a better sales organization. Sales managers engaged in "self-criticism" sessions at the Dynamite Club and Typhoon Club, as their associations were called. Training and retraining sessions were put into effect, as were bonuses and awards for breaking quotas. There were negative incentives as well: Those not making their sales couldn't invite their wives to the semiannual sales conferences.

Underlying Clough's sales campaign was a sweeping corporate reorganization. The new Abbott president set up or strengthened committees in a host of areas — packaging, personnel, safety, research, production planning, and improvement, among others. "In this way," remarked Clough, "views of many individuals are obtained and help to shape company policies."

Through E.H. Ravenscroft, now the board chairman, he established a practice, which lasted until the late 1950s, by which only long time Abbott employees could serve as board directors. For years, the directors met at the cafeteria lunch table every day to go over company business. A batch of multivitamin capsules was kept at hand, leading to the common request: "Pass the bullets!"

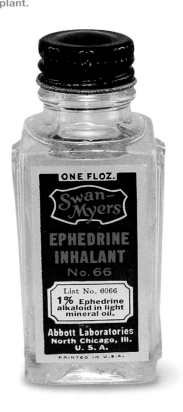

> ## "It is rare indeed that one finds these days a common stock that is selling as high as it did in 1929."
>
> — *COMMERCE* MAGAZINE

Where his predecessors had walked the halls to poll employees, Clough set up a committee for employee activities, and another for worker suggestions on how to improve operations. A suggestion box became an Abbott staple: good recommendations were put into practice, and their originators got cash awards. These totaled about $100,000 over two decades, sometimes resulting in savings of like amounts.

Workers of a studious bent got help from their president: Clough founded the Abbott Study Club, whose night time classes at the plant ranged from simple mathematics to industrial psychology. Those attending more formal courses at area schools were reimbursed for half their fees. Abbott was years ahead of other firms in providing such tuition reimbursement.

Fervent promotional efforts paid dividends in every sense. During the heart of the Great Depression, from 1932 to 1935, revenues went from $3,622,000 to $6,118,000, and profits rose from $298,000 to $1,135,000.

"It is rare indeed," commented *Commerce* magazine on Abbott, "that one finds these days a common stock that is selling as high as it did in 1929."

Ephedrine

One cause of the swelling sales was a product that both Swan-Myers and Abbott had produced. It was ephedrine, the popular decongestant and weight-loss drug. An alkaloid, it is derived from the Chinese *ma-huang* plant, and China's emperors had employed it to treat colds and weak hearts for thousands of years. In 1925, pharmacologists at the Peking Union Medical College ascertained its medical uses and, soon, Swan-Myers and Abbott Laboratories were making ephedrine. With the merger of the two firms, Abbott became the largest manufacturer of the medicine in the world.

A production concern, however, was that a thousand pounds of *ma-huang* were required to make just five pounds of ephedrine. Abbott already had vast expertise in making alkaloidal substances. So it contracted with Chinese middlemen to procure great quantities of the plant, and figured out methods of making pure ephedrine from them. Company pharmacologists cleverly combined ephedrine with other medicinals. It was formulated with the antiseptic *Metaphen* to yield *Metaphedrin*, an oil spray for sinus afflictions. Another spray, of ephedrine and the anesthetic *Butesin*, was aimed at hay fever.

Company editor Lillian Adams sang the praises of ephedrine's precursor plant in the company publication *Abbograms*, to the tune of the traditional song, "Believe Me If All Those Endearing Young Charms":

> *"Believe me Ma Huang those endearing young*
> *charms*
> *That you bring from the East of my dreams,*
> *Soft nestle me down to sweet sleep in your arms*
> *Mid poppies and lantern gleams.*
> *And you draw the night veil of Ephedra mare-tail*
> *'Til my nightmare of asthma's at rest;*
> *Let me drink to you Ma Huang in flagons of ale*
> *For you stop the damned wheeze in my chest!"*

Another cause of Abbott's continuing financial success was a new product resulting from its ongoing work in vitamins.

Wide-ranging Abbott researcher Charles F. Lanwermeyer, at the controls of halibut liver oil processing gear, in Prince Rupert, British Columbia.

Trolling the Seas for Vitamins

In the spring and summer of 1930, Abbott's Charles Lanwermeyer ranged throughout the Pacific Coast of Alaska and Canada in search of, of all things, livers from the guts of halibut. The genesis of his odd journey lay in the unpalatable taste and smell of cod liver oil.

A Proud Tradition in Nutrition

1920s
Viosterol

Abbott entered the then-new field of vitamins — or, as they were originally known, "vita-mines" — with *Viosterol* in 1929.

1930s
Haliver Oil

During the Great Depression, Abbott's revenues swelled from vitamin-rich *Haliver Oil*, derived from the livers of halibut.

1950s
Dayalets

Since the 1950s, Abbott has produced multivitamins such as *Dayalets*.

A substance rich in vitamins A and D, it had for generations been forced down the throats of sick youngsters. Dr. Burdick had noted that the yellow liquid "was a disagreeable substance for disagreeable children."

Like other firms, Abbott realized profits could be had from finding a similar, but better-tasting, substance. A large survey of promising plants and animals was undertaken. Carl Nielsen, Abbott's head of pharmaceutical research, had worked on the *Viosterol* project. Now he put to use his encyclopedic knowledge of the medical literature. In 1929, he noted an article by Signe and Sigval Schmidt-Nielsen, two Norwegian researchers, in *The Biochemical Journal* that detailed their search for vitamins A and D in seafood. They had examined perch, salmon, shark, even whales — and halibut. The livers of the latter were packed with vitamin A.

With Dr. Burdick's backing, Nielsen had commercial fishermen send him frozen halibut livers, and he and his researchers picked through the rotted remains. Preliminary results backed up the findings of the Norwegians. But to conduct thorough bioassays of the organs, large amounts of livers were needed. The obvious place to go was the "Meadows of the Sea," in the fish-rich northeastern Pacific.

The head of Abbott research met with his top assistant, Lanwermeyer, who had joined Abbott through the Milliken acquisition.

"Charlie," Nielsen ordered him, "you're going fishing. Get up to Canada or to Alaska if you have to, because we're going to need a lot of halibut livers, especially if we find we can do this commercially. And try to keep why you're up there a secret!"

So Lanwermeyer lugged a camera and typewriter to numerous shoreline fishing towns, writing up daily notes to Nielsen, and meeting a wall of skepticism.

"You're on a fool's errand," officials of fishing companies told him. "You'll never get what you need." Crews had no use for the livers, dumping them into the oceans by the thousands after catching and gutting the halibut. "They ain't no good to anyone," the Abbott researcher was informed.

Then, at the halibut fishing mecca of Prince Rupert, in British Columbia, Lanwermeyer tried a new tack. At a tavern, he plied local fishermen with rounds of Black Horse Ale. After softening them up, he urged:

"Tell you what I'll do. If you'll go out and get me some livers, every one of you, when you come back, you can have as much ale for yourself as you all got tonight."

"They ain't worth a damn," the fishermen's chief replied. "But if you really want them, we'll get you some."

Encouraged, Lanwermeyer set up waterfront shop at an enterprise for smoked herring. He went out with other fishermen, saw them stick salmon bait on the 200 hooks of their endless fishing lines, and winch up the catch. Back ashore, he mixed halibut livers with solvents to separate out the oil, which he shipped to Nielsen's waiting team for analysis.

1960s
Similac

The 1964 acquisition of M&R Dietetic Laboratories, makers of the popular infant formula *Similac*, made Abbott a major nutrition company.

1970s
Ensure

Abbott in 1973 introduced *Ensure*, which would soon be the most used medical nutritional for adults.

1990s
Glucerna

The *Glucerna* line of snacks, cereals, and drinks, first offered in 1998, was aimed at the unique dietary needs of people with diabetes, one of a number of "disease-specific" nutritionals developed by Abbott.

2000s
ZonePerfect

In 2003 , Abbott acquired the *ZonePerfect* line of performance nutrition bars, providing a high level of nutrition in a convenient form. It would enhance its Healthy Living franchise with the addition of the EAS line of performance nutritionals.

At this 1934 sales convention, Abbott's third president,
Simeon DeWitt Clough, background, busily fielded business
on the phone while salesmen in the foreground posed
for the camera.

Abbott eventually combined its two successful vitamin-rich products, *Haliver Oil* and *Viosterol*, into one, and promoted it "tongue-in-cheek."

At this time, Lanwermeyer had his run-in with the Royal Canadian Mounted Police. When the Mountie confined the Abbott man to his rooming house, he wrote Nielsen:

"The redcoats have got me. If I go to jail, please send some tobacco and oranges."

Another time, forgetting his vow of silence to Nielsen, Lanwermeyer discussed his project with an Alaskan reporter, whose article, "Chemist Seeks Liquid Sun in Alaska Waters," appeared in the *Ketchikan Tribune*. Abbott, its secret out, raced to beat its competitors to the punch.

Back in Illinois, Nielsen had his own worries. Cod liver oil was readily extracted through steaming or boiling. Producing oil from halibut, in contrast, was like squeezing water from rocks. But after innumerable experiments, and the expenditure of $200,000, Abbott researchers, working with Parke-Davis company scientists, found a profitable means to extract copious amounts of the oil.

It was worth the effort. Halibut oil, according to a presentation by Nielsen before the American Chemical Society, had 20 times the vitamin D content of cod liver oil, and 100 percent more vitamin A.

In Seattle, Abbott built a factory to extract, refine, and store the stuff. It took in fish from across a large and icy

expanse off Alaska's Kodiak Island and in the Bering Sea. Fishermen were instructed to separate the vitamin-rich livers from the catch's entrails. The precious commodity was kept in glass tanks filled with nitrogen or carbon dioxide to fend off vitamin-destroying oxidation.

By early 1932, physicians were prescribing *Haliver Oil* — as Nielsen dubbed it. It had been only two short years from conception to production. Company sales and profits got a major boost during pressing economic times.

That year, Abbott launched a crash program to mass-manufacture *Haliver Oil*.

Production commenced at the new North Chicago liquid manufacturing building, M2. The plant was known for making root beer extract, elixir of pava pepsin, camphor and chloroform liniment, mouth wash, even cod liver oil. But now its focus changed.

Fifty employees were put to work every day and night of the week. They mixed fish oil, made gelatin, and molded, sorted, cleaned, and weighed the capsules. Shifts included Christmas and New Year's Eve. The company's Christmas dinner was brought directly to the employees.

Some faced drawbacks other than missing the holidays. Elmer Krueger, a production worker and recent

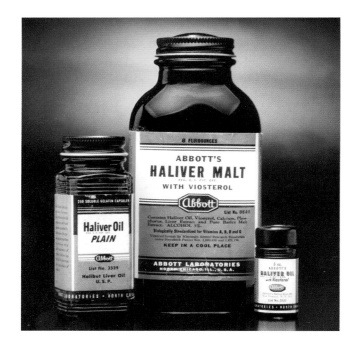

Haliver Oil was available in multiple forms.

University of Wisconsin graduate, found it hard to wash away the scent of the fish oil — a particular embarrassment, as he was just about to go on his honeymoon.

After *Haliver Oil* became a hit, imitations flooded the market. Abbott struck back with a campaign that foretold the product labels of a later era. It bought samples of 34 of Haliver's imitators, and conducted bioassays to determine if the content matched the claims on the labels. Most flunked the test, while *Haliver Oil*, also scrutinized, exceeded the vitamin units displayed on its label.

Haliver Oil was, in time, processed with *Viosterol*, Abbott's original vitamin product. It took the form of a small capsule equivalent to three teaspoons of cod liver oil, but with no ill taste or gagging.

Nielsen continued the research into nutrition, bringing aboard top students of Dr. Conrad Elvehjem, a food expert from the University of Wisconsin, and later its president. Nielsen's pioneering work led to his appointment to Abbott's board of directors in 1934, and sowed the seeds of Abbott's long-term leadership in nutrition science.

On his retirement, in 1946, Nielsen worked as a scientific advisor in his native Scandinavia. In 1948, King Frederick IX of Denmark dubbed him a Knight of the Order of Dannebrog.

To celebrate the *Haliver Oil* saga, a wag — likely an Abbott employee — published the following verses in the *Chemical Bulletin*:

> *From cold Pacific waters,*
> *To North Chicago plains*
> *They send us halibut livers*
> *To ease our growing pains.*
>
> *A blessing to the suffering,*
> *Rich source of vitamins.*
> *Our Haliver delivers*
> *From dietary sins …*
>
> *… We like to tell the story,*
> *To sick ones and their friends.*
> *It's a solace to the weary*
> *And pays us dividends.*

Abbott senior managers (from left to right) Director of Sales Raymond E. Horn, Vice President and Treasurer James F. Stiles, Chairman Edward H. Ravenscroft, President and General Manager S. DeWitt Clough, Executive Vice President and Assistant General Manager Rolly M. Cain, and Director of Marketing Charles S. Downs show unwavering dedication to innovative employee benefits. Abbott has remained a leader in this area.

"Happiness and Peace of Mind" in Pioneering Employee Benefits

As Abbott's revenues rose, the company expanded what Clough called its "Happiness and Peace of Mind Program," or benefits for its employees. They were especially welcome during the uncertainty of the Depression years. "Sunny Jim" Stiles, then the human resources chief, worked out the details of various programs, and fought for their enactment.

They grew steadily throughout the decade as Abbott innovated new employee benefit ideas:

▷ *1933*. Health and accident insurance costing 52 cents to $2 a month.
▷ *1936*. Accidental death and dismemberment insurance; company-paid; on or off the job.
▷ *1938*. Hospital-based surgery or treatment; small employee fees; for both employees and dependents. Abbott was the first such company to supply such coverage.

Further, a "blessed event" program handed an employee a $50 check at the birth of each child.

While expanding benefits at Abbott, Clough pressed for voluntary insurance programs in other firms. He wrote many magazine and trade articles on the virtues of group health insurance.

Reported the *St. Louis Dispatch*: "For about $60 a year, an Abbott employee can get himself insured against practically everything except being divorced by his wife and drafted in case of another World War."

Continues on page 112 ▶

What's New
A Sophisticated Publication from an Innovative Company

Rising revenues combined with unique talent helped Abbott launch the industry standard for high-quality educational and marketing publications. In the fall of 1935, Abbott debuted its toney corporate magazine, *What's New*. Aimed at physicians, it was created for highly educated readers with refined tastes. A success from the start, by the early 1950s it had 312,500 physicians among its readers, as well as the millions of patients in their waiting rooms.

From the start, *What's New* had a standout layout and design — the better to showcase the world-famous artists, from the straightforward to the surreal, commissioned to decorate its pages with original paintings and illustrations. Its artist rolls included the likes of Grant Wood, Raoul Dufy, and Thomas Hart Benton.

What's New also enlisted noted authors to write short stories for its monthly issues. Filling its pages were the verses of America's best-known poets: Robert Frost, Edna St. Vincent Millay, and, fittingly, Carl Sandburg, the champion of Chicago, the "city of big shoulders" that Abbott made its home. "Abbott is a favorite among artists," noted an industry observer, "who know they won't be hampered by style limitations."

The art for this cover of *What's New* was painted by Raphael Soyer. Titled "Modern Dancer," this realistic painting is distinctive as the abstract movement became popular during this time period.

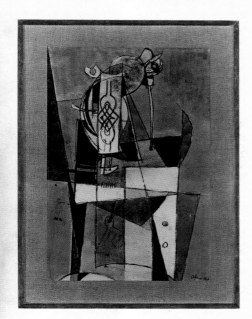

The changing times are captured in the changing styles of *What's New* cover art. This 1958 cover by Afro Basaldella captured the spirit of post-World War II movements in American and European art.

What's New combined leading ideas in both medicine and art to create a high-quality publication that benefited doctors and patients as well as the company.

Every issue of *What's New* was put together by a talented staff of varied backgrounds. One of *What's New*'s supervisors was editor Joseph S. Dungan, an ex-Parisian musician and former *Chicago Tribune* ad writer. Another was advertising mastermind Charles S. Downs, a former Swan-Myers copywriter who was largely responsible for the first-rate look and content of *What's New*. A mainstay at Abbott into the 1960s, Downs was critical in establishing the nation-wide War Bonds campaign of the 1940s.

Top-notch writers, such as Conrad Aiken and William Saroyan, were also represented.

Style aside, the magazine's primary purpose was conveying medical information. Editors gleaned nuggets from hundreds of professional publications, and placed them into three-by-five-inch "Brief Summaries and Abstracts" that were easily clippable by doctors, the publication's target audience.

What's New was well known for its annual Christmas issue, which shined particularly bright in its 1952 edition. It featured works — both classic and new — of renowned artists like Pablo Picasso and writers like Ogden Nash.

In addition to seasonal fare, the issue included articles on leukemia, inflammation of the eyes, and weight gain worsened by holiday eating. One piece featured a lavish display of historical microscopes.

A medical editor during the Second Word War was Gordon Hoard, a premedical student whose financial woes led him to play saxophone for the famous Tommy Dorsey jazz band.

Sometimes the editors performed their own writing and research. Notable was an article on the problems of Native American Indian healthcare, backed by data gathered by researchers taking trips that stretched from the Mexican jungles to near the Arctic Circle. From 1935–1962, Abbott produced 229 editions of the magazine. ■

The chemical formulas of the *Nembutal* and *Pentothal* molecules were very similar, differing by only one critical sulfur (S) atom.

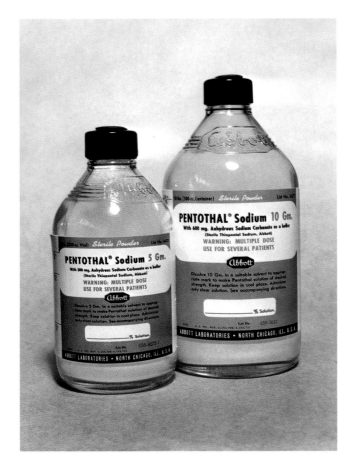

NEMBUTAL   PENTOTHAL

Bottles of *Pentothal* sodium quickly became a best-seller for Abbott and a boon for surgeons.

Breakthrough: *Pentothal*

Chairman Edward H. Ravenscroft noted in 1937: "Abbott Laboratories was built on a foundation of more definite and accurate medicine. Research in the past, research in the present, and research in the future is the rock on which this foundation rests." Indeed, in the second half of the decade, research into a follow-up to *Nembutal* bore spectacular fruit.

For six years Dr. Tabern, again with Dr. Volwiler's direction, had pursued an anesthetic that could be injected directly into the bloodstream. The pair also sought a drug powerful enough to carry through surgery, yet one whose effects quickly wore off. In the pre-war period scientists had thought barbiturates with sulfur atoms might do the trick, and Volwiler had noted this research as part of his intense surveys of medical literature.

For three years the Volwiler and Tabern duo sifted through 200 compounds. Ironically, the very first compound examined hit gold. "We injected it into a dog," Tabern remembered, "and he went to sleep fast and woke up in 10 minutes feeling fine — and we were sure we had it."

But the usual, meticulous battery of tests for any new drug had to take place. With the compound, called "Barbiturate A," Abbott very much followed the track taken with *Nembutal*. First, chief pharmacologist Henry C. Spruth tested out the substance, along with other promising new anesthetics, on animals. The University of Wisconsin's Dr. Tatum was again enlisted, to try Barbiturate A on monkeys, rats, rabbits, and canines. Each test animal became unconscious before the injection was finished. Each one woke up within minutes, clear-headed. In these, as in all its animal tests required in research and development, Abbott strove to avoid unneeded discomfort among the test subjects.

In 1933, Dr. Biehn again called on the Mayo Clinic's Dr. Lundy, the so-called "Warrior against Pain." This time Lundy did not have a heavyweight champion on hand to try the drug, but he tested it on 700 other patients.

The results were striking. No muscle twitching. No dizziness. No sense of suffocation as seen with other anesthetics. Patients were out cold before they could count to 20. They were awake within 20 minutes, with little or no nausea.

Thousands of further clinical tests were done in Great Britain, Canada, and South Africa. In 1937, Abbott announced its new drug — *Pentothal*, or sodium thiopental — in an article in *What's New*. The publication carefully noted the substance should be supplied "only by competent, experienced anesthetists in hospitals where all facilities are at hand to meet problems involved in anesthesia, such as carbon dioxide and oxygen administration."

As with *Nembutal*, Dr. Tabern again took to the road, this time with an instructional movie about the new anesthetic. Tabern spent additional overtime hours in North Chicago ironing out the manufacture of *Pentothal* in quantity. Dr. Harry E. Sagen, a former University of Wisconsin bacteriology professor, imposed exacting standards of quality control for the powdery yellow substance.

> "Research in the past, research in the present, and research in the future is the rock on which this foundation rests."
>
> — E.H. RAVENSCROFT

Abbott hardly expected the widespread success of its new drug, readily administered in water solution intravenously. Eye surgeons found they no longer had to anesthetize patients with unwieldy face masks. Dentists could dispense with less reliable "laughing gas." Brain surgery was also eased. Because *Pentothal* worked so fast, cancer surgeons found it ideal for quickly performed biopsies, especially with very ill patients lacking strength to endure a longer-lasting anesthetic. The drug was also tailor-made for tonsillectomies and Caesarian sections.

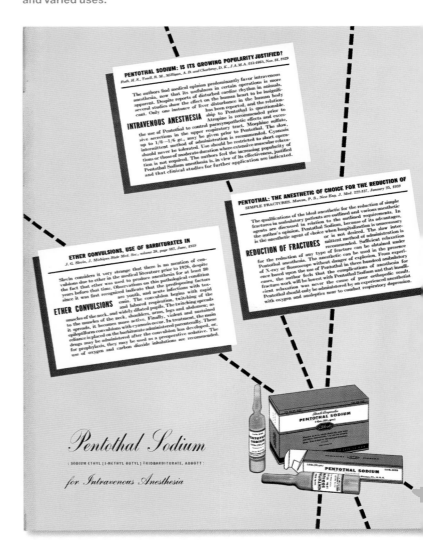

Sodium *Pentothal* soon was known for its many and varied uses.

Pentothal went on to dominate its field. Records from 1934 to 1955 of some three million cases of anesthetics applied intravenously show that it was used 94 percent of the time. In the 1940s, it was to find other applications, including in psychiatry. As late as the 1960s, a clinical booklet on anesthesia advised physicians, "To know intravenous anesthesia is to know *Pentothal*." Twenty years later, it was still the world's most used anesthetic, and is commonly used to this day.

An IV Kind of Solution

A product closely related to an intravenously administered drug like *Pentothal* was the bottle and tube that drips the solution into a patient's vein. Although Abbott became a major producer of these intravenous (IV) administration sets, it entered the field largely by accident.

Continues on page 116 ▶

Edward H. Ravenscroft

Edward Hawks Ravenscroft was the company's first master engineer and first corporate cost analyst. He was also part of an esteemed Abbott father-son pair.

In the early years of the company, Edward H. Ravenscroft, an engineer by trade, helped manage the recovery from the 1905 fire that gutted the Abbott publishing plant.

In 1908, he supervised the building of the new research and manufacturing complex, the sister edifice of the publishing plant that rose from the ruins of the fire. Later, in the 1920s, he located the site, and expertly designed, with Fred Young, the new North Chicago headquarters. His skillful placement and layout of buildings was vital to the swift distribution and processing of the scores of chemicals and tons of exotic plants continually shipped into the facility, then transported around the world after manufacture.

Moreover, for more than two decades, after assuming a leading financial role, Ravenscroft analyzed and trimmed the myriad cost inputs for Abbott's processes and products. He made decisions on final selling prices, pared manufacturing expense, and continually improved cost accounting. In so doing he laid the foundation for the intricate system of tying costs to productivity that presidents George R. Cain and Edward J. Ledder were to institute in later decades.

Edward Hawks Ravenscroft excelled in construction management and cost analysis. He married Dr. Abbott's sister, Lucy, producing a son who would also have a notable Abbott career.

Edward A. Ravenscroft, son of Chairman E.H. Ravenscroft, rose to the position of executive vice president and was involved in many critical Abbott initiatives.

During the First World War, he took under his wing the young James "Sunny Jim" Stiles, tutoring him in finance. Stiles would rise to become company treasurer as well as board chairman.

Ravenscroft had a distinguished career in construction long before he joined Abbott. Born in Edinburgh, Scotland, in 1871, the son of an accountant, he settled in Chicago and attended the University of Michigan. As a railroad and civil engineer, he managed the reconstruction, in 1896, of freight houses in East St. Louis after a tornado flattened them. He was chief assistant engineer of the 3,959-foot Thebes Bridge, built in 1905, a double-track railway construct spanning the Mississippi River. Anticipating an increase in traffic from the newly invented motor car, Ravenscroft's team built the bridge double-strong.

As chairman of the board during the crisis times of 1933 to 1946, Ravenscroft's financial and engineering acumen proved of great benefit. His knowledge of finance was a boon during the lean Depression years, and his experience with building assisted in the rapid ramp-up of production during the war.

Ravenscroft and his son Edward composed, with Rolly and George Cain, Abbott's most celebrated father-son duos. Their long familial history at Abbott was fitting, for Edward H. Ravenscroft was a literal member of the Abbott family. In 1896, he wed Dr. Abbott's sister, Lucy May, in Dr. Abbott's house. Lucy helped underwrite Ravenscroft's university education in civil engineering. They had four children, including Edward Abbott Ravenscroft.

The younger Ravenscroft took after his father in engineering and finance. He too was a University of Michigan graduate, in chemical engineering. At Abbott he served as vice president of Engineering. His position was chief engineer when his father, as company chairman, in 1936 turned the first spade of earth for the new research center in North Chicago. He even took after his father's early work as a railway engineer, becoming a builder of intricately designed model railroads, and president for a time of the National Model Railroad Association.

The elder Ravenscroft, having long mastered construction and finance, excelled in another career after retiring from Abbott. At his 900-acre Ravenglen Farm in northern Illinois, he bred Holstein-Friesian cattle of distinction. His King Bessie Senator bull won the All-American award on six straight occasions. In keeping with Abbott's tradition of local citizenship, the farm eventually became Lake County's Raven Glen Forest Preserve as a place of public recreation. ∎

Bottle handling at Abbott's
new IV production plant.
The process would later be
completely automated.

In 1932, Dr. Biehn and biological research head Edgar B. Carter, who had joined Abbott in the Swan-Myers acquisition, studied whether Abbott should get into the manufacture of IV bottles and solutions. Dr. Burdick rejected the idea, in part because the bottles in question had rubber stoppers that gave the solution a rubbery smell. The scent was harmless, but off-putting to purchasers.

Three years later, an Evanston, Illinois, pharmacist proposed to Carter that Abbott supply the nearby St. Francis Hospital with IV bottles filled with dextrose-and-salt solutions. The one-liter containers had to be sterile, and

thus free of fever-inducing pyrogens. Each bottle was to have a screw-on cap and, in place of a rubber stopper, an insoluble, odorless liner.

Soon Abbott had skipped over the middleman pharmacist, and was selling directly to hospitals nationwide. Company salesmen had a pitch that couldn't be beat: They would suggest that a potential buyer open the IV bottle of a rival manufacturer, sniff its inevitably rubbery scent, and ask:

"How would you like to have some of that stuff injected in your veins?"

Due to their distinctive labels and bottles, the company's offerings during this period were collectively known as "Abbott blue."

Equipment was purchased for the screw-on caps, and special molds were crafted for the bottles. As sales increased, the production team of Fred Young and George R. Ryan, the latter also from Swan-Myers, expanded and enhanced the processes for making the IV bottles. Over time Abbott became the biggest supplier of IV solutions in the United States.

Sound production techniques also played a key role in the related manufacture of ampoules, the sealed glass containers holding small amounts of solution or drugs.

Dr. Sagen, the *Pentothal* quality chief, headed up a group that applied Swan-Myers' facilities and skilled personnel in making the tiny vials.

Sagen put every worker through six months of apprenticeship. Laborers knew how to precisely calibrate the amount of solution, and how to seal each ampoule with an oxygen gas flame. The filled, sealed ampoules were sterilized anew, then stored in metal boxes for a week or more, then examined again for contaminants. Nothing was left to chance.

Dr. Joseph Favil Biehn was medical director and, as "the sand in the gearbox," a stern proponent of quality control.

Developing many of the stringent guidelines for production and marketing was the formidable Dr. Biehn. He insisted on comprehensive animal tests of new pharmaceuticals before their use in human clinical trials. He ensured the use of the most experienced clinicians, such as Dr. Lundy. Biehn also formulated rules for the safe infusion of drugs. A stickler for quality and consistency, Dr. Biehn was nicknamed, "the sand in the gearbox," a moniker he relished.

Biehn created policies on what salesmen could ethically claim about a product. And long before laws requiring such disclosure, he had Abbott publish details on the use, misuse, and possible side effects of all its pharmaceuticals.

An important quality assurance official was future chairman of the board Elmer B. Vliet, second from right. In this photo from the mid-1940s, Vliet, then manager of the control department, met in a control lab with, left to right, E.F. Shelberg, L.F. Reed, and J.A. Gordon.

Director of sales Raymond E. Horn, departing for a business trip, pushed to extend Abbott's global reach. Horn would become Abbott's president, driving strong worldwide expansion.

Becoming an International Enterprise

In the late 1930s, despite the severe recession of 1937, sales kept on rising. They were helped by Abbott's dramatic expansion abroad, catalyzed by the singular Manuel Doblado.

Doblado began with Abbott in 1930, in the poor-selling Oklahoma region. He was an eager salesman, and President Clough agreed to mail sales literature bearing the image of Doblado to every doctor in the Sooner State. The marketing piece promised Doblado would soon pay a visit to promote *Sodoxylin*, a hardly cutting-edge saline remedy for indigestion. The energetic fellow wound up winning a gold watch for taking weak sales to new heights.

When Raymond E. Horn took over as sales chief, he assigned Doblado to Pittsburgh, where he again blew out his quotas. An impressed Horn asked him to headquarters for a chat. He asked Doblado what he wished to do next.

Doblado replied that he wanted to get into the Export Department and go to Mexico to open a branch.

Sales vice president Rolly M. Cain was paying heed. Unusual for an American executive of his time, Cain was of a cosmopolitan bent, having traveled much in Europe.

Director of sales Raymond E. Horn, departing for a business trip, pushed to extend Abbott's global reach. Horn would become Abbott's president, driving strong worldwide expansion.

Manuel Doblado drove the company's early expansion into Latin America, demonstrating the powerful potential of developing markets.

The Depression had rocked the Old World's currencies, with England abandoning the gold standard, roiling the exchange rates between the United States and Canada, the latter a British dominion. To handle this, in 1931 Cain set up Abbott's first affiliate outside the United States, Abbott Laboratories, Ltd., of Canada, based in Montreal, and with a sales office in London. The newly incorporated company produced and distributed Abbott products throughout most of the British Empire.

Now Cain turned his sights on Latin America. He knew Abbott's sales representative in Mexico City was moonlighting for another firm, and seemed more interested in playing tennis than moving product. So he was receptive to Doblado's urgings, and assigned him to take over sales in Mexico.

Continues on page 123 ▶

Golden Jubilee — Abbott Marks its 50th Anniversary with a New Research Center

As Abbott entered its 50th year as a company, it rushed to commemorate the milestone with an ultra-modern research center at its North Chicago complex.

By autumn 1938, the three-story 53,000-square-foot brick structure was finished. The cost: $500,000.

Raymond Loewy, the father of American industrial design, planned the interior of the building.

It held laboratories for botany, bacteriology, hormonal research, and pharmaceutical and chemical science. Employees thought the research facilities "a sort of scientific workers' paradise."

The impressive exterior of the new research facility, fashioned from Minnesota granite and tapestry brick. The symbols displayed on the building represent common metals, such as the looking glass of Venus, the symbol for copper, from the legend that Venus had risen fully formed from the ocean foam on the shores of Cyprus, famous for its copper mines.

When ground was broken, on December 21, 1936, things came full circle. In 1920, Dr. Abbott had turned the first furrow of earth for the North Chicago complex, which engineer E.H. Ravenscroft went on to design. For the new edifice, Ravenscroft — now chairman of the board — turned the first shovelful of soil. Predicted President Clough: "In this research building … discoveries may be made of great importance."

The force behind the construction initiative was Dr. Volwiler, the leader of the *Nembutal* and *Pentothal* projects. He wanted to consolidate the greater part of the firm's research into one building.

Abbott enlisted Raymond Loewy, the famed designer of the Coca Cola bottle and, late in life, NASA's Skylab space station, to plan the building's interior.

One ultra-sensitive balance was placed in an air-conditioned, always-lit room to keep the temperature and the equilibrium ever constant. A micro-analytical lab was "micro" indeed — its weighing tubes, beakers, and "casseroles" could fit in the flat of a hand. It was suitable for weighing compounds down to a fifteen-thousandth of an ounce.

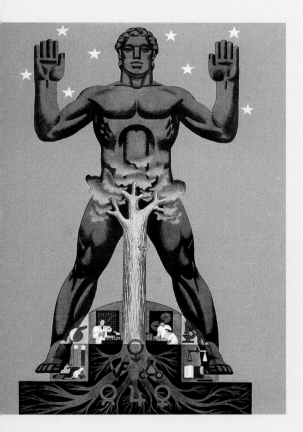

The "Abbott Tree," by Weimer Pursell, depicted a majestic figure of Man drawing his courage and sinews from a great tree, with its roots among scientific workers and symbols. The Tree is an enduring symbol of Abbott's pioneering research.

The new research center placed an emphasis on speed. New devices could measure, for instance, the nitrogen content of a drug in 20 minutes, not six hours as before, or the amount of a nutrient right away, not only after weeks of testing.

The lab instruments would sound futuristic even decades later:

▶ Fluorophotometers to measure the condition of the blood-retinal barrier.
▶ Polariscopes that shot rotating beams of sodium vapor light through a prism, and identified the strength and purity of substances in solution.
▶ Colorimeters to determine a solution's absorption of light.
▶ Spectrophotometers to illuminate biological samples with wavelengths of light.

Along with its labs the research center sported a 720-person auditorium and stage, suitable for speeches on medical topics — and tap-dancing at company galas. An annual spring talent show, with names like "Ghost-Capades," was made a company tradition. The Abbott Medicine Men, a quartet of harmony singers, were the stars. More than a few Abbott employees married after meeting up at these events.

A 15,000-plus-volume library was festooned with artist Weimer Pursell's murals of great scientists. Those depicted included: Lavoisier, the father of modern chemistry; Doctors Morton and Long, the discoverers of anesthesia; Avicenna, the medieval Persian thinker on the contagion theory of disease; and Paracelsus, the Renaissance-era chemist and mineralist.

But Pursell's biggest contribution to the building was his floor-and-a-half-high "Abbott Tree" mural, which dominated the lobby.

Speaking at the center's opening ceremonies were Thomas Parran, Jr., the Surgeon General of the United States, Dr. Morris Fishbein, editor of the *Journal of the American Medical Association*, and MIT president Dr. Karl Compton, among other luminaries. Raymond Loewy struck a medallion for the dedication ceremony.

Also on hand was President Clough, who stated: "Fit and Fifty is a phrase well to our liking." ∎

TOP

Labs were filled with state-of-the-art scientific instruments like the vitameter, which used ultraviolet light to precisely measure amounts of vitamin A in a solution.

BOTTOM

A silver-and-gold medal was struck for the building's dedication, inscribed with the ceremony's motto: "Changing Ideas — Changeless Ideals."

The Depression decade ended with Abbott prospering, as this company sales convention indicated. In the front row are top executives, from left to right: production manager Fred Young, sales head Ray Horn, marketing chief Charlie Downs, sales chief Rolly Cain, treasurer "Sunny Jim" Stiles.

In early 1934, Cain and Clough pressed Doblado on his sales strategy for Abbott Laboratories de Mexico, S.A., as the fledgling south-of-the-border subsidiary was called. As in Oklahoma, Doblado's approach would be comprehensive. He replied he would advertise extensively, and make sure Abbott products filled the inventory of every "jobber," or middleman, in Mexico.

"Our business in Mexico brings in about $5,000 a year," noted Cain. "Can you predict what you'll do in your first year, if given the opportunity?"

Doblado's reply: "One hundred thousand." Cain and Clough were startled.

The wide-ranging salesman was good to his word, reaching $100,000 in sales that year despite the late start. He was promoted to export manager. The nervy marketing man then drew up a scheme to expand into Latin America's largest and most affluent nations, Argentina and Brazil.

Doblado again met with Clough and Cain, as well as "Sunny Jim" Stiles and other executives, and asked for $200,000. He wanted to rent offices, hire salesmen, and advertise widely in Buenos Aires and Rio de Janeiro. The sum was very large for its time, but Cain backed his man. Doblado got his cash and, in 1937, Abbott subsidiaries were set up in those cities and in Havana, Cuba, as well. That same year saw an office also open in Manila, the capital of the Philippines, and a spanking new manufacturing center in Ealing, near London, England.

In 1933, Abbott's sales abroad had totaled all of $62,000. By 1939, they had reached $1,624,000, equal to 14 percent of gross revenues. That year, Abbott had branches in more than a dozen locales outside the U.S., more than double its reach at decade's start. In the years ahead, the company would become a fully global enterprise. But the process of becoming a multinational started in the 1930s, long before the term was in common use.

At decade's end, the results for Abbott as a whole were equally gratifying. Total sales, which stood at $3,502,000 in 1929, were $11,485,000 by the end of 1939 — a 328 percent increase during the Great Depression. Profits stood at $2,048,000. During the decade following the great stock market crash, a share purchased in 1929 for $32 soared to $236 by 1939, an increase of more than 700 percent.

The loading docks in North Chicago were testament to Abbott's bustle. From all over the planet came in vast quantities of raw material for fashioning hundreds of finished products. Arriving were rolls of gold foil from the Yukon; selenium from Chilean mines; bales of *ma-huang* leaves from China; perfume oils from France; as well as tons of precursor chemicals, among other goods from around the world.

In 1939 a writer for *Fortune* magazine, observing the war that had broken out in Europe, and its possible effect on United States companies, noted that: "Abbott is ready for anything."

In the years ahead, the Second World War would fully test and confirm that assertion.

Decade at a Glance
1930–1940

1930

Abbott acquires medical products maker Swan-Myers. Its president, Rolly M. Cain, and his son, George R. Cain, both will become Abbott presidents.

Dr. Donalee L. Tabern and Dr. Ernest H. Volwiler create the fast-acting anesthetic *Nembutal*. *Nembutal* rarely produces nausea or stupor in patients. Tabern goes on trips throughout the Midwest to market the drug to hospitals and clinics. *Nembutal* will be used in surgery, during childbirth, and for insomnia and seasickness. Following a common practice of Abbott scientists, Tabern, shown below, puts together a model of the *Nembutal* molecule.

▼

1931 ▲

Due to the Swan-Myers acquisition, Abbott is now the world's largest maker of ephedrine, the decongestant and weight-loss remedy. A thousand pounds of the Chinese *ma-huang* plant must be procured to make just five pounds of the drug.

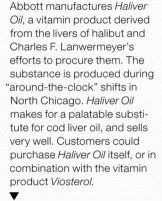

1932

At the height of the Great Depression, Abbott manages to rapidly expand. "Few of the leading industrial organizations of the country," notes *Nation's Commerce*, "can show a sounder record for the past year than the Abbott Laboratories."

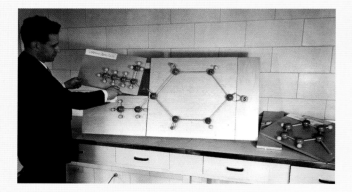

Abbott manufactures *Haliver Oil*, a vitamin product derived from the livers of halibut and Charles F. Lanwermeyer's efforts to procure them. The substance is produced during "around-the-clock" shifts in North Chicago. *Haliver Oil* makes for a palatable substitute for cod liver oil, and sells very well. Customers could purchase *Haliver Oil* itself, or in combination with the vitamin product *Viosterol*.

▼

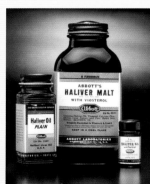

1933

Abbott offers its employees inexpensive health and accident insurance. Clough encourages other firms to introduce similar programs for their workforces.

Dr. Alfred S. Burdick dies. Simeon DeWitt Clough succeeds him as president. Clough quickly launches a campaign that yields more than a million dollars in sales.

Edward H. Ravenscroft becomes chairman of the board. ▶

1934

Steering Abbott through the Great Depression is S. DeWitt Clough, a former sales chief who proves a strategically brilliant chief executive.

▼

Under sales executives Manuel Doblado and Raymond E. Horn, Abbott greatly expands its sales presence in Mexico, then throughout Latin America, paving the way for significant international expansion.

1935

Abbott begins to manufacture intravenous (IV) fluids. The bottles have an odorless liner, and are filled with dextrose-and-salt solutions. In time, Abbott will become the largest supplier of IV solutions in the United States.

Abbott debuts *What's New*, a high-quality medical journal and corporate magazine. Along with scientific articles, it boasts artwork and works of fiction by world-renowned painters and authors, including Grant Wood and Robert Frost.

WHAT'S NEW

Employee handling bottles at IV manufacturing plant.

1936

The company breaks ground for a new research center, building R1, in North Chicago.

A leader in employee benefits, Abbott provides company-paid accidental death and dismemberment insurance.

1937

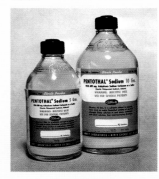

After six years of research by Drs. Volwiler and Tabern, Abbott introduces *Pentothal*. A fast-acting anesthetic injected directly into the bloodstream, *Pentothal* will become the world's most widely used anesthetic. Eye and brain surgeons, obstetricians, even dentists, find the drug very useful.

Abbott sets up operations in Buenos Aires, Argentina; Rio de Janeiro, Brazil; Havana, Cuba; and Manila, the Philippines.

Director of sales Raymond E. Horn, below, boards an airplane to market Abbott products across its growing international range.

A new manufacturing center is established near London, England.

1938

Abbott is the first company to provide its employees and their dependents, for a small fee, hospital-based surgery or treatment. "For about $60 a year," states a newspaper, "an Abbott employee can get himself insured against practically everything except being divorced by his wife and drafted in case of another World War."

The company commemorates its 50th anniversary with a new, state-of-the-art research facility, in North Chicago. The research center is filled with the latest scientific apparatus. Famed designer Raymond Loewy plans the building's interior.

1939

Despite the Depression, Abbott's company sales are $11,485,000, up from 1929's tally of $3,502,000. Abbott's overseas sales totals reach $1,624,000, up from just $62,000 in 1933. The value of a hundred shares of its stock has soared from $3,200 in 1929 to $23,600 in 1939.

The company prospered even during the Great Depression, as signified by this Abbott sales convention.

President Clough, at the urging of the U.S. War Department, establishes a Drug Resources Committee. It makes plans for large-scale production of medical supplies in the event of a widespread war.

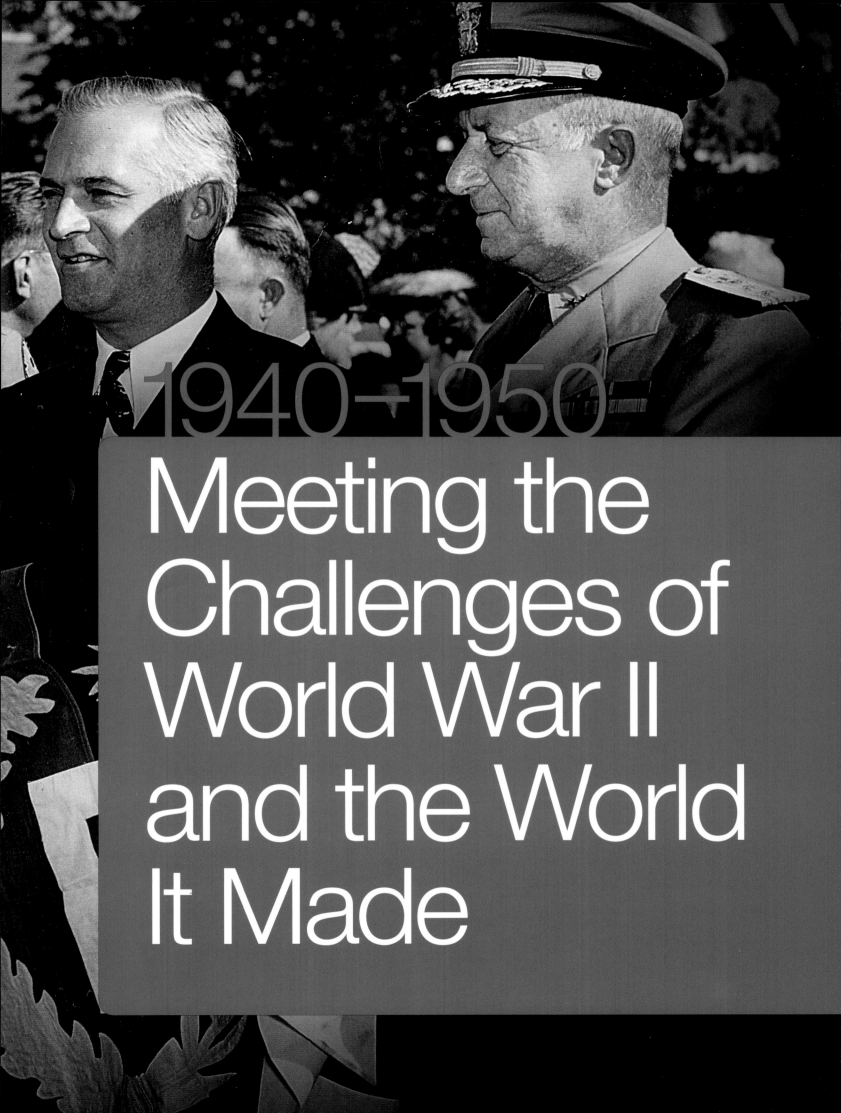

1940–1950

Meeting the Challenges of World War II and the World It Made

"Drugs are as important as munitions," President Clough told an all-hands meeting of Abbott's employees at the company's headquarters in April 1942, just five months after America's entry into the Second World War.

The atmosphere at the packed gathering of 1,600 employees was tense yet energetic. America was at war, and some of Abbott's own international branches, notably in Manila and Shanghai, had been captured. The firm was revving up to supply vital pharmaceuticals to the nation's 10-million-strong armed forces. Some would date from the First World War, while some would be newly developed under the most urgent of circumstances.

Clough read a telegram from the U.S. Army's Surgeon General, urging Abbott to produce greater quantities of drugs for the military. Clough also announced, to cheers and applause, pay increases to deal with soaring costs of goods from wartime shortages.

"Production at Abbott," pronounced Clough, "is war production!"

PREVIOUS SPREAD
A grateful Army and Navy presented Abbott with five "E" Awards for excellence in wartime production. President Clough, left, accepted one of the "E" banners. Many Abbott employees also entered the military. By 1944, some 554 were in the armed forces, and nine had died in service.

Of Abbott's many contributions to the war effort, none was more important or impressive than its work to scale up production of the new wonder drug penicillin to meet the government's wartime need.

President Clough inspired sales representatives with a silver coin likeness of Gen. Douglas MacArthur, who led the U.S. armed forces in the Pacific theater of action.

GENERAL HEADQUARTERS
SOUTHWEST PACIFIC AREA
OFFICE OF THE COMMANDER-IN-CHIEF

October 14, 1942.

Dear President Clough:

Thank you so much for sending me one of your "lucky pocket pieces." I shall carry it with me. Perseverance and will, courage and skill, together with God's help should bring victory.

Most cordially,

DOUGLAS MacARTHUR.

Mr. S. DeWitt Clough, President,
Abbott Laboratories,
North Chicago, Illinois.

To President Clough's surprise, Gen. MacArthur wrote a letter thanking him for the medallion bearing his image.

To ward off shock, medical personnel administered plasma to a wounded corporal in the South Pacific. Abbott innovated production methods to ensure its availability.

In 1940, Nazi Germany conquered France and launched the airborne bombing blitz of Great Britain. The United States remained an uneasy neutral observer. However, President Clough was ahead of the game. The War Department, at his urging, had in 1939 authorized Abbott to set up a Drug Resources Committee. Its job: plan scaled-up production of medical supplies if and when America entered the conflict.

Skill, Perseverance, Courage, Will

In December 1941, after the bombing of Pearl Harbor, that moment came. Abbott was directly affected: Its branches in Manila and Shanghai, cities occupied by the Japanese army, were shuttered. The company itself swiftly moved to a wartime footing. In summer 1942, to boost the spirits of salesmen at their semi-annual conference, Clough had the ad department give out sterling-silver coins. They bore the likeness of Gen. Douglas MacArthur, commander of the Allied war effort in the Pacific.

The medallion's motto: "Work To Win." The reverse side of the "pocket piece" bore a clover leaf reading, "Skill Perseverance Courage Will." MacArthur was the subject of Clough's conference talk. Almost on a whim, Clough sent him one of the coins.

That October, a letter arrived in the president's office. "Thank you so much," the general wrote, "for sending me one of your 'lucky pocket pieces.' I shall carry it with me."

Making a Life-Giving Substance for the Troops

The U.S. armed forces urgently requested a raft of products, in large quantities, from Abbott. These included sulfa drugs, the anesthetics *Butyn*, *Nembutal*, and *Pentothal*, the antiseptics *Metaphen* and *Acriflavine*, and Abbott vitamins.

One of Abbott's first challenges was supplying wounded troops with a life-giving substance, plasma. But deriving dried plasma from human blood was tricky. The substance has more than 100 chemical constituents,

none of which can afford to be damaged in the sensitive process of freezing and drawing off the water from the blood. Fortunately, Abbott had a crack team to tackle the job.

The science side was handled by assistant director of research Dr. Edgar B. Carter, who was instrumental in Abbott's related, and industry-leading, line of intravenous products. Carter was aided by Dr. Donald W. MacCorquodale, a contributor to Nobel Prize-winning work on synthesizing Vitamin K, vital to blood coagulation. Also on board was Edward A. Ravenscroft, the son of Edward Hawks Ravenscroft, the engineer and company chairman. The younger Ravenscroft was the holder of many patents, including one for the first bottles with a screw-cap and pour lip. He was to build the high-pressure vacuums for making the plasma. Riding herd was George R. Ryan, top aide to the kinetic production director, Fred Young.

Shifts of workers were on around-the-clock production lines; labor shortages were relieved by bringing in servicemen's wives, including those of generals, as well as off-duty sailors from the nearby Great Lakes Naval Training Center. Abbott made plasma from almost one million pints of blood collected from Red Cross centers stretching from Milwaukee to Kansas City, then shipped it to military bases worldwide.

Continues on page 135 ▶

An Eloquent Contribution to the War Effort

Thomas Hart Benton, one of America's foremost artists, was in Los Angeles delivering a lecture when news arrived of the Japanese attack on Pearl Harbor. The emotional Benton, the son and the grandnephew of United States Congressmen, stopped in mid-sentence, then strode off the speaker's platform. After holing up in his Kansas City, Missouri, studio for nine weeks, he emerged with a series of paintings entitled, "The Year of Peril." Abbott's promotion of these striking images began a singular contribution to the U.S. war effort.

Artist Thomas Hart Benton intended his wartime paintings to shake people out of complacency. Abbott presented his work to startled readers of *What's New*.

Benton commented on his New Realism-style work:

> *"I might be of help in pulling some Americans out of their shells of pretense and make-believe. There are no bathing beauties dressed up in soldiers' outfits in these pictures. There is no hiding of the fact that war is killing …"*

Charles Downs, Abbott's marketing chief, took notice. He bought up all seven of Benton's paintings — and put them in the April 1942 issue of *What's New*. They appeared next to an article on ragweed and hay fever, titled, with an arch wartime twist, "Enemy Aliens and Native Saboteurs."

Moving fast, Downs recruited other noted artists, and sent them overseas with pay to depict the work of the Army, Navy, and medical corps for Abbott periodicals. More than 100 paintings were composed about naval aviation alone, showing carrier pilots in training, on reconnaissance, or in dogfights.

Abbott-sponsored artists like Kerr Eby were "subject to the same hardships and dangers as the front-line units."

The government made millions of reproductions of this war bond painting by Lawrence Beall Smith, which appeared in *What's New*.

A painting by Lawrence Beall Smith in the January 1943 *What's New*, depicting children cowering under a Nazi swastika, caught the attention of the U.S. Treasury Department. With Abbott's approval, it used the image in war bond drives. Three million posters were made of it, and 50 million were printed of other Abbott-sponsored paintings. The government asked Abbott to create a "comprehensive record of war activities," spurring much more artwork. Company employees dreamed up the names of the posters. Many of them were displayed during an April 1943 bond drive at the Brooklyn Museum, which drew an astonishing $800,000,000 in pledges.

Abbott printed and distributed color reproductions of such posters around the country. Department stores, car dealerships, and pharmacies displayed them in their windows.

Wrote the owner of one drug store to Abbott: "The display vividly portrayed to the civilian population what our boys are going through, and what a sacred obligation we have to back them up with the purchase of bonds."

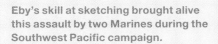

Eby's skill at sketching brought alive this assault by two Marines during the Southwest Pacific campaign.

Abbott sponsored creation of one of the most popular war bond posters, "Till We Meet Again." Its message spoke to millions of loved ones of departing servicemen.

In "Battalion Aid Station" by the artist Franklin Boggs, medical personnel minister to sick and wounded soldiers in a makeshift jungle hospital.

"I can't remember when I didn't draw," recalled Abbott-sponsored artist Franklin Boggs, pictured here in the Southwest Pacific. "I was always challenging myself. Is this the best I can do? Is this good enough?"

"One particular night when I arrived back from the front," recalled artist Boggs, "I asked the doctor, 'Where can I sleep?'" He said, "Why don't we just put you into the ward with the patients?" The result was this dreamy sketch of wounded men lying at night under mosquito nets.

Franklin Boggs was an Abbott-sponsored artist whose work has appeared in New York's Metropolitan Museum of Art.

In lauding the Abbott-sponsored artists, Maj. Gen. Norman T. Kirk — the Army's Surgeon General — stated:

> "They were subject to the same hardships and dangers as the front-line units to which they were attached. Armed with only palette and brush, they lived in New Guinea foxholes and Normandy cellars. They took everything the enemy had to offer and risked their lives voluntarily and repeatedly to complete their mission."

In June 1945, during a ceremony at Washington's Corcoran Gallery of Art, the company donated its collection of war art to the War Department, the precursor to the Department of Defense.

Army Surgeon General Kirk termed the work "an eloquent contribution to the war effort which will be far-reaching and everlasting." ∎

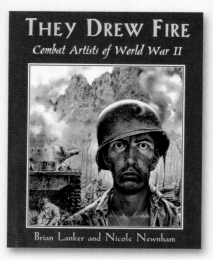

In 2000, the Public Broadcasting Corporation aired a documentary entitled "They Drew Fire," about the U.S. combat artists of the Second World War. Abbott artists Franklin Boggs and Kerr Eby were among those featured.

An Abbott shipping case for blood plasma served as an improvised cradle for Theresa, a baby born in a U.S. Army hospital during the battle for Italy.

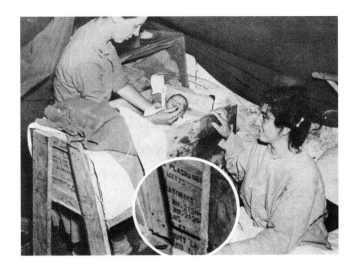

A surgeon stationed in the Italian theater commented on the results: "Plasma is quite the wonder treatment of this war. A patient goes sour as you watch. You are seeing him die. Pallor develops, pulse weak. Plasma is administered and, presto, the harbingers of death disappear." Thousands of stricken soldiers were saved.

Fighting Malaria, Leprosy, Sepsis

Production challenges of a different sort were found with *Quinacrine*, a synthetic substitute for quinine, the natural, alkaloidal antidote to malaria. The drug's yellow color readily stained the clothes and skin of those handling it.

"When next you see a fellow," reported Abbott's employee publication *Pharmagraph*, "looking as though he had recently fallen into a vat of yellow paint, remember that undoubtedly he is a man who works on *Quinacrine*."

The production squad installed equipment that turned out the drug automatically. For good measure, *Quinacrine* tablets were given shiny coatings that did not crumble at the touch.

Abbott had obtained a government license to manufacture *Quinacrine* after the submission of several thousand chemical compounds to Washington's Office of Scientific Research and Development, the powerful wartime agency that oversaw development of radar and the atomic bomb. The Office's medical staff screened the compounds for solid leads, and forwarded them to pharmaceutical firms, resulting in *Quinacrine's* successful synthesis. With troops fighting in tropical climes throughout the southwest Pacific, a remedy for malaria was welcome indeed.

Another drug, aimed at the civilian sector, ended up treating military personnel, as well as the poorest of the world's poor. One of the foremost scientists from the First World War, Dr. Raiziss, of the company's DRL wing, had conjured up another substance of great promise: *Diasone*, a compound that seemed to work against the bacterial scourge of tuberculosis. Six expensive, exacting years of measuring the drug's metabolization and toxicity ensued. One and a half million doses were dispensed in clinical tests. In the end, however, *Diasone* was judged not effective enough against tuberculosis.

Happily, however, it was found to reduce the lesions and ulcers of leprosy, the dreaded skin disease. The medicine was given to sufferers at the United States Marine Hospital National Leprosarium in Carville, Louisiana. Ahead of its time, *Diasone* became an "orphan drug" of sorts (see page 277). Although it brought Abbott little profit, the firm produced it for less advantaged parts of the world where leprosy was still widespread.

Diasone was derived from sulfa drugs, the sulfonamide-based "wonder drugs" that block the ability of microbes to reproduce, and which proved extremely effective at treating certain wounds. Abbott's contribution was *Sterilopes*, packaged for ease of use. The sulfanilamide powder was sealed in a small, sterilized envelope, which in turn was placed in a sealed, larger envelope. The smaller packet had a sieve to dispense the sulfa, sprinkled loosely and evenly over the injury. Infections were rampant amidst the filth of the battlefield, but *Sterilopes* allowed GIs with scant medical training to stop an infection in its tracks.

Continues on page 138 ▸

Sulfa drugs were packaged to let soldiers easily dispense them to wounded comrades.

Abbott on the Home Front

During the war the ever-busy loading dock of Building M1 serviced both trains and trucks, which pulled right up to the dock.

Armies moved their troops by train, and so Abbott did its workers. Faced with gas rationing, and located near the Chicago and Northwestern rail line, Abbott constructed its own train depot on its property.

An Army is said to march on its stomach — so, apparently, does a company. During the war Abbott built a bustling new cafeteria for its North Chicago employees.

The conflict's pressing production requirements made avoidance of accidents and errors more important than ever. An employee admired the banner awarded Department 5 for the best monthly safety record.

An army's performance depends on its morale, and Abbott boosted employee spirits with companywide contests for the best patriotic slogans. Lorraine Calhoun of Department 25 earned a $4 prize with: "Do your part in times of strife/Your work well done will save a life."

THE
Contest Winners!

Magazine Title Winners: *Betty Larsen, John Calhoun, Marjorie Moody, Katherine Zuttermeister, Caryl O'Neil, Ed Twentyman and Mabel Peters.*

Here's a picture of some of the slogan winners: First row: *F. L. McOmber, Warren Miller, Jr., E. M. Schriner, Carl Landree, D. V. Frost, Archie Bookless, Jim Rundell, and Ray Anderson.* Second row: *Angie Sojer, Elsie Meyer, Edna Peters, Barbara Lewis, Emily Tschappat, Nannie Fischer, Irene Chinn, Eileen Dresen, Ruby Boegen, Chet Ensley and Ruth Lindout.*

How the Winners Were Chosen

A difficult task faced the judges of the Abbott magazine name and slogan contest. To choose four appropriate names from more than 600, or cull out the 25 best slogans from more than 250 submitted, proved far from easy. The procedure and basis for making the awards were as follows:

It was necessary first to apply a method of elimination. Names related directly or indirectly to the war effort, of which many were submitted, were ruled out because they would not be appropriate at some future date. Next in order of elimination came many suggested names coined from an Abbott product or built around a certain department or activity. We eliminated next, for obvious reasons, all names which were stereotyped: names of well known magazines with which the word "Abbott" had been combined.

We considered the remaining names from the standpoint of their originality, descriptiveness, simplicity and a final consideration applied which might be termed "artistic adaption."

Slogan Selection

In choosing the 25 best slogans we were guided primarily by brevity, originality, and applicability to Abbott activities. As they are to be used in the near future many are phrases that are applicable to the war effort.

After careful deliberation the undersigned committee has made a choice, one perhaps with which some may disagree, but which was honestly arrived at and based on fundamental considerations.

The Judges: Edla Peterson, Robert Jones, Carl Sine, Louise Johnson and Al Taff.

Here are the judges hard at work! Names of senders were not listed on entry forms the judges studied.

The "Abbott PharmAgraph" is the keenly awaited title of the new magazine, and first prize of $50 goes to Katherine Zuttermeister of Dept. 36!

Second prize of $25 went to Ed Twentyman of Dept. 10 for his name of "Abbott Cross Section."

"Abbott News Capsule," conceived by John Calhoun of Dept. 5, received third honors and $10.

Four individuals thought of the title "Abbott High Lights," which the judges selected for fourth prize. Winners were Betty Larsen, Dept. 45; Marjorie M. Moody, Dept. 7; Caryl O'Neil, Dept. 36 and Mabel H. Peters, Dept. 5. Each will receive $5.

In the slogan contest, those who were good were very, very good. Of 25 prizes Mabel Peters of Dept. 5 took three! This was in addition to her prize in the title contest. Ruby Boegen of Dept. 2 also scored three bulls eyes. Carl Landree of Dept. 46 had two winners.

Other winners of the $4 slogan prizes are:

Lorraine Calhoun, Dept. 25;

Halazone tablets for purifying water, one of Abbott's successes from the previous global conflict, were again sent in immense quantities to thirsty troops abroad. Sometimes they were delivered by unusual means. Artillerymen supplied the cut-off men of one battalion by wrapping *Halazone* tablets in heavy gauze, then firing the "cloth cannonballs" toward the soldiers' positions. The beleaguered men survived for almost a week, until reinforcements arrived, by mixing *Halazone* with otherwise undrinkable water from streams.

The Anesthetic of Choice for Soldiers — and Psychologists

Also of great impact was *Pentothal*, the liquid sedative developed so painstakingly before the war by Drs. Tabern and Volwiler. It proved much safer and more transportable than ether, chloroform, or nitrous oxide. Non-flammable, *Pentothal* could be readily administered without the use of masks or cumbersome equipment. Only a syringe, distilled water, and ampoules of the drug were required. Surgeons could operate on the injured on the spot, without first moving them to medical facilities.

The sedative was applied in about 50 percent of all rear-area military treatments, and about 60 percent of the time in forward military hospitals. The mortality rate: a thankfully minuscule 0.018 percent.

The drug had an important impact on the psychic, as well as physical, treatment of the wounded. In 1940, during the British Army's evacuation from the French town of Dunkirk, doctors gave *Pentothal* and *Nembutal* to soldiers and civilians who had been traumatized or wounded. After falling into a semi-conscious state, these patients some-times released stored-up emotions of fear and shock. Earlier, in 1934, the Mayo Clinic's Dr. John Lundy — who conducted clinical tests on *Nembutal* and *Pentothal* — had found that patients given either drug, or morphine, sometimes awoke during operations, answered questions posed them, and retained no memory of the queries. After the U.S. entered the war, two Chicago psychiatrists serving in the military applied these insights to the treat-ment of combat neurosis. Lt. Col. Roy R. Grinker and Maj. John P. Spiegel studied cases in which afflicted soldiers could not recall terrifying battlefield experiences. Under their Grinker-Spiegel method, psychiatrists would place a mentally wounded soldier in a darkened room, inject him with a small amount of *Pentothal*, and have him count

backwards. After quickly reaching a semi-conscious state, the patient was encouraged to act out his battlefield trauma. Through such "narcosynthesis," the soldier might relive the death of a comrade, or the shell shock of enemy artillery fire. Psychiatrists used this method to aid the mentally stricken by exposing hurtful, buried memories to help the patient understand the reason for what was then called "battle fatigue."

In 1944, Dr. Grinker was placed in charge of the 900-bed Don Cesar Place convalescent hospital in St. Petersburg, Florida. The following year, narcosynthesis aided the recovery of more than 80 percent of the military personnel sent there for treatment. Deputy air surgeon Gen. Charles R. Glenn lauded Grinker as the "leader in the field of rehabilitation of combat fliers."

Abbott's continuing research into *Pentothal* led to fascinating related discoveries. Since the voyages of Sir Walter Raleigh, science had known that certain indigenous tribes in the Americas had tipped poisoned darts with extracts from the curare plant. The insidious poison brings on asphyxia by paralyzing the skeletal muscles, while keeping the victim conscious and horribly aware of his predicament. However, a crystal of its alkaloid extract can be employed to relax and anesthetize stomach and head muscles. (Curare, truly a double-edged sword, means "to cure" in Latin.)

In 1944, the indefatigable Dr. Tabern discovered a means to extract sufficient quantities of the crystalline curare from its fatal precursor paste. He built on earlier chemistry work by Abbott's Irving Sangrelet and E.J. Matson's exhaustive survey of the medicine's sources of supply. By 1947, physicians were using the extract in head, eye, and abdominal surgery.

Around this time, some law enforcement officials began to use *Pentothal* to try to elicit information from criminals or suspects. In a sensational 1947 murder case, authorities arrested Chicagoan William Heirens for the murder of an eight-year-old girl. The police reportedly obtained Heirens' confession to this and two other killings by injecting him with *Pentothal*. Abbott criticized this use of its product, noting that a person could be misled into false answers during interrogation, and that non-medical uses of *Pentothal* could be dangerous. The Illinois Supreme Court affirmed these views by supporting Heirens' conviction on alternate grounds. Judicial rulings in other states have backed up this view.

Continues on page 144 ▶

This arresting wartime ad for *Pentothal*, with the human anatomy as background, noted the anesthetic's effectiveness for treating wounds of the extremities, face, and abdomen.

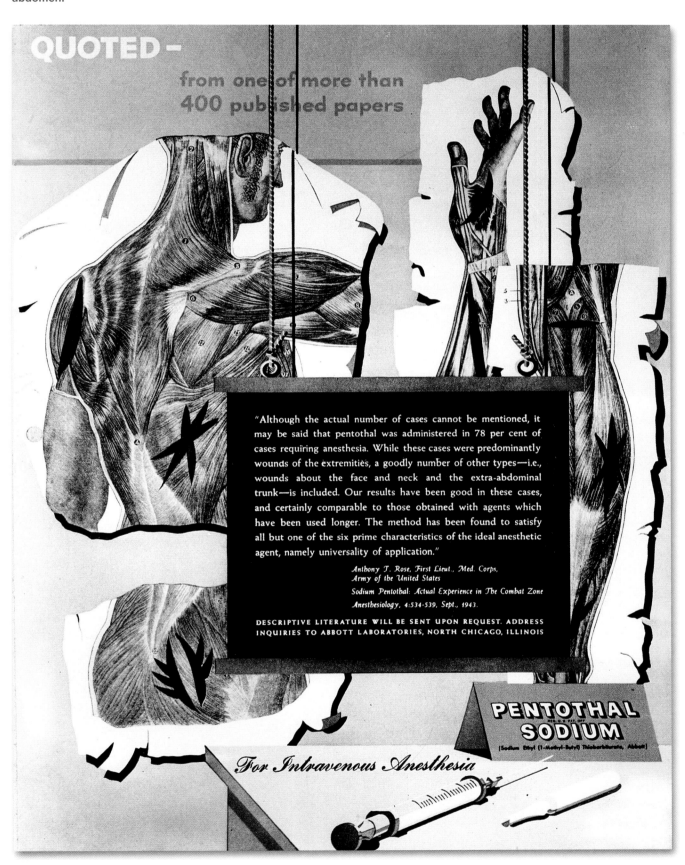

Mass-Producing Penicillin in Record Time

The most important drug of the war, and the one demanding the greatest exertions from Abbott, was penicillin. Penicillin proved extremely effective against streptococci, pneumonia, gangrene, and gonorrhea and syphilis. And penicillin often worked where sulfa drugs failed. The government's Office of Scientific Research and Development poured $30 million into the nationwide project to scale up production.

Chief Bacteriologist Dr. Hobart W. Cromwell directed much of the research and output of the high-production penicillin project.

Dr. Robert D. Coghill performed high-level research on penicillin for the U.S. Department of Agriculture, and later at Abbott.

With casualties stoking demand, the United States government commissioned companies, Abbott and Charles Pfizer & Co. among them, to ramp up mass production of penicillin. Abbott also formed a group with Eli Lilly, Upjohn, and Parke-Davis to exchange information on antibacterials for the effort.

In three months, Abbott erected research and production quarters on the new fifth floor of North Chicago's Building M3. The work drew on studies by Dr. Robert D. Coghill, a future Abbott director of research, at the federal Northern Regional Research Lab in Peoria, Illinois.

The Abbott team, led by Dr. Hobart W. Cromwell, determined which of some 100 penicillin strains could best kill bacteria, and which would produce the greatest amount of the drug. Donald W. MacCorquodale, the chief of biochemical research, labored on purifying the raw mold of the penicillin strain into a usable drug.

The highest yield, in fact, came from a mold found on a rotting cantaloupe at a Peoria, Illinois, fruit stand. The mold was isolated by Coghill's team in Peoria, then X-rayed to make an improved, mutant strain at the Carnegie Foundation's lab in Cold Spring Harbor, Long Island. Researchers at the University of Wisconsin then employed ultra-violet light to make yet another, better strain for companies to work with.

The process for making penicillin was difficult, and was constantly improved. To start, penicillin spores were put in glass bottles filled with sugars and liquid. In a week or more, Abbott's workers transferred the mold to another receptacle for mixing with a second liquid. After seven days, the mold was thrown out, leaving a "broth." What was left was refrigerated. Then the broth was dehydrated. This made penicillin, a powder that was sealed in a glass vial.

Dr. Donald W. MacCorquodale (right) and Dr. W.C. Risser purified penicillin in the lab.

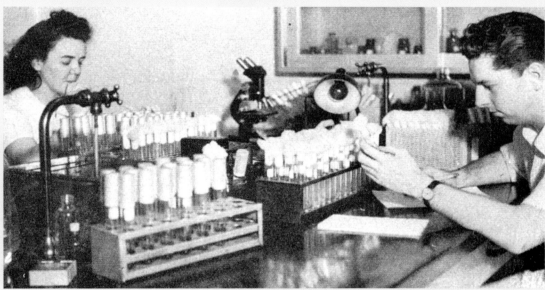

Abbott employees Virginia Sholty and Dave Evans test the potency of a penicillin strain against staphylococcus.

Louise Bandie, Dorothy De Long, Louise Kynoch, Louise Wachs, and Gertrude Currier filled and capped "seed bottles" of penicillin spores. Seed bottles were filled with corn and sawdust, then sterilized. Next, a spore suspension was added. The filling machine was on the right.

By growing penicillin in large submerged tanks instead of small, shallow pans, Abbott produced higher yields and far greater amounts of the precious substance.

Abbott employees operating complex production equipment.

Unsolicited advice from outsiders lacking knowledge of biology was ignored, such as the farmers who offered up their soil as an ideal growth culture. It was harder to refuse the desperate pleas of doctors seeking penicillin, and offering large bounties for deathly ill patients. Yet the law reserved all penicillin for sailors and soldiers overseas or for researchers at home. This would not be the last time Abbott faced steep demand for a life-giving drug of limited supply.

Two gallons worth of broth were required to make a pinch of the yellowish drug. Production chief Fred Young forced through faster means of production. Squat bottles that held the spores were replaced with pans. Thirty-liter fermenters were tried, their contents constantly shaken, and plied with sterilized air.

Then 5,000-gallon tanks were installed to further stoke fermentation. Molds were grown "submerged," instead of on the surface of the culture, which cut their growing time in half, and pared costs of labor and material.

The difficult work paid off as yields of the drug skyrocketed. In 1943, the United States made a total of 15 pounds of penicillin. By April 1944, it was making *9 pounds a day*. Prices were slashed from $20 to $0.06 for 100,000 units. By March 1945, the supply crunch had eased enough for Abbott to make penicillin vials, capsules, and ointments available to drug stores. ■

THE UNITED STATES OF AMERICA

TO ALL WHO SHALL SEE THESE PRESENTS, GREETING:

THIS IS TO CERTIFY THAT
THE PRESIDENT OF THE UNITED STATES OF AMERICA
IN ACCORDANCE WITH THE ORDER ISSUED BY GENERAL
GEORGE WASHINGTON AT HEADQUARTERS, NEWBURGH,
NEW YORK, ON AUGUST 7, 1782, AND PURSUANT TO ACT
OF CONGRESS, HAS AWARDED THE MEDAL

FOR MERIT
TO

DR. ROBERT D. COGHILL

FOR EXTRAORDINARY FIDELITY AND EXCEPTIONALLY
MERITORIOUS CONDUCT

GIVEN UNDER MY HAND IN THE CITY OF WASHINGTON
THIS   SECOND   DAY OF FEBRUARY 1948

SECRETARY OF STATE   COMMANDER-IN-CHIEF

Citation and letter from
President Harry S. Truman
awarding the President's
Medal of Merit to Abbott
Director of Research Dr.
Robert D. Coghill. Coghill's
wartime research at the
Department of Agriculture
fueled Abbott's success in
mass-producing penicillin.

CITATION TO ACCOMPANY THE AWARD OF

THE MEDAL FOR MERIT

TO

DR. ROBERT D. COGHILL

DR. ROBERT D. COGHILL, for exceptionally meritorious conduct in the performance of outstanding services to
the United States during the recent war period. Dr. Coghill,
as Head of the Fermentation Division of the Northern Regional Research Laboratory, Bureau of Agriculture and Industrial
Chemistry, planned and directed methods for seeking high
yielding strains of penicillin molds and methods of recovery
and purification of penicillin, which proved to be an invaluable contribution to the war effort of the United States.

THE WHITE HOUSE

February 2, 1948.

From the 1910s into the 1960s, the venerable Dr. Roger Adams served Abbott as a consulting expert in chemistry. He also served the United States government and the science community in high-level roles. Dr. Adams was awarded the Priestly Medal in 1946 (below). Chemistry's highest award, the medal is named after Joseph Priestley, the discoverer of oxygen.

From the start, Abbott disavowed the popular but misleading term "truth serum" for its famed anesthetic. Hundreds of medical papers on *Pentothal* have not demonstrated an ability to overcome a willful concealment of the truth.

Post-War Changes

As in the First World War, Abbott rose to the challenge, greatly expanding its research and manufacturing efforts, and contributing much to the allied victory.

And in the person of Dr. Roger Adams — the long time consultant who had set up the company's synthetic drugs program of the First War World — Abbott helped in the reconstruction effort following this second global conflict. In 1945–1946, Adams served as scientific advisor to Gen. Lucius Clay, the military administrator of post-war Germany. Adams identified German chemists who might serve as consultants for Abbott. In 1946–1947 Adams was chairman of the scientific advisory mission to Gen. Douglas MacArthur, the military administrator of post-war Japan, and made recommendations on bringing Japanese scientists into a democratic society. The following decade, when Abbott would first explore joint ventures in Japan, Adams offered ready advice on that country's top scientists, companies, and research institutes.

The multitalented Adams, who had headed the American Chemical Society in 1935, went on to be president of the American Association for the Advancement of Science.

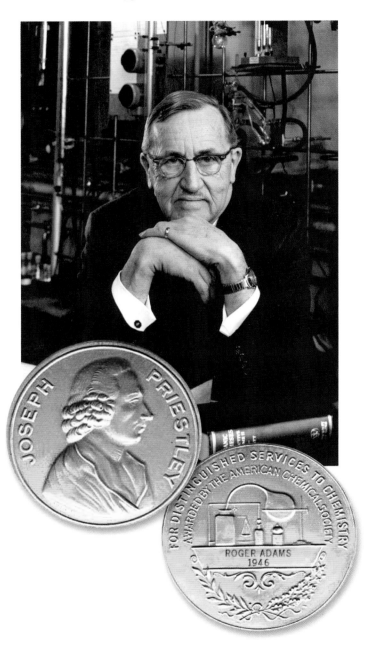

"The energy, initiative, and efficiency which industrial concerns like yours have demonstrated in the war effort give me complete confidence that the problems of transition to normal peacetime production will be met with the same effectiveness."

— GEN. BREHON SOMMERVELL

Adams also continued his work mentoring chemists at the University of Illinois, where, from 1926 to 1954, he headed the department of chemistry and chemical engineering, and trained 184 Ph.D.'s including the inventor of nylon. He also schooled his charges in non-academic pursuits. A colleague noted that Adams also managed to "educate many of his graduate students in gin rummy and poker at their expense."

In 1945, Gen. Brehon Sommervell, the logistics officer responsible for building the Pentagon, wrote President Clough: "Your company has played a very important part in producing the equipment and supplies which have been such a decisive factor in winning the war."

Looking past the war's imminent end, Sommervell added in his letter to Clough: "The energy, initiative, and efficiency which industrial concerns like yours have demonstrated in the war effort give me complete confidence that the problems of transition to normal peacetime production will be met with the same effectiveness … and will be as swiftly and successfully solved."

President Clough did his best to fulfill the general's prediction. After the First World War, Abbott had fared much better than most firms in overcoming the post-war recession. Now, in 1946, joblessness in the United States rose as millions of military personnel returned home to seek civilian work. Yet again, as other companies stumbled, Abbott launched into a peace-time expansion, largely due to its management's careful preparations.

In 1943, even as Abbott geared up full wartime production, Clough drafted the Abbott 1950 Plan, a road map for prospering in the post-war world. To ensure its success, he believed it critical to put the right people in the right jobs. So, in establishing 17 subcommittees for the Plan, Clough appointed: Dr. Volwiler to run the R&D committee, "Sunny Jim" Stiles to head the finance committee, Floyd K. Thayer to head the chemical expansion committee, and Raymond E. Horn to head up the sales expansion committee. These proved to be the right men in the right places.

The passing of the war saw
Rolly M. Cain follow S. DeWitt Clough
as company president.

Groups of Abbott employees, after a busy day's work, bustle out of the North Chicago site. While other companies were hurt by the dislocations of wartime's end, Abbott kept on growing.

An annual sales target of $50,000,000 was set. Stiles had already salted away $4,000,000 to fund future operations.

The war's end brought on a bigger realignment of management. Dr. Volwiler moved up to executive vice president, and Charles S. Downs was made vice president in charge of advertising.

The most significant change saw Clough end his long presidency, becoming chairman of the board. Worldly sales chief Rolly M. Cain, the former head of Swan-Myers, became Abbott's new president.

In early 1946, at the annual shareholders meeting, Clough made his final shareholder report as president. "You have seen the records," he told those assembled. "All departments are fortified, and geared for greater growth in the future." In 1940, Abbott sales had stood at $12,981,000. After five years of war, at the end of 1945, sales had rocketed to $37,930,000, an almost threefold increase.

The New World of Antibiotics

A major area of growth after the war was Abbott's continued drive to produce penicillin and related drugs. Given the spectacular wartime success of penicillin in treating infections, many companies rushed to find the next big bacteria killer. The payoff could be huge: U.S. sales of the drug were approaching $100 million.

But the competition was fierce. To keep its market share, Abbott had to continually devise reformulations of penicillin, some 16 in the decade. At times, it had to cut its price for the drug by more than 50 percent.

TOP LEFT
TOP LEFT
Large amounts of the antibiotic streptomycin, for fighting tuberculosis, were made through a complex array of filters.

BOTTOM
Abbott sprinted into a post-war expansion, erecting structures like Building F1 in North Chicago to meet an ever-growing demand for antibiotics.

TOP RIGHT
Abbott formulated penicillin into a powder that a patient could self-administer through the *Aerohalor*, saving patients and doctors trouble and time. Previously, penicillin was injected into patients, or forced into their lungs via bulky air compression equipment.

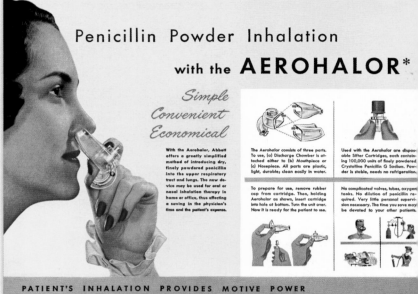

Countless thousands of microscopic organisms can kill or stem the spread of harmful bacteria. But the vast majority are useless as medicine; they may not be potent enough, or perhaps are harmful to the many beneficial bacteria in the human body. Another problem that came to light in later decades is that penicillin itself can increase the resistance of bacteria to antibacterial drugs.

Companies went to great, and inventive, lengths to find useful antibacterial organisms. Some firms scoured the deep seas for unusual molds. Others asked shareholders to mail in bits of promising soil from their garden plots.

Research labs turned out thousands of promising antibiotics: Abbott itself identified more than 3,000 antibiotic-making organisms in the 1940s. Yet few fulfilled their promise.

However, there were exceptions. One was streptomycin, which Abbott helped produce in quantity. In 1944, Rutgers University students, under Dr. Selman Waksman, had located it in the throat of a chicken. With his discovery, Waksman actually coined the term "antibiotics," which in this case, halted the spread of *Mycobacterium tuberculosis*, the cause of tuberculosis.

In 1946, Abbott constructed a fermentation building, F1, and an extraction building for the manufacture of penicillin and streptomycin. The fermentation structure's 10,000-gallon tanks were put in first, then walls were built around the giant containers. The building cost almost $500,000, and its equipment cost $1 million. Meanwhile, Dr. Robert Coghill, the Department of Agriculture scientist whose investigations had helped Abbott's wartime mass production of penicillin, joined the firm as associate director of research.

The company introduced related products during the penicillin boom. One was devised by Mack Fields, an Abbott engineer and pharmacist. He came up with an alternative to the inefficient gear for dispensing mist or powder into a patient's nose and throat to fight upper respiratory infections.

Up to that time, compressed air machines and unwieldy oxygen tanks with multiples valves were employed to force penicillin in powdered form into a person's lungs. Working with a trio of Chicago doctors, Fields invented the *Aerohalor*. The hand-held plastic inhaler held a disposable cartridge for spraying powdered penicillin into the nasal and throat passages.

Abbott strove in other ways to make its anti-infectives go down more easily. It supplied dentists and eye surgeons with penicillin ointments. Veterinarians could treat animals with liquid-based antibiotic solutions. Mothers concerned about their children's reluctance to stomach ill-tasting medicine could opt for *Dulcets*, sulfa-drug and penicillin tablets that were literally sugar-coated.

Sailors apparently were as finicky as kids: The Great Lakes Naval Training Center near North Chicago treated trench mouth and sore throats with penicillin-laced ice cream. Abbott's researchers themselves tested troches — small lozenges containing penicillin that dissolved in the mouth. The testers hailed themselves the Guinea Pig Club of Volunteers.

A problem with penicillin was its quick exit from the body: A watery solution of the drug stayed in the blood for just an hour. Thus nurses had to constantly re-inject it. During the war, Army Captain Monroe J. Romansky thought of a way to lengthen the drug's endurance. His "Romansky Formula" was a medium of penicillin mixed with peanut oil and beeswax. After injection into a muscle, it remained in the blood for six or seven hours. Abbott adapted the Romansky Formula into its own product.

Another Abbott formulation lasted for 24 hours by combining penicillin with *Procaine*, Abbott's version of Novocaine. The low solubility of *Procaine's* salt slowed the absorption of the antibiotic even as its anesthetic properties eased the pain of deep-muscular injection. It was called *Penicillin G Procaine in Oil*, and it was versatile. The drug treated secondary infections in tooth extractions and tonsillectomies, as well as heart inflammations and even anthrax. Later came *Abbocillin* 800M and *Abbocillin*-DC; the effect of these products' highly concentrated penicillin lasted 48 hours.

Continues on page 152 ▸

Many Abbott drug variants have been pediatric reformulations to help children take needed medicine. One was the sugar-coated *Dulcet* tablet for sulfadiazine, an antibacterial sulfa drug promoted in this comical ad based on an old English nursery rhyme.

The fruits of Mrs. Clara Abbott's philanthropy

The Clara Abbott Foundation was established with 12,000 shares of company stock donated through the will of Dr. Abbott's wife, Clara. According to the terms of the will, funds were to be used "in furtherance of my beloved husband's profession and work," and included a provision that provided for the establishment of a "charity" to help Abbott employees.

Clara Ingraham Abbott.

The trustees of Clara's estate honored her request by determining that the formation of a foundation would be an appropriate means to help those who continue to advance the work to which Dr. Abbott devoted his life. On July 5, 1940, the "Abbott Foundation" was established with the stipulation that the funds "be used for the benefit of employees comparatively the more in need thereof." The name of the foundation was officially changed to "The Clara Abbott Foundation" in 1976 to more clearly distinguish its services from Abbott and the Abbott Fund, and provide necessary legal separation from the company.

Upon its formation, and before Abbott's implementation of comprehensive benefits packages, The Foundation's initial programs provided assistance for health benefits and pensions for Abbott families in need. Throughout the years, The Foundation's programs and services have continued to evolve and change to meet the growing needs of Abbott families; yet, the original philosophy of the organization has remained unchanged. Today, the three core

In 1939, the Clara Abbott Trust endowed Abbott Hall, an expansive student dorm and training facility on the Chicago campus of Northwestern University.

Foundation programs include need-based financial assistance and scholarships, as well as financial education.

Financial Assistance
The Financial Assistance Program, the Foundation's first major program, was established to provide assistance to Abbott families who could not meet basic living needs or who sustained severe property damage, most often resulting from catastrophic natural disasters.

The Foundation provides financial assistance to Abbott people who cannot afford food, clothing, or shelter as a result of medical bills, unexpected loss of income, natural disaster, and family crisis. Over the years, The Foundation has provided more than $75 million in assistance to Abbott employees and retirees. In addition, The Foundation has provided financial support to more than 2,600 employees impacted by disasters around the world.

Scholarship Program
Shortly after The Foundation was established, its board of directors recognized that increasing college costs for children of Abbott employees and retirees was a growing concern. In response to this need, The Foundation established the Clara Abbott Scholarship Program in 1953. In the early years, scholarships were awarded to dependents attending a private college or university, but were quickly expanded to include public (tax-supported) institutions, as well as technical and vocational schools

not affiliated with a college or university. Since the program's inception, scholarships have been awarded based on financial need. In the last 10 years alone, The Foundation has awarded more than 35,000 scholarships to children and dependents of employees worldwide.

Financial Education
In 1999, to help Abbott families develop and foster positive, long-term financial habits, The Foundation established the Clara Abbott Financial Education Program. Personal financial education classes were developed to help empower Abbott employees and retirees to become financially independent in a preventive and proactive manner. More than 53,000 Abbott employees and retirees have attended classes.

The logo of the foundation that Clara Abbott endowed, which helps Abbott employees and retirees in need.

Simeon DeWitt Clough

If S. DeWitt Clough hadn't been so adept as an advertising, marketing, and high-level business manager, he might have founded the self-help movement. In his spare time he published a compilation of inspirational verse, *Everyday Courage*, featuring quotations from the famous and successful. He also put out a book of adages and aphorisms called *Backbone*, with the subtitle: *Hints for the Preventions of Jelly-Spine Curvature and Mental Squint. A Straight-Up Antidote for the Blues and a Straight-Ahead Sure Cure for the Grouch.*

Simeon DeWitt Clough joined Abbott the same year, 1904, as his predecessor president, Dr. Alfred S. Burdick, but could hardly have differed more in personality. Where Burdick was soft-spoken, a scientist-scholar, Clough was outgoing, energetic, a natural salesman. He was the product of Chicago's rough streets, "who pulled himself up by his bootstraps."

Fittingly for a marketing man, he started work as a newspaper delivery boy. After high school, he found a job as a clerk, and took college accounting and stenography classes at night as well as correspondence-school classes in advertising.

Dr. Abbott, impressed by his drive and colorful writing style, appointed Clough, at age 25, to be sales manager. Dr. Abbott could have been describing Clough when he urged his salesmen: "It is the fellow with the cheery voice and the broad smile ... that makes the best impression." Clough was commonly described as "ebullient." As he himself put it, "Enthusiasm is the

A zestful writer of commercial advertising and amateur verse, President and Chairman Simeon DeWitt Clough was, above all, a superb leader in any kind of business climate.

Ever the communicator, Chairman Clough went back to his roots as an ad man, working with communications head Charles Downs to aid the war effort.

power that lifts men out of themselves." The ads he crafted — and for years he composed most of Abbott's advertising copy — reflected his trademark style: bold and cheery, with a vivid typeface to match.

From a young age, Clough took on much of Abbott's heavy lifting. When the firm's press plant burned down, in 1905, he co-wrote, with Dr. Abbott, a brochure pleading for renewed subscriptions. During the financial depression that soon followed, Clough was made business manager in addition to his sales duties. And it was Clough who quietly conducted negotiations and arranged a truce to end Dr. Abbott's feud with the *Journal of the American Medical Association*. In 1915, Clough became a member of Abbott's Board of Directors.

In 1930, he initiated the key Swan-Myers acquisition in classic Clough style. He chatted up Swan-Myers president Rolly M. Cain at a convention, amicably building a rapport by conversing about the start-up days of the two companies. He was made vice president as a result of the deal.

During his long and eventful leadership, Clough showed remarkable foresight in steering Abbott through three extremely challenging periods. The first was his marketing campaigns and product development efforts to boost sales during the Great Depression. The second was his pre-war planning for the Second World War. And the third was his wartime planning for the post-war economy. By his own words, Clough had served through "the most protracted difficult period for management in the entire history of American business."

When the Great Depression hit, Clough was the right man in the right place. His relentless salesmanship was exactly what Abbott needed when growth was impossible for many other firms. But he was just as effective a leader in the starkly different time of war. Critical then were management skills to run a vast manufacturing ramp-up. His meticulous approach, which his ebullience tended to mask, became evident. So did his penchant for managing by committee, when cooperation to meet wartime production goals was key. When the war ended, he had already hatched plans for the post-war period, allowing him to leave his position with Abbott in outstanding shape.

When Clough took over as chief executive, in 1933, Abbott's sales were $4,000,000. When he relinquished the reins, in 1945, they stood at nearly $38,000,000. Earnings during the period went from about half a million dollars to more than $3 million; the number of workers quintupled, to almost 5,000. Even the company's income taxes paid, an indicator of prosperity, exploded, from $85,000 to $6 million.

"You have seen the records," Clough stated in his final, 1946 report to stockholders. "All departments are fortified and geared for greater growth in the future."

As a business visionary and top-level executive, Clough proved himself worthy of his illustrious predecessors Drs. Abbott and Burdick.

Perhaps recalling his hardscrabble days as a paper boy, Clough never forgot what it was like to start on the ground floor. He took pride and pleasure in expanding Abbott's employee benefits, what he called the "Happiness and Peace of Mind Program."

To the end, the irrepressible Clough had heart, in many ways. On stepping down as president, in 1945, Clough served as Abbott's chairman of the board. After retiring in 1952, he spent the next eight years as chairman of another important organization, the Chicago Heart Association. ■

In the post-war era, Abbott's bottom line got off to an impressive start, despite a tragedy in the executive suite. In 1947, just 11 months after taking Abbott's reins, President Rolly M. Cain died from a heart attack. As vice president of sales, the former head of Swan-Myers had helped establish a worldwide presence for Abbott.

Rolly Cain was succeeded by director of sales Raymond E. Horn, the manager who had supercharged Abbott's sales a decade earlier.

Horn had acquired high-level executive experience even before joining the medical products industry. After working as a top aide in President Taft's administration, he had served for four years as deputy chief of the Federal Bureau of Investigation. During the First World War, Horn supervised military intelligence offices in Pittsburgh, then became an inspector of the Office of Naval Intelligence.

Abbott maintained a presence in India from 1910. India is now home to the second-largest concentration of Abbott employees worldwide. Because transportation of product in India was most often done by hand, the office chief wrote North Chicago: "I would like to impress upon you the necessity for our overseas boxes to be shipped in smaller sizes to enable one or two men to handle them."

With the transition to Horn, Abbott's revenues continued to increase rapidly. In 1947, 61 new products were introduced. In 1948, growing sales permitted the expansion of group life, health, and accident insurance as well as a new employee pension program.

Launching a Legacy in Epilepsy Care

Scientists at Abbott were working on many products other than penicillin. The company furthered its leadership in the IV arena with *Aminosol,* an intravenous solution that contained amino acids — the building blocks of proteins. Via a dripping tube, patients could now receive practically all required nutrition: water, salts, proteins, dextrose for sugars, minerals, and vitamins. And the company's pioneering work in vitamins themselves continued. Abbott developed the first stable solution of Vitamin C. It also rolled out *Surbex*, a vitamin containing vitamins B and C complex.

An important new product line, which would expand much in the next decade and form the foundation of a major new business, was radio-chemicals. These were medicines that the versatile Dr. Tabern was deriving from radioisotopes engendered by the wartime atomic bomb project.

Also in 1946, other research bore fruit against the scourge of epilepsy. Since the time of Julius Caesar, a prominent victim of "the falling sickness," this disease had gone largely untreated.

A physician outside Abbott took a keen interest in solving the epilepsy riddle. Dr. William Gordon Lennox, while serving as a Methodist medical missionary in China, had observed a friend's young son stricken with epilepsy, and how little could be done for him.

With funding from the Rockefeller Foundation, Lennox later established the Harvard Epilepsy Commission, and studied the disease at Boston's Children's Hospital. In 1937, he had written, "To the epileptic writhing on the road of medicine, the investigator has perhaps given a cup of cold water, but then has passed by to succor those with illnesses which seemed more likely to reward his efforts." Lennox would find his mission significantly advanced by Abbott science in the years to come.

Abbott's own involvement in epilepsy treatment began, as promising research often does, indirectly. Dr. Marvin A. Spielman, a former University of Wisconsin assistant

Dr. Marvin A. Spielman examined substances at his lab in Abbott's chemical research department, where he discovered the anti-epileptic *Tridione*.

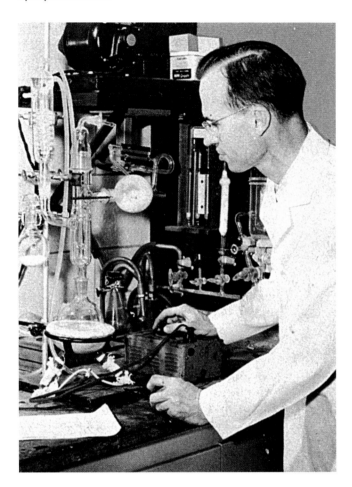

professor of chemistry, had joined Abbott in 1940. An early assignment was to find a painkiller better than aspirin. Spielman sorted through countless compounds and sent the sixteenth, called AN-16, soon named *Tridione*, to the pharmacology shop. There Dr. Richard K. Richards and colleagues confirmed *Tridione* was non-toxic, and had potential to alleviate menstrual cramps, stomachaches, and gall bladder pain.

Richards knew that other departments were looking into another new substance, designated AP-43, later called *Amethone*. Heavy doses of it touched off convulsions. However, in much smaller amounts *Amethone* stopped spasms in the muscles of the stomach, uterus, and urinary tract. Muscle spasms and pain, Dr. Richards knew, were often related. So he thought of combining the muscle relaxer *Amethone* with the painkiller *Tridione*.

In summer 1943, his team tested a combination of the drugs that had enough *Amethone* to touch off deadly convulsions. Based on the test results, Richards reasoned

that the *Tridione* prevented the convulsions. It occurred to him the substance might work against epilepsy.

A researcher at the University of Vermont had written Richards, asking, "Do you have any new drugs we ought to try?" Richards shipped a supply of *Tridione* to Brandon State School for Mental Defectives in Brandon, Vermont. There, Dr. F.C. Thorne found the drug significantly reduced the effect of epilepsy in nine of 11 patients.

In Boston, meanwhile, a glum Dr. Lennox reflected that therapies for epilepsy were, he said, "stranded in a maze of blind alleys." Then, in 1945, he was supplied a batch of *Tridione*, and conducted tests. An 11-year-old boy who had previously suffered 20 epileptic convulsions a day had no convulsions after two months of treatment. A girl who had experienced 40 seizures a day for six years had only one each day after similar treatment.

Lennox applied *Tridione* to patients at Children's Hospital. At the yearly conference of the American Medical Association in 1946, he reported that the drug had ended seizures for 33 percent of the cases, and much reduced them in 51 percent. "In my experience, it has been most dramatic," Lennox told the conferees.

Because of the relative smallness of the epilepsy patient population, *Tridione* made very little money for Abbott. However, executives and employees alike were proud to have produced a remedy for a theretofore largely untreatable malaise, and continued efforts to develop improved treatments.

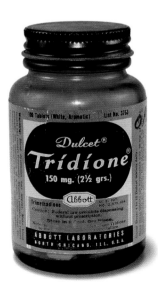

***Tridione* began a long tradition of Abbott treatments for epilepsy.**

From his development lab, Norm Hansen, left, ran numerous pilot projects with new drugs before they were approved for large-scale production. In his lab, Hansen discussed an issue with, left to right, Jim Rundell, Walt Hoffman, and Julian Phillip.

In pharmaceutical research, Carl Nielsen and Charles Lanwermeyer — the heroes of the *Haliver Oil* saga — joined the effort. Lanwermeyer solved the unpleasant scent of *Tridione* by chance. A salesman with a flavoring company left him samples of an artificially flavored liquid that tasted like coconut. Lanwermeyer squirted drops of the stuff onto a test batch of *Tridione*. The unpleasant odor disappeared without hurting the drug's efficacy.

Heavy lifting continued in pharmacology and the chemistry labs. Dr. Richards, Dr. Spielman, and many others poured over more than 2,000 different chemical formulations and permutations of *Tridione*. This work yielded an improved version of the drug that was more effective against petit mal.

After years of more hard work, in 1956, Richards and Spielman's team came up with a new, related drug, *Peganone*, which was more effective against grand mal seizures. Formulated by swapping an ethyl group for a

Pharmacologist Dr. Richard K. Richards was instrumental in formulating *Tridione* and its sister drug *Peganone*, remedies for the petit mal and grand mal forms, respectively, of epilepsy. The author of more than 170 scientific papers, Richards was described by a reporter as walking "at a speed just under a dog trot, his lab coat flying behind him, like a jet-propelled Groucho Marx."

Discovered in 1956, *Peganone* was another in Abbott's growing armamentarium of treatments for epilepsy. It was particularly effective against grand mal seizures, and had few side effects.

Employees Jerry Maloney,
left, and Wally Thomas wield
a centrifuge to separate out
Tridione crystals from a
liquid solution.

methyl group in an early form of *Tridione*, *Peganone* also had few side effects. Abbott would continue to develop remedies against the "falling sickness," such as the blockbuster drug *Depakote*, for decades to come.

The End of an Eventful Decade

At the conclusion of the 1940s, the numbers showed Abbott to be among the most innovative and successful of companies. In 1949, the company put out 74 new medical devices, drugs, or drug reformulations, the most products it had ever introduced in a single year. Fully 70 percent of its record sales that year were of products less than 10 years old. In the decade, Abbott boasted 518 new products, more than 50 per year.

In the decade to come, Abbott's innovative ways continued. The 1950s would see the creation of further breakthrough antibiotics, a blooming of the new product line in radioactive drugs, a vast expansion of the North Chicago complex paired with marked growth overseas, and a comprehensive corporate rebranding.

Decade at a Glance

1940–1950

1940

The Clara Abbott Trust, established by Dr. Abbott's widow, begins to distribute funds to aid Abbott employees in financial distress. Further, the Trust starts to allot funds to worthy medical and scientific organizations. A gift of more than $1.5 million is granted to Northwestern University for Abbott Hall, a 20-story residence for students and faculty.

▼

1941

Abbott goes into full wartime production footing as the United States enters World War II.

1942

At the behest of the United States government, Abbott works with a consortium of pharmaceutical makers to ramp up production of penicillin for wartime use. As a result, U.S. penicillin production goes from 15 pounds per year in 1943 to 9 pounds per day in 1944.

▼

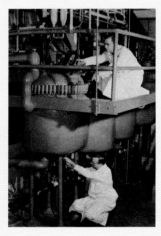

Medicos give plasma to a soldier wounded fighting in the South Pacific. Abbott ramped up production of the life-saving substance to meet wartime need.

▼

Abbott starts to produce for the military large quantities of medical supplies and pharmaceuticals such as sulfa drugs, *Nembutal* and *Metaphen*.

1943

Pentothal, being non-flammable and both safer and more transportable than ether or chloroform, proves a boon on the battlefield. Readily administered without masks or cumbersome equipment, it allows surgeons to operate on the wounded without first moving them to the rear.

Abbott continues work on a massive production project to make large amounts of penicillin for the war effort. The project is headed by Dr. Hobart W. Cromwell and draws on studies by Dr. Robert D. Coghill, later Abbott's director of research.

▲

Abbott commissioned popular artists to create paintings like this one that were used in war bond sales drives.

Far-sighted President Clough sets up planning committees to draw up the Abbott 1950 Plan, a blueprint for transitioning and expanding Abbott in the post-war world.

1944

During the Second World War, Abbott is a medical goods provider to soldiers around the globe.

▲

Artist Kerr Eby, commissioned by Abbott to paint battle scenes in the South Pacific, has a number of sketches published. Throughout the war, Abbott continues to commission the war-related work of many talented artists, such as Eby, Thomas Hart Benton, and Franklin Boggs, which it subsequently donates to the United States government.

Simeon DeWitt Clough becomes chairman of the board.

Dr. Tabern discovers a means of extracting crystals from the poisonous curare plant that are useful in relaxing and anesthetizing muscles.

1945

The Grinker-Spiegel method for treating battle-fatigued soldiers with *Pentothal* achieves great success.

For much of the decade, Abbott scientists such as Dr. Marvin A. Spielman, pictured here, and Dr. Richard K. Richards, conduct research leading to the anti-epileptic drug *Tridione*.

Abbott's benefits plan is extended to non-occupational ailments among employees.

1946

Rolly M. Cain is appointed president as S. DeWitt Clough becomes company chairman.

Abbott's long-time collaborator Dr. Roger Adams serves as scientific advisor to the military administration of post-war Germany.

Dr. Adams is awarded the Priestley Medal, the field of chemistry's highest honor.

Abbott constructs a fermentation building with 10,000-gallon tanks and an extraction building for the manufacture of penicillin and streptomycin.

Dr. Tabern sets up an exploratory division within Abbott to make radiomedicines.

1947 ▶

President Rolly Cain dies from a heart attack just 11 months after assuming office. He is succeeded by director of sales Raymond E. Horn (pictured here).

Dr. Roger Adams is chairman of the scientific advisory mission to Gen. Douglas MacArthur, the military administrator of post-war Japan.

Sixty-one new products are introduced. Two employees shown below are processing *Tridione* in a large centrifuge.

1948

Abbott becomes the first U.S. drug firm to make radiopharmaceuticals for medicine and research.

Group life, health, and accident insurance are offered to employees, as is a new employee pension program.

A new pharmaceutical lab characterizes Abbott's post-war expansion and building boom.

1949

Abbott puts out 74 new medical devices, pharmaceuticals, or drug reformulations, its biggest single-year introduction of products to date. For the decade, there are 518 new Abbott products.

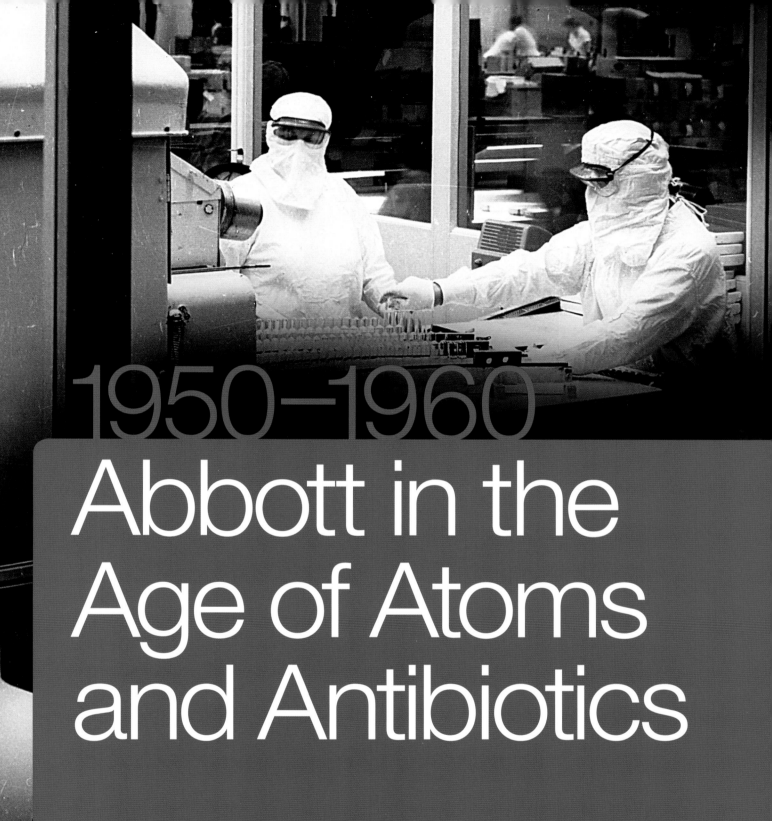

1950–1960

Abbott in the Age of Atoms and Antibiotics

For a high-tech science lab, the pace was more like a pizza parlor at lunchtime. "Can we give Dr. Elkins some gold for Monday?" Abbott's Ruth Felker barked over an intercom. Orders that poured in from 20 branch offices were handled with dispatch. In the shipping room, stacks of cartons were labeled "Rush: Emergency Medicine." The requests were sent via teletype, the email of its day, from all over the world. Felker continued reading from the teletype printer, calling out: "Can Dr. Asper have some iodine for use on Monday morning?"

The processed gold, chromium, and other elements in this unique product line were shipped within hours, by fast truck, to the airport of Oak Ridge, Tennessee — where fissile material was produced for the Manhattan Project during World War II — and flown to their destinations.

PREVIOUS SPREAD
Abbott was a leader in the new Atomic Age field of radio-pharmaceuticals. Its pioneering work would lead to the foundation of one of its most important businesses in the years to come: diagnostics.

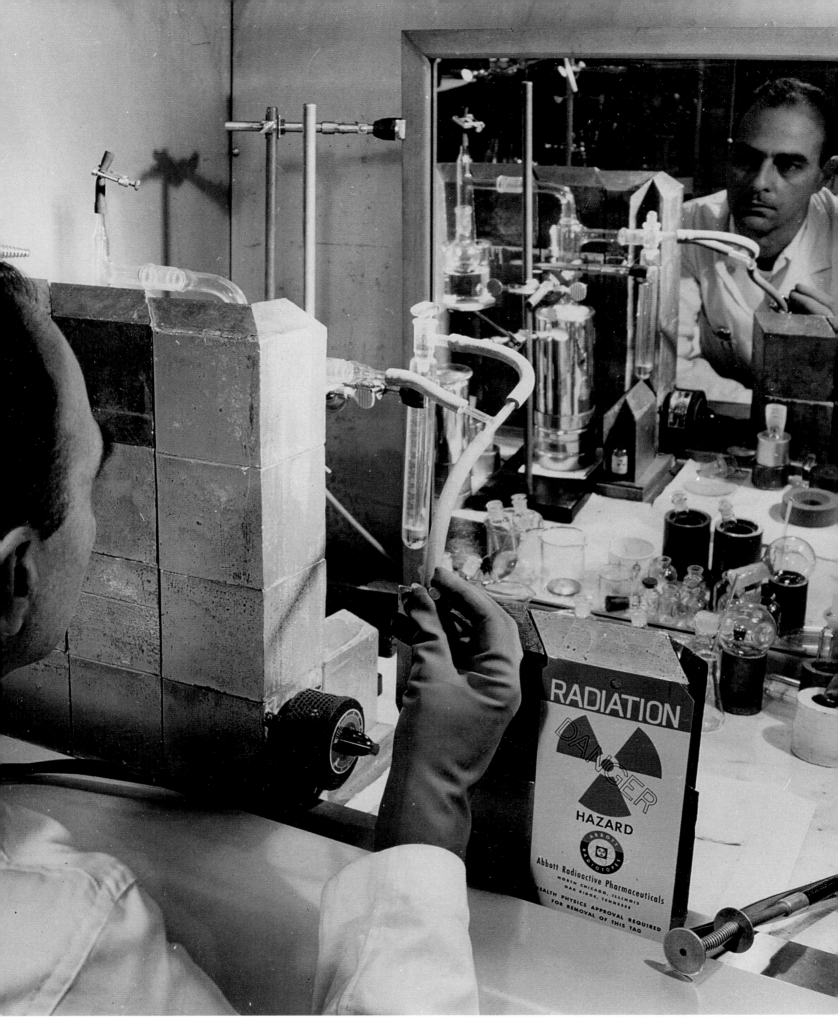

An Abbott technician carefully handled radiomedicine from behind a protective shield, his own image reflected by a rear mirror.

The cause of the frenetic activity at Oak Ridge was that these substances were radioactive, with "half lives," and in most cases decayed rapidly. Radio-gold, for instance, has a half life of just 2.7 days, meaning half of it literally disappears in that time, transmuted into mercury. Radio-phosphorus, with a half life of 14.3 days, quickly turns into sulfur. It was Abbott's latest product line, and as the 1950s began, perhaps its most innovative.

A New Industry for the Atomic Age

So, if a doctor requested 200 millicuries of radio-gold, Abbott would ship him 431 millicuries three days before, to make up for the loss of the irradiated gold in transit! Curies are the units of measure for irradiated medicines, named after Pierre and Marie Curie. Each curie equals 37 billion disintegrations per second of the element's atoms.

"The real trick of this business," noted Richard Leitner, the lab's assistant manager, was to "keep enough [of the drugs] on hand to fill prescriptions, yet not enough for time to gobble our scant profits."

The original elements were turned into isotopes by zapping them with extra neutrons from the uranium and plutonium at "X-10," the United States Atomic Energy Commission's nuclear "furnace." The government's civilian agency reactor was located just a few hundred yards from the Oak Ridge lab. Then they were turned over to Abbott for processing, measuring, and shipping.

The first atomic bomb, the most powerful weapon yet seen, had first been tested in 1945. Now, in summer 1952, just seven years later, Abbott had founded an "atomic drugstore" for the peaceful pursuit of healing. Its Department of Radioactive Pharmaceuticals was the first facility to make irradiated materials for commercial purposes.

Dr. Donalee L. Tabern hands off the first package of commercially produced radioactive isotopes to be shipped abroad.

Richard Leitner, assistant manager; Geoffrey Gleason, manager; and Charles Hobson, the general contractor, at ground-breaking of Abbott's Oak Ridge lab in February 1954. An unidentified man operated the bulldozer.

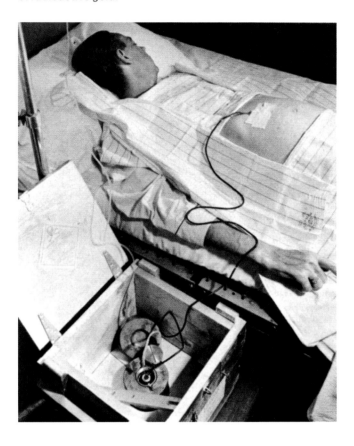

Hospitalized cancer patients
were treated with solutions
of radioactive gold.

A doctor used a Geiger counter to measure the radio-iodine
in a patient's thyroid gland, located near the throat. The
amount emitted indicated the thyroid's level of activity, an
indicator of disease.

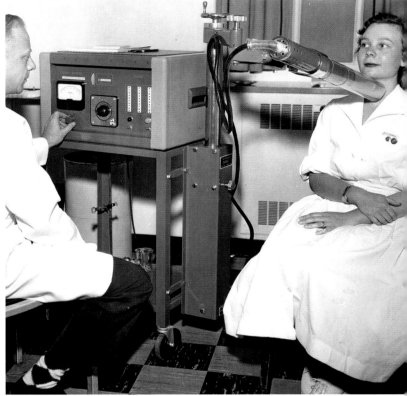

The obvious location for the lab was Oak Ridge, one of
the federal labs that had helped produce the atomic bomb.
Washington needed an experienced commercial firm to take
its raw nuclear materials and fashion them into medicines,
and Abbott had the experience. "Materials from the [govern-
ment's] nuclear reactor could be handled more speedily,"
stated new Abbott Board Chairman James F. Stiles, "and
without loss of activity through the limited half life."

Radiopharmaceuticals, scientists found, served many
purposes. "Radio-gold" was injected into the tumors of
cancer patients to destroy the growths without harming
surrounding healthy tissues. Cobalt, when irradiated and
placed in the abdomens of cancer sufferers, performed
similar work, as if bombarding the malignant matter with
billions of tiny X-rays. Radio-phosphorous was useful for
killing the excess of white blood cells in leukemia, and the
surfeit of red cells in the blood disorder polycythemia vera.

Some substances, when taken by a patient, allowed
Geiger counters to trace the flow of food through the
intestines, or blood through the circulatory system. Radio-
tagged amino acids traced the function of those vital
proteins. Radiomedicines were especially useful for
analyzing the liver, the only organ that cannot be X-rayed.

Abbott followed very strict
new procedures for the safe
handling of nuclear materials.

Chemist Charles Estep used a mechanical finger to lower a processed isotope into a lead-shielded container. A fellow employee held a counter to measure the level of radiation.

Physicians used thick rubber gloves and a heavy-metal syringe to siphon radio-drugs from lead-lined canisters.

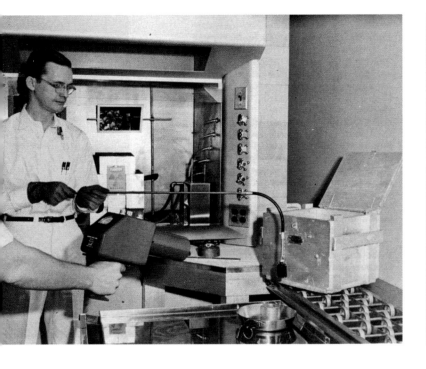

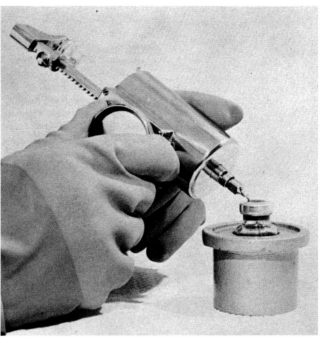

The atomic drugstore also processed radio-iodine. An overactive thyroid gland absorbs more iodine than a normal thyroid. So, after injecting a patient with radio-iodine, a physician could measure the thyroid's level of activity by placing a Geiger counter near it.

At the height of the Korean War, Abbott shipped albumin irradiated with iodine to front-line MASH (Mobile Army Surgical Hospital) units. After a doctor injected the albumin — the largest component of blood plasma — into the veins of a wounded soldier, a Geiger counter indicated the amount of blood in the patient's system, and how much he needed transfused. Abbott's irradiated albumin was the first radioactive substance issued a license by the National Institutes of Health.

Abbott's Oak Ridge lab was sited at a former funeral parlor which, it was said, had closed due to a lack of business. This was a good omen. To continue that happy tradition, the atomic drugstore had many safeguards to protect its employees from radioactivity. Workers wore pocket meters and film badges to record the amount of radiation to which they had been exposed. Beakers holding radioactive elements were covered with leaden hoods. Items for shipment were themselves encased in lead; in the case of radio-gold, 100 pounds of the hefty metal covered a fingernail's worth of medicine.

The United States Atomic Energy Commission had turned to Abbott to make radiomedicines because the firm had worked with such materials since the early 1940s. At that time, the Mayo Clinic's Dr. John Lundy, who had run the initial clinical tests for *Pentothal*, had bought some radio-sulfur with $585.90 of his own money. He asked Abbott's Dr. Tabern, a force behind *Pentothal's* development, to use the sulfur to trace *Pentothal's* flow through the body. For once, the brilliant Tabern was stymied. Lacking an adequate knowledge of radioactivity, he failed at tracing the anesthetic's course.

However, this spurred the tenacious Tabern to learn as much as he could about atomic medicine, becoming one of the world's foremost experts in the process. He enrolled in a class at the University of California, where Ernest Lawrence — as in the Lawrence Livermore National Laboratory — had done pioneering radiation work. To learn more, Tabern even experimented on himself, frequently taking X-rays of his body.

When the government's Oak Ridge lab began making radioisotopes, in 1946, Tabern was ready. He set up a small division within Abbott to make radioactive materials, driving to the Argonne National Laboratory outside Chicago to pick up irradiated samples for study.

Tabern became a tireless missionary for nuclear medicine, preparing movies and lecturing constantly on his passion before organizations like the American Chemical Society. "If you trailed him with a Geiger counter," noted future chairman Elmer Vliet of Tabern, "you'd have a map of the United States." Added a journalist: "So intensive is his salesmanship, that some people wonder whether he may not be radioactive himself."

In 1948, Abbott became the first U.S. drug firm to make radiopharmaceuticals for medicine and research.

At first, Tabern's team made radioisotopes at Abbott's North Chicago plant. Profits were negligible, yet scientific discovery considerable, and prestige high. As its business and product line grew, Abbott moved its atomic lab to Oak Ridge, next door to the isotopes made at the federal furnace.

Geoffrey Gleason, who had long worked closely with Tabern on radiation, was dubbed lab manager. A deceptively shy fellow who sported wild Hawaiian shirts,

"Jeff" Gleason remodeled the old funeral home into a state-of-the-art nuclear lab, and devised a "hot lab" for making radio-iodine. By summer 1952, the atomic drugstore was shipping product, literally as fast as it could.

Two years later, Abbott's nuclear team achieved another breakthrough with *Radiocaps*, capsules containing an invisible film of radio-iodine. No injections were required, nor special protections against radiation. The patient simply swallowed a *Radiocap*, and the following day a physician would stand next to him with a scintillation counter — 100 times more sensitive than a Geiger counter — to measure the thyroid's absorption of the iodine. Abbott made no profit on *Radiocaps*, charging but $1 apiece.

In 1955, the U.S. Pharmacopoeia, the standard-setting authority for medications, formally listed its first atomic medicine — Abbott's radio-iodine. Abbott had pioneered a whole new field of medicine.

The company would continue its cutting-edge work in nuclear medicine for years to come.

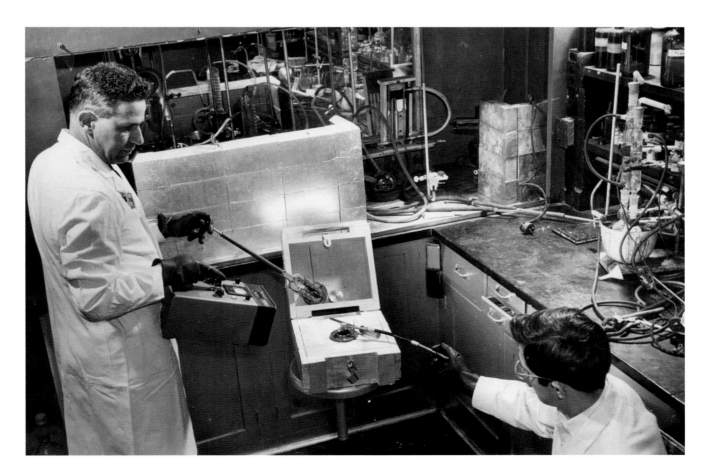

Dr. Donalee L. Tabern and assistant moved radiomedicines carefully — with rubber gloves and metal prods. Tabern also held a radiation counter.

During the midst of the baby boom, 1955, employees held a shower for Carol Hale of Dept. 345.

Visitors awaited a tour of the North Chicago headquarters from one of Abbott's team of tour guides.

A Dynamic Place in a Deceptively Placid Time

The 1950s are often remembered as a sedate time of predictable suburban living and conformist men in gray flannel suits. In fact, the decade teemed. The arts pulsed with plays like "A Streetcar Named Desire" and novels like *The Caine Mutiny*. America boomed with a record number of babies and with industries second to none. At the same time, fallout shelters reflected widespread angst over the hydrogen bomb. Other world-shaping creations — television, the polio vaccine, space satellites, the mainframe computer — sprang into use.

Abbott paralleled the decade's image, and reality. On the surface, the company was steady and unspectacular. Growth was mostly solid, if not at the rates of earlier decades. Yet, Abbott grew faster, with no severe downturns, than most of its rivals, and greatly expanded its product line, production facilities, and personnel. It strode into whole new arenas like agricultural research. And it dominated the highest high technology of its time — "radioactive" medicines.

A Proud Tradition of Diagnostic Tools

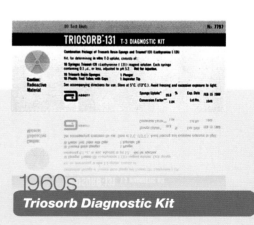

1950s
Radioisotopes

Abbott was the first company to make radioactive medicines to diagnose and treat disease.

1960s
Triosorb Diagnostic Kit

Abbott's experience with radiopharmaceuticals gave it unique expertise in the medical application of radioactive materials. By the 1960s, this led to the introduction of the *Triosorb Diagnostic Kit,* which tested blood samples without exposing patients to any radiation.

As Dr. Volwiler, then president, commented in an annual company message in the internal publication *Pharmagraph*: "You will find the word 'new' appearing frequently throughout this report."

A Changing of the Guard

Abbott began the decade with another change at the top, when President Raymond E. Horn resigned due to illness after just 36 months in office. Dr. Volwiler, the third president in four years, took over. Volwiler, now 56, had been a mainstay of Abbott's research since 1918, and was the first scientist to serve as president since Dr. Burdick.

One of Dr. Volwiler's first moves was to consolidate the company's product line, reducing 1,000 products down to 700. He seemed to follow Burdick's approach of the 1920s: Items that were unprofitable or that other firms produced more efficiently were phased out.

"We can best serve the medical profession and our stockholders," stated the pragmatic Volwiler, "by continuing to emphasize the general line of products we make best." When Abbott did introduce a new product, and it continued to launch many, it was after long research and due consideration to potential return.

Indeed, less than four weeks after Volwiler became president, in 1950, a breakthrough product some 13 years in the making was announced. Volwiler himself had been responsible for bringing it to Abbott. Called *Sucaryl*, the artificial sweetener was to help create a new food industry — and to eventually embroil the company in controversy.

A Search for Sugar-Free Foods

In 1937, Ph.D. candidate Michael Sveda was working in a University of Illinois lab. Searching for a drug to reduce fevers, he tested derivatives of sulfamic acid. Sveda was about to make an accidental discovery reminiscent of Alexander Fleming's chance finding of penicillin. The young man paused, took a drag on his cigarette, and laid the butt down on the lab bench, which was covered with sulfamic acid and salts. When he took another puff, he was surprised to find the cigarette had a sweet taste.

Continues on page 170 ▶

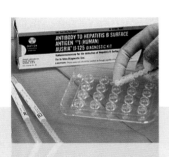

1970s
Ausria Immunoassay

The *Ausria* diagnostic kit to measure antibodies to Hepatitis B, launched in 1972, marking the beginning of Abbott's leadership in the field of immuno-assay. Its Diagnostics Division is formed the following year.

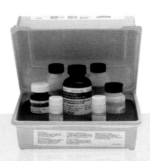

1980s
HTLV-III EIA

In 1985, Abbott's *HTLV-III EIA* became the first licensed test for identifying HIV. Coming at the height of the AIDS scare, this was the first medical success in combating the virus.

1990s
AxSYM

The *AxSYM* diagnostic device, launched in 1994, returned results from multiple immunoassays in as little as eight minutes. It expanded the variety and volume of tests an instrument could perform, as well as its speed.

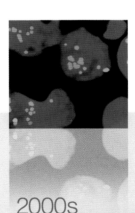

2000s
Molecular Testing

Today, the leading edge of testing is in molecular diagnostics, which reads a patient's DNA to provide physicians the best information to guide care. For instance, Abbott's *PathVysion* test can help identify patients who will respond best to a particular drug for breast cancer.

Breakthrough Advertising

In the heyday of Madison Avenue, Abbott followed in the tradition of S. DeWitt Clough and Dr. Abbott himself with memorable and highly creative advertising campaigns.

Abbott had helped create the vitamin industry in the 1920s and '30s with the research that created *Viosterol*, *Haliver Oil*, and other nutrient-rich substances. In the 1940s and '50s, it expanded its vitamin line into multivitamins, known variously as *Vita-Kaps*, *Dayamins*, flavored *Dayalets*, and chewable *Vi-Daylin* for children. They were aimed at people on the go who might not have the time to prepare a proper meal.

To boost sales of *Dayalets*, marketing and advertising chief Charles S. Downs devised striking ad campaigns. One (right) featured photographs of nutrition-deprived personality types — such as junk-food eaters. But instead of human models or drawings as subjects, the ads centered around actual foods artfully arranged as people.

Characters included; "Mr. Meat and Potatoes," " Dainty Doris from Lake Forest," "Burger Billy Out of Philly," and each made a different point about good nutrition.

"The *Pentothal* postcard promotional program (p.169) is a powerful example of '50s marketing genius," wrote the author of a book on the campaign. To demonstrate the universal availability and acceptance of the anesthetic, Abbott mailed physicians postcards "from" locations around the world, from 1954–1968. ∎

Mr. Meat and Potatoes

He's a musical sensation
Whom we hasten to applaud,
But his habits in nutrition
Have been singularly odd;
Though he's mellow with a cello
And a fiddler with a flair . . .
Mr. Meat and Potatoes is a Dietary Square

Dainty Doris from Lake Forest

She's a tidy little spinster,
Too meticulous for words,
But the problem's to convince her
That her diet's for the birds;
While her feeling for Darjeeling
Is unwavering and pure,
Dainty Doris from Lake Forest needs some Dayalets for sure!

Burger Billy Out of Philly

Oh, his wife is home a knittin'
And his day is never done;
While his shares are busy splittin'
He's a chokin' down a bun.
Though he'll barter tooth and garter
His nutrition's near collapse . . .
Burger Billy out of Philly needs some Dayalets, perhaps!

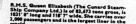

R.M.S. Queen Elizabeth (The Cunard Steam-Ship Company Ltd.) is of 83,673 tons gross, is 1031' 9" long and 118' 7" wide. She carries over 2,000 passengers and is the largest liner in the world.

PRINTED MATTER

"At sea"

Dear Doctor:

Every comfort is provided aboard the R. M. S. Queen Elizabeth, including first-rate medical care. The ship's doctors demand—and get—the utmost in dependability and safety in their medical supplies. One of their choices is PENTOTHAL—agent of choice the world over in intravenous anesthesia.

PENTOTHAL® SODIUM
(Thiopental Sodium for Injection, Abbott)

Abbott

DR. WILLARD S. SMALL,
960 E. GREEN ST.,
PASADENA 1, CALIF.
U. S. A.

R.M.S. "Queen Elizabeth"

Native sealers from Greenland, picture from the Greenland film "QIVITOQ" taken by Nordisk Film Ko.

Dear Doctor:

In vast and sparsely populated Greenland you'll find PENTOTHAL in use, as it is wherever modern medicine is practiced. There is no safer, more effective and versatile intravenous anesthetic the world over.

Abbott

PENTOTHAL® SODIUM
(Thiopental Sodium for Injection, Abbott)

DR. WILSON M. SHAW,
BEVERLY HOSPITAL
HERRICK & HEATHER STS.,
BEVERLY, MASS., U.S.A.

Unlike saccharin, *Sucaryl* was unaffected by boiling or broiling, and could be dropped right into a kitchen pot.

Then followed the careful, lengthy process of examining and testing a novel compound. Hundreds of preparations of *Sucaryl* were tried. Dr. Richard K. Richards, so vital to the development of the epilepsy drug *Tridione*, traced *Sucaryl's* progress through the digestive tract of laboratory rats. He did this using radioactive sulfur, one of the substances employed in Abbott's new radiochemical line. Richards also performed nearly three years of toxicity tests. He showed that the heart muscle of rats fed *Sucaryl* exhibited no changes compared to rats given placebos.

The United States Food and Drug Administration (FDA) conducted its own tests over two years. The FDA found that, even when low-caloric *Sucaryl* made up five percent of a lab rat's diet — an astronomically high amount no human drinker could ever approach — it had practically no effect on the animal's growth. After a dozen years of careful examination from both it and industry, the FDA pronounced the product safe for human use.

To help customers find ways to use its new product, Abbott published a cookbook using *Sucaryl* as the sweetener instead of sugar.

Intrigued, he identified and tasted all the compounds on the bench. He and his professor eventually identified the substance responsible; sodium cyclohexylsulfamate — later called cyclamate. Sveda wrote a report on his findings, and, in 1940, went on to work for the DuPont company's Cleveland office.

Abbott was then looking for compounds to mask the sometimes bitter taste of its barbiturates. And Dr. Volwiler, then director of research, was seeking an alternative to saccharin, for diabetics or others on sugar-restricted diets. Volwiler was well known for his command of new developments in pharmaceutical science. He learned of and studied Sveda's work. He then made a deal with DuPont, which had the rights to the sweet substance. Abbott got permission to test and make sodium cyclohexylsulfamate, which Abbott named *Sucaryl*, for commercial use.

Sucaryl was Abbott's first major product with broad consumer appeal. The company promoted the product for popular uses and designed distinctive, user-friendly packaging for it.

In spring 1950, Dr. Volwiler invited a group of reporters to a luncheon, which was topped off with a dessert of sponge cake. Abbott's new president then announced: "You have just had lunch prepared without a grain of sugar. Instead of sugar, a new Abbott product called *Sucaryl* was used!"

Reaction was positive from the start. Kirsch Beverages in Brooklyn took just two months to sell out 100,000 cases of its *Sucaryl*-sweetened soda pop. By 1952, some 150 firms were selling six million cases of *Sucaryl*-flavored drinks. Later in the decade, Abbott built a large chemical factory in Wichita, Kansas, to make cyclohexylamine, a precursor ingredient for *Sucaryl*.

It was Abbott's first major product with appeal to a broad consumer market. Yet it reflected its owner's roots in pharmaceuticals. Abbott marketed the product to druggists, who could dispense it without a doctor's prescription. Abbott's Dr. David J. Jones and wife wrote a *Sucaryl* cookbook for distribution by pharmacies.

Unlike saccharin, *Sucaryl* did not decompose when baked in an oven or boiled in water. Thirty times sweeter than sugar, manufacturers put it in pies, cakes, jams, and cookies. An eight-ounce glass of ginger ale contained 120 calories, but the same amount of the beverage sweetened with Sucaryl held only seven calories. And, unlike its rival synthetic sweetener, *Sucaryl* had no bitter aftertaste.

Makers of sugared drinks began to worry about their market share, although sales of *Sucaryl* at this time were less than one percent of total beverage sales by volume. Addressing the Carbonated Beverage Manufacturers of Illinois in 1954, Abbott chemical sales chief Floyd Thayer assured: "*Sucaryl* has no quarrel with sugar, nor do we promote it as a substitute for sugar in normal food supply. It is on the market for diabetics and overweight people who normally do not consume products containing sugar." Yet, despite its auspicious beginnings, the product would face a tempestuous future.

Though Abbott was seeking a
route to the broad consumer
market, it continued to rely
on its tried-and-true methods
learned through the ethical
promotion of pharmaceuticals.
Later, it moved to mass
distribution channels like
other popular shampoos.

Dusting off Dandruff

In the past, Abbott had sometimes looked for "volume sellers" with wide consumer appeal, and the year after *Sucaryl's* introduction it put out a dandruff remedy that became a household name. Like *Sucaryl*, it was found by chance. Also like sodium cyclohexylsulfamate, it took a long time to reach the marketplace.

In 1926, Birger Nordlander was asked by his company, General Electric, to find a means of detecting mercury vapors, the gas form of that quicksilver liquid substance. In so doing he formulated, from the elements selenium and sulfur, a stable form of the compound selenium sulfide. Nordlander discovered that paper coated with the compound turned to black in the presence of mercury vapor. His assignment complete, the chemist pondered applications for selenium sulfide. He knew that sulfur was a treatment for skin ailments. His firm began to employ it in salves and shaving creams, and tested it as a treatment for dandruff. But General Electric shied from entry into consumer pharmaceuticals.

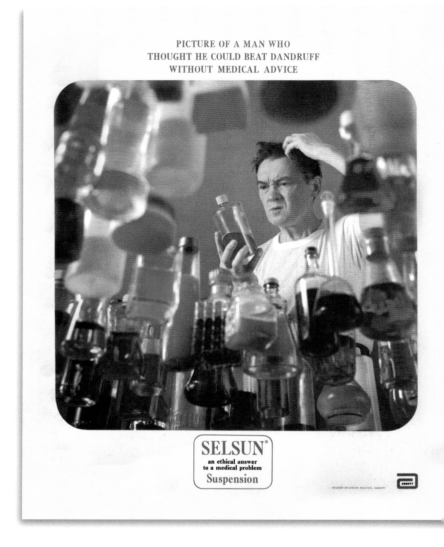

Abbott's popular dandruff shampoo, *Selsun*, was discovered accidentally through a quest for a means of detecting mercury vapors.

Abbott however was quite interested. As with *Sucaryl*, it forged an agreement to take over the research and production tasks, and brought selenium sulfide, which it called *Selsun Suspension*, into the marketplace. Abbott conducted clinical tests on the remedy with 400 people. Approximately eighty-five percent of those tested with dandruff and oily hair found a marked decrease in dandruff; and an even greater percentage of those with dandruff and non-oily hair found relief as well. The product was initially made available with a prescription. Years later, a variant known as *Selsun Blue* became a very popular consumer product.

Abbott researcher Alma W. Goldstein, pictured here in her lab, collected mold samples while on vacation that led to an important new antibiotic. Scientists often grew samples of new antibiotics in agar, a gelatin that provides nutrients to the organism. Here, Abbott researchers grow cultures in test tubes stuffed with cotton, agar, and microbes.

Advancing Antibiotics

The industrywide scramble for new antibiotics continued throughout the 1950s. And once again, luck — and pluck — played a role in an important new Abbott product.

Abbott microbiologist, Alma W. Goldstein, was on vacation in 1951 in a Colorado park known as the Garden of the Gods. Vacation or no, she was ever watchful for new molds that might mean new antibiotics. She described her work in a way both poetic and prosaic: "[I was] searching through a Lilliputian garden of fantastic shapes and gorgeous colors for bigger and better germ killers." Goldstein scooped up into a bottle a sample of the area's characteristic red soil. Back at Abbott, she got down to work.

Goldstein mixed the soil with sterile water, and placed the solution in an agar dish, a pan containing a seaweed-derived gelatin that serves as a nutrient. Over several days, colonies of microscopic molds started to form. The molds were transferred to shaker flasks — tapered, nutrient-rich containers automatically shaken to optimize growth.

Paper chromatography was used to determine if a sample was a dead end or a potential new antibiotic. Paper chromatography is a technique that allows a scientist to identify the constituent substances in a mixture by measuring how far they travel on a specially prepared strip of paper. One substance identified was dubbed ristocetin. An evaporator produced a concentrate of it, which was placed into fermenters to make sufficient amounts for detailed analysis.

Next, Goldstein began working with Norm Hansen's development lab. His team determined the proper nutrients, temperature, and other factors for optimal production on a mass scale. Then the antibiotic, which Abbott dubbed *Spontin*, was tested on white mice. Over three more years, pharmacologists studied the interaction of *Spontin* in the bloodstream of humans, and clinicians in 20 hospitals tested it on humans.

Among those managing these tests was Dr. Monroe Romansky, deviser of the Romansky Formula for prolonging the action of penicillin, which Abbott had earlier adapted in a product of its own.

Dr. Romansky found *Spontin* stopped the recurrence of endocarditis, bacterial infection of the heart valves. When *Spontin* reached the marketplace, in 1957, physicians hailed it as "the antibiotic of last resort," for use when other antibiotics failed. It was a particular help against some types of pneumonia, meningitis, and blood poisoning.

Another important antibiotic came out in 1952 after three years of testing. Abbott called it *Erythrocin*, which Eli Lilly and the Upjohn Company, which also marketed it, called Ilotycin and Erythromycin, respectively. The last name is also its common medical name. In time *Erythrocin* became a top seller for Abbott, and remained the heart of its pharmaceutical business for decades.

Continues on page 177 ▶

James F. Stiles, Jr.

James F. Stiles, Jr., known to all as "Sunny Jim," was, among other achievements, the father of Abbott's progressive benefits system, drawing up innovative, generous health insurance and workman's compensation programs that led the way for Abbott employees. A 44-year Abbott man, no one knew the company better.

Health insurance and an accident plan came first, in 1933, and cost as little as 13 cents a week. Three years later, Jim Stiles instituted accidental death benefits, paid fully by Abbott, for accidents inside or outside the workplace. Several years later, employees and their dependents could obtain insurance for hospital treatments and surgery. By 1945, Stiles drew up a plan that covered non-occupational ailments. In time, at his direction, Abbott paid for up to 75 percent of the medical expenses of workers and their families. The highly progressive comprehensive benefits drew many talented workers to the firm, particularly in the depths of the Depression, when jobs themselves, not to mention work benefits, were scarce.

Then, in the 1950s, Stiles put together a forward-looking contributory stock plan that would help secure the future of generations of Abbott employees. Beginning in 1951, employees with at least three years' experience at Abbott could purchase company stock for less than half the market price. A third of the firm's workers signed up

Delivered into the world by Dr. Abbott himself, James F. "Sunny Jim" Stiles created progressive employee benefits that were sometimes the first to be offered by any company in the nation. He was an affable extrovert who excelled at the minutiae of finance.

Chairman Stiles addresses a group of the employees for whom he did so much by championing the company's growing benefits package.

immediately, and the vast majority within 24 months. Abbott's employees prospered along with the firm's steadily rising stock price.

In such a giving role, Stiles was an easy man to like, which made his ready smile all the more habitual.

"Sunny Jim" had an Abbott pedigree second to none. He was delivered into the world, in 1892, by Dr. Abbott himself, when the Doctor was still making house calls on his bicycle.

Twenty-one years later, in 1913, Stiles started at the company humbly, as a packer of boxes in the shipping department. His timing was propitious. The next year, the First World War erupted, and Stiles found himself an aide to future Board Chairman Edward H. Ravenscroft, a man gifted in financial affairs.

Stiles' work in employee benefits revealed his own considerable talent for numbers. It was natural for him to move up to company comptroller; then, in 1930, to company treasurer. Stiles took on other company responsibilities. He was part of a management team, for example, that advised on the highly successful Latin American expansion of the 1930s.

In an extracurricular financial role, he became president of the Chicago branch of the National Association of Cost Accountants. During the Second World War, he served as chairman of a Department of the Treasury war finance committee. After his retirement he went on to other important financial work for Uncle Sam. He was appointed assistant secretary of the Department of the Treasury, to direct the savings bond division that Abbott had so bolstered with its war bonds campaign of the 1940s.

After 39 years of Abbott service, Stiles was rewarded in 1952 with the board chairmanship, a post he held for five years.

It was natural for a "people person" like "Sunny Jim" to be a joiner. In a company whose leaders were known for their membership in many industrial and charitable organizations, Stiles led the pack.

For his church, he was Sunday School superintendent for 18 years, and was elected for his philanthropic work to the Methodist Hall of Fame. For his company, along with many other duties, he was treasurer of the Clara Abbott Foundation and trustee of the Abbott Fund. For his locality, he was secretary of the Lake County Tuberculosis Sanitarium and a director of Chicago's Regional Planning Commission. For his state, he was president of the Illinois Chamber of Commerce. For his country, he earned, in 1953, the National Industrial Man Award from the National Council of Industrial Management Clubs.

"Sunny Jim" bestowed countless benefits to many organizations, but none more than the company he served so long and so well. ■

Paper chromatography was used to screen for potential new antibiotics. Each specially prepared strip was dipped in a solvent — the liquid that dissolves a material, the solute, to make a chemical solution. The length traveled up the strip helped identify biological matter.

Researchers would transfer the antibiotics through sterile needles from agar to shaker flasks, covered temporarily with paper cups to prevent contamination. The aerated canisters at the top of the lab bench served as mini-fermentation tanks for the expanding colonies of microbes.

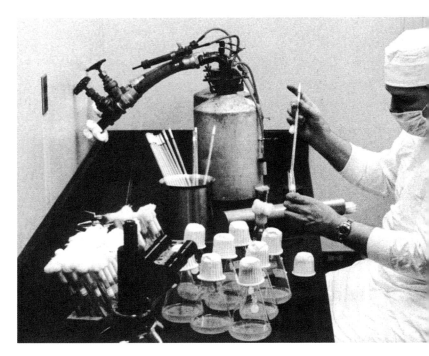

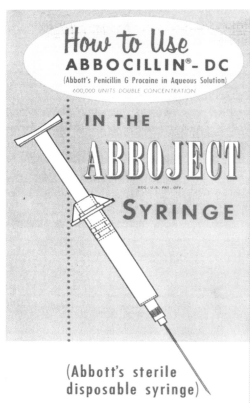

While developing new antibiotics, Abbott also devised new means for infusing them. An example was a disposable syringe for administering a longer-lasting form of penicillin through the Romansky Formula, which suspended the drug in beeswax and peanut oil.

An antibiotic discovered from a sample found near Abbott's headquarters, *Fumidil* addressed amoebic dysentery — better known as "Montezuma's Revenge" — and the variant *Fumidil B* prevented parasites from reproducing in bee colonies.

In the '50s, Abbott became a leading provider of antibiotics. Its penicillin-based medications included the popular *Compocillin*, a form of penicillin used in treating strep throat and chest infections in children.

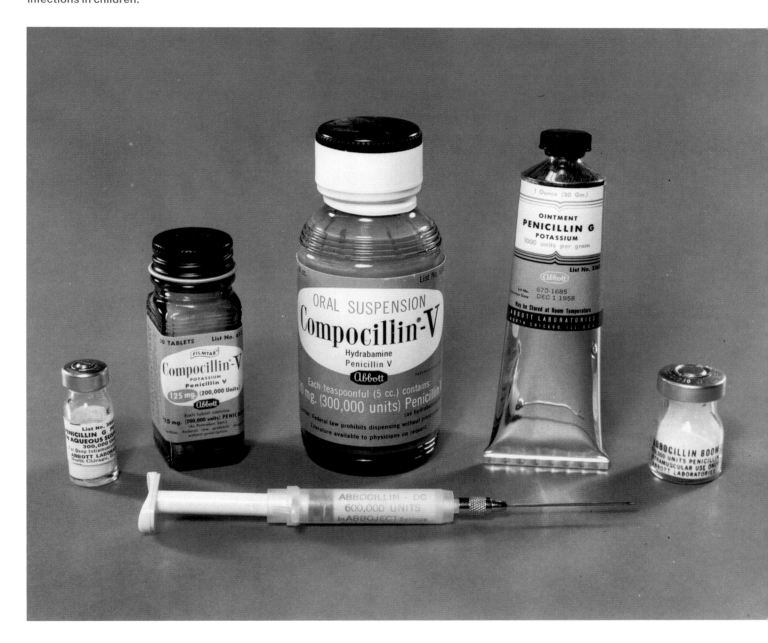

Derived from a mold 6,000 miles away in the Philippines, the antibiotic was safe and versatile. By 1957, five years after its introduction, not one serious reaction had been reported from its use. *Erythrocin* did not generate side effects, such as kidney damage or blood cell disorders, that other antibiotics sometimes did. At the same time, the drug worked against more kinds of bacteria than penicillin, and against some kinds of bacteria that had formed an immunity to penicillin.

Despite the countless dry holes drilled by various firms in the search for new antibiotics, Abbott produced a third major find. Known as *Fumidil*, it was discovered by an Abbott scientist in a small sample of soil collected from the Illinois Beach State Park, just a few miles from his lab located along the shores of Lake Michigan. It was the first antibiotic to be marketed for the treatment of a single disease. The ailment was the scourge of travelers known as "Montezuma's Revenge" — amoebic dysentery. In 1954, Abbott made a variant, *Fumidil B*, which prevented parasites from reproducing in colonies of bees.

Ground-breaking for a vast new warehouse in North Chicago on June 10, 1952, assembled Abbott's leadership. Standing on the shovel, left to right, were engineer W.F. Shattuck; engineering director E.A. Ravenscroft, the son of former Chairman E.H. Ravenscroft; plant superintendent H.D. Robinson; and President Ernest H. Volwiler. In foreground, left to right, are architects Joseph Hennessy and Charles Rummell and contractor Martin F. Carroll; chemical sales director Floyd K. Thayer; Board Chairman James F. Stiles; production director Fred H. Young; and executive vice president and future CEO George R. Cain, the son of former President Rolly M. Cain.

An Early Environmental Advocate

As a noted scientist, Dr. Volwiler was pleased — from the start of his presidency — to oversee a major expansion of North Chicago's research facilities. Norm Hansen's development labs were enlarged, and a new structure erected for the finishing of antibiotics. Abbott also put up a very large warehouse and expanded the existing buildings. The funds poured into the largest of these construction projects regularly exceeded $5 million.

As part of its infrastructure buildup, Abbott entered into the field of environmental management — before that term was coined. Communities near North Chicago

had reported a musty taste and smell in some local water supplies. Abbott studied the matter for three years, and was unable to identify the cause. However, it decided to construct a waste-water treatment plant. In this new company complex, chlorination and settling of solid wastes were used to process up to 50,000 gallons a day.

Furthermore, Abbott, with Jim Stiles as deal maker, agreed with the city of North Chicago to purchase bonds to construct a brand-new municipal waterworks.

Abbott created a new agricultural products business including the purchase of this farm in Long Grove, Illinois, used as a living laboratory for products in development.

Sometimes one department would obtain its products from another. At the end of the fermentation cycle, the culture was harvested and a byproduct of the process known as liquid streptomyces solubles or LSS was sold for use as a poultry feed additive.

Flora and Fauna

Abbott had, at times, formulated products for animals. In 1956, it went whole hog. It purchased a dairy farm near North Chicago, and outfitted it as a research center for the development of drugs for farm animals and improved agricultural products. Manager Charles Less stocked the 220 acres of grounds with turkeys, ponies, pigs, chickens, and cattle.

Product development followed the rigor of Abbott's established drug processes. Chemical compounds from many company research programs were gleaned for possible use. Lab workers tested promising ones for safety and efficacy. Then employees at the center tested various dosages of, and ways of administering, the drug or supplement on the animals. Instead of hospitals, clinical tests were held at agricultural colleges and veterinary schools. Finally, the new product would go to the U.S. FDA for review.

Henry C. Spruth, Abbott's chief pharmacologist during *Nembutal's* development, headed up the research. In overall charge was Abbott's associate research director, chemist Dr. Marlin T. Leffler. His place was later filled by Dr. Gilbert Otto, a Johns Hopkins expert on parasitology, as Abbott's director of Agricultural and Veterinary Research.

Abbott continued its tradition of support for science education and its local community through its sponsorship of the exhibit "The Conquest of Pain" at Chicago's Museum of Science and Industry.

The farm poured out new products for fauna and flora. An example was *Caparsolate*, to treat heartworm in dogs. A variant of *Erythrocin* called *Gallimycin* addressed lung and sinus infections — as well as head colds — in poultry. *Pro-Gen* stimulated growth in animals. *Phenurone* was an anti-convulsant to treat epileptics; it proved to be of use with animals experiencing epilepsy-like conditions. Other offerings included hormones and feed nutrients.

A cornucopia of offerings poured out of the agricultural research center. Gibberellic acid was used in fermentation and, in time, helped make better grapes, oranges, and cherries. Another fermentation aid was a microbe, *Bacillus thuringiensis*, which destroys pest larvae without the use of insecticides.

More Beneficial to Employees

Jim Stiles continued to grow the benefits programs offered to Abbott's workers. In 1951, an employee stock ownership program was initiated. After three years on the job, a worker could buy stock at less than half the market price. After two years, 95 percent of eligible workers, about 6,000 employees, had signed up. Moreover, health insurance was broadened to cover up to 75 percent, and later more, of the medical costs of workers and their families.

Benefits were extended to the children of employees. In 1954, the Clara Abbott Foundation began a College Student Aid program, allotting financial assistance to high-school graduate children of company workers.

Another feature of employee life was the annual Christmas dinner in the company cafeteria. By 1957, the affair was serving 3,000 people, and dishing up 3,486 pounds of turkey. The event always took place on a Monday, as it took a weekend to manage the logistics. The tradition continues to this day, bigger and better than ever.

Abbott also strove to develop internal talent and foster two-way communications between managers and employees. The firm rotated talented young employees through different departments. The aim was to nurture future executives by exposing them to all aspects of the company's operations.

In addition, at periodic suppers for employees of all levels, a dollar was paid for each question asked of management. A similar sum was given to those who asked about rumors making the company rounds. Management responses in these Q&A sessions were printed in the employee publication *Pharmagraph*.

Abbott continued its tradition of support for science education and its local community through its sponsorship of the exhibit "The Conquest of Pain" at Chicago's Museum of Science and Industry.

Abbott opened its facilities, including its labs, for employees to show off their work on its annual Family Day.

Singing stalwarts of sales
conferences were the
Abbott Medicine Men.
Harmonizing from left to
right: Bill Ehnert, Herman
Schaefer, Roy Truelsen,
Les Biere.

Abbott continued to offer many "unofficial" benefits in the
form of extracurricular organizations. An employee modeled
for the aspiring artists of the Abbott Art Club.

These Abbott performers
at the annual spring variety
show, circa 1950, had plenty
to smile about thanks to ever-
growing company benefits.
During professional, as
opposed to social, events,
the stage was the speaker's
platform of the company's
Research Center auditorium.

Employee perks of various kinds were on the increase.
Company picnics grew to become company fairs. By 1955,
more than 5,000 employees and family members attended
the yearly event at Foss Park in North Chicago.

In a related vein, Abbott continued to heed many of the recommendations placed by employees in company suggestion boxes. In fact, in 1958, Abbott received an award for its suggestions program — from the National Association of Suggestions Systems. Later known as the Employee Involvement Association, the organization lauded employee Mrs. Nell Stahl, who suggested improvements in the assembly of disposable syringes, resulting in annual savings of $2,900.

Dr. Volwiler termed these far-sighted benefits and programs: "research in people."

Soaring Investment and Growth Around the World

From 1950 to 1957, Abbott's sales rose from $74 million to $111 million, while profits increased somewhat less rapidly, from $10,880,000 to $12,681,000. In 1951, 1952, and 1954, profits actually fell — a rarity for Abbott. This was largely due to a sharp hike in taxes, and a sharp drop in the price of antibiotics due to increased competition and greater industrywide production. The price of streptomycin, for instance, fell by more than 90 percent in just five years.

> "In the drug industry obsolescence is high due to the productivity of research. Consequently, a great deal of research is required just to keep even. To get ahead requires more than that."
>
> — DR. ERNEST H. VOLWILER

Another cause was Abbott's growing rate of investment in its business. By 1957, the company was spending $7 million on equipment, buildings, and other capital projects, and another $5 million for research. During Volwiler's tenure, R&D spending was three times the industrial average.

"In the drug industry," President Volwiler noted, "obsolescence is high due to the productivity of research. Consequently, a great deal of research is required just to keep even." He added pointedly: "To get ahead requires more than that."

Capital spending meant more than investments in modern buildings and the latest scientific gear. It also meant fixing up existing stock, like the 30-year-old rail spur into the North Chicago loading docks. Here Abbott's gang of rail workers replaced the tracks.

Abbott was ever adding new buildings to its North Chicago site. The dotted line at the top shows acreage purchased from the American Can Company and slated for expansion. Eventually this site would grow to include more than 2.5 million square feet of floor space devoted to pharmaceutical and chemical production, hospital products manufacturing, research and development, engineering, and employee services.

Despite high research and investment costs, Abbott's sales and profits grew due, in good measure, to its burgeoning international presence. Products were crated and shipped to destinations around the world, this stack alone representing five continents.

Dr. Volwiler discussed the production of bottled product with two employees of Abbott's Colombia production plant.

Harold D. Arneson, left, president and general manager of Abbott Laboratories International Co. and Abbott Laboratories Export Corp., and Tomas G. Coarasa, manager of Abbott's Mexican subsidiary, discuss Abbott's growing presence in Latin America.

Abbott's international expansion encompassed a large new manufacturing complex in St. Remy, France.

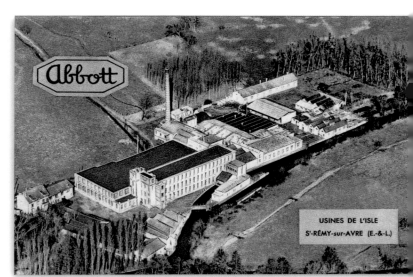

Yet, even as the falling price of penicillin and other antibiotics squeezed profit margins, sales in other divisions boosted revenues. Floyd K. Thayer, in his third decade as manager of the Chemical Sales Division, continued to significantly boost that unit's revenues.

Under the tutelage of Harold Arneson, Manuel Doblado's worthy successor in the international division, growing sales outside the United States made up fully 23 percent of all company revenues by 1956.

Abbott was now selling goods in 116 countries and had subsidiaries or factories in 35 nations. Construction began in 1956 on its largest international plant to date, in Buenos Aires, Argentina. The next year, Abbott opened a new plant in St. Remy, France.

Sales were also aided by medical director George R. Hazel, who selected a group of medical service representatives to offer doctors educational programs on company products. And despite not having the "blockbuster" drugs of some other firms, Abbott more than held its own.

"We have grown steadily," stated the *Pharmagraph* in 1957, "and gained new highs not through the success of just one or two products, but through constant application of the most up-to-date research, production, and marketing methods for our entire line.

"Each Abbott product plays an important part in the overall picture. No product contributes more than 8 percent of our total net sales."

Continues on page 191 ▶

Italian drivers have long been known for operating smaller vehicles, including these trucks that transported Abbott products in Rome.

Dr. Ernest H. Volwiler

Ernest Henry Volwiler was the scientist-chairman and an Abbott Legend.

Abbott's able president for most of the 1950s, Ernest H. Volwiler was best known as a research scientist for his work creating *Pentothal* and other vital drugs.

Like another Abbott researcher turned executive, Dr. Burdick, Ernest Volwiler started out as a teacher. Born on a farm near Hamilton, Ohio, he became an instructor at the Reilly Township Public School in Butler County. There he taught every subject, and earned money for college tuition. His life changed as an undergraduate at Miami University in Oxford, Ohio, when he attended an eye-opening lecture on chemistry.

Inspired, he finished a chemistry degree with honors in three years, and enrolled in a doctoral program at the University of Illinois. He oversaw fellow students and conducted experiments on synthetic chemicals. During the First World War, Dr. Roger Adams recruited him into Abbott. In 1918, Volwiler started as a research chemist at $35 a week, working on anesthetics and answers to the global flu pandemic that erupted that year.

The young Volwiler would arrive at five in the morning to check on chemical tests, sometimes the only person in the building, other than Dr. Abbott, himself. He quickly climbed the company's research ladder.

In the First World War he helped develop *Procaine* and *Barbital*, the analogs for the German-made drugs Novocaine and Veronal. By 1920, he was head chemist and, with Dr. Adams, developed *Butyn* and *Neonal,* improvements on *Procaine*, *Barbital*, and cocaine, the last then widely used as an anesthetic.

By 1930, he was director of research, by 1933, vice president of Research and Development, holding that position until 1946. He was responsible for consolidating Abbott's R&D in the North Chicago research center. After his 1950–1958 stint as president, he served as chairman of the board until 1959.

Dr. Volwiler graced the cover of *Forbes* magazine for a 1956 profile of Abbott.

Dr. Volwiler was the Abbott scientist best known to the scientific community. He was — with Dr. Tabern, whom he recruited — one half of one of the most heralded and productive scientific duos of the century.

The pair created the anesthetics *Nembutal* and *Pentothal*. For the latter feat they were inducted, in 1986, into the National Inventors Hall of Fame.

Outside honors were showered on him. The American Chemical Society awarded Volwiler its highest honor, the Priestley Medal; he was later the Society's president. He also headed the American Drug Manufacturers Association. Presented the Gold Medal of the American Institute of Chemists, he joined other winners such as George Eastman, of Kodak fame, as well as his own mentor, Dr. Adams. The American Association of Colleges of Pharmacy named the Volwiler Research Achievement Award after him. United States President Dwight Eisenhower appointed him to the National Science Foundation.

Like Dr. Burdick, Dr. Volwiler proved an able executive as well as scholar. When he moved up to company president in 1950, his calm manner provided stability after Abbott had a succession of three presidents in just four years. In his pragmatic way, he first consolidated the product line, then steadily expanded it.

He was also responsible for bringing the sweetener *Sucaryl* into the Abbott line. Under his leadership, Abbott continued its surge forward as the worldwide leader in radiomedicine. During his tenure, a very large proportion of the company's offerings were new-to-market products, including the easily administered radio-medicine, *Radiocaps*, as well as the antibiotics *Spontin* and *Erythrocin*.

During this period, Abbott also established a new agricultural research center, which led to innovations in naturally occurring pesticides, growth enhancers for fruits, and medicines for farm animals and pets. International expansion continued with major overseas plants established in Buenos Aires, Argentina, and St. Remy, France.

Volwiler, like many leading Abbott figures, lived a very long life. Perhaps it was the proximity to medical products, perhaps it was his work ethic and sense of purpose. But when he died in 1992, at age 99 — following the passing of Lillian, his wife of 71 years — Volwiler left 13 great-grandchildren, two great-great-grandchildren, and a remarkable legacy in chemical medicine. Abbott celebrates that legacy to this day with its Volwiler Society, an honorary organization to recognize the achievements of the company's leading scientists. ∎

In 1955, Abbott entered the digital age, with the installation
of its first computer. In 1959, came the Burroughs 200 series,
pictured. At the time the calculating machines were still
large in size, stored data on perforated paper tape, and made
only 2,000 calculations per second. The analysts here used
a computer to calculate absorption rates of substances in
the bloodstream.

George R. Cain became
Abbott's president in 1958.
He would lead the company
to a new level of success.

A Son Takes on His Father's Work

In April 1958, Dr. Volwiler, age 64, was named chairman of the board, succeeding "Sunny Jim" Stiles. One year later he would be followed by his long-time colleague, Elmer B. Vliet. Volwiler had joined Abbott when its laboratory workers numbered six; now they totaled more than 700. The world-recognized researcher went on to work at the National Science Foundation. The irrepressible Stiles, after retiring from Abbott, served for several years as head of the Saving Bonds Division of the U.S. Treasury, continuing the great work he had done during World War II.

Earlier, research director Dr. Robert D. Coghill, the former Department of Agriculture scientist, went back into government service. His role was taken by Dr. Arthur W. Weston, one-time assistant to Norm Hansen. Weston led up new focus areas of research. Dr. Leffler headed agricultural research. A division of microbiologic research was also set up. And an experimental therapy division was established, run by Dr. Richard K. Richards, of the *Sucaryl* and *Tridione* projects.

In a harbinger of things to come, in 1957, the first non-Abbott employee joined the company board. This was Continental Illinois Bank president David M. Kennedy, later a U.S. Treasury Secretary.

Taking over as president was self-assured George R. Cain, the son of former President Rolly Cain. The younger Cain had served as an aide to President Raymond Horn and later as executive vice president under Dr. Volwiler, after rising up the ranks in various commercial positions.

In immediately boosting support for research and infrastructure, George Cain carried on the tradition of Volwiler and, indeed, every Abbott chief executive, before and since. Just two months after assuming the presidency, he oversaw the start of an eight-story add-on to North Chicago's research center — 20 years after the original building's construction.

It was the start of a projected five-year, $20 million capital expansion program. At the ground-breaking, Cain noted:

> "The building will be at the same time a legacy
> from those Abbott people who made such
> progress possible, and a workshop for the Abbott
> scientists today and tomorrow who will carry on
> the quest for new weapons against suffering and
> disease. We look upon it as a symbol of our faith
> in the future."

In 1958, research spending increased to $5.6 million. A hundred new scientists and researchers would be brought in. Lab scientists focused on circulatory and nervous disorders, viral afflictions, the then-novel field of steroids, and cancer.

For the latter, Abbott cooperated with other drug makers and with thousands of hospitals, universities, and foundations, in an early "war on cancer." At the behest of the National Institutes of Health, the company rushed to screen 40,000 chemicals and filtered antibiotics for the way they interacted with tumors. Abbott also granted $300,000 to schools and research organizations to conduct general research.

Continues on page 195 ▶

The Evolution of Abbott's Mark

The making of a lasting and distinctive brand.

1904–1915

The first official Abbott logo appeared in 1904, in the 19th edition of the company's product catalog. The catalog cover had a circular icon with the phrase, "PURITY-ACCURACY GUARANTEED" around its outer edge. Entwined in its center were Dr. Abbott's initials, "WCA." The logo was imprinted on the corks of medicine bottles and on company stationery.

1915–1928

In 1915, the company changed its name from The Abbott Alkaloidal Company to Abbott Laboratories, reflecting its increasing scientific sophistication as it moved into production of synthetic drugs. While the Purity-Accuracy Guaranteed motto was retained, Dr. Abbott's initials were replaced with the banner "Abbott" in the Doctor's handwriting.

1928–1930

In 1928, the cover of the price list featured a new Abbott logo in modern script. It was similar to Dr. Abbott's handwriting (right) from his student days at the University of Michigan.

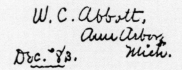

1928–1929

The back cover of the 1928 price list had tried out another new logo featuring contemporary art deco lettering and a new motto, "The House of QUALITY and SERVICE," inscribed in a circle containing a pharmacist's balance.

1931–1932

A new logo introduced in 1931 reflected two corporate acquisitions. That year, Abbott acquired the Swan-Meyers company. In 1922, Abbott had acquired The Dermatological Research Laboratories, or DRL. The insignia of both enterprises were placed inside an octagonal Abbott logo.

1932–1959

The following year, an eight-sided, black-and-white Abbott logo appeared. The year after that, in 1933, the Swan-Meyers and DRL insignia were dropped. For more than a quarter century, the Abbott octagon was well known throughout the medical products industry.

1959–Present Day

In 1959, the company undertook a major rebranding effort, including packaging, signage, and the greatest departure ever from its long-established corporate identity. The new logo was created by the famed industrial design firm George Nelson Associates. The "A" symbol remains in use to this day. In 2005, a new corporate rebranding effort enhanced it for a new era (see pages 342-343).

The company's burgeoning growth of the late 1950s got an extra push in 1959, when Abbott undertook a companywide redesign of its packaging and corporate identity. The genesis of this move was the repackaging of the artificial sweetener *Sucaryl* and vitamin products like *Dayalets* and *Vita-Kaps* (see page 194).

"Over the past several years the design of graphic materials produced by the parent company has become increasingly chaotic," explained advertising vice president Charles S. Downs, who had headed the Second World War bond poster campaign. "There is a lack of instantly recognizable, strongly integrated family feeling."

Packaging at Abbott was complex. In 1959, the packaging standards department wrote and maintained the specifications for 8,000 packaged items. Packaging for such disparate items as ampoules, bottle caps, IVs and plasma bags, and mailing tubes had to be specially engineered. Chemicals and export goods received extra attention due to stricter or unusual requirements.

For a new symbol, Abbott turned to the New York firm of George Nelson Associates, which had helped found American modernist design after studying the deans of modern architecture, Walter Gropius and Mies Van der Rohe.

In 1959, the old company symbol was still the script "Abbott" enclosed by an octagon, a variation on a theme used since 1931. To replace it, George Nelson Associates considered an ancient medical symbol, the serpent on the staff of Asclepius, the Greek god of medicine. This motif had been on the commemorative coins Raymond Loewy made for Abbott's 50th anniversary. Designers twisted the snake to conjure up an abstract letter "A," which remains the company's symbol to this day.

"It is decorative and pleasing to the eye," commented Downs. "It is adaptable to letterheads, invoices, samples, direct mail, and journal advertising."

The symbol "permits quick and easy identification," added Downs. "No small matter when one considers the multitude and variety of packaging on pharmacists' shelves and in storerooms."

"Thematic Abstraction," by Hans Moller, from the Abbott Art Collection.

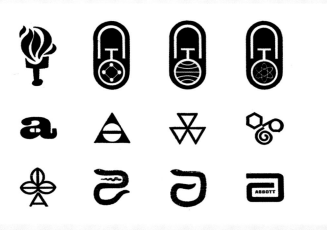

Graphic designer Don Ervin developed a number of different approaches to updating Abbott's brand in 1959. The winning idea, as shown above, was an abstracted letter "A" derived from the snake on the staff of Asclepius, the ancient symbol of medicine.

Repackaging Abbott's Look

To match the new corporate branding, Abbott redesigned its consumer products packaging with a similarly updated look.

Previously, as with most vitamin makers, the containers for such products were mundane, and resembled milk cans and apothecary jars. Abbott determined "to get the products out of the kitchen and onto the dining room table." It turned to the design firm of

Raymond Loewy, the renowned industrial designer of Abbott's Research Center. Its director of packaging design, William Stark, completely revamped the containers for five vitamins and the artificial sweetener *Sucaryl* with a sleeker, more decorative, and modern-looking style.

The strategy was successful. Vitamin sales rose, while *Sucaryl* solidified its position as the country's most popular artificial sweetener. The marketing team was inspired to redesign and unify all the company's products. It would center them around the new corporate logo. ■

The refashioned *Sucaryl* bottle had rounded labels echoing the container's contours, and a cone top that was eye-catching as well as functional: It let the user drip, instead of pour, the sweetener.

The line of vitamins went from dumpy and utilitarian to "wasp-waisted" and stylish — reflecting the traditional pharmacist's mortar — with an hourglass makeover. The containers were intended to be attractive enough for display on dining table or countertop.

New President George R. Cain expanded research with an eight-story addition to the North Chicago R&D center, making it a company icon.

New products poured forth in the late '50s, including *Pramilets*, a nutritional supplement for pregnant women.

Growing Products, Growing Revenues

All this research generated major new products — 15 in 1958 and 40 more in 1959.

Some broke new ground in hospital equipment and drugs. *Pliapak* was a disposable plasma bag. *Pulmo-Pak* was an artificial lung that pumped blood cells with oxygen. *Gradumet* enabled the "controlled release" of medicine for drugs like *Tral* for peptic ulcers, permitting more precise and less burdensome dosing. Controlled-release remedies for diseases like diabetes would, in time, become widespread.

> "We have built thoughtfully with money we have earned, not borrowed."
>
> — GEORGE R. CAIN

The nutritional supplement *Pramilets* was offered for pregnant women. *Norisodrine Syrup with Calcium Iodide* opened the air passages of those suffering from asthma, bronchitis, and certain allergies. Yet another drug helped patients recover from barbiturate overdose or anesthesia.

Other entries were new and improved formulations of existing drugs. *Erythrocin-I.M.* was injectable to help sufferers who could not tolerate taking the antibiotic orally. Also, an Abbott-developed potassium-penicillin granule entered the bloodstream faster and with greater potency than previous penicillin offerings.

The new products and years of investment proved successful. In the decade's final year, Abbott sales were a record $122,602,000, with earnings of $12,989,000. The company achieved this performance even with record research expenditures that year of $6,900,000 — a 20 percent boost. President Cain summed up the decade: "We have built thoughtfully with money we have earned, not borrowed."

These financial milestones were reached despite ferocious competition from other health products companies. Cain noted that in other industries a few firms made up the great bulk of production. In automobiles, for instance, General Motors and Ford had few rivals. "No one company in our field," contrasted Cain, "has as much as 10 percent of the total market. It is this intense competition that has pressed our industry into world leadership. American companies are now supplying about 75 percent of the world's pharmaceuticals." Abbott's involvement in the global market would only grow in the years ahead.

Decade at a Glance
1950–1960

1950 ▲
Ernest H. Volwiler, a scientist noted for his work creating *Pentothal* and other anesthetics, is Abbott's president for most of the decade.

The company opens a registered business entity in France, and enters into business in Spain.

▲
Abbott introduces *Sucaryl,* an artificial sweetener, helping to create a new food industry.

1951
The company offers employees a contributory stock plan. Employees with at least three years' experience at Abbott could purchase company stock for under half the market price.

In a move into a mass consumer market, Abbott introduces *Selsun Suspension* shampoo for dandruff control.
▼

Dr. Donalee L. Tabern, working with radioactive elements in his lab, followed up his success with *Pentothal* by leading Abbott's entry into nuclear medicine.
▼

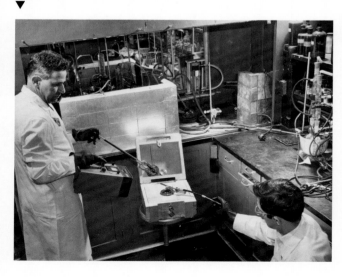

1952
James F. Stiles moves up to chairman of the board.
▼

Abbott's nuclear lab for making radiomedicines begins shipping product to customers.

1954
The Clara Abbott Foundation starts its College Student Aid program, allotting financial assistance to high-school graduates of company employees' children.

▲
The nuclear medicine team devises *Radiocaps*, capsules with an invisible film of radio-iodine used to treat thyroid disorders. Patients require neither injections nor special protections against radiation.

1955
Abbott installs its first digital computer.
▼

The U.S. Pharmacopoeia, the standard-setting authority for healthcare products, formally lists its first atomic medicine: Abbott's radio-iodine.

1956

Abbott outfits a purchased dairy farm in Long Grove, Illinois, creating a new agricultural products division for the development of drugs for farm animals and improved crops.

▼

Research teams develop another drug for epilepsy, *Peganone*. It proves more effective against the grand mal form of the malaise.

Construction begins on Abbott's largest international plant to date, in Buenos Aires, Argentina.

Throughout the decade, Abbott adds new buildings to its North Chicago site.

▼

1957

The company launches the antibiotic *Spontin*, "the antibiotic of last resort." It is useful against pneumonia, meningitis, and blood poisoning.

The first non-Abbott director joins the company board: Continental Illinois Bank President David M. Kennedy, later a U.S. Treasury Secretary.

Abbott's international expansion extends to a new manufacturing complex in St. Remy, France.

▼

1958

George R. Cain, the son of an Abbott president, is himself named president of the firm.

▼

Dr. Volwiler moves up to chairman of the board. Chairman James F. "Sunny Jim" Stiles retires to lead the Savings Bond Division of the U.S. Treasury.

On his retirement, Dr. Volwiler relaxes to reflect on the Priestley Medal bestowed on him by the American Chemical Society.

▼

1959

Abbott introduces 40 new products.

Company sales reach a record $122,602,000, and research expenditures reach a new high of $6,900,000.

Elmer B. Vliet succeeds Ernest H. Volwiler as chairman of the board.

▼

Abbott introduces a new logo, a stylized "A." It appears as a part of a major new corporate identity initiative. A classic of industrial design and one of the industry's most recognizable marks, it is still in use today, the centerpiece of a major rebranding effort almost 50 years later.

▼

1960–1970
From Good to Great

In the 1960s, American society was changing rapidly. The same was certainly true of Abbott, in its internal organization, its regulation by the federal government, its construction of a vast new headquarters, and its acquisitions at home and expansion abroad.

PREVIOUS SPREAD
The eight-story research building in North Chicago, construction of which had begun in 1958, was up and running by 1961. The top of the building sported the new Abbott "A" logo.

As it matured into a multinational corporation, Abbott broke with tradition by bringing in outside executives to its Board of Directors, seen here in the early 1960s. Members of the Board and Abbott executives shown here include: Seated from left to right: Dr. Charles S. Brown, Robert V. Jaros, Paul Gerden, Elmer B. Vliet, George R. Cain, Edward A. Ravenscroft, Willis Gale, and Arthur W. Weston PhD. Standing from left to right: Lowell T. Coggeshall, M.D., Charles S. Downs, Frederick J. Kirchmeyer, James L. Allen, Harold D. Arneson, George R. Hazel, M.D., Herbert S. Wilkinson, Floyd K. Thayer, and Norman A. Hansen.

Abbott began the decade with unaccustomed bad news on the bottom line. In 1960, despite sales of $125 million, profits dropped 4.6 percent to $12,385,000. In 1961, sales increased a modest 3 percent, while profits again fell, to about $12 million. Clearly, it was time for a change.

Changing Internally and Reaching Out

The company had grown faster in the late 1950s, but over that decade some of its rivals had gained ground. "Our competitors experienced an average yearly increase of almost 8 percent as compared with our 5.5 percent," President George R. Cain stated in fall 1961. "We have not kept pace. Aggressive action is needed."

In the same period, administrative, advertising, and sales expenses had doubled. Operating costs were also higher, and research expenditures in 1961 hit $9,600,000, or 7.4 percent of sales, the highest proportion in Abbott's history to that time. Competition was continuing to squeeze the profits of vitamins and antibiotics, including the flagship *Erythrocin*.

There was a sense that Abbott was slipping behind its competition. "We weren't getting new products," commented Cain. "Scientific management," he concluded, "is most likely to yield desired results." The consulting firm Booz Allen Hamilton was brought in to make a management and organizational analysis of the firm.

The company's worldwide expansion under President George R. Cain was represented by the painting "Abbott City." It brought into one busy frame more than 50 Abbott buildings from around the globe. The artist was Society of Illustrators Hall of Fame member Franklin McMahon.

Abbott's surge in this era was featured in the 2001 best-seller *Good to Great: Why Some Companies Make the Leap ... and Others Don't.* Author Jim Collins researched 1,435 companies, and settled on just 11, including Abbott, that practiced the discipline and attention to product and service quality that brought about truly great performance. Abbott first made the leap in the 1960s under President George R. Cain.

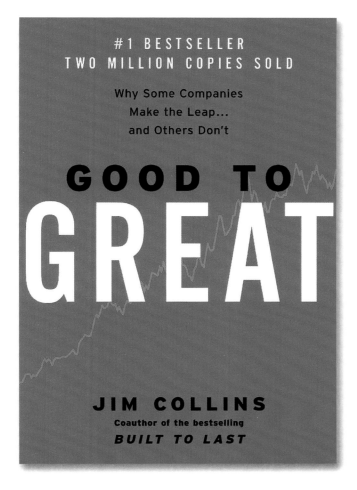

Cain moved to restructure the company. In 1961, he reduced the nine senior officers reporting to him to five vice presidents of impressive background. Frederick J. Kirchmeyer was made head of product planning and development. Kirchmeyer was a 22-year Abbott veteran and former head of pharmaceutical research who held patents in sulfa salts and derivatives of quinone, an oxidizing agent. Cain picked Charles S. Downs, the marketing talent behind *What's New*, as head of public relations. Dr. Charles S. Brown had served with Abbott for 17 years as a chemical engineer and as head of manufacturing. He became the new chief of United States and Canadian operations. General counsel Paul Gerden became the head of administration.

For the first time, an executive from outside Abbott was selected to lead a major Abbott division. This was Albert R. Wayne, who had led the international division of Mead Johnson, a maker of infant nutrition, a field in which Abbott would come to specialize. Cain appointed Wayne to lead the fast-growing international operations group.

The new vice presidents, save Downs, joined President George R. Cain and Edward A. Ravenscroft in a new operations committee that took on policy planning. Ravenscroft had been the company's director of engineering, then its comptroller and supervisor of cost analysis. The son of a former board chairman, he was, like Cain, a true Abbott insider. Ironically, it was Ravenscroft's father who had instituted the tradition of seating only Abbott officers on the board, a tradition the younger Ravenscroft would help to change. Edward Ravenscroft was to serve as an executive vice president in Cain's operations committee as well as a reorganizer of international operations.

Consolidation and administrative efficiency were the watchwords. Many of S. DeWitt Clough's old committees were disbanded. Profit per employee was made into an important metric, and remained so. At the same time, the highly profitable Chemical Sales Division expanded. And a Grocery Products Division made the briskly selling sweetener *Sucaryl* available to outlets other than pharmacies.

In reshuffling Abbott internally and bringing in outside managers, Cain played no favorites. He replaced several of his own relatives working at the company. He did not hire any of his three working-age sons. "We are anti-nepotic," he noted.

The sense of change had been heightened the previous year by the retirement of several long-term Abbott figures, including noted researcher and quality assurance expert Elmer B. Vliet, who had risen to chairman of the board from 1959–1962. The new era was further underscored by the death of two former leaders: Chairman of the Board S. DeWitt Clough and President Raymond E. Horn.

Congressional Contretemps

In Washington, D.C., the United States Congress helped start a decades-long trend toward greater government involvement in the healthcare industry. Tennessee Senator Estes Kefauver, chairman of the Antitrust and Monopoly Subcommittee, held highly publicized hearings beginning in late 1959. The hearings raised issues that presaged the healthcare debates of later years. The subcommittee looked into allegations of price fixing, excess profits, exaggerated advertising claims, high-pressure marketing tactics, harmful side effects, and the higher cost of brand-name drugs compared to generics.

Continues on page 206 ▶

Elmer B. Vliet

Elmer Vliet's long Abbott career mirrored that of his predecessor as Board Chairman, Ernest H. Volwiler. In fact, he was a chemical engineering student of Volwiler's at the University of Illinois, and started at Abbott in 1919, one year after Volwiler joined up. Volwiler spent 40 years at Abbott, Vliet 42 years. Both lived to vigorous old age, Volwiler to 99, Vliet, 96, and both served the company with dedication and great distinction.

A lifelong Abbott man, Elmer Vliet joined the company from the U.S. military, and over a long and dedicated career rose steadily to become its chairman.

After working during the First World War in the research group of the U.S. Chemical Warfare Service and at the U.S. Department of Agriculture's Fixed Nitrogen Laboratory, Elmer Vliet was hired by Abbott as a research chemist.

From the beginning, the talented young man handled important duties. In 1920, Vliet, along with Roger Adams, brought in from the University of Illinois chemist Floyd K. Thayer, the future head of the vital chemical sales unit. In 1928, Vliet was charged with examining the labs and plant of John T. Milliken and Company, prior to its merger with Abbott.

Some projects were starcrossed. In 1920–1921, Dr. Abbott himself directed Vliet to Philadelphia, to help out a friend, Dr. S. Lewis Summers, who was trying to perfect a manufacturing process for an arthritis remedy. Vliet thought the process doomed, and the initial foray at making the medicine resulted in an explosion that mangled the equipment. When Vliet asked to return to Chicago, Dr. Abbott ordered him: "Stay there.

Shown working in a control lab in 1929, Elmer Vliet, was the Abbott chairman most experienced in quality assurance.

If this works, I'll make you manager of that plant." For a month, while the apparatus was repaired, Vliet played pinochle with Dr. Summers. Only after a second failure, and a third, was Vliet, frustrated but unhurt, finally recalled.

By 1935, he was manager of the control laboratories, a role critical to quality assurance. In 1946, he became the control labs director. Along the way Vliet earned several medical patents. He was appointed vice president and scientific director in 1952. From 1959 to 1962 he was chairman of the board.

As Abbott chairman, Vliet, drawing on his many years in quality assurance, was an eloquent spokesman on the role and responsibilities of pharmaceutical makers. As he once stated before the Association of Food and Drug Officials: "Our responsibility is to make the best possible drugs, to present them in a straightforward manner, honoring our obligation to point out limitations along with virtues, and to make these drugs under such conditions of quality control that qualified physicians can use them with confidence for the benefit of patients."

"He exemplified Abbott Laboratories' commitment to innovative scientific research," noted Abbott CEO Duane L. Burnham in 1994, on Vliet's death that year, "and to achieving consistent high quality in production of healthcare products."

At his death Vliet left behind nine great-grandchildren and a great-great grandchild.

Outside Abbott, his most noted community service was building and chronicling the history of Lake Bluff, Illinois, near North Chicago, the village where he lived for 47 years. Vliet learned about the community in assorted capacities, serving as head of zoning on the board of commissioners, and as president of the local high school board, the park board, and the village itself. He went on to write *Lake Bluff: The First 100 Years*. Vliet donated the proceeds from his book to help found the Vliet Museum of Lake Bluff History. ∎

Senator Estes Kefauver, who had run for both President and Vice President of the United States, mounted an investigation of the pharmaceutical industry, raising issues that continue in today's ongoing healthcare debates.

The drug industry mounted a vigorous response. Dr. Austin T. Smith, president of the Pharmaceutical Manufacturers Association (PMA, today known as PhRMA, the Pharmaceutical Research and Manufacturers of America), noted the price of drugs had risen by just three percent in the previous decade — compared to 22 percent for all U.S. industrial products. Dr. Smith pointed out that the vast majority of the regulatory actions of the United States Food and Drug Administration (FDA) were aimed at non-PMA members, who made cheaper drugs under less rigorous standards.

Abbott was not called on to testify at the hearings, although, like a number of other companies, some of its corporate records were subpoenaed. The company did prepare pamphlets in early 1960 for employees and executives that responded to the Kefauver hearings.

One pamphlet noted that, when a profitable new product is introduced, "There is a lightning-like reaction on the part of competing firms to improve upon the original breakthrough, to the benefit of patient and physician." An example cited was the introduction, in 1950, of cortical steroids. By 1958, 27 companies provided such steroids, and the market share of the company that originally introduced the product had plummeted from 100 percent to 17 percent. Such fierce competition cut prices and spurred innovative reformulations, Abbott contended.

Further, the cost and risk of drug development was high. "In 1958, firms tested some 115,000 substances," the booklet stated. "Of these, 1,900 showed enough promise to reach clinical trials. From them came just 365 new products. The price of pharmaceuticals and the cost and difficulty of developing them would be lasting themes. By the 2000s, the estimated R&D costs to a company of developing a single drug averaged more than $1 billion.

The Second Battle of the Square Deal

As a result of interest raised by the hearings, Abbott had a run-in with a national periodical that recalled Dr. Abbott's 1908 fight with the *Journal of the American Medical Association*. On February 15, 1960, *Life* magazine published a seven-page feature, entitled "Big Pill Bill to Swallow," on the Kefauver hearings. The story launched what President Cain considered an unfair attack on the drug industry. He had advertising manager William D. Pratt and public relations supervisor William Cray contact *Life's* general manager to point out errors in the article.

Continues on page 210 ▶

BIG PILL BILL TO SWALLOW

The wonder-drug makers get handsome profits from their captive consumers

Jimmy Porter was taking a 30¢ pill, a Temaril pill prescribed to relieve the itching of his chicken pox. He took one every three hours and so did his sister and his three brothers. When the family's little epidemic was over, it had cost the Porters more than $50 in drugs alone, which they felt was too expensive. The Porters' problem, on a vast scale, is a problem of all American families. Last year Americans spent $2 billion on prescription drugs, half as much as on doctors. And this price, even considering the miracles modern drugs accomplish, is too high.

The high cost results from a unique and freakish business situation which began to form 20 years ago. The prescription drug business was always a profitable one, but in those days it was conducted by small conservative companies in a restrained way. When the wonder drugs came along, offering new cures for the ill, vast new markets opened up. The character of the industry changed. As chemical know-how increased, the companies were caught up in a race to develop new drugs which they could patent. As the market broadened, competition grew fierce and selling pressure high. In two decades total sales increased by 1,000% and drugs became big business. In 1958 the score of companies which dominate the industry averaged 25% profit on sales before taxes—more than twice as high as the average for industry in general. The reason for such profits has now come into sharp focus. Unlike other major industries, this one has the advantage of selling to captive consumers—sick people who cannot shop around but must buy what the doctor orders.

Now the drug companies are being attacked for their fatness before congressional hearings conducted by Senator Kefauver. Their spokesmen defend their free-enterprise right to make big profits for stockholders and justify them by the huge research risks they take. But this defense has not yet convinced the investigators or the public who must pay the price.

A *Life* magazine article that criticized the pharmaceutical industry on the cost and availability of drugs drew a spirited response from Abbott.

Abbott's response to a *Life*
magazine article attacking
its industry recalled its
response through the public
press to the 1908 broadside
by a noted medical journal.

A PAID EDITORIAL

REPORT TO THE NATION'S DOCTORS ON A "BIG PILL BILL TO SWALLOW"

On February 15, **Life** Magazine carried a 7-page editorial feature on the ethical pharmaceutical industry. Implicit in this article were errors of fact, affecting both the medical profession and the pharmaceutical industry.

In the March 7 issue, **Life** carried this correction in the "Letters to the Editor" column:

- **Life** misfilled its pill bottle. Our reporter was told there were only 10 pills in each $3 Temaril bottle. The correct figure is 20—ED.

Unfortunately, **Life** misfilled more than its pill bottle. The first sentence of the February 15 article told of four-year-old Jimmy Porter taking a "30¢ pill, a Temaril pill prescribed to relieve the itching . . . of chicken pox." **FACT:** This tablet (which is not made by Abbott Laboratories, incidentally) sells on prescription at an average price of 11.3¢—not 30¢.

Life said the tablets were given to each of the five Porter children every three hours. **FACT:** If this happened, the children were getting twice the dosage recommended by the manufacturer.

Life said the chicken pox epidemic in this family cost "more than $50 in drugs alone." **FACT:** To spend $50, it must be assumed that all five children took the anti-itching tablets for more than four days at twice the recommended dosage and at a cost of 30¢ a tablet. Typical treatment for five youngsters with this particular drug, even for a full week, would cost $15.40 in all, not $50.

Life said the Porters spent a tenth of their income on medical care last year, and that their problem, on a vast scale, is a problem of "all American families." **FACT:** Per capita expenditures for drugs in 1959 came to about $18, and about $94 for all medical care. The average prescription price last year was only $3.08. We do not know whether the Porters had more, or less, illness than usual.

What is important—to all Americans—is how many illnesses and hospital stays were shortened or prevented by doctors and drugs, how much pain was alleviated, how many lives were saved. Can present drug expense of $18 per person be too heavy in a nation that spends $52 per person (over 14 years of age) on tobacco and $87 per person (over 21 years of age) on alcoholic beverages?

Life implied that drug prices are too high because of the "advantage of selling to captive consumers." **FACT:** The physician, who is ethically bound to prescribe in the best interests of his patient, is the only man professionally capable of diagnosis and treatment. If the patient has a real financial problem, the physician, as part of his obligation, may provide drug samples he may have on hand or, in extreme cases, he will contact social or government agencies.

Life said that "in a single day a doctor may collect $40.00 worth of free drug samples." **FACT:** This figure might be true—if the doctor opened all of his mail, and interviewed all detail men, on just one day of the week. Samples inform the doctor about new drugs or remind him of old ones. **Life** did not mention what eventually happens to samples. Physicians treat patients with them—the indigent, the aged, the unfortunate, those in charitable institutions.

Life compared the costs of drug promotion (14 per cent) to the "less than 3 per cent" spent on new car promotion by manufacturers. **FACT:** Ethical drug advertising in medical journals and direct mail varies from year to year between 3.9 and 4.7 per cent. And this, of course, is carried on entirely by the manufacturer. New car advertising is sponsored by manufacturer *and* dealer, so there is no comparison here at all.

Life said "the average doctor is deluged with sales talk, either through direct mail or visits from drug firm representatives known as detail men." **FACT:** It is true that the doctor receives, and reads, a lot of direct mail, and many medical journals. He also sees, and listens to, many detail men. This is one way he can keep up with the rapidly changing pace of medical progress . . . one form of education which enables him to give his patients the best possible medical attention. Medical advertising already is, and must continue to be, the best-policed of all advertising. It deals with human lives.

Life quoted a pharmacologist to the effect that new products are introduced "because they are profitable, not because they have a medical advantage over the products of preceding years." **FACT:** Pharmaceutical houses routinely produce drugs which have a limited market—and at little or no profit. The criterion is simply whether the drug is needed to prevent or cure disease. Products which do not deliver real benefits to doctor and patient alike soon pass out of the medical market. Good products survive.

Life quoted another pharmacologist to the effect that "extraordinarily few important new drugs have been originated by American drug houses." **FACT:** In the last decade alone, American pharmaceutical houses have developed 392 new medicinal chemicals, including tranquilizers, steroids, antibiotics, diuretics, antihypertensives, etc. Useful drugs discovered elsewhere have been developed to clinical usefulness within the industry. Penicillin is a classic example. So was insulin. So are some of the new tranquilizers. Without tremendous research and production efforts by the industry, many modern drugs would still be just medical curiosities.

Life showed a pie chart allocating the consumer's drug dollar, with company profit taking 15 per cent of this dollar. **FACT:** This is reasonably accurate—but only when you consider just a few products. Further, **Life** neglects to mention that half of this profit goes into taxes. On these products the purchaser pays about 7 cents toward profit. On others he pays much less. These are the pennies which provide the incentive for developing effective drugs—drugs which ease pain, prevent or cure illness, prolong life.

Life said "a good part . . . of the blame for the high price of prescriptions must be borne by the physician," and that "better informed consumers" should "pressure the doctors into using finer discrimination." **FACT:** Such assertions belittle the scientific knowledge and judgment of every doctor. He is indicted for prescribing medications only he is competent to judge as best for each patient. The pressure **Life** suggests would bring chaos to medical practice.

Life stated there is no "real difference" between brand name drugs and equivalent generic name drugs. **FACT:** Many unbranded drugs have been proven inferior, as a scrutiny of Food and Drug Administration citations would show. A physician typically prefers not to take a chance on unbranded drugs, especially with those turned out by firms operating within a state and therefore not subject to Federal food and drug laws. With most things we buy, we rely on the quality and integrity of brand names. In the case of drugs, this is even more important than with other consumer items, since the health, and even the life, of a patient may be at stake. The brand name is the physician's assurance that the drug he prescribes is the exact drug the patient receives.

Abbott Laboratories believes the American people want to retain and improve our present system of medical care. We believe they want to keep the same kind of doctor-patient relationship, with its freedom of choice, which has done so much to take us to our present astonishing levels of national health. Progress depends upon further effort and teamwork among all the health professions. This must continue. To this all of us are dedicated by tradition, purpose, and training. For the greatest medical challenges—and the greatest triumphs—still belong to the future.

This is our report. It is not our intention to vilify **Life**. We accept that it has the right to a viewpoint. Our concern is that the conditions it reported, and the interpretation put to them, are not consistent with the facts.

If you would like to have a booklet we prepared for our own employees, *Abbott Laboratories and the Pharmaceutical Industry*, just send this coupon to Public Relations Department, Abbott Laboratories, North Chicago, Illinois.

Name_____

Street_____

City_____ Zone_____ State_____

ABBOTT LABORATORIES NORTH CHICAGO, ILLINOIS

CAPSULES

An Obsession with Quality

Abbott's intense commitment to quality started with Dr. Abbott, himself, whose oft-repeated admonition to employees was, "You cannot talk merit into a product. You must put it there!" One of his favorite slogans was, "Make it right!" Early product labels sported the motto: "Purity, Accuracy Guaranteed."

Later, under sticklers for precision like Dr. Joseph Favil Biehn, medical department head in the 1930s, quality control at Abbott became an ever-more precise and methodical science. By the early 1960s, overlapping levels of quality assurance provided the most rigorous safeguards.

Quality control and assurance with healthcare goods began with inspection of raw materials arriving at the company loading dock. Chemical tests followed for identity, purity, and potency. Ingredients for blending were carefully weighed. Each stage of production had meticulous control checks. Even bottle caps were inspected for tiny amounts of contaminant.

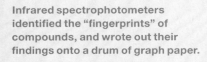

Infrared spectrophotometers identified the "fingerprints" of compounds, and wrote out their findings onto a drum of graph paper.

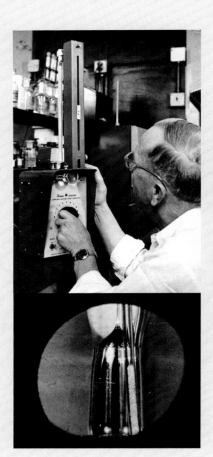

Critical melting points were one control check on the purity of chemical compounds. A technician placed a substance for testing into a capillary tube, where it was heated. The melting-point temperature was read off a thermometer peep hole just above a magnifying glass.

Abbott took two years to perfect this machine for handling and bottling *Sucaryl*. Four-ounce bottles of the sweetener were conveyed from the left. In the middle they were filled from a drum tank, and then the row of caps that emerged from the top right were twisted on top. Some 5,000 bottles an hour were then conveyed to the right for inspection and packaging.

Technicians carefully inspect bottles of parenteral solution. They held the containers of liquid up to intensely bright light to check for stray specks of contaminant.

Samples of every lot of finished goods were scrutinized. The chief of "quality control," Elmer Krueger, was authorized to impound and destroy a batch of any drug for any deviation from strict standards. Even after a product was released to pharmacies, a record of its batch numbers, test results, and a sample, were kept for five years. With the increasing complexity and growing regulation of healthcare, quality control would only become more stringent in the years ahead.

Stated medical affairs head Dr. George R. Hazel: "The best protection for the public will be the manufacturing integrity of the company, its concern for reputation."

Quality control wasn't all about plant machinery. It also involved careful planning of, and interaction with, the management of the clinical trials for new drugs. The planning was by Abbott staff physicians.

They devised the studies, evaluated results and claims, and fielded queries about the trials from such interested parties as outside scientists, clinicians, hospital administrators, and regulators.

A true record of quality control lay in the thousands of pages of documentation typical of the clinical trials for a new drug. Such reportage contained human drug trials, animal toxicity tests, formulations, dosages, manufacturing processes, methods of testing, standards of purity, and packaging techniques.

Chairman of the Board Elmer B. Vliet noted: "Quality is only achieved when it is made the inflexible policy of a concern. And when every person in each department has the ability, the ambition, the incentive, and the persistence to perform his task properly." ∎

Products could be sterilized by heating or pressurization. Baskets of IV solution bottles rode a slow-motion conveyor into a 20-foot-long autoclave, or oven. In 1960, an intravenous solution underwent 36 separate quality tests.

In reply, *Life* printed a three-sentence statement in its letters to the editor section. Referring to a Pfizer anti-inflammatory drug Tamaril, it read: "*Life* misfilled its pill bottle. Our reporter was told there were only 10 pills in each $3 Tamaril bottle. The correct figure is 20."

Feeling slighted, Abbott responded aggressively. Pratt and Cray put together a full-page "paid editorial" that appeared in the magazine's March 21 issue. It refuted the 13 statements and interpretations in "Big Pill Bill to Swallow."

The article had lamented the high cost of medical care. Abbott's response countered: "Per capita expenditures for drugs in 1959 came to about $18, and about $94 for all medical care." (By 2011, per capita healthcare spending in the United States had risen to $8,680, only about 10 percent of which was for pharmaceuticals.)

The article also charged that drug firms put out new products for reason of profit, not due to substantive medical advancements. Abbott's riposte: "Pharmaceutical houses routinely produce drugs which have a limited market — and at little or no profit … Products which do not deliver real benefits to doctor and patient alike soon pass out of the medical market. Good products survive."

The magazine responded to the piece, with some aspersion. Abbott pulled its *Sucaryl* advertising out of *Life*, and put it into the magazine's archrival, *Look*. Further, Abbott mailed reprints of the editorial to thousands of physicians, pharmacists, and Congressmen. Many doctors placed them in waiting rooms; some druggists paid to place them in local newspapers.

Abbott had gotten in its licks, but at a price: Its editorial cost $32,060. Cain called it "the world's most expensive letter to the editor." The Second Battle of the Square Deal ceased, and attention returned to Congress.

Pending Legislation

In early 1961, Sen. Kefauver and New York Congressman Emanuel Celler proposed sweeping drug legislation. Their bill proposed to cut companies' 17-year period of patent protection to three years; also to authorize the U.S. Department of Health, Education, and Welfare (HEW) — the precursor to the Department of Health and Human Services — to rule over the patenting of drug reformulations. Such patents would only be allowed for changes that, in the government's view, significantly improved a drug's therapeutic impact.

In counterpoint, Abbott brought out its most renowned scientific authority — Dr. Volwiler. In testimony before Congress, he noted that changes to the *Nembutal* molecule had been responsible for the creation of the vital drug *Pentothal*. These chemical changes, Volwiler noted, were of "the kind that some witnesses before this committee have stressed to be simple, trivial, devoid of risk, and of little or no value to medicine." Similar changes to the *Tridione* molecule, it was noted, led to successful new treatments for epilepsy.

Company ads in medical publications supported Volwiler's view. "It is assumed," stated one, "that the Secretary [of HEW] has the omniscience to determine the quantity and variety of drugs that should be on the market … But there is copious evidence in history that the negative judgment of 'experts' has sometimes delayed medical progress for years, and even for generations. This historical list would include Jenner's smallpox vaccine, Pasteur's anthrax vaccine, Lister's theory of antisepsis — even the sulfas and penicillin."

Abbott also published a pamphlet, "Molecular Modification — Gateway to Better Drugs," that questioned letting the Secretary of HEW decide whether a new drug was superior to its original formulation. Such a process of decision making "would make invention unrewarding, dry up research, and even deny potentially useful products to physicians," the booklet stated. Another Abbott pamphlet, "Let's Not Cripple the Patent System," questioned why the Senate was singling out the drug industry for patent law changes.

President Cain weighed in with speeches and op-eds. The Congressional proposals, he stated in the *Chicago Daily News*, "are based on foolish, emotional, and often distorted facts … Disregarded are the values of the patent system, dynamic competition … and the freedom of physicians to select their drugs of choice."

Abbott counterattacked when it saw its own products under unfair assault. In summer 1961, the chairman of the Federal Trade Commission, in testimony before Congress, chided Abbott for an ad that supposedly did not fully disclose the side effects of *Oretic*, a diuretic. Abbott's chief counsel, Paul Gerden, replied that Abbott had taken out eight pages in the *Journal of the American Medical Association*, or *JAMA*, that detailed *Oretic*'s dosages, side effects, clinical studies, and much else. Abbott had also mailed out copies of the lengthy insert to thousands of physicians with the tagline, "In case you missed it, in *JAMA*, Doctor …" Abbott stressed it had always backed full disclosure of its products' uses, composition, and effects.

Two Abbott biochemists, Dr. Jacob C. Holper (left) and
Dr. Alvin J. Glasky, broke important ground on how to spur,
and prevent, the growth of viral disease.

Research Fundamentals

The completion of a new research center doubled the
amount of research space in the expansive — yet now
crowded — grounds of North Chicago. Cain decided yet
more space was needed. Five miles southwest of its
headquarters, Abbott bought 420 acres of farmland. The
acreage had consisted of two gentleman farms, one built
by a Chicago "cream pie king," the other of which served
as a day school. There, throughout the decade, construction of new facilities, and transfer of existing operations,
would take place. This site would become Abbott Park,
the new and even larger company headquarters of the
future. Meanwhile, scientific research, sometimes of the
most fundamental nature, continued apace.

In June 1963, the cutting-edge research of two
Abbott scientists, Dr. Alvin J. Glasky and Dr. Jacob C.
Holper, was splashed across front pages. The two had
added an enzyme to a batch of chemical ingredients. As
a result, viruses exploded in number in their laboratory
dish. Headlines screamed, rather inaccurately, that the
research duo had created life.

What the Abbott scientists had done was to add the
enzyme RNA synthetase to a laboratory "soup" composed
of man-made nucleotides, the compounds that make up
RNA and DNA, and that also serve as the ingredients of
viruses. Viruses are the tiny, infectious agents that exist
in a gray area between life and non-life. The researchers
incubated their soup, then mixed it with living cells. Viruses
exploded in number in the broth.

Continues on page 214 ▶

Scientists Create 'Life' in Lab

Viruses Formed from Chemicals, Chicagoans Say	Achievement Is Hailed as a Milestone BY ROY GIBBONS [© 1963: By The Chicago Tribune]

Glasky (left) and Holper

The work on viruses by
Abbott scientists was met
with screaming headlines,
such as this one in *The
Chicago Tribune*.

State-of-the-Art Research and Development

In the late 1950s, the world had witnessed the birth of the Space Age, with the Soviet Union and the United States launching into orbit the Sputnik and Project Mercury satellites, respectively. Yet by the early 1960s, as major investments in research and equipment kicked in, Abbott's scientific personnel, instrumentation, and biochemical research methods were as cutting edge as any "space shot."

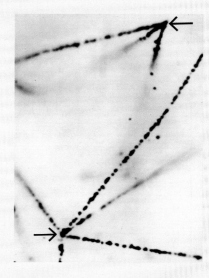

The autoradiography lab could make photographic emulsions of the paths of radioactive particles, gleaning clues on the speed and function of such objects. The arrows indicate the nuclei, or centers, of the atoms.

With magnifications up to one million, far more powerful than any optical microscope, the electron microscope permitted examination of objects theretofore never seen, even minuscule viruses operating within cells.

Scientists performed nervous-system research on chick embryos under sterile conditions. On the right, a researcher at the microscope manipulated instruments on chick tissue within the glass box, after slipping his hand through the tube leading into the box.

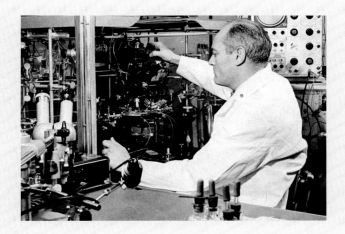

A technician, left, operated this complex set of electronic devices to study, among other things, the electrical conductivity of nerve cells.

Another way to study the nervous system was to observe the reactions of lab animals administered drugs that affected the nerves. Rats were placed in "Skinner boxes," named after behavioral psychologist B.F. Skinner, and conditioned to react in certain ways, for instance, to depress a bar to receive a drink of water. Researchers then observed how a drug affected such behaviors. Abbott has always strictly complied with FDA regulations on the care and use of animals in research.

This counter-current extractor, left, used a forest of intricate, interconnected glass tubing to separate out the components of chemical mixtures. The machine's continuous rocking action performed hundreds of successive extractions from liquids moving in opposite directions.

An automatic amino acid analyzer, left, separated, analyzed, and recorded amino acids, the building blocks of protein molecules and of DNA. The device worked around the clock unattended, freeing up researchers for higher-level work.

Abbott radiomedicine staff were trained on safe and effective handling of radioisotopes. The recording gamma spectrometer at the right identified and measured gamma rays emitted by isotopes. The three-month class was recognized by the United States Atomic Energy Commission.

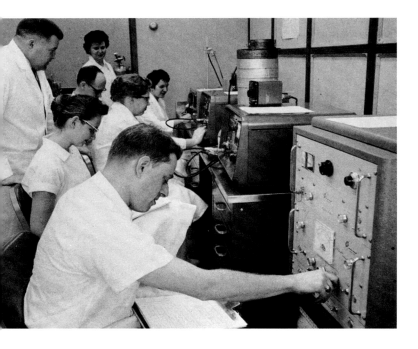

Glasky and Holper went on to discover that enzymes responsible for the growth of viruses are blocked by interferons. These are the natural proteins the immune system produces to enhance the body's response to viruses and other invaders, that is, to "interfere" with these interlopers. Such research had considerable impact down the road, as a number of companies have produced interferon drugs to fight cancer, multiple sclerosis, and other diseases.

By this time, much of Abbott's R&D was in fundamental science or, as Cain called it, "our search for more basic knowledge of the cause of disease." The research labs featured esoteric apparatus like the analytical nuclear magnetic resonance spectrometer. Its high-frequency radio wave and strong magnetic field could crack the code of a molecular substance in less than five minutes. Abbott scientists were investigating such subjects as the nature of the immune system, brain and nerve regeneration, the biochemistry of enzymes and cancer-fighting compounds — and the very code of life itself, DNA.

In 1963, product planning and development chief Kirchmeyer took note of the healthcare industry's sense of progress. "When we look back to 1939 now," he stated at a St. Louis College of Pharmacy alumni gathering, "it is hard to believe that we lived in dread of tuberculosis, pneumonia, scarlet fever, polio, and a host of ailments that have since been conquered or alleviated by better drugs and advancing medical techniques."

Radioactive Medicine Comes Home

The decade brought a big change to Abbott's innovative radiopharmaceutical business — a change in location. Since 1952, Abbott had manufactured and shipped its radioactive medicines from its facility in Oak Ridge, Tennessee, the "Atomic City," where raw isotopes were readily available from the nearby federal nuclear lab. But over time Abbott was able to produce, or to obtain from General Electric and Union Carbide, 90 percent of its raw radioactive materials.

Given the short half lives of radiomedicines, and the resultant need to quickly transport them, it made sense to move the business and most of the 50 Abbott workers back home.

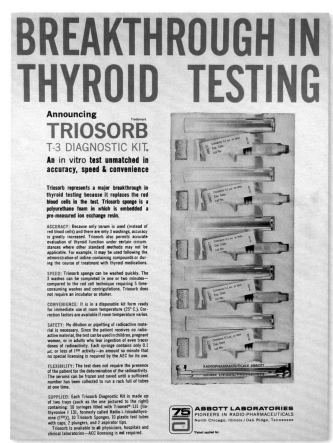

The *Triosorb* testing kit represented a technological milestone on Abbott's path from radiomedicine to modern medical diagnostics and the formation of its world-leading diagnostics business.

The newly positioned nuclear facility was sited at the new headquarters under construction in Abbott Park, in Lake County, Illinois, five miles from the North Chicago site. The 44,000-square-foot atomic installation contained six "hot labs" for making raw isotopes, as well as sterile preparation areas and a quality control space.

The facility had the strictest safety codes. Workers donned leaded hoods and protective gloves to manipulate radioactive materials shielded behind thick blocks of glass. Thousands of yards of ventilation pipe whisked away any stray radioactive air particles. By the mid-1960s, Abbott was making 30 isotopes for more than 130 different pharmaceuticals. It was also supplying about 50 items of equipment for storing and administering the medicines.

Innovative work continued at the new site. Its scientists produced small amounts of radio-iodoinsulin for studying the action of insulin in diabetics. And the *Triosorb* Diagnostic Kit tested blood serum without exposing a patient to radiation, exposure that required a license from the government's nuclear watchdog agency. With the kit, a physician took a sample of a patient's blood, placed into it a radioactive form of a thyroid hormone, then tested and compared that to healthy serum. It was easier, and safer, for all concerned.

Greater Diversity, Faster Growth

Under George Cain, Abbott moved aggressively to acquire other firms, a strategy the company had not followed since the 1930s.

One deal that was not to be, began in a way somewhat reminiscent of Dr. Burdick and S. DeWitt Clough's 1930 purchase of The Dermatological Research Laboratories.

Then Burdick and Clough had rushed off from a golf course for a meeting vital to the acquisition. In this instance, in 1963, Cain was playing at the Old Elm Golf Course in Lake Forest, Illinois, with Jack Searle, General Manager of the pharmaceutical firm G.D. Searle & Co. In between shots, Cain brought up the notion of a merger. The companies seemed almost destined to combine, given their closely shared history. It was the Searle firm that had bought the old Abbott Ravenswood print and production plants in 1925. Both companies had started up in Chicago the same year, 1888. Both were very successful, and had bought up large, adjacent tracts of land to expand in Lake County. Further, the companies' product lines were highly complementary.

Abbott was trending toward a more consumer-oriented product line at the time, and Searle offered two of the day's best-known over-the-counter medicines: the motion sickness drug Dramamine, and the laxative Metamucil. Searle was also known for a substance of growing popularity in the '60s — Enovid, an oral contraceptive popularly known as "The Pill."

In the summer of 1963, the boards of Abbott and Searle agreed on the financial aspects of a merger. George R. Cain was to be president and chief executive officer, and his friend Jack Searle would be chairman of the board. Even a new name was agreed on: Abbott-Searle, Inc. It seemed a done deal.

The sticking point came in trying to merge the personnel of the two companies into one smoothly operating concern. For 10 weeks, Abbott and Searle puzzled over how to resolve this matter. In the end they could not, and the "match made in heaven" was called off.

With the Searle proposition ended, Abbott resumed negotiations that had been taking place with M&R Dietetic Laboratories. This Columbus, Ohio-based firm was prominent in consumables, notably Similac, a popular infant formula and Pream, a well-known coffee creamer.

M&R Dietetics had started up in 1903, as the Moores & Ross Milk Company after founders Harry C. Moores and Stanley M. Ross. In 1925, they began making a milk-based infant formula, soon named Similac. It proved so in-demand that Moores and Ross sold their milk business to a well-known, neighboring firm, Borden, and changed their company name to M&R Dietetics, which focused on formula. Stanley Ross' son, Richard, headed the firm at the time of its negotiations with Abbott.

By the late 1940s, Similac had become the most popular infant formula in the United States. By 1956, M&R Dietetics was performing research into improved, more nutritious milk-based formulas. In 1959, the innovative nutrition firm had introduced Similac with Iron, which addressed anemia in babies who were not receiving mother's milk.

In 1961, to meet growing demand for Similac in Europe, M&R built a plant in the Dutch city of Zwolle. In the 1960s, M&R scientists created Isomil, a soy-based formula for children who could not digest cow's milk. The firm also developed Pedialyte, an electrolyte and carbohydrate solution for children affected by dehydration brought on by diarrhea or vomiting.

As a "tot," M&R President Richard M. Ross (below) had appeared on the label of his father's new baby formula. Called Franklin Infant Food, it was named after a former brewery that had occupied the company's plant. Ross grew up to head his father's firm, M&R Dietetics, and then Abbott's Ross Laboratories Division after Abbott acquired the company.

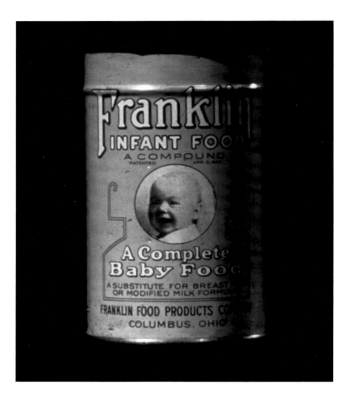

The next year, backed by its acquired resources, Abbott's new Ross Laboratories Division broke ground on a $3.2 million technical center in Columbus, Ohio. Its centerpiece was a five-story, 60,000-square-foot research center. A two-story pilot plant and an office building were also constructed.

Some might have thought sales of infant formula would fizzle, as the product was acquired at the end of the "baby boom." Yet, even as the U.S. birthrate fell by 18 percent from 1961 to 1967, sales of *Similac* rose almost 50 percent, due largely to Ross' strong relationship with the pediatric medical community.

With Abbott's business in radioactive medicine growing, another natural acquisition seemed to be Nuclear-Chicago, a maker of radiation monitors, film badges, and even a "nuclear slide rule" for making complex atomic-related calculations. By November 1964, the boards and shareholders of both firms had agreed on a merger. But days before it was slated to happen, the Justice Department filed an antitrust suit. Both Abbott and Nuclear-Chicago protested that the coupling would not hurt competition in the nuclear medicine industry.

Continues on page 219 ▶

Similac, the United States' leading infant formula, was the chief prize in Abbott's 1964 acquisition of M&R Dietetic Laboratories, its largest to that time.

M&R and Abbott had been close to a merger until the Searle situation had intervened and, in February 1964, the two firms struck a major deal. To acquire M&R, Abbott exchanged 365,000 shares of its stock, worth $42 million. M&R's president, Richard M. Ross, became Abbott's largest shareholder, and president of the new Ross Laboratories Division of Abbott. M&R products received the benefit of Abbott's worldwide distribution network. Abbott got entree into major consumer markets. In the years ahead, *Similac* would spearhead Abbott's growing role in nutrition.

In the 1920s, chemist Dr. Alfred Bosworth created Similac, the first human-milk infant formula, on the Boston Floating Hospital. The ship was built in 1906 to aid indigent women with sick children. The firm M&R Dietetics commercially produced Bosworth's formula. In acquiring M&R, Abbott gained Similac.

Ohio Governor James A. Rhodes cut the ribbon during ceremonies for Ross Labs' new technical center, opened in 1966. Dick Ross, president of Abbott's Ross Laboratories Division, happily looked on at right.

A Diamond of an Anniversary

In 1963, Abbott marked its 75th anniversary as a company. The milestone was celebrated with exhibits, artwork, company gatherings, and other commemorations.

In the 1960s, multimedia exhibits became all the rage, and Abbott created one called "Chemical Man" as its diamond anniversary "gift to the American people." It depicted the molecular and microscopic underpinnings of human life through microphotography, animation, narration, and three-dimensional models. Of "Chemical Man" President Cain stated: "We hope that at the very least the exhibit creates a sense of wonder and awe at the miracle of life. At the most we hope it stimulates younger people toward an interest in scientific careers." The exhibit debuted in 1963 at Chicago's Museum of Science and Industry. A duplicate was created for the 1964–65 New York World's Fair.

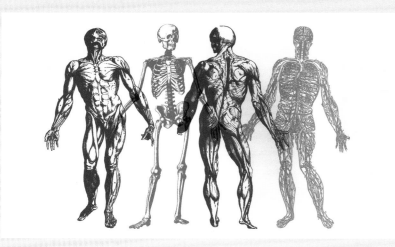

A companion brochure to the exhibit explored the biochemistry of man from different angles. It started with man as a whole, then delved into smaller components of life: cells, molecules, DNA.

As a diamond anniversary gift, Owens-Illinois, the world's largest maker of bottles, presented Abbott with a mounting of the 200,000,000th IV bottle that had rolled off of Abbott's assembly lines.

For six years, one of Abbott's most unusual products was a golf ball. It was one of the products acquired along with Faultless Rubber, a company purchased by Abbott to produce rubber for medical uses such as tubing, hot water bottles, and nipples for baby bottles. U.S. Open golf champ Lee Trevino sang the praises of its Faultless golf ball: "Endorse it?" said Trevino. "Hell, man … I play it!"

That year another move, on the surface an unexpected one, was made into consumer products. Abbott bought Faultless Rubber — makers, among many other products, of the Faultless golf ball.

Back in 1923, Faultless founder T.W. Miller, Sr. had worked out the production process for a one-piece golf ball. It was glued together out of rubber, sulfur, and zinc oxide. The ball was placed in registered molds to form the dimples, then vulcanized. After the fringe at the equator of the sphere was removed, the ball was boiled, dipped in a gutta-percha and balata solvent, and lacquered. Sadly, when struck, the ball often broke into pieces. But four decades of refinements had rendered the Faultless golf ball the choice of the pros.

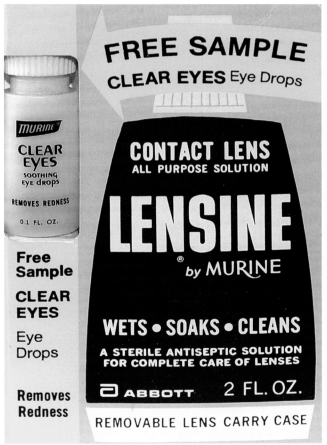

As part of its movement into consumer products, Abbott acquired the Murine Company of Chicago, a well-known maker of eye-care products.

A trial was set for May 1965. Then the government postponed the case until autumn. Meanwhile the judge who was to preside over the trial retired, causing another delay. Faced with legal uncertainty and high legal costs, Abbott and Nuclear-Chicago that autumn called off the deal.

Ironically, Nuclear-Chicago was eventually acquired by G.D. Searle & Co., the firm with which Abbott had also almost merged.

In the 1960s, Abbott had various products aimed at a broader consumer market. The fourth row of this array of Abbott product families featured such popular examples as *Sucaryl, Pream,* and vitamins like *Vi-Daylin.* Yet the company held to its enduring strength in pharmaceuticals. The bottom row includes such mainstays as *Eutonyl* for hypertension, the antibiotic *Erythrocin,* and the anesthetics *Pentothal* and *Penthrane.*

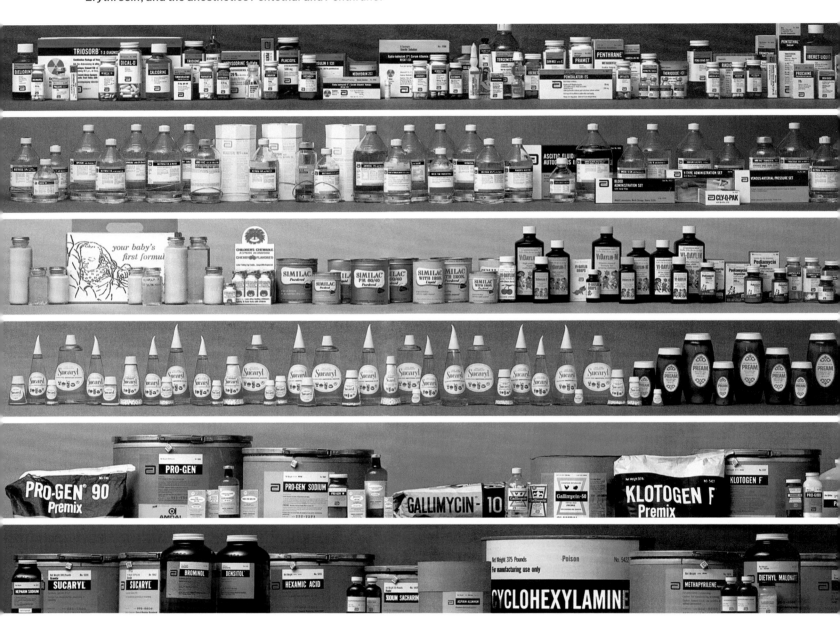

The acquisition of Faultless was done for 110,554 shares of stock, worth $4 million. The purchase was not quite the odd-couple match that it seemed. Faultless was a rubber manufacturer based in Ashland, near Akron, Ohio, the home of Goodyear Tire and Rubber Co. and many other firms making rubber-related products. It had developed many hospital products, such as the first medical tubing for battlefield wounds, as well as the first molded hot water bottle, and household gloves, catheters, and nursing nipples for baby bottles, a good fit with the new Ross Laboratories Division.

Abbott ended the decade with another foray into household-name consumer products, with its 1969 purchase of Chicago's Murine Company. Entering its stable were *Murine* eye drops, *Lensine* solution for contact lenses, and *Clear Eyes* to relieve dry, red, itchy eyes. To make the deal, worth $13.2 million, Abbott again drew on its reserves of stock, some 171,000 shares' worth.

Abbott's first joint venture, and Japan's first endeavor in radiopharmaceuticals, took the form of Dainabot Radioisotope Laboratories, Ltd., located near Tokyo. The deal showcased Abbott's ever-growing international presence.

A Global Concern

George Cain intensified Abbott's ongoing growth in the global marketplace. Like his global-minded father, Cain was very aware of the importance of international trade.

"Up to the present time," he stated, "we have operated as have so many typical American companies — as an American organization, domiciled in the United States, with a splinter organization out to the side that we called a 'foreign operation.' I don't like the word 'foreign' because I think it connotes strangers, who perhaps aren't particularly welcome."

In 1962, an Abbott subsidiary in Switzerland forged a joint venture with Dainippon Pharmaceutical Co., Ltd, a Japanese firm based in Osaka. Called Dainabot Radioisotope Laboratories, Ltd., it manufactured radiopharmaceuticals at a processing plant set up in a suburb of Tokyo. Coming 17 years after the atomic bombing of Hiroshima, it was Japan's first company operating in the nuclear field. It was also Abbott's first joint venture.

The enterprise was highly unusual for the time, as few U.S. firms had penetrated the Japanese market. "Normally the Japanese government prefers that Japanese firms hold majority interest in any joint operation," stated President Cain. But because of Abbott's unique skills with isotopes, the venture equally split investment and earnings between the two firms.

Two years later, in 1964, Abbott joined a second venture with Dainippon to market Abbott's products in Japan. The company, called Nippon-Abbott K.K., was another mark of Abbott's long-established, and fast-growing, skill in setting up shop overseas. The three companies merged in 1983 to form Dainabot Co., Ltd.

Also in 1965, Abbott followed up on its earlier construction of plants in France and the United Kingdom. It formed another joint venture, Deutsche-Abbott GmbH, with the large German drugmaker C.H. Boehringer Sohn. In three years, Abbott had set up three companies in the two largest Asian and European markets.

Abbott was on its way to becoming a truly global manufacturing concern. Abbott Laboratories, Ltd. of England started up operations in a massive new plant in Queenborough, Kent. The site served as a gateway for Abbott's strategic and growing presence in Europe. Other plants went online in Italy and Australia.

Back in 1957, Dr. Volwiler had helped lay the foundation for the cooperative venture with Dainippon Pharmaceutical Co. by meeting with its president, Mr. Tokujiro Miyatake.

President Cain's determination for overseas expansion was underscored by a new, 250,000-square-foot manufacturing plant in Kent, England.

Cain sounded like a prophet of the coming world of multinational corporations: "It is my firm conviction," he stated, "that this company, to maximize its greatest potential, must become truly an international company … You can't run a large company today by just sitting in North Chicago … This world is shrinking. If we are going to make investments overseas and do the job we should do both here and overseas, we must begin to think of ourselves as a truly integrated, international company."

By the mid-1960s, *Abbottempo*, a new medical journal oriented toward an international audience, had replaced the revered, long-running *What's New*. As the cover art indicates, the new publication retained the sophistication of the old. This 1965 cover uses the painting "At the Moulin Rouge" by Henri de Toulouse-Lautrec.

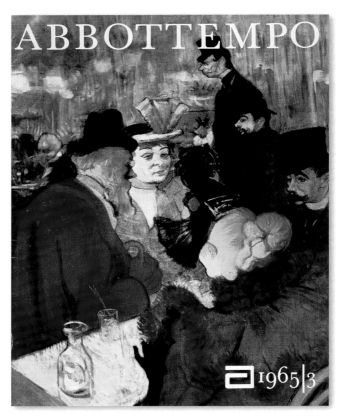

While Abbott Park was under construction, the North Chicago research center continued to house the company's R&D organization. Here the entire staff gathered outside of the now-venerable facility, which was cutting edge when it opened in 1938.

The Products of Research and Investment

Seven years of research and commensurate investment in R&D generated the hypertension drug *Eutonyl,* launched in 1963. Hypertension is the long-term constriction of blood vessels and arterioles, their smaller cousins. In Abbott's labs, scientists had formed more than 1,800 compounds. The 911th compound, called MO-911, proved to be an inhibitor of monoamine oxidase, which blocks chemicals that loosen up blood vessels.

Ironically, MO-911, which became *Eutonyl,* while increasing the blocking chemicals, had the mysterious effect of loosening blood vessels and arterioles. With adjustments to dosage, common side effects of other anti-hypertensives — drowsiness, depression, and a "washed out feeling" — were minimized. The drug had the bonus of increasing the alertness and even the mental spirits of patients, thus its name, from the Greek "Eu" (good) and "Tonos" (tone).

By 1968, yearly spending on research was up to $22 million, then $32 million just four years later — about six times more than when Cain became president, in 1958. It was spread around many areas: cardiovascular, glandular and metabolic systems, anti-infectives, and mental health.

"It's like betting on a quinella," noted Cain, "and not knowing which horse will come in."

R&D was a never-ending race. In 1963, 90 percent of Abbott's 600 products had not been around 20 years earlier.

By the late 1960s, the expansive new headquarters at Abbott Park was substantially occupied. Some 4,000 employees were working in the almost three million square feet of building space. The complex contained a three-building research center that housed pathology, toxicology, pharmacology, and other specialties, and a trio of buildings for vaccine production. A radiopharmaceuticals research and manufacturing facility replaced the old one at Oak Ridge. There were also administrative offices, a power plant, and a warehouse that covered seven acres.

Bolstering the Product Line and the Bottom Line

Cain's broad revamping of Abbott started to deliver results as early as 1962. That year, earnings per share rose by 22 percent, the most since 1946, as sales increased by $14 million to $144 million. Profits rose a record 22 percent to $3.72 a share, even as research spending exceeded $10 million. International revenues stood at $39 million, 27 percent of the total, a new high.

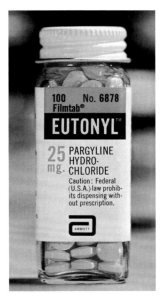

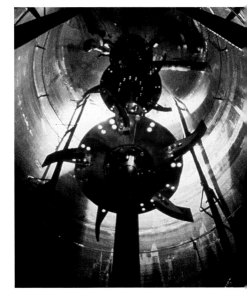

ABOVE
Introduced in 1963, *Eutonyl* not only reduced hypertension, it also increased alertness. Thus its name, from the Greek "Eu" (good) and "Tonos" (tone).

RIGHT
A look down into the giant maw of a 35,000-gallon fermenter. It was used to make such products as the plant growth regulator *Pro-Gibb* and the biological insecticide *Dipel*, as well as *Erythrocin*. Abbott's skill in fermentation allowed it to provide manufacturing services to peer companies. It would also lead to the company's first billion-dollar product, the antibiotic clarithromycin, in the 1990s.

This airborne view from 1965 shows Abbott Park, the company's future world headquarters, under construction. The foreground indicates that Abbott was once again strategically locating its major facilities adjacent to transportation infrastructure. The view is to the northeast, with Lake Michigan and the North Chicago site in the distance.

"This company must be built around individuals; ideas must come from individuals who refuse to be discouraged by company size and bric-a-brac. The contribution of the scientific man, the uncommon man, the man with a sense of urgency, these are the very keystones of our future."

— GEORGE R. CAIN

Industry analysts took notice. Stated *Value Line*: "Heavy research outlays of recent years are on the verge of bearing fruit in immediate and long-term growth for Abbott."

In 1963, the year of merger talks, the stock market viewed Abbott, and Cain's strategy, very favorably. The company's shares reached a record high of $124, gaining 38 percent in a year, and the board announced a three-for-one stock split. Since its stock was first offered in the market crash year of 1929, the value of an Abbott share had risen more than 8,000 percent.

The fruit of research, new products, continued to roll out. *Inpersol* was a dextrose solution set that permitted treatment of acute kidney failure without artificial kidneys. *Enduron* was a once-a-day oral diuretic effective against hypertension and edema, or dropsy, fluid buildup under the skin.

During the Vietnam War, Abbott kept up its tradition of supplying U.S. service personnel near the front lines. A medic made use of donated *Butesin*, the topical anesthetic, to treat a Vietnamese woman left injured and homeless after a fire burned down her refugee camp.

Anesthetics continued to be a mainstay, including the perennial *Nembutal*, first introduced in 1930, and the newer drug *Placidyl,* a treatment for insomnia. *Penthrane* was a powerful, very safe, inhalation anesthetic put on the market after tests in more than 4,000 surgeries.

By the late '60s, pumped by the booming Vietnam War economy nationwide, a stunning surge in sales had occurred. Revenues for 1967 climbed more than $300 million, double those of just five years earlier.

All this growth was achieved without the momentum of any true blockbusters. Said Cain in 1968, with characteristic honesty: "We haven't had a major product introduction since the antibiotic *Erythrocin* eleven years ago." He attributed this in part to the slowness of the drug development and approval process.

Acquiring Strength in Diagnostics

Meanwhile, in October 1967, Abbott made another acquisition, this time in an innovative area of diagnostics. It purchased Courtland Laboratories of Los Angeles. Courtland was a leader in the detection of Rubella, or German measles. If contracted during the first three months of pregnancy by a woman without immunity to the disease, Rubella can cause a high incidence of birth defects.

Courtland also pioneered in blood fractions, or components of blood, such as immune gamma globulin for hepatitis, normal serum albumin for shock and burns, and another blood fraction to treat hemophilia. The company also produced blood collection tubes and anti-coagulants.

The Rubella Antibody Detection Kit contained all nine components for detecting the disease's viral antibodies in pregnant women. It was the first in a projected series of diagnostic sets. The kits helped establish a trend in diagnostics: They were not only accurate and inexpensive, they were easy to use. In future years, patients would increasingly self-test, and self-administer medications, saving much time and expense.

The newly acquired concern also performed research on reagents, the substances that help trigger a chemical reaction. Abbott established a new production facility at its headquarters complex to make diagnostic reagents to identify and diagnose microbial and viral diseases, as well as those related to rickets. Within two years, the center had developed a diagnostic kit to detect hepatitis as well as a line of blood grouping and typing serums and reagents essential to diagnostic testing.

In the coming decades, Abbott's radiomedicine operation, the talent and expertise acquired from Courtland, and other testing operations, would blossom into an industry-leading global diagnostics business.

Continues on page 228 ▶

An Abbott employee fielded questions at a local elementary school. As part of its community service programs, Abbott sent employees into schools to lecture on such diverse topics as careers in biology and chemistry and the dangers of illicit drug use.

George R. Cain

Mild, even diffident in person, George Cain took Abbott, in the words of the best-selling business analyst Jim Collins, from "Good to Great."

George Cain restructured Abbott along more rational reporting lines, and devised financial metrics to more accurately measure performance. Yet Cain was vigorous behind the scenes, often an advocate, as he termed his problem-solving approach, of "just plain putting more push and muscle into it."

He was born in Noblesville, Indiana, and attended Williams College. Although his father, Rolly Cain, had been president of Swan-Myers, George Cain started his working life as an insurance broker. The tall, lanky young man labored for seven years in insurance. He mastered health statistics and, at Abbott, would apply numerical analysis to great effect.

He joined Abbott in 1940, rising in seven years to assistant sales manager. He then undertook something rather like a "presidential training program." He served as assistant to President Raymond Horn, as executive vice president, and as secretary, and then chairman of the Executive Committee for Dr. Volwiler.

President George R. Cain brought Abbott into the modern era. Courtly yet dynamic, Cain broke with precedent by bringing in outside leadership, and made the firm's first major acquisition in decades. He applied the scientific method to gauge results and reorganize the company. The results: Shareholder returns that beat the market 4.5 to 1.

> "He could not stand mediocrity in any form and was utterly intolerant of anyone who would accept the idea that good is good enough."
>
> — JIM COLLINS IN HIS BLOCKBUSTER BOOK *GOOD TO GREAT*

When he was made company president in 1958, at age 48, Cain broke with tradition at the tightly knit firm by bringing in high-profile executives from outside the company. Going against type and expectation, it may have taken a consummate insider to bring in new blood from outside.

"Cain made it clear," wrote Jim Collins in *Good to Great*, "that neither family ties nor length of tenure would have anything to do with whether you held a key position in the company." Serving as chairman for 10 years, Cain completely changed the makeup of the board of directors, from Abbott-only to a group with high-level executive and scientific talent from a range of outside organizations.

Nonetheless, in choosing his own successor as president, Cain went with an Abbott man who knew the company inside-out: Edward J. Ledder, who had worked at Abbott for almost three decades at the time.

Cain also kept his focus on the future and the world beyond Abbott by acquiring outside firms, most notably M&R Dietetic Laboratories, which became Abbott's Ross Laboratories Division and now, as Abbott Nutrition, remains a major growth driver to this day. "From 1929 until 1964 there was no major diversification at Abbott," Cain noted. And with the purchase of Courtland Labs, Faultless Rubber, and the Murine Company, he laid the groundwork for a major shift to consumer products and pointed the direction for the company's growing diagnostics business. Cain also advanced new hospital products, which would be a driving force of the 1970s and 1980s.

Through it all, Cain hewed to the highest standards. "He could not stand mediocrity in any form," noted Collins, in his study of the highest-performing corporations, "and was utterly intolerant of anyone who would accept the idea that good is good enough."

Still, Cain knew how to kick back. He was "very good with a gun and a fishing rod," noted executive vice president Paul Gerden. "And also with a pool cue and a deck of cards." The Abbott leader had a special fondness for duck hunting. Such pursuits showed perhaps the influence of his father, a man responsible for Abbott's Rod and Gun Club.

Assured and confident, Cain often lent his expertise to other organizations. He served on the boards of International Harvester and Illinois Bell Telephone, was a trustee of Northwestern University, an officer of Evanston Hospital in Illinois, and a director of the Hospital Research and Education Trust. When he died suddenly in 1972, at age 61, he left behind his wife Jane, his three sons, and three grandchildren — as well as a bigger, stronger Abbott and a rock-solid foundation for the many challenges faced by his successor. ∎

Abbott's tour guides pose in front of the North Chicago research center. This corps welcomed visitors — including pharmacy students, physicians, and customers — and led them on tours of the company's ever-expanding manufacturing, research & development, and distribution operations.

A Period of Transition

As the son of an Abbott president, Cain had been born to manage, and he continued refining his leadership team. In 1966, he promoted Dr. Charles S. Brown, the United States and Canada chief, to executive vice president, with lead science and manufacturing duties. Cain made pharmaceutical marketing vice president Edward J. "Ted" Ledder part of the key Operations Committee.

Ted Ledder carried a heavy load: He was put in charge of pharmaceuticals, the nutrition division, other consumer products, and a revamped radiopharmaceuticals group. Ledder had started with Abbott in 1939 as an assembly line worker, his starting wage at 47 cents an hour. Continuing a remarkable ascent through the ranks, Ledder was made executive vice president the succeeding year.

Abbott now had five major segments: pharmaceuticals, hospital products and services, pediatric products like *Similac*, consumer and industrial brands, and the fast-moving international group.

In 1967, Cain made an even bigger move. He vacated the position of president — and filled it with Ted Ledder. Cain remained chief executive officer and chairman of the board while he groomed his successor. The two were to make a formidable team, with each complementing the other's strengths. Cain, an executive's executive, a man of vision and foresight; Ledder, up from the factory floor, a shirt-sleeved, pragmatist who knew how to get things done right.

In 1969, Dick Ross retired as head of the Ross Laboratories Division, and joined the board. Ross was replaced by the high-energy David O. Cox, who, 31 years prior, had joined M&R, Ross' precursor, as a salesman.

In 1968, Cain revealed another reorganization. Abbott now had six divisions: pharmaceuticals, hospital products, Ross, consumer products, international, and group operations. Each division had its own staff for research, manufacturing, and marketing. Each was its own profit center. Thus, the costs and revenues of each could be readily calculated. Cain had, in large measure, achieved the scientifically managed firm he had long envisioned.

To add expertise to the revamped, ever-growing corporation, Cain kept bringing in outside talent to the Board. These included: Dr. Emanuel M. Papper, dean of the University of Miami's School of Medicine, who had earlier been a noted anesthesiologist at Columbia University; Donald M. Graham, chairman of Continental

Edward J. "Ted" Ledder was named Abbott's president in 1967, highlighting an extraordinary rise from the shop floor, where he had joined the company in 1939.

Chief Financial Officer Bernard H. Semler provided the disciplined business systems that allowed George R. Cain to take Abbott "from good to great."

Illinois National Bank; Gilbert H. Scribner, Jr., president of the publisher Scribner & Co.; Boone Powell, vice president, and later CEO, of Baylor University Medical Center; and James L. Allen, a pioneer of professional management consulting, and chairman of Booz-Allen & Hamilton, Inc., the consulting firm that advised Cain on Abbott's restructuring. By 1970, six of the 14 board members were from outside the company, up from two in 1958, a quantum leap in corporate governance.

In Cain's favored field of metrics, Abbott further linked the performance of employees to the bottom line. In 1968, it brought in Bernard H. Semler as vice president, Finance, who developed a new approach to corporate finance called "responsibility accounting." Semler tied every cost and revenue, however small, to an individual employee responsible for it. Every manager was held responsible for his or her "return on investment." The approach helped Abbott drive down its administrative expenses to the lowest among its rivals.

> ## "Things don't just happen, they must be made to happen, therefore, they must be planned."
>
> — BERNARD H. SEMLER

Yet, at the same time, creativity was strongly encouraged. "On the one hand," noted the book *Good to Great*, "Abbott recruited entrepreneurial leaders and gave them freedom to determine the best path to achieving their objectives. On the other hand, individuals … were held rigorously accountable for their objectives. They had freedom, but freedom within a framework." But a flexible framework. Stated a company executive, "We recognized that planning is priceless, but plans are useless."

Great Taste, Bad Data

As the 1960s closed, even as Abbott was enjoying record sales, a problem cropped up that soon became one of the largest product issues in Abbott's history.

In October 1969, an Abbott-funded study found that laboratory rats fed an extraordinary amount of cyclamate, the sweetener in *Sucaryl,* had developed an abnormal number of bladder tumors. The amount of cyclamate consumed in the study was equivalent to a human drinking 350 cans of diet soda per day. Abbott immediately turned over the findings to the U.S. FDA, the National Cancer Institute, and the Department of Health, Education, and Welfare.

Abbott had been concerned about the possibility of tighter regulation of *Sucaryl* for some time. In 1968, Cain had stated, "There have been some scare headlines on the effects of cyclamates." He attributed these to "sugar interests." But, he added that, "We have done as much research on *Sucaryl* and cyclamates as on any other product. They are completely safe and the FDA has repeatedly supported this."

But now, in fall 1969, the federal authorities announced: "We have no evidence at this point that cyclamates have indeed caused cancer in humans.

"Even so, we have no recourse but to restrict their use."

Under this order, *Sucaryl* had to be pulled from the shelves. Its use was restricted to those with a medical need.

The *Sucaryl* issue would vex Abbott. But a more urgent product issue was soon to arise that would test the company to its core and make it a stronger and better competitor for the future.

Decade at a Glance

1960–1970

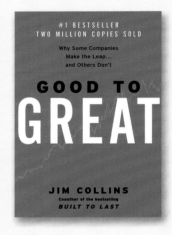

1960 ▲
Abbott's restructuring in the 1960s under President George R. Cain would be featured in the 2001 best-seller *Good to Great: Why Some Companies Make the Leap … and Others Don't*. Author Jim Collins chose Abbott as one of 11 companies – out of 1,435 – that had the product, service, organizational, and people quality to engender truly great performance.

The year is also marked by the deaths of former Board Chairman S. DeWitt Clough and former President Raymond E. Horn.

Tennessee Senator Estes Kefauver continues highly publicized congressional hearings that criticize the pharmaceutical industry for the allegedly high cost of its products.

In response to a *Life* magazine article critiquing the drug industry, Abbott takes out a paid editorial in the publication that points out the relatively low cost of healthcare (in 1959 roughly $94 per person in the United States, just $18 of which is from pharmaceuticals).

1961
President Cain restructures the company, reducing the number of senior officers and disbanding various committees. Profits per employee are made an important performance metric.

▲
President Cain parts from tradition by bringing in many outside executives to Abbott's Board of Directors. This image shows the board, reconstituted in the early 1960s.

Dr. Volwiler testifies before the U.S. Congress, warning that proposals to reduce patent protections for medical products could decrease incentives for developing them. Abbott publishes various ads and op-ed pieces highlighting the value of market competition and physicians' free choice of medical goods.

The eight-story research building in North Chicago, construction of which had begun in 1958, is occupied by 1961. The top of the building sports the new Abbott "A" logo.

▼

1962
Chairman of the Board Elmer B. Vliet, retires.

▼

In response to the tragedy of "thalidomide babies," infants born in Europe with birth defects due to a sedative taken by their mothers, the Pharmaceutical Manufacturers Association sets up a Commission on Drug Safety. The chairman is Dr. Lowell T. Coggeshall, an Abbott Board member and University of Chicago vice president.

Abbott opens a large new manufacturing site in France.

Abbott's first joint venture, and Japan's first endeavor in radiopharmaceuticals, is with the Japanese firm Dainippon Pharmaceutical Co., Ltd. The venture is called Dainabot Radioisotope Laboratories, Ltd.

▼

1963
Abbott scientists Dr. Jacob C. Holper and Dr. Alvin J. Glasky conduct cutting-edge research with RNA, DNA, and interferons — proteins that enhance the body's immune system. They perform important work on spurring and preventing the growth of viral ailments.

▼

Abbott introduces the hyper-tension drug *Eutonyl*.

The company comes close to merging with nearby pharmaceutical firm G.D. Searle & Co., but the planned merger falls through.

1964
The company moves its radio-medicine business from Oak Ridge, Tennessee, to the new headquarters under construction at Abbott Park, in Lake County, Illinois. Throughout the decade, building continues apace at Abbott Park.

The company acquires M&R Dietetic Laboratories, the manufacturer of Similac and other infant formulas. M&R's president, Richard Ross, becomes president of the new Ross Laboratories Division of Abbott. Ross spearheads Abbott's growing role in nutritionals.

Abbott joins a second joint venture with Dainippon, called Nippon-Abbott K.K., to market Abbott's products in Japan.

1965

Ohio Governor James A. Rhodes cuts the ribbon during ceremonies for Ross Labs' new technical center, complete with a five-story, 60,000-square-foot laboratory. Richard M. Ross, president of the division, looks on at the right.

Abbott purchases Faultless Rubber, maker of hot water bottles, catheters, nursing nipples, and Faultless golf balls, endorsed by U.S. Open golf champ Lee Trevino.

Abbott forms a joint venture, Deutsche-Abbott GmbH, with the major German drugmaker C.H. Boehringer Sohn.

New buildings are constructed in Abbott Park, soon to be the company's new world headquarters, throughout the decade.

1967

Abbott's continuous international expansion is highlighted by construction of an antibiotics facility in Puerto Rico that has a processing plant, fermentation building, and a facility for concentrating waste material.

Edward J. "Ted" Ledder takes over George Cain's role as president, with Cain remaining as chief executive officer and chairman of the board.

Abbott acquires the diagnostics firm Courtland Laboratories, a leader in the detection of Rubella, or German measles.

1968

CFO Bernard H. Semler applies to Abbott "responsibility accounting" in corporate finance. Every cost is tied to an individual employee responsible for it, and every manager is responsible for his or her "return on investment."

Spending on research reaches $22 million, roughly five times more than in 1958.

Chairman Cain reorganizes Abbott into six divisions: pharmaceuticals, hospital products, Ross Laboratories Division, consumer products, international, and group operations.

1969

An Abbott-funded study finds that laboratory rats fed extraordinary amounts of cyclamate, the sweetener in *Sucaryl*, have developed an abnormal number of bladder tumors. The federal government orders that use of *Sucaryl* be restricted to people with a medical need.

Abbott buys Chicago's Murine Company, acquiring its *Murine* eye drops, *Lensine* solution for contact lenses, and *Clear Eyes* for dry, red, itchy eyes.

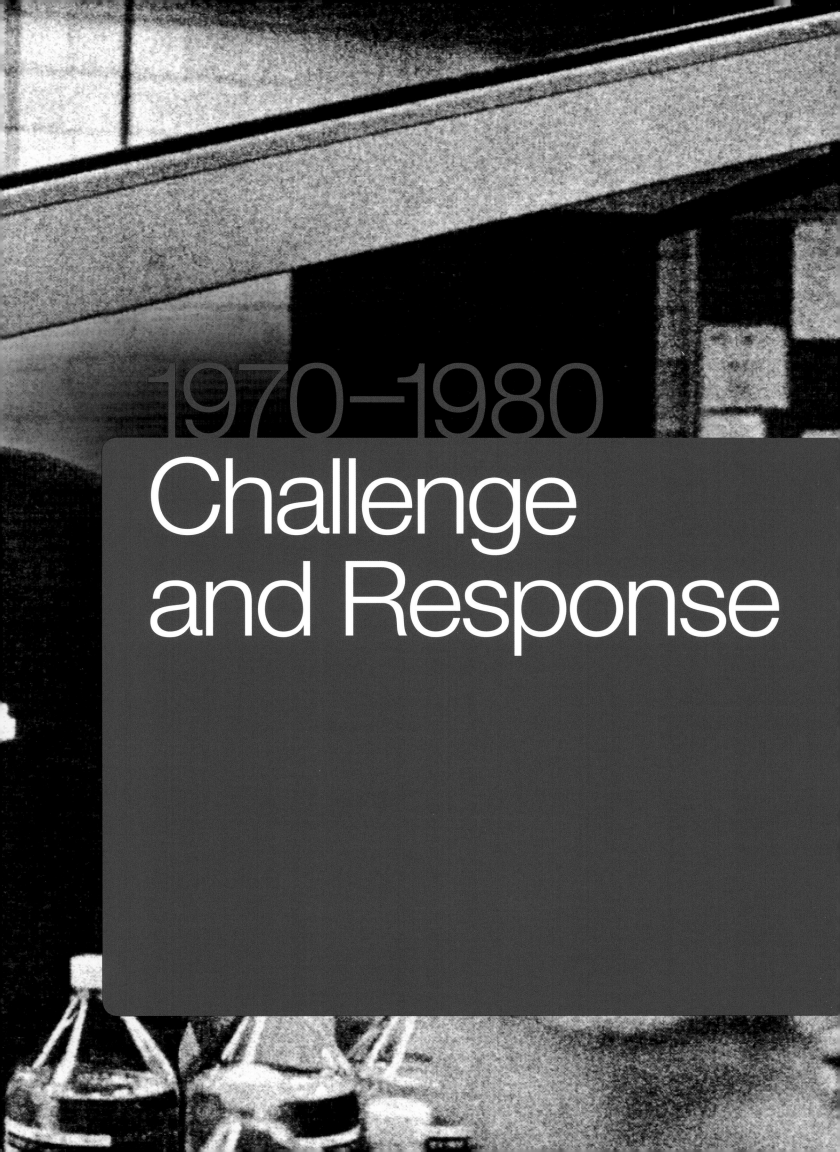

1970–1980
Challenge and Response

Throughout April 1971, President Edward J. Ledder drove to the office with little but dire news in mind. For Abbott, the early 1970s recalled the 1905–1908 period. Then, the company had endured a great fire, a financial panic, and a spat with a leading medical journal, only to grow bigger and more prosperous. Now, Ledder reflected, it faced a ban on its profitable sweetener *Sucaryl*, a recall on an industry-topping line of hospital goods, and contention with regulators seeking to impose restrictive measures. Later, President Ledder would admit, "There were days when I didn't even want to drive to work." Yet, as before, Abbott would take on the most trying circumstances, and, in the end, come out ahead.

PREVIOUS SPREAD
Chairman George R. Cain and President Edward J. Ledder inspect a solutions bottling line. Ensuring the quality and safety of these products would provide a major challenge, which would spur the company to a new level of success.

An Abbott icon was revealed at the company's growing Abbott Park headquarters in 1969. The "A" tower stood 100 feet high with 164 bulbs in its four "A"s. Facing in all directions, it announced the company's presence as Lake County's largest private employer. In 1973, the tower temporarily went dark in recognition of the energy crisis gripping the country.

Chemical & Engineering NEWS

OCTOBER 27, 1969

CYCLAMATES

Shock, confusion follow ban   20

At the start of the 1970s, the U.S. FDA forbade the use of cyclamate, the sweetener in *Sucaryl*. For two decades, the substance had been a widely used ingredient in confections and diet colas, prized by dieters and people with diabetes, and no harm to humans was ever suggested.

In August 1970, the United States Food and Drug Administration (FDA), following on its restriction of *Sucaryl*, Abbott's low-calorie sweetener, to medical needs, banned use of the cyclamate sweetener in the United States altogether. Financially, it stung. Abbott lost almost four percent in annual sales as a result. The agency based its action on the 1958 Delaney Amendment to the Food Additive Laws. The Amendment stated that no additive can be sold that, when fed to a lab animal or person, causes an above-normal incidence of tumors. The science behind the ruling was puzzling to many.

From Sweet to Sour

For 25 years Abbott had conducted extensive research, started by none other than Dr. Volwiler, which showed the inexpensive food additive and table sweetener to be safe for human consumption.

Abbott suspected that competitive interests threatened by *Sucaryl* favored its prohibition. Sugar companies were already conducting research trying to impugn the safety of artificial sweeteners.

The director of research for a sugar industry foundation even admitted: "We are funding research on cyclamates because if anyone can undersell you nine cents out of ten, you'd better find some brickbat to throw at him." The sugar interests, reported *The New York Times*, had spent more than $500,000 since 1965 on such research.

Ensuing research indicated cyclamate was safe. In 1973, for example, the German Cancer Research Center reported on a study in which laboratory rats were fed, for their entire lives, amounts of cyclamate equivalent to about 300 bottles of diet cola a day. Of 882 rats, only one got bladder cancer — from a condition unrelated to consuming cyclamate.

In the 1970s, Abbott expanded its two production plants in Rocky Mount, North Carolina. The facilities would play a big role in reviving the company's line of IV products, temporarily recalled due to concerns over contamination. The installations included quality control labs and an 87,000-square-foot warehouse.

Through the rest of the decade, Abbott requested, at considerable legal expense, that the U.S. FDA reinstate cyclamates as a non-prescription sweetener. After its petition was denied in 1980, Richard W. Kasperson, Abbott's vice president of Regulatory Affairs, stated: "The FDA's decision does a disservice to science and the American public, particularly to diabetics and others who for health reasons need an artificial sweetener." Kasperson noted that many European and Latin American countries allowed commercial use of cyclamate "because their governments have evaluated the same evidence and found cyclamate safe."

In 1984, the FDA, based on new evidence, concluded that cyclamate was not cancer-causing. Its Cancer Assessment Committee reported "that the collective weight of many experiments … indicates that cyclamate is not carcinogenic." From Abbott's perspective, the agency's conclusion was moot, as by then it was essentially out of the synthetic sweetener business in the United States.

The Recall

On top of the *Sucaryl* ban, another full-blown crisis erupted. In March 1971, eight hospitals reported blood infections from evidently contaminated cap liners on Abbott's IV solution bottles. Government agencies noted that, although the unopened solution bottles were sterile, they might have been contaminated by putting the caps back on after removal. Tragically, nine deaths were reported from patients administered intravenous fluids.

"A lot of hospitals loved the screw caps," ruefully recalled Charles J. Aschauer, Jr., who served as head of the Hospital Products Division and Abbott's executive vice president. "They could unscrew the cap and drop something in, an additive, and then screw the cap back on."

Abbott immediately suspended all shipments of its IV solutions. It started a massive and painstaking recall of IV solutions from hospitals around the United States.

IV kits were at that time Abbott's biggest product line. The company had held 45 percent of the American IV solutions market. Overnight, its share dropped to 0 percent.

The IV woes knocked $19 million off of Abbott's 1971 before-tax profits. The toll was higher in direct and indirect costs; all losses amounted to perhaps $50 million, more than 10 percent of total sales. Sales for 1971 were flat. For several years, the company's earnings and stock price registered the impact.

Things were grim. But Ledder was intent on rising to the occasion, as had his predecessors — Dr. Abbott, during the panic of 1907 and President Clough, during the Great Depression. He knew that Abbott, as the nation's largest maker of life-supporting IV solutions, had to move fast.

Inside of two weeks, Ledder negotiated a deal with Berkeley, California-based Cutter Laboratories. Cutter would help convert Abbott's massive production lines from the screw-cap IV closure, in use since the mid-1930s. In their place would be Cutter's state-of-the-art vacuum-rubber stoppers.

By mid-April, pilot production of the new stoppers began at Abbott plants in Rocky Mount, North Carolina, and in North Chicago, Illinois. In June, the U.S. FDA approved the production processes at Rocky Mount. In July, both facilities ramped up to full-scale production.

Ledder did what he had to in order to regain market share. "You cut price," he recalled, "you reduce your product to commodity status." The tactic worked. By the end of 1971, the company had shipped hospitals 15 million containers of solution, equal to 57 percent of the former volume.

Abbott's plants not only replaced the suspect caps, but expanded into additional hospital products. Ledder noted this neat turning of a "sow's ear to a silk purse": "We started distribution with a limited line of key products, but we're now producing a line which meets more than 90 percent of a hospital's needs."

But Abbott and Ledder were not out of the woods yet. In mid-1972 they received another blow, when Chairman George R. Cain died suddenly of a heart attack.

During dedication ceremonies for the expansion of Abbott's Rocky Mount plant, Chairman George R. Cain, left, met with executives of another high-tech hub in that state. Former North Carolina governor Luther H. Hodges, center, was chairman of the fledgling Research Triangle Park, which would grow into a major research hub, and Ned R. Huffman, right, its executive vice president.

To bounce back from the financial impact of the IV recall and *Sucaryl* ban, Abbott relied on the innovation of its rapidly growing diagnostics group. Lab workers in hospitals and clinics used the *ABA-100* system to determine enzyme levels and analyze blood components.

Cain had been chairman of the board for 10 years and, up to 1967, had served nine years as president. The company was left without the architect of its modern structure, and without the senior half of its successful management team. Ledder was left without his mentor and close partner.

Fortunately, Cain's 1960s reorganization and decentralization of the company served his successor well. Due to Cain's clearly defined lines of responsibility, President Ledder did not have to take on many additional duties. To be sure, he already had more than enough on his plate.

The Next Big Thing: Diagnostics

Despite this series of unexpected blows, Ledder and Abbott rapidly regained their stride.

The comeback from the IV debacle proceeded steadily. Remarkably, by the end of 1972, one year after the recall, Abbott's IV sales had regained their previous levels. Plans were laid to replace the glass IV bottles altogether, with durable plastic ones. Within a few years, new factories for IV containers and tubes were to be built in Barceloneta, Puerto Rico; Altavista, Virginia; and North Chicago, Illinois.

Just as remarkably, in 1972 Abbott's sales hit a new record — exceeding half a billion dollars. Soon the company would enhance not just the IV containers, but their contents, by adding electrolytes and amino acids to the solutions.

But the biggest key to the company's recovery was diagnostics, long an area of accomplishment, and of strategic investment, it would be the next great driver of Abbott's growth.

The year 1972 saw two new diagnostic offerings. One was the *ABA-100* blood chemistry analyzer. The first computer-controlled blood analysis systems were soon monitoring and generating reports from *ABA-100s*. The other offering, from the radiomedicine part of the business, was *Ausria*, a breakthrough radioimmunoassay test for detecting serum hepatitis.

The big news in diagnostics arrived the following year. "We are bringing together all our activities in diagnostic products and services in a new diagnostics division. The functions included biologicals, radiopharmaceuticals, and clinical instrumentation," announced President Ledder.

Among the goals of the consolidation was to devise diagnostic tests that were simple, automated, accurate, and low-cost. A major Abbott focus was now to be disease prevention as well as treatment.

This emphasis on price and on early diagnosis and prevention proved a wise one in the 1970s, a time of inflation, especially regarding the cost of healthcare. Products that held down such costs, by preventing the need for expensive, long-term care, were especially valued by hospitals, doctors, and clinics.

Another societal trend working in Abbott's favor was an explosion in healthcare litigation. In the first half of the 1970s, the cost of medical malpractice insurance rose by more than 500 percent.

"With so many malpractice suits," Ledder explained, "doctors are turning more and more to diagnostics to be sure" their diagnoses were as accurate as technology allowed.

Further, the potential market was immense, with labs and hospitals conducting hundreds of millions of tests each year on tissue and blood samples.

To head up the diagnostics drive, Ledder, as his predecessor Cain was wont to do, tapped new talent. Appointed head of the diagnostics division was *wunderkind* James L. Vincent. Just 35 years old, and with Abbott for less than a year as head of radiopharmaceuticals, Vincent had been president of the Asian division of the large electronics firm Texas Instruments. His background with an electronics firm reflected the increasingly computerized field of diagnostic systems.

Vincent reported to Robert A. Schoellhorn, who held the newly created position of executive vice president of the hospital group. Schoellhorn had joined Abbott after a long tenure with American Cyanamid, the large chemical manufacturer, as president of its Lederle Laboratories division, which made vitamins.

"We recognized that we needed to be more than a pharmaceutical company to grow," recalled Schoellhorn. "We had few new drugs in the pipeline, so we put a heavy banking on diagnostics."

> "We recognized that we needed to be more than a pharmaceutical company to grow."
>
> — ROBERT A. SCHOELLHORN

Both Schoellhorn and Vincent would quickly "earn their spurs," and eventually become Abbott presidents.

New diagnostic products began pouring forth. A follow-up to *Ausria* was *Ausria II*. This radioimmunoassay test cut by 15 hours the incubation time of blood tests. A test now took but a few hours. Blood banks and hospitals could now provide blood for transfusions the same day that the blood was drawn. *Ausria II* was also more sensitive than older tests at detecting possible contaminants.

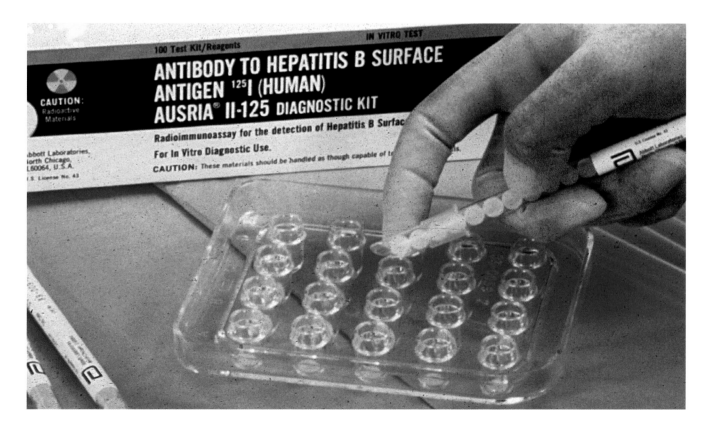

Even as Abbott faced some setbacks in the early 1970s, its new diagnostics division went from strength to strength. Once again, Abbott's business diversity saw it through challenges in other parts of its operations.

At a time of surging success in diagnostics, Abbott's VP clinical analyzer was the most successful diagnostic tool to date. It analyzed blood chemistry at unprecedented speeds.

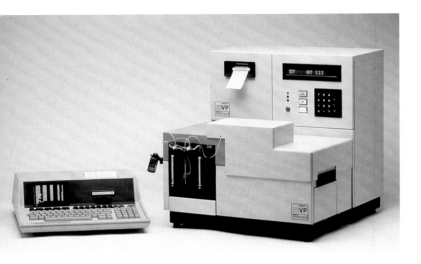

A pioneer in diagnostics since the days of radiomedicine, Abbott continued to advance medical detection technology with new systems such as *Quantum*.

Another new diagnostic tool was *Auscel*. This device had the advantage of employing no radioactive material. It was also inexpensive; even small blood banks could afford it.

Both tests demonstrated the company's growing expertise in detecting hepatitis, which was vital to securing a reliable and safe blood supply. In fact, the federal Bureau of Biologics mandated that all donated blood must be tested only with these advanced tests. In time, Abbott's diagnostics would be used to assure the safety of the majority of the world's blood supply.

By 1975, sales from Abbott's Hospital Products Group, including diagnostics, were up to $350 million annually, fully 38 percent of the company's total revenues. The Hospital Products Division sold intravenous solutions and kits, anesthetics, injectables such as syringes, bladder care products like catheters, and various sterile disposable items such as surgical gloves.

One success followed another. In 1977, a diagnostic device, lightning-quick for its time, reached the market. The *VP* clinical analyzer could accurately and inexpensively test 400 blood samples an hour. With its printouts and electronic displays, the *VP* reflected the revolution in "mini-computers" and electronics miniaturization then under-way, led by the likes of Wang Laboratories and Digital Electronics Corp.

Toward the end of the 1970s, to meet the swelling demand for nonradioactive diagnostics, Abbott introduced *Quantum II*, an automated system for conducting immuno-assays. *Quantum II* was a programmable spectro-photometer consisting of a spectrometer, for measuring a certain color or wavelength, and a photometer, for measuring the intensity of the light. Instead of measuring amounts of radioactivity, it measured the enzyme reactions in a test liquid.

All the products were promoted by a knowledgeable, 2,400-person-strong sales and marketing staff. Despite the large roster, the sales approach remained personal, as it had been since Dr. Abbott's day. In 1978, for instance, to sell an innovative spray-on bandage for burns, a team of 12 fanned out to leading burn centers from Ohio to Texas. The sales reps demonstrated the product to top burn specialists, winning their confidence. Word about the bandage trickled down to regional and municipal hospitals, ensuring market success.

In the aftermath of the IV recall, Abbott replaced its venerable line of glass containers with flexible, plastic ones. At the North Chicago facility, workers, their hair carefully covered, inspected new IV solutions on the assembly line.

In the 1970s, efficient, cost-effective, automated production lines became the order of the day, a trend that only intensified over time.

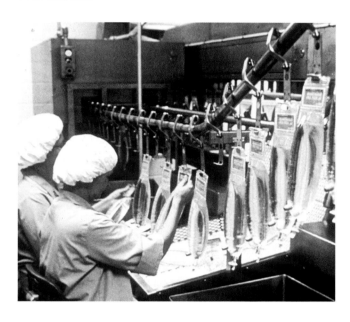

"That's really a key to our operation," noted Ledder who, along with Abbott, garnered a 1978 Marketer of the Year award from the American Marketing Association. "We're very good at direct selling. Our people are detailed on the products, and they can answer any questions that come up."

Still thought of by many as "just a pharmaceutical company," Abbott's biggest-selling and fastest-growing product lines now lay in other areas.

Controlling Costs, Returning Profits

In the early 1970s, with sales of IV units temporarily down and sales of *Sucaryl* gone, Ledder found another road to renewed success — tightening costs. The strategy proved prescient. By 1974, the oil embargo by the Organization of Petroleum Exporting Countries (OPEC) led to fuel short-ages and soaring costs for raw materials and other goods, as well as a severe economic downturn. Abbott responded with stringent measures to boost productivity.

By the end of 1974, Abbott's sales surpassed $750 million, up two-thirds from the crisis year of 1971, when the IV and *Sucaryl* problems depressed sales growth. Profits rose almost 20 percent.

For the economy as a whole, 1975 was one of the decade's worst years of "stagflation" — recessionary economic stagnation combined with high inflation.

Yet Abbott pulled strongly in the opposite direction. Sales soared 23 percent in 1975, and earnings went up 28 percent. Two dividend increases and a two-for-one stock split followed. Revenues were twice those of 1971, and three times greater than those of the booming late 1960s.

A technician inspects metal cans of the Ross Laboratories Division's products. A switch to high-speed canning of Abbott's nutritionals boosted assembly line speeds by more than a third.

Abbott worked with the NASA space agency to conduct zero-gravity research on the enzyme urokinase during the 1975 United States–Soviet Union joint space mission. This research resulted in the creation of Abbott's highly successful clot-busting drug, *Abbokinase*.

Still, vice president and treasurer James A. Hanley, and executive vice president of finance Bernard H. Semler, the latter the creator of "responsibility accounting," were not satisfied. They noted that some in the financial media chided Abbott for its product recalls and its issues with the U.S. FDA. As with any publicly traded company, its price to earnings ratio was scrutinized, and found lacking compared to some of its rivals.

So Hanley and Semler hosted a day-long investor seminar at company headquarters. Some 100 leading healthcare financial analysts attended a series of presentations and question-and-answer sessions. They left impressed.

"The company has clearly come a long way since the dark days of 1971," commented David McCallum of Faulkner, Dawkins and Sullivan, a large institutional brokerage house. "Abbott changed some minds," noted one New York City analyst, "and overcame some worries on the part of investors." Abbott's investor seminars became a successful and long-lasting tradition.

Old Standbys, New Innovations

In addition to productivity measures and the focus on diagnostics, pharmaceuticals — including the old reliable of anesthetics — contributed to the recovery. One example was a new tranquilizer, approved by the U.S. FDA in 1972, called *Tranxene*. It had a calming effect on the central nervous system, relieving short-term anxiety.

Another Abbott mainstay came to the rescue in 1976. Hundreds of people were afflicted with a mysterious infection that led to pneumonia-like symptoms, the death of 29 people, and a near panic. Most of the victims had attended a meeting in Philadelphia's Bellevue Stratford Hotel, of the veterans' group the American Legion. The ailment, soon dubbed Legionnaire's disease, was attributed variously to a virus, a bacterium, and even a terrorist attack aimed at the former soldiers. Many treatments were attempted, and at first none was successful.

The federal Centers for Disease Control and Prevention mounted a giant effort to track down the source and identity of the disease. Finally, a virus-like bacterium was pegged as the cause.

But a proper remedy was lacking. Finally, the drug that turned out to be most effective in fighting the malaise was erythromycin — the Abbott antibiotic of 30 years' standing.

The deadly outbreak of "Legionnaire's Disease" was one of the biggest health stories of 1976. The cure proved to be Abbott's standby antibiotic, erythromycin.

Several years later, a high-profile endeavor in pharmaceuticals drew the attention of company researchers to outer space. This project related to urokinase, a natural enzyme that breaks up blood clots. The space agency NASA selected an Abbott proposal, over many other solicitations, to isolate the cells that produce urokinase.

Abbott conducted its experiment in zero-gravity space, aboard the Apollo spacecraft. On Earth, the cells cannot be isolated, due to the effects of gravity. In space orbit, however, the cells could be separated by directing an electrical current through their solution. Back on Earth, the cells were used to produce cultures for research.

The successful experiment occurred during the historic 1975 American-Soviet mission where the Apollo craft docked with the Soviet Soyuz spacecraft. Urokinase, under the name *Abbokinase*, was approved for medical use in 1978, and became an important Abbott product.

Abbott was able to make these breakthroughs because it continued to build its scientific capability. By mid-decade, research expenditures reached $50 million a year. Areas of focus were drugs to fight inflammation, infections, heart disease, mental disorders — and epilepsy, through another Abbott-developed drug for the disease, *Depakene*.

Difficult times spawned an effort to realign the company along established business lines like drugs and diagnostics. In this vein, Abbott had, in 1972, sold off many of its Faultless rubber products, including the Faultless golf ball. The buyer seemed much better suited to the sports-oriented side of its product line. It was Globetrotter Communications, Inc., owner of the famed Harlem Globetrotters basketball team.

Abbott remained active in household products, however. Its *Selsun Blue* dandruff shampoo became available as a consumer product instead of by prescription only. It rang up an annual $10 million in sales, placing second in that market segment behind consumer products giant Procter & Gamble's Head & Shoulders shampoo.

Meanwhile, Abbott continued to build up its line of nutritional products. A prominent entry was *Ensure*, a vitamin- and mineral-rich liquid for use between meals or as a food supplement, and *Ensure Plus*, a fortified meal replacement. These products were designed in part for the growing number of people "on the go," who had less time to prepare meals themselves. This new product category, adult nutritionals, would grow into a major Abbott-led market in the years ahead.

Continues on page 246 ▶

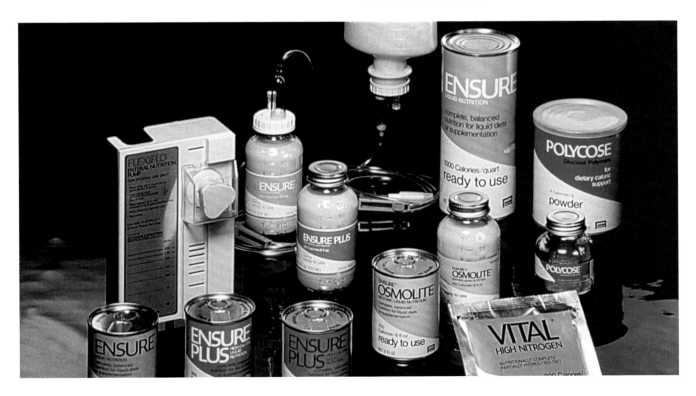

The Ross nutrition business was built on infant formula; but, in the 1970s, it branched out aggressively into adult nutritionals, with *Ensure*, and into specialty medical products.

Abbott Strikes Another Blow Against Epilepsy

During the hot summer days of 1977, Dr. Bernard Abrams of Columbus, Ohio, found himself on a mission. His six-year-old daughter, Felice Beth, suffered from a severe form of petit mal epilepsy. The girl, subject to seizures and falls, had to wear a helmet to protect herself.

A drug known as sodium valproate, available in Europe for 10 years, was known to be effective against the malaise. Yet, the compound had not been approved in the United States. A frustrated Dr. Abrams mounted a one-man media campaign to draw attention to Felice Beth's woes. An NBC television series profiled the Abramses, and various newspapers and radio stations featured them as well.

Back in December 1974, Abbott had become interested in marketing and manufacturing sodium valproate in the United States. The company had been involved since the 1920s in developing a means to combat epilepsy.

In January 1975, Abbott filed with the U.S. FDA an "IND," or Investigational New Drug application, for sodium valproate, later called *Depakene*. The IND, the start of the typically years-long process of drug approval, provided the agency with background data on the remedy, and indicated that Abbott could begin clinical studies.

As part of the approval process, a manufacturer had to submit a minimum of two clinical studies supporting a drug's safety and effectiveness. For *Depakene*,

The heart-rending story of Felice Beth Abrams helped compel the U.S. FDA to speed approval of Abbott's *Depakene* to make sodium valproate available to people with epilepsy in the United States.

Abbott submitted one conducted by the pediatrics department of Tokyo University. The other was a joint study, begun in summer 1976 by Abbott and the National Institute of Neurological and Communicative Disorders, called the Penry-Dreifuss study after its NIH- and University of Virginia-based directors.

By the 1970s, the entire approval process for a drug could take from 7 to 12 years. The FDA's review of an application alone, by 1978, averaged 34 months, despite a law mandating a maximum six-month review. By summer 1977, Abbott had already been involved in *Depakene's* approval regimen for two-and-a-half-years, for a drug

Depakene overcame early obstacles to gain approval as an epilepsy treatment in the United States. Its successor compound, *Depakote*, would become a blockbuster, also addressing migraine headaches and manic episodes in bipolar disorder.

Once approval was gained Abbott moved quickly to supply the estimated 300,000 petit mal sufferers in the United States.

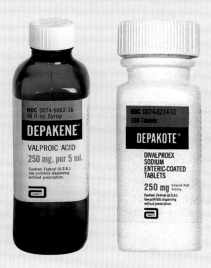

that had been on the world market for more than 12 years. At this juncture, however, Dr. Abrams' crusade made an impact.

He and Felice Beth traveled to England, where they were able to obtain sodium valproate, and the girl's condition improved considerably. The continued media attention got Congress involved; in the *Congressional Record* legislators complained about the length of the approval process for sodium valproate.

Normally, the next step for Abbott would have been to request the filing of a New Drug Application, or NDA. However, as media attention on Felice Beth intensified, the FDA took the nearly unheard of step, in July 1977, of itself asking Abbott to file an NDA. Abbott quickly complied, providing the FDA in September with literature on more than 200 ex-U.S. studies and 600 research citations, as well as its two clinical studies. NDAs had, by this time, grown to about a thousand two-inch-thick documents in length.

On October 12, the FDA's Neurologic Drugs Advisory Committee recommended approval of the NDA. The FDA then threw out the Penry-Dreifuss study and, on December 13, asked Abbott for data on another study taking place at the University of Florida. On January 30, 1978, Abbott presented the data. On February 28, the FDA approved the drug. It had been 160 days from start to end of the filing, as opposed to the years typically required.

With the regulatory hurdles now past, Abbott moved quickly. Within two weeks, *Depakene* capsules were available to the estimated 300,000 petit mal sufferers in the United States.

Abbott would continue its work in this field, developing the following decade a version of the drug called *Depakote*, truly a "triple threat." Along with epilepsy, *Depakote* was to prove effective for some sufferers of migraine headaches and of bipolar disorder. In fact, it was the first chemical treatment for manic episodes in bipolar disorder, or manic-depressive illness, in 25 years, since the introduction of lithium as a treatment. This quickly became the drug's leading indication, as *Depakote* grew to be a billion-dollar blockbuster. ∎

In 1976, Edward J. Ledder, left, was named chairman of the board. Succeeding him as president and chief operating officer was Robert A. Schoellhorn, right, formerly the hospital group's executive vice president, well versed in the diagnostics line making up a growing part of Abbott's business.

Maintaining a Formula for Success

By 1976, Abbott's financial situation had improved — and then some. When Ted Ledder took over as president in 1967, company sales stood at $303 million. In 1976, they burst past the one-billion-dollar mark. Ledder determined the time was right to turn over the operating reins of the company.

As Ledder became chairman of the board, hard-charging Robert A. Schoellhorn, fresh from his success with the company's fastest growing business, diagnostics, was named president and chief operating officer. In 1979, Schoellhorn would become chief executive officer.

As he had with George Cain, Ledder found in Schoellhorn a partner with whom he could form a hard-to-beat leadership team. The latter was tough, aggressively expanding market share; the former was detail-oriented and tenacious, while serving as the company's elder statesman.

It was almost an Abbott tradition to test a new leader with trial by fire. For Schoellhorn, this emerged in the form of major media controversy, concerning the marketing of infant formula in developing nations.

Throughout 1976, a spate of articles, television features, and congressional hearings criticized what was termed heavy-handed marketing of formula in developing countries, to impoverished mothers of infants and their healthcare providers. Such "Third World" nations often lacked modern water systems or the proper means to sterilize water. Some mothers, unaware of proper hygienic practices, fed their infants formula mixed with contaminated water. The tragic result could be infectious diarrhea, a leading cause of infant death in poor countries.

Critics also asserted that mothers unable to afford formula should not be pressured into buying it. In such cases they might dilute the formula to make it go further, resulting in insufficient nutrition for a child. Moreover, medical officials noted that, if possible, infants should be breast-fed, as breast-feeding was less expensive and supplied nutrients and benefits to the immune system that formula lacked.

Abbott was not the major industry player in the controversy. That role was filled by Nestlé, which was the largest supplier of infant formula to developing nations. However, Abbott did market *Similac* in some of the countries in question.

Abbott decided to take the offensive to reduce any misuse of *Similac* or other infant formulas. In this, Abbott drew on its own long-standing, and still-existing, code of marketing ethics. The Abbott code prohibited advertising formula to mothers. It also recommended that doctors or other trained medical personnel advise a mother on an infant's nutrition.

The Abbott Code of Marketing Ethics for Developing Countries:

▶ Affirms the superiority of breast milk.

▶ Confines promotion of infant-formula products to health-care professionals.

▶ Specifies that product labels stress the importance of breast-feeding.

▶ Displays graphically the proper techniques for preparation and use of infant formula.

Abbott also changed its *Similac* labels, clearly stating that breast-feeding was preferred. It printed the labels in the language of every country in question.

The point man in Abbott's campaign for the proper use of infant formula was Ross Laboratories Division president David O. Cox. He urged all the other makers of formula to adopt a code of ethics similar to Abbott's.

In May 1978, Cox testified before the Senate Health and Scientific Research Subcommittee, chaired by Massachusetts Sen. Edward M. Kennedy. Cox spoke along with representatives of the Nestlé Corporation, Bristol Myers Company, and American Home Products Corporation. Reminiscent of the Kefauver hearings in 1959–1962, the encounters between the industry officers and the congressmen were sometimes contentious.

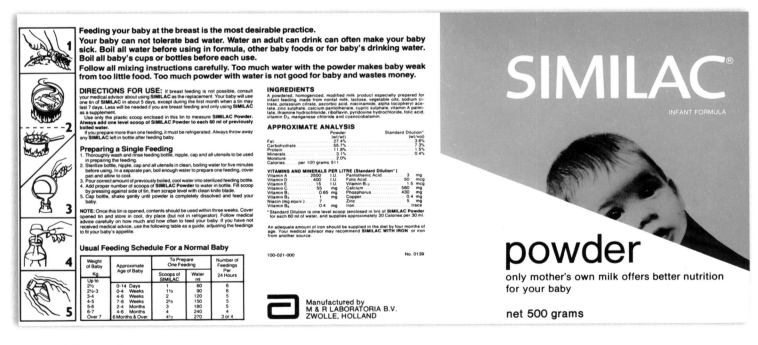

Labels of Abbott infant formula *Similac*, in accordance with the company's Code of Marketing Ethics, clearly affirmed superiority of breast milk, and demonstrated the proper preparation and use of the product.

In a strong statement, Cox said, "We … disagree strenuously with critics that promotion to the health-care profession in the Third World should be stopped. In our opinion there is no better group to care for sick or malnourished infants." He averred that many charges against Abbott were "circumstantial, anecdotal, exaggerated, or biased, although very effective in stimulating controversy." He added that any problems linked to infant formula occurred even more with other food bases, such as gruels, paps, evaporated milk, and fresh animal milk, commonly found among the impoverished.

In a follow-up letter to Sen. Kennedy, Cox noted that water should be boiled for all food preparations in developing nations. "To suggest that the contamination of infant formula is a special case," Cox wrote, "is to misunderstand Third World conditions." Cox emphasized: "Education to aid in the safe delivery of food, no matter what the mother chooses to feed, is universally essential."

During this period, Abbott pointed out that many organizations that were highly sympathetic to poor mothers and their children were providing them infant formula. These included foreign-aid agencies, local governments in the affected countries, and charity and church groups.

So Abbott was pleased when Dave Cox received a letter from Sister Karen Burns, a nun with the Franciscan Sisters, who were helping malnourished children in the jungles of Bolivia.

"I am writing in reference to your product, *Similac*," the Sister's missive began. Cox remembered: "Two photographs were enclosed with the letter. One was of a shriveled infant suffering severe malnutrition; the other, a later photograph of the same child on the way to recovery."

The letter described how the mother of the infant had breast-fed the baby until her milk dried up. The infant lost much weight, and was in danger of starving to death. Then a Franciscan nun provided the mother with *Similac*. Six weeks later, the child was healthy again.

In her letter, Sister Burns went on to thank Cox and Abbott for "the good you are doing for the people throughout the world who are in need of nourishment — if and when we can get your product to them."

Sen. Edward M. "Ted" Kennedy of Massachusetts, left, and president of Abbott's Ross Laboratories Division David O. Cox, right, at a 1978 subcommittee hearing on the marketing of infant formula to mothers in developing countries.

Abbott has worked with leading public figures to ensure the safe use of its products. Minnesota Senator Hubert Humphrey, center left, the former Vice President of the United States, spoke with Abbott vice president of Public Relations William D. Pratt, center right, before both took part in a 1974 Abbott-sponsored television program on nutrition. Pratt was a government affairs veteran of the early-1960s Kefauver hearings controversies.

International Intrigues

In the 1970s, Abbott pursued its long-standing strategy of expansion abroad with great success. By 1975, international sales made up 36 percent of all revenue.

And, at a time that saw the thawing of the Cold War, Abbott's most unique foreign operation took root in the Soviet Union. U.S. firms such as Pepsi-Cola were starting to build entire factories in the U.S.S.R. The country actually produced two kinds of formula, but was not happy with the results. The chairman of the Soviet's Technopromimport, Georgi Konoplev, noted: "*Similac*, with its high nutritional properties, is considered a particularly good substitute for mother's milk soon after birth."

So Chairman of the Board Ledder cut a capitalist deal with the communist state. Under a $25 million contract made final in 1978, Abbott and manufacturer FMC Corporation supplied the equipment, engineering, and product expertise to build a *Similac* plant in the Soviet Socialist Republic of Moldavia, near Romania. The factory was outfitted to make sufficient *Similac* powder to feed a million and a half infants — 14,000 tons' worth per year.

Continues on page 252 ▶

Abbott opened its first Irish facility in 1974, in county Sligo (pictured here). Today, Ireland is one of the company's largest manufacturing centers around the world.

Edward J. Ledder

Like predecessor S. DeWitt Clough, Edward J. Ledder was Chicago-bred. Also like Clough, he started at the bottom of the workforce. And like Dr. Abbott himself, Ted Ledder was a Horatio Alger story, rising to the top by his "bootstraps." This experience gave him the strength and perspective to see the company through a crisis that threatened its very survival.

Edward J. "Ted" Ledder was a working-man's hero, an unpretentious leader who rose up from the shop floor and helped right the company during the most difficult of times.

He began at Abbott in 1939, at age 22, on the production line of the finishing department, earning just 47 cents an hour. Ted Ledder moved on to the shipping and pricing departments. Then, in 1944, he shipped out for three years with the U.S. Navy. He was discharged as a lieutenant, junior grade.

On his return he was promoted to his first supervisory job at Abbott: assistant manager of pricing and quotes. In 1953, he was assigned to the innovative rotation training program that Dr. Volwiler promoted, by which promising employees were shifted around divisions and functions to gain managerial experience. At this time he also earned his Masters of Business Administration (MBA) degree from the University of Chicago.

After gaining some knowledge of production planning, Ledder transferred to his real métier, sales and marketing, working in the southeastern Wisconsin territory. By 1960, he was Assistant Sales Director for product promotion; by 1961, Director of Pharmaceutical Marketing. In 1965, he was elected to the Board of Directors, and the next year made vice president of Marketing Operations. In 1967, Chairman George R. Cain appointed Ledder president of Abbott, 28 years after his humble start with the firm.

Chairman and CEO Ted Ledder signing an agreement to build a *Similac* infant formula plant in the Soviet Socialist Republic of Moldavia.

Over the next four years, Ledder had to deal with the ban on *Sucaryl*, the recall of the entire IV solutions line, post-Vietnam War recession and inflation, and the death of his mentor and management partner, George Cain. Over the succeeding four years, he transformed the IV business and brought in new talent to build a spectacularly successful diagnostics business, while controlling costs and fighting for every inch of market share. Abbott attained previously unreached heights of success.

His sales and marketing background helped make the best of a dire situation. In fact, of the IV recall, he once said, "It was one of the best things that ever happened around here. It toughened up the workforce, and really welded them together."

With IVs temporarily, and *Sucaryl* permanently, out of production, Ledder urged his salesforce to make up the losses with sales of other products, including ampoules and vials. "There is no secret to [sales]," he said, "but you sell what you got, whether it's a new product or not."

Ledder was named chairman of the board in 1976, and retired in 1981 with more than 42 years of service, and served on the board until 1986.

Seemingly tireless, Ledder, despite a sometimes crushing Abbott workload, belonged to many outside organizations. He was at various times a member of the Business Advisory Council for the University of Denver, a trustee of the Illinois Institute of Technology, an advisor to the University of Chicago, a member of the executive committee of the Pharmaceutical Manufacturers Association, a director of the chemical maker FMC Corporation and the energy firm Enserch Corp., and chairman of the Heart Association of Lake County. After his retirement, Ledder also served as a director of the then-new biotech company Amgen, and of PR Pharmaceuticals. He was also a governor of the University of Miami School of Medicine.

Ledder and his predecessor, George Cain, worked during an era of large organizations growing ever bigger. Yet, Cain was a firm believer in the ability of one person to affect major organizational change.

He could have been describing Ledder when he said:

"Ideas must still come from individuals who refuse to be discouraged by corporate size and organizational bric-a-brac. The contributions of the scientific man, the uncommon man, the man with a sense of urgency — these are the keystones of our future." ■

Abbott joined with Japan's Takeda Chemical Industries to form TAP pharmaceuticals to market Takeda-discovered drugs in the United States. It would go on to become one of the most successful joint ventures ever formed.

The agreement was another unusual feather in Abbott's international cap, but didn't come easily.

"They're the toughest negotiators in the world," a weary Ledder commented afterward of his Soviet counterparts. "In fineness of detail, in insisting on specifics," he stated, "I have great admiration for their negotiators and their thoroughness."

Just the year before, Abbott had struck another international agreement that would have large and long-lasting impact. In 1977, the company entered into a joint venture with Takeda Chemical Industries, Japan's largest pharmaceutical company. The new entity, Takeda-Abbott Pharmaceuticals, would market Takeda-discovered drugs in the United States. In the decades ahead, TAP would become one of the most successful joint ventures in business history.

Success despite Economic Stress

In the late 1970s, annual inflation in the United States rose as high as 13 percent, and interest rates soared into double digits, too. The high price of goods and services pummeled many companies across industries. Meanwhile, generic drugs cut into the profits of many pharmaceutical firms. But, as it had in the Great Depression, Abbott prospered in hard times.

Despite the economic challenges around them, President Schoellhorn and Chairman Ledder kept to their successful strategy. They aggressively pushed into new diagnostics markets with an expanding array of testing devices. From 1973 to 1979, sales of diagnostic equipment soared about 300 percent. And, in an era of high prices, the pair stressed productivity and cost controls. These benchmarks built on George Cain and Bernie Semler's disciplined policies of measuring profits and sales for each employee.

In the late 1970s, for all U.S.-based companies, sales per employee rose by an average of 1.8 percent. At Abbott, in 1977, the increase in sales per employee was 6 percent, and went up from there. It was 8 percent in 1978, and 10 percent by 1979.

Sales and administrative expenses were also pegged to sales. From 1974 to 1979, this ratio fell from 27 percent to 22 percent. In real terms, this meant a savings of $80 million a year. In real impact, this meant more money for shareholder dividends, laboratory research, and capital investment.

Indeed, the sales and marketing effort in this era re-created the lofty results of S. DeWitt Clough's campaigns of the Depression-era 1930s. Through hustle and smarts. Abbott's sales reps were requested, for efficiency's sake, to make one more visit a week to a physician. This was comparable to adding 19 more sales personnel, at no additional cost.

"When you set your objectives for the year, you record them in concrete," noted vice president for diagnostics research George B. Rathmann on Abbott's analytical approach. "You change your plans through the year, but you never change what you measure yourself against. You don't get a chance to adjust and finagle, and decide that you really didn't intend to do that anyway, and readjust your objectives to make yourself look better." Rathmann later went on to co-found and serve as CEO of biotech leader Amgen.

In 1979, employees at Abbott's Hospital Products facility in Laurinburg, North Carolina, passed three million consecutive hours without one loss-of-time accident in a period spanning three years.

A worker adjusted recovery equipment to isolate the products of fermentation for alternate uses. Chemical manufacturing at Abbott was becoming both more complex and more efficient.

For Wall Street, the financial results were startling. Early in the decade, as it faced the *Sucaryl* ban and IV solution recall, Abbott had lagged behind its industry peers in terms of stock market performance. Yet, from 1973–1977, during rough economic times, the worth of the company's stock rose 61 percent. In comparison, the shares of other healthcare firms decreased on average by 42 percent.

When Abbott held its second investor seminar, in 1978, the earlier skepticism of industry observers toward the company's performance had dissolved.

An analyst with Alex Brown & Sons, the United States' first investment bank, remarked of Abbott: "The company's past record of operating results, by almost any measurement, is among the best compiled in American business."

After beginning the '70s with a streak of crises, Abbott was on solid footing to start the decade ahead.

While sales and operational efficiency were stressed, standards of safety were heightened further. In 1979, for example, the hospital products plant in Laurinburg, North Carolina, reached a noteworthy milestone: It passed three million consecutive hours without one loss-of-time accident — about a three-year stretch of perfection.

Another sure way to curtail expense in a time of runaway prices was through conserving use of oil and natural gas. Abbott started up an energy savings program and, within a year, the U.S. Department of Commerce presented the company with a SavEnergy Citation. In a related area, in 1977 the federal Environmental Protection Agency, or EPA, identified as "exemplary" in pollution control the Abbott plants at North Chicago and Barceloneta, Puerto Rico. The EPA used the plants to set effluent standards for the rest of the pharmaceutical industry.

Decade at a Glance

1970–1980

1970 ▲

Leading Abbott through the crises of the early 1970s are President Edward J. Ledder (left) and Chairman of the Board George R. Cain (right).

At the start of the 1970s, the U.S. FDA forbids the use of cyclamate, the sweetener in *Sucaryl*. As a result, Abbott loses $19 million in annual profits. For two decades, the substance had been a widely used ingredient in confections and diet colas. After its removal from the market, *Sucaryl* is proven to be safe and harmless.

▼

1971

After reports of contaminated cap liners on its IV solution bottles, Abbott suspends shipments and recalls its IV solutions from hospitals. The recall of Abbott's biggest product line leads to a major sales loss and a decline in stock price.

President Ledder makes a deal with Cutter Laboratories to convert the production lines for Abbott's screw-cap IV closure to Cutter's modern, vacuum-rubber stoppers. Ledder also slashes prices to regain company market share.

▲

Chairman Cain (far left) meets North Carolina officials during the dedication of Abbott's Rocky Mount plant for making new IV solution bottles.

1972

Chairman of the Board Cain dies of a heart attack.

Abbott's IV sales regain their previous levels, and total sales reach a record of more than half a billion dollars.

The recall of Abbott's IV solutions leads to new manufacturing plants and new bottle types, and to intensified scrutiny of the company's manufacturing processes.

▼

The *ABA-100* blood chemistry analyzer is introduced. Abbott also introduces *Ausria*, a breakthrough radioimmuno-assay test for detecting serum hepatitis.

Abbott sells off its line of Faultless Rubber products, including the Faultless golf ball.

1973

A new diagnostics division is formed that encompasses biologicals, radiopharmaceuticals, and clinical instrumentation. The aim is to devise automated diagnostic tests that are accurate, simple, and low in cost.

The company introduces *Ensure*, its first adult nutritional.

▼

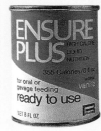

Abbott sales soar in the economically challenging 1970s in large part due to its introduction of many innovative diagnostic tools, such as the *ABA-100*.

Extensive laboratory research by the German Cancer Research Center indicates that the consumption of *Sucaryl* is safe. The product remains banned in the United States.

1974

Abbott International opens a new plant in Sligo, Ireland. In the years ahead, Ireland will become a major manufacturing center for the company.

Abbott's sales surpass $750 million, with profits rising almost 20 percent.

1975

Overseas sales now make up a new high of 36 percent of all revenue.

Sales of hospital products, including diagnostics, represent 38 percent of the company's revenues.

1976

Robert A. Schoellhorn, formerly executive vice president of the Hospital Group, becomes company president.

The antibiotic erythromycin, available since the 1940s, proves effective in fighting the deadly outbreak of Legionnaire's disease, which is one of the year's top healthcare stories.

The company publicizes the Abbott Code of Marketing Ethics for Developing Countries, aimed at avoiding misuse of infant formula in developing nations.

Abbott sales exceed one billion dollars.

Abbott opens a 94,000-square-foot manufacturing plant in Barceloneta, Puerto Rico, employing about 500 people, making IV kits, vitamins, and antibiotics.

1977

The *VP* clinical analyzer reaches the market; it can inexpensively and accurately test 400 blood samples per hour.

The U.S. Environmental Protection Agency (EPA) identifies as "exemplary" the pollution control of Abbott plants in North Chicago and Barceloneta, Puerto Rico. The EPA uses the plants as models to set effluent standards for the rest of the pharmaceutical industry.

Since 1973, during difficult economic times, the worth of Abbott stock has risen 61 percent, while the shares of other healthcare firms have decreased, on average, by 42 percent.

Depakene is approved in the U.S. for the treatment of epilepsy.

TAP Pharmaceuticals is formed as a joint venture between Abbott and Takeda Chemical Industries, Ltd. of Japan. It will become one of the most successful joint-venture companies ever.

1978

Abbott finalizes a contract to help supply the equipment, engineering, and product expertise for a *Similac* plant in the Soviet Socialist Republic of Moldavia, near Romania.

Abbokinase, also called urokinase, is approved for medical use.

Sen. Edward M. "Ted" Kennedy of Massachusetts, left, and president of Ross Laboratories Division, David O. Cox, right, speaking at a 1978 U.S. Senate hearing on the marketing of infant formula to mothers in developing countries.

1979

Robert A. Schoellhorn is named chief executive officer.

Abbott introduces the anticonvulsant *Depakene*, the tranquilizer *Tranxene*, and *Abbokinase*, a treatment for blood clots in the lungs. The company has an annual earnings growth rate of 16.5 percent and a sales growth rate of 15.5 percent.

Abbott sales per employee average 10 percent, up from an already high 6 percent in 1977 and 8 percent in 1978.

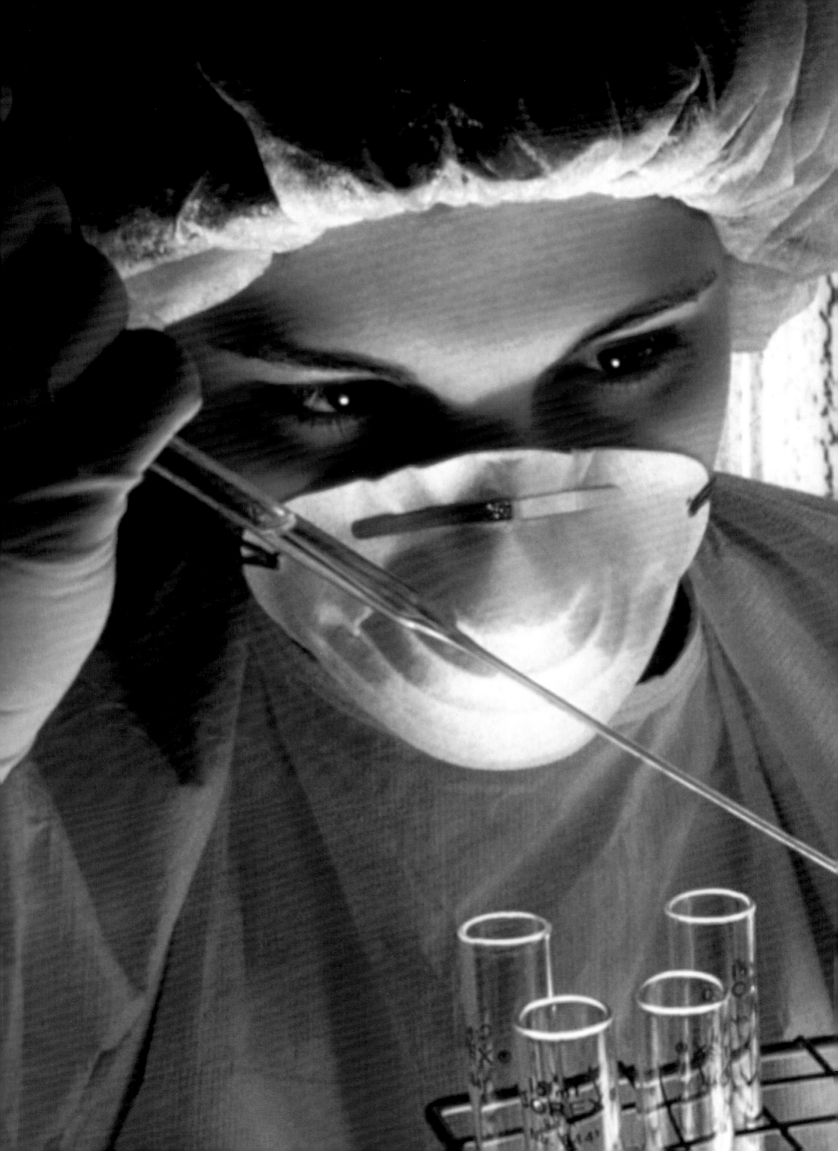

1980–1990

Reaching New Scientific and Commercial Heights

In the predawn chill of an early March morning in 1985, Abbott leaders left headquarters en route to Washington, D.C. The scientists and high-ranking executives were in a jubilant mood. In the early 1980s, the new scourge of HIV/AIDS was exploding, afflicting ever-larger numbers of victims around the world, and placing the blood supply at risk. An effective remedy to the mysterious disease was sorely needed. So was a reliable test to detect the virus that caused it. The federal government had given five companies, Abbott included, samples of the newly-isolated HIV virus. Washington promised an expedited approval process for the firm that created a test to identify the antibodies produced by the body in reaction to the virus. After months of late-night work by a special research task force, Abbott succeeded in developing the first licensed diagnostic to detect the antibody to the AIDS virus. Then, team members flew off to Washington to join the United States government in announcing this breakthrough — medicine's first major victory against the mysterious and deadly new disease.

PREVIOUS SPREAD
The 1980s saw a tremendous effort in the development and production of new diagnostics, Abbott's prime driver throughout the decade. An Abbott scientist manipulated DNA samples with a pipette to help create a novel diagnostic technology.

U.S. Secretary of Health and Human Services Margaret Heckler and U.S. FDA Commissioner Frank Young hold a press conference to announce the approval of *HTLV-III EIA*, Abbott's new test to detect the presence of HIV.

In a storied career, Edward J. Ledder, left, had risen over four decades of service from the assembly line to the executive suite, providing rock-steady leadership during the most trying of times. After much success in hospital products and diagnostics, Robert A. Schoellhorn, right, advanced in 1981 from president and CEO to chairman of the board.

The year 1981 brought the end of the management tandem of Chairman Ted Ledder and President Bob Schoellhorn. Ledder retired after 42 years at Abbott, having climbed from the factory floor to head the Board of Directors.

Management Transition

The new president, Abbott's tenth, was G. Kirk Raab, age 45. Raab hailed from the increasingly important international division, moving up from leadership of Latin American operations. He had much experience in hospital goods, drugs, and nutritionals. In firm overall charge was Robert A. Schoellhorn, as chairman of the board and CEO.

By the Numbers

Abbott had come out of the economically difficult 1970s in fine form. It entered the new decade with results that were no less than spectacular.

In 1980, revenues topped $2 billion. Even accounting for inflation, the numbers impressed.

The momentum kept building. In 1981, shareholders received their third two-for-one stock split in five years. Over just the previous seven years, since 1974, the market value of a share of Abbott stock had increased 800 percent. One hundred shares of 1929 stock worth $3,250 had now grown to 40,128 shares valued at about $1.1 million. Not to mention the $235,000 that those shares would have paid in dividends. For a company like Abbott, "buy and hold" was a winning investment formula.

At the start of the 1980s, the United States economy entered a steep recession, even as healthcare costs continued to rise. It made sense to continue the firm's winning strategy, with the focus on diagnostics and its ability to reduce medical expenses while growing company earnings.

Stated Chairman Schoellhorn: "Success will be directly proportional to a company's ability to offer products and services that reduce overall healthcare costs, and that make the healthcare system itself more productive."

G. Kirk Raab was named Abbott's tenth president in 1981. He would go on to be CEO of biotech leader Genentech.

The business press took notice. *Dun's Business Month* named Abbott one of the five best-managed companies in the United States.

Ounces of Prevention

Throughout the decade, the company leveraged its broad strengths to roll out or improve a dizzying array of successful diagnostics. In 1982, Abbott introduced 25 new diagnostic tools; in 1986, 70 of them, as diagnostic technology reached a new peak.

A Quantum Leap in Testing

Quantum II, Abbott's spectrophotometer for performing immunoassays through non-radioactive means, had been introduced in the 1970s. By 1982 it could run 16 different tests, 20 by 1985.

Later in the decade, political pressures grew to clamp down on the ever-rising cost of providing healthcare. In 1984, *Business Week* noted the striving of healthcare providers "to become less vulnerable to cost-containment pressures."

In the mid-1980s, it was clear Abbott was more than holding its own. Against stiff competition, it had climbed past some 20 competitors to the number-one rank in the $4 billion worldwide diagnostics market. In the U.S. market, it ranked first in medical nutritionals as well.

While market shares grew, productivity increased, according to the internal metrics that Ledder and Schoellhorn had devised. From 1979 to 1984, Abbott hired 15 percent more employees. During this time, sales for each worker rose 35 percent. Earnings per employee rose 92 percent. Abbott was a big machine, but a lean and productive one.

"We have some of the most detailed productivity goals you can imagine in each operation of the company," stated Schoellhorn. "One of our objectives is to be the low-cost producer wherever it is possible."

The numbers were striking. By 1984, helped by a recovered U.S. economy, total sales climbed to a lofty $3 billion, up a billion dollars from just 1980. An ongoing company mantra became, as Schoellhorn termed it, "a compound growth rate of at least 15 percent per year in earnings per share over the next five years."

The year 1986 was a particularly strong one for Abbott financially. Sales for the year increased $450 million. There was the almost expected two-for-one stock split. And dividends went up for the 14th straight year.

By the 1980s, instruments like the *Quantum II* made Abbott the world's leading diagnostics company, and diagnostics the company's leading business.

Diagnostic systems such as the *TDx* for therapeutic drugs got smaller in size as the number of substances they could analyze grew. Chairman Schoellhorn commented of such tools: "Diagnostic testing is inherently cost-effective. Earlier, more accurate detection of disease allows for earlier and often less costly treatment."

The benefits of dispensing with radiation-based testing were many, especially in cost savings. Laboratories could do without special licenses and equipment. And, because the substances used in testing were not rapidly decaying isotopes, they had longer shelf lives.

Quantum II was also fast, giving results in just a few hours. "It is … important to reduce the cost of diagnosing and monitoring diseases," noted Schoellhorn. "This is precisely what we are doing."

Perhaps its most noted assay of the time was PAP, not the Pap smear, but a test that analyzed enzymes to monitor prostate cancer. PAP was Abbott's first diagnostic to employ monoclonal antibodies. Such antibodies bind to, and readily identify, a substance. Many more applications of such antibodies would ensue.

TDx: Monitoring Therapy

In 1981, the diagnostics division introduced the *TDx* therapeutic drug monitoring system — therapeutic in that it allowed attending physicians to check the levels of medicines in a patient's bloodstream and adjust doses accordingly. Adverse reactions and expensive hospital stays could be avoided. Small enough to fit on a lab countertop, *TDx* neatly followed Abbott's diagnostic guidelines: fast, precise, reliable, and easy-to-use.

The *TDx* steadily expanded its menu to include tests for immunosuppressants, toxins, and hormonal and endocrine functions, more than 60 tests in all. Its sales soared. By the late 1980s it was used in two-thirds of U.S. clinical labs and hospitals, making it one of the company's most commercially successful diagnostic systems. Around the same time, Abbott also entered into its first multiyear agreement with the American Red Cross, as the sole supplier of hepatitis and AIDS screening tests for Red Cross blood centers.

Continues on page 264 ▶

Breakthrough: Detecting HIV

As the incidence of HIV/AIDS grew exponentially in the early years of the 1980s, the United States Food and Drug Administration (FDA) estimated that more than 1.6 million HIV tests would be required at blood centers — if such a tool existed. The lethal virus remained, at this time, highly mysterious, and medical science, thus far, had no success in combating it.

That was when, in May 1984, the federal agency requested, and gave incentives to, medical products innovators to develop such a test.

Abbott rolled up its sleeves. A task force of 40 employees worked around the clock to crack the code. Researchers worked on samples of the isolated HIV virus, then called HTLV-III. The team delivered, developing and producing a test called *HTLV-III EIA* (enzyme immunoassay). Clinical tests affirmed the accuracy of the HIV test.

The following March, the government issued Abbott a license for the test. It was the first diagnostic to detect the antibody to the AIDS virus. From start of research to full-scale production,

the project took only eight months. This was a remarkably short time for a project that resulted in the first major medical breakthrough against the seemingly implacable disease. It was one of the most noteworthy scientific achievements of its time, and in Abbott's history. ∎

Chicago Tribune Monday, March 4, 1985

Abbott jubilant over FDA award

Test gets 1st license in AIDS fight

By Michael L. Millenson

Don't kid yourself—Goliath likes to win a few, too.

Officials of Abbott Laboratories were jubilant Saturday after the North Chicago-based firm was awarded the first government license to produce a diagnostic test to screen blood for acquired immune deficiency syndrome [AIDS].

Company scientists and top brass rose in predawn darkness to hop a corporate plane to Washington for a press conference featuring Margaret Heckler, secretary of health and human services, and Frank Young, commissioner of the Food and Drug Administration. The ceremony capped a competition that began last May, when the

government gave a sample of the newly-isolated virus for AIDS, HTLV-III, to five companies and promised expedited approval for a test to spot HTLV-III antibodies.

Abbott earned a comfortable $402.6 million last year on sales of $3.1 billion and was the nation's leading maker of diagnostic products, but the AIDS test victory was no less sweet for that.

In phone interviews Saturday, company officials took particular pleasure in pointing out that they had beaten competitors said to be more agile.

"We get hammered so much [with the accusation] that the smaller biotechnology companies are faster moving than the big multinational companies," said Jack W. Schuler, the

Abbott executive vice president who oversees diagnostics. "We're feeling real good about ourselves."

Added Robert A. Schoellhorn, Abbott's chairman and chief executive officer: "We *are* an entrepreneurial company. We are not a small biotechnology company."

Entrepreneurial merit notwithstanding, Abbott's size means that the economic impact of the AIDS test on the company will not be great by itself. The FDA estimates that 1.6 million AIDS tests will be needed monthly at blood centers. An undetermined number of tests will also be given at "alternative sites" to high-risk individuals who wish to see if they have AIDS antibodies without having to donate blood and risk

Heckler   Schoellhorn

contaminating the public blood supply.

Peter Drake, an analyst at Kidder, Peabody & Co., puts the size of the U.S. market for the AIDS diagnostic test at $90 million. Abbott won't give its own

Continued on page 2

One of the great scientific achievements in Abbott's history was its development of the first licensed test to detect HIV. This was one of medical science's first successes in combating the virus, and saved untold lives.

A task force of 40 employees worked on the team to create the world's first licensed test to detect HIV. Shown here (from left) are Scott Weber, Robin Gutierrez, John Heller, and George Dawson.

HCG-Urine TestPack, a diagnostic product used to detect early pregnancies, was small enough to fit in a doctor's palm. Results came back within minutes and were easy to interpret, appearing as a plus or a minus sign on the exterior of the *TestPack* disc, a format that would become ubiquitous in years to come.

Identifying STDs

In 1983, the U.S. FDA approved *Chlamydiazyme* — as in "Chlamydia," the most common sexually transmitted disease in the United States, and "zyme," as in enzyme. It was an enzyme immunoassay to detect the bacterial infection, which often occurs without visible symptoms and that, if untreated, can cause infertility in women.

Good Things in a Small Package

In June 1985, Abbott introduced *Vision*, an automated whole-blood analyzer. The watchword was "small." *Vision* was about the size of a microwave oven, and fit neatly in a doctor's office.

Vision let physicians test blood on the spot. Previously, doctors and lab workers had to wait 24–72 hours for the results of blood work to return from the lab. Now they could get test results for cholesterol, glucose, and other common blood components in as little as *eight minutes*. If the results were troubling, caregivers could treat patients or adjust their medications right away. Patients were also saved a great deal of time making repeat visits to the doctor's office.

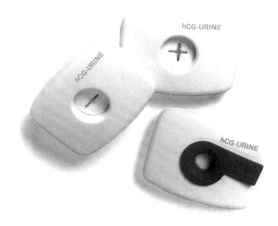

Thanks to its compact size, the *Vision* diagnostic system allowed physicians to test blood on the spot rather than sending samples out to a lab.

Rapid Testing

Abbott quickly followed up in January 1986 with another innovative diagnostic tool for the doctor's office. Called *TestPack*, it could quickly examine blood, urine, and culture samples for conditions like strep throat, Chlamydia, and viral infection.

TestPack was compact, consisting of a small disc to which reagents were added. It was "fail-safe": After a test, the disc displayed a plus or minus sign to show the outcome of the test, the first device to ever use this now standard reporting format. But it displayed a sign only if the reagents were active and proper procedures had been followed. If a mistake was made in running the test, no result was shown.

A *TestPack* early pregnancy test supplied accurate results for an anxious patient within just three minutes. Using monoclonal antibody technology, first employed by Abbott with the *Quantum II* device, it detected elevated levels of hCG, or human chorionic gonadotropin, the female hormone the placenta secretes soon after fertilization. A plus sign on the *TestPack* disc meant the presence of hCG and, therefore, pregnancy. In clinical trials, a comparison of standard serum pregnancy tests with *TestPack* showed 100 percent agreement — with no false positives or negatives.

Blockbuster: The IMx

Introduced in 1987 was the *IMx* blood chemistry analyzer for medium-sized laboratories. The *IMx*, as in IM for "immunoassay," would become the world's leading automated immunoassay system and one of Abbott's best-selling products.

A technician examining the sample-holding carousel of the *IMx* immunoassay system. The popular system considerably sped up diagnostic testing conducted by medical labs.

TDx system was employed to detect substances such as cocaine and phencyclidine, or PCP.

In 1988, hospital and laboratory products, with its emphasis on diagnostics, amounted to 47 percent of Abbott's total revenues and 58 percent of its international sales. The company held about 80 percent of the market in testing for HIV. It was, by far, the world's leader in testing blood donated for blood banks. By the end of the decade, Abbott would stand at the head of an $8 billion global diagnostics market.

Schoellhorn noted with some pride, "We became the world's largest diagnostics manufacturer by providing systems that make it practical and cost-effective for smaller laboratories and those in hospitals to perform a number of different tests rapidly and economically … we're doing the same thing for the physician's office."

The analyzer, building on the *TDx* system platform, could process and print information on a carousel of 24 samples in half an hour. The cost of supplies and labor, and the number of manual steps for preparing immunoassays, were much reduced. It had tests for cancer, heart conditions, pregnancy, thyroid function, anemia, HIV, and hepatitis, among others.

Fighting Drug Abuse

With growing use of illegal drugs such as cocaine, "drug-free zones" and employee drug tests became a sign of the times. By 1986, more than 30 percent of Fortune 500 companies administered some type of drug testing. That year, the United States federal government proposed mandatory drug testing for federal employees in sensitive positions.

Abbott addressed this concern. In 1986, it entered the growing market for blood tests of illegal or abused drugs, introducing tests that were accurate and inexpensive. The

Abbott's Ross Laboratories Division marked the 25th anniversary of *Similac with Iron* in 1984 with a commemorative poster. Ross steadily improved the nutritional content of its formula products, and spent a large annual budget informing caregivers and mothers on proper infant nutrition.

The recall of 1971 a fading memory, IV production was ever-more high-tech. Carefully cloaked workers in the "clean room" of the Austin, Texas, production plant made Abbott IV solutions.

Abbott's *ADD-Vantage* intravenous drug delivery system allowed hospitals to store medications more effectively in powdered form, mixing them into solution only at the time of use. The product was adopted by many pharmaceutical companies.

Less Invasive = More Convenient

During the decade, profits for Abbott's line of hospital products, such as IV solutions, were squeezed in several ways. The United States government imposed cost caps on items reimbursed through Medicaid, the federal healthcare program for the poor.

Abbott was placing less stress on basic IV solutions, which were becoming a lower-priced commodity good, focusing instead on differentiated specialty hospital products such as pumps and patient monitors. In fact, after United States President Ronald Reagan was shot by a would-be assassin in 1981 and rushed to a hospital for surgery, he was given intravenous solutions in controlled amounts with the aid of Abbott's *LifeCare II-D IV* pump. The pump accurately measured the flow rate of solutions and medications, often a critical concern during and after surgery.

Further, during this time Abbott helped advance an area that sought to reduce medical costs and patient trauma by making surgery and treatments less invasive.

A major example was a technique for patients suffering from kidney failure, often brought on by hypertension or diabetes. Previously, sufferers had to make periodic hospital visits to be hooked up to complex, costly kidney and blood dialysis gear. Now, a small tube was placed in the patient's abdomen, and dialysis fluid was infused, then drained. A patient performed this action himself four times daily.

The exchange was called CAPD, or continuous ambulatory peritoneal dialysis, with peritoneal meaning "of the abdomen." Patients were freed from hospitalization, and were able to eat, work, and travel more normally.

To further develop and market less-invasive technologies like this, Abbott, in 1983, invested $7 million in an alliance with Boston Scientific Corporation, a technology innovator in the medical device field. Tools included endoscopes that permitted removing gallstones and kidney stones without incisions. Abbott's investment helped build Boston Scientific into a major device maker with a significant benefit to Abbott. Another innovative procedure was dilation of arteries and blood vessels through balloon catheters, as an alternate to coronary bypass surgery. Such devices would make up an increasingly important product line for Abbott.

Abbott acquired the medical device firm of famed Salt Lake City-based inventor James LeVoy Sorenson, the creator of the computerized heart monitor, among many well-known medical inventions.

In 1983, Abbott consolidated three of its Japanese operations into one unified healthcare firm, called Dainabot, K.K., an offshoot of Dainabot Radioisotope Labs, Abbott's original Japanese joint venture from two decades earlier. As part of the consolidation, Abbott boosted its majority interest in Dainabot. It also gained a foothold for marketing the products of its own research in Japan, the world's second-largest economy. In 2002, it would acquire full ownership of Dainabot and begin to build the Abbott name in Japan.

Convenience and more sophisticated know-how extended to the company's long-standing work with IV kits. In fall 1985, the U.S. FDA approved, and Abbott introduced, an intravenous drug delivery system, named *ADD-Vantage*. Some pharmaceuticals are unstable in solution. *ADD-Vantage* allowed such drugs to be mixed just prior to infusion into a patient. The new application was highly valued by hospital customers. Within 12 weeks, 12 major pharmaceutical firms, including Wyeth and Hoffman-LaRoche Inc., signed up to use the *ADD-Vantage* method to provide their drugs to hospitals, too.

Abbott's hospital products group made a significant acquisition in 1980, which further bolstered its position in the hospital market. Abbott purchased the medical device firm Sorenson Research, of Salt Lake City, Utah. The acquisition significantly benefited the firm by providing it with the first catheters that, by warding off blood clotting, could remain in the body for extended periods. The devices formed a foundation for Abbott's Critical Care business.

Abbott added to its expertise in higher-end patient technology by acquiring Oximetrix Inc., a producer of intravenous pumps, in 1985. The Mountain View, California, firm also made systems to continuously monitor blood oxygen levels in the critically ill.

Healthcare Worldwide

Another driver of Abbott's success in the '80s would be international growth, which it made clear from the decade's onset. In 1980, Abbott acquired full ownership of its West German affiliate, Deutsche-Abbott GmbH. It thus reinforced its presence in the world's third-largest economy.

It also fully acquired Sáo Paulo, Brazil-based Prevaz Recordati Laboratorios, S.A. Brazil, along with Argentina, made up Latin America's largest markets.

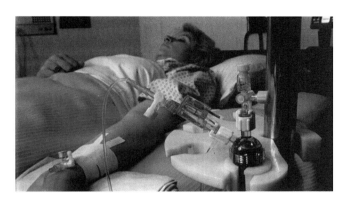

Abbott's Sorenson Research subsidiary manufactured the Intraflo hemodynamic line, which monitored arterial blood pressures, cardiac volume output, and blood gases.

Fingers flew, and outfits were stylish, on the finishing line of the production plant in Argentina.

In the early 1980s, Abbott continued its rapid global expansion. Its operations in Delkenheim, near Wiesbaden, West Germany, included a gleaming glass-and-steel facility for both commercial and manufacturing operations.

This image, from the mid-1980s, told the story of Abbott's growing personnel and production base in Puerto Rico, one of its largest locations, worldwide. Some of Abbott's 2,000 Puerto Rican employees manned this float during the island's Constitution Day parade.

Abbott began to see pharmaceutical payoffs from its joint venture work in Japan, which was consolidated under the corporate name Dainabot Co., Ltd. A Dainabot scientist monitors her experiment.

These actions would "increase substantially Abbott's position in the important Japanese healthcare market," noted Schoellhorn. In 1987, Abbott was listed on the Tokyo stock exchange. Together, Abbott and Dainabot developed important new diagnostic tools.

Some 70 years earlier, Abbott had been one of the first U.S.-based companies to set up shop in then-British India. Now it formed its first operation in another Asian giant, mainland China, which was reopening its economy to the world, and on the path to becoming an economic superpower.

In June 1988, Abbott created a joint venture, Ningbo Abbott Biotechnology Ltd., with three Chinese entities. These were the Shanghai Institute for the Pharmaceutical Industry (SIPI), the Ningbo Special Free Trade Zone, and the Ningbo Pharmaceutical Company, a major Chinese producer of pharmaceuticals, based in the large Chinese seaport city of Ningbo.

For 50 percent of the equity, Abbott helped set up a manufacturing plant and offices for Ningbo Abbott Biotechnology. Abbott also supplied management expertise. The enterprise focused at first on diagnostic tests for detecting substances such as triglycerides and urea nitrogen in the blood.

Ningbo proved somewhat ahead of its time, and Abbott's involvement in the venture concluded in 2001. However, it provided Abbott with its first modern experience of doing business in China, laying a foundation for the significant presence it would build there in years to come.

Continues on page 272 ▶

TAP Pharmaceutical Products

Abbott's Japanese Joint-Venture Blockbuster.

Since the 1960s, Abbott had a presence in the fast-growing Japanese market through its joint venture with Dainippon Pharmaceutical to make radiomedicines. Then, in 1977, President Robert A. Schoellhorn had formed another joint venture, with Japan's largest drug firm, Takeda Chemical Industries.

With Dainippon, Abbott had lent its expertise with radioisotopes. With Takeda, it would benefit from the scientific knowledge of its partner. Through TAP, Abbott won the rights to market in the United States and Canada any human pharmaceutical products stemming from Takeda's research.

The Japanese firm had a number of intriguing pharmaceuticals in its pipeline, and Schoellhorn was betting, successfully, that one or more would pan out. TAP would later market blockbuster Takeda-discovered products like the hormonal therapy *Lupron* and the acid-reflux treatment *Prevacid*.

In 2008, Abbott and Takeda concluded their joint venture — one of the most successful in business history — with Abbott retaining the rights to *Lupron*, along with substantial payments, and Takeda the rights to *Prevacid*. ∎

Dr. Ira Ringler was the first president of TAP, Abbott's joint venture with Japan's Takeda Chemical Industries. The cooperative venture became one of the most successful ever formed. The worldly Ringler had worked a decade before on the *Similac* venture with the Soviet Union.

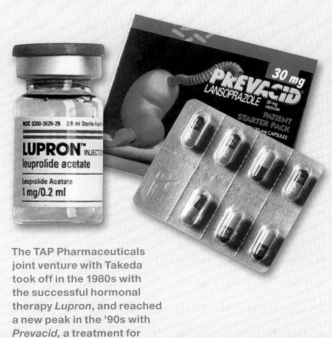

The TAP Pharmaceuticals joint venture with Takeda took off in the 1980s with the successful hormonal therapy *Lupron*, and reached a new peak in the '90s with *Prevacid*, a treatment for acid reflux that would become one of the top five pharmaceuticals in the United States.

Robert A. Schoellhorn

Of all of the company's chief executives, Bob Schoellhorn had the longest career outside Abbott. Once inside, however, he presided over extraordinary growth and sowed the seeds of major new Abbott business to come.

Born in 1928, Bob Schoellhorn graduated in chemistry from the Philadelphia College of Textiles and Science. He then launched into a 26-year career with chemical maker American Cyanamid, starting as a lab technician for $140 a month. After working with dyes and organic chemicals, he was promoted to district manager in Canada in intermediate chemicals. Offered other district manager slots in California, New York, or Chicago, his venturesome streak led him to choose the latter: "Chicago I knew absolutely nothing about … it was new territory."

Later, he was a manager in the international division of the chemicals group. Then, for more than two years, he served as president and general manager of Lederle Laboratories, American Cyanamid's pharmaceuticals and vitamins group.

When Abbott made Schoellhorn a job offer, his penchant for adventure and novelty took over. "It was a difficult decision to go to Abbott because I had a good future at Cyanamid," he recalled. But "Abbott was almost entirely in the healthcare business,

Action-oriented Robert A. Schoellhorn had a long and varied chemical industry career before joining Abbott. At Abbott, he was instrumental in putting front and center its diagnostic and hospital product lines, in reviving its pharmaceutical business, and in delivering explosive sales and profits.

and anything they did outside of healthcare was an exception. So Abbott was very appealing.

"The other thing was that I quickly saw in Ted Ledder that Abbott was a company that operates with individuals making decisions and delegating responsibilities — an action-oriented company. American Cyanamid was a more committee-operated company."

Schoellhorn's rise up Abbott's chain of command was rapid. When he joined up, in 1973, he was named executive vice president of the hospital group. The next year he was on the board of directors.

Schoellhorn and diagnostics division chief and eventual Abbott president James L. Vincent soon did wonders in boosting the product lines and profits of the key diagnostics and hospital enterprises.

But Schoellhorn's focus and contributions were not restricted to these businesses. Under his leadership the company also began a renaissance in its pharmaceutical business, which had taken a back seat over the years. Schoellhorn began to reinvest in the business, particularly in renewed R&D. He

also brought in new leadership for the business. The result: In the following decade pharmaceuticals would again become the company's largest and most profitable business.

By 1976, Schoellhorn was president and chief operating officer. In 1979, he was made chief executive officer. Two years later he replaced the man he so admired, Chairman Edward J. Ledder, upon his retirement.

With Ledder, Schoellhorn had expanded on George R. Cain's performance metrics, tying performance to sales and earnings per employee. Sterling results made Abbott one of the 100 largest U.S.-based companies, as measured by revenues and earnings.

Bob Schoellhorn was known for taking aggressive action. Under his leadership Abbott made major ventures into new businesses and geographies. It became a key investor in Amgen, which would become the world's leading biotechnology company; and in Boston Scientific, paving the way for Abbott's later medical devices business. He also oversaw critical international ventures, including the creation of the remarkably successful TAP joint venture with Takeda Chemical Industries, of Japan. And he introduced the company to China, a key market for the long-term future, through its Ningbo joint venture.

The decision-making process "needs to be quick," he once noted. "You'll make some mistakes, obviously. Everybody does. But if you recognize them quickly and correct them, why, it's often better than to have … made no decision at all."

After departing Abbott in 1990, Schoellhorn's venturesome nature won out again. He went into an entirely new field — the luxury recreational vehicle business — when he became the owner and CEO of Marathon Coach, Inc., a maker of customized RVs. ■

At age 93, a spry Dr. Volwiler was on hand for his induction, along with late colleague Dr. Donalee Tabern, into the National Inventors Hall of Fame for their breakthrough work in anesthetics, especially *Pentothal*.

Dr. Volwiler's legacy lives on at Abbott in the Volwiler Society, symbolized by the award above, an honorary organization recognizing the company's most distinguished scientists and engineers.

The Start of a Pharmaceutical Renaissance

While Abbott had been building up extremely successful sectors like diagnostics, its pharmaceutical business had declined significantly. Its leading medication continued to be erythromycin, its more-than-30-year-old antibiotic. Some of Abbott's competitors had moved ahead through robust R&D investment that was taking the science and business of pharmaceuticals to a new level. During this period the company's Board even debated the notion of exiting the drug business. It chose instead to rebuild, by forging alliances with other firms, bringing in new pharmaceutical products, and by revitalizing the company's historic strength in pharmaceutical R&D.

To this end, Abbott poured money into drug research. Some of the funds went into new technologies for finding promising new chemical substances. "The old ways of random screening of compounds," said Chairman Schoellhorn, "are giving way to the new, computer-assisted technologies." The R&D effort bore fruit, as the Pharmaceutical Products Division delivered several important new products.

A significant result of this effort was the hypnotic *ProSom*, with the chemical name estazolam. The drug, whose name means "for sleep" in Latin, was a successful treatment for insomnia.

Other pharmaceutical innovations sprang from Abbott's long-term investments and alliances overseas, particularly in Japan.

Prostate cancer is a leading cause of death among older men. Offering hope in the mid-1980s was the first product emerging from TAP, the joint venture between Abbott and the Japanese firm Takeda Chemical Industries.

This was the drug *Lupron*, approved by the U.S. FDA in 1985. It consisted of leuprolide acetate, a man-made hormone that mimics GnRH, the gonadotropin-releasing hormone, which triggers production of other sex hormones. *Lupron* directly affected the pituitary gland, and stimulated, then reduced, in men the generation of testosterone. Most prostate cancer tumors are maintained by that male sex hormone.

Therefore, the goal of prostate cancer treatment "is to turn off or counteract the body's production of testosterone," noted Dr. Ira Ringler, then president of the joint venture. *Lupron* achieved that aim — without the severe side effects of other therapies.

A pharma veteran despite his youth, Paul N. Clark was brought in at age 38 to lead Abbott's return to pharmaceutical excellence.

Nobel Prize winner Dr. Ferid Murad was recruited to reinvigorate the company's research effort as part of its pharmaceutical renaissance of the 1980s.

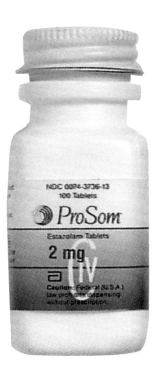

The sedative *ProSom* was an early product of the pharmaceutical renaissance Abbott began in the 1980s.

One alternative to *Lupron* treatment was surgical castration. "The emotional upset and trauma of surgical removal of the testes are avoided," added Ringler. A second option had been estrogen therapy, the administration of female sex hormones, which led to breast enlargement, nausea, and a higher risk of heart disease or stroke.

The patient, like a diabetic who self-administers insulin, injected *Lupron* into himself daily. *Lupron* treated advanced forms of prostate cancer, reducing tumor size and related urinary tract blockage. When a new "depot" formulation allowed patients to inject just once a month, rather than daily, *Lupron* became a blockbuster. Later formulations would help patients by reducing injections to just once every six months.

Another important alliance with a Japanese firm took place in 1985, with Taisho Pharmaceutical. Abbott and Taisho formed a partnership concerning an antibiotic the latter had developed, known as clarithromycin, which would later become Abbott's most successful product to that date, under the brand name *Biaxin* in the United States, and *Klacid* or *Klaricid* in international markets.

Continues on page 276 ▶

Celebrating Abbott's First Century

Abbott marked its centennial, in 1988, in style, with celebrations and publications to commemorate 100 years of remarkable scientific and commercial success.

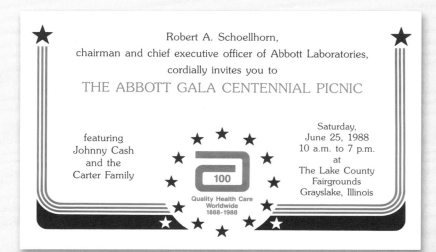

Robert A. Schoellhorn,
chairman and chief executive officer of Abbott Laboratories,
cordially invites you to

THE ABBOTT GALA CENTENNIAL PICNIC

featuring
Johnny Cash
and the
Carter Family

Saturday,
June 25, 1988
10 a.m. to 7 p.m.
at
The Lake County
Fairgrounds
Grayslake, Illinois

Quality Health Care
Worldwide
1888-1988

Hearkening back to the company's earlier days, Abbott threw a family picnic to mark its big anniversary. But the family had grown so large that it now filled the entire Lake County, Illinois, fairgrounds. And rather than the entertainment being provided by singing salesmen, it was music legends Johnny Cash and the Carter Family. More than 22,000 Abbott people and their family members attended.

This group of retirees, gathered at Abbott's celebration at the Lake County Fairgrounds, were all veterans of the company's 50th anniversary, in 1938.

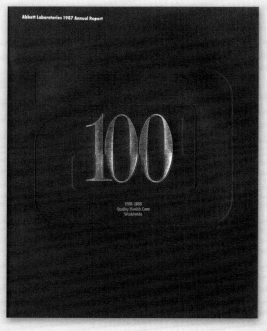

Abbott's Annual Report noted the company's milestone with elegant understatement.

Johnny Cash, the Man in Black, presents Chairman and
CEO Bob Schoellhorn an autographed guitar to mark the
occasion. Today, the guitar is displayed at Abbott House,
the company's heritage center.

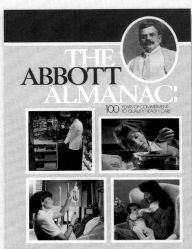

*The Abbott Almanac: 100 Years of
Commitment to Quality Care* was
published to recount the tale of the
company's first century in business.
It told Abbott's story year by year,
and provided a foundation for this
expanded exploration of Abbott's
history.

"Abbott today is still driven by the same sense of
purpose that drove our founder — Dr. Wallace
Abbott. For 100 years we have held to his credo of
looking for better ways of providing quality healthcare through advanced, cost-effective
technology."

— ROBERT A. SCHOELLHORN

The Abbott-discovered hypertension drug *Hytrin* would find an even larger application the following decade as a treatment for benign prostatic hyperplasia.

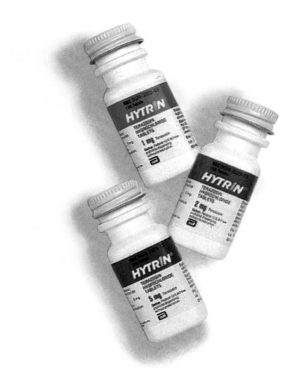

While developing and marketing entirely new drugs, Abbott also reformulated successful, existing drugs for important new uses.

Depakote, for instance, was a patented successor to *Depakene*, the drug for treating epilepsy. Launched in 1984, its coating permitted slow release of the drug, bypassing absorption by the stomach, thus relieving gastric distress.

In the year ahead, *Depakote* would be approved for use in bipolar disorder, or manic depression, which became its primary use, eventually making it a billion-dollar product. By 1998, *Depakote* would surpass lithium, long the leading treatment for bipolar disorder, in addressing the manic episodes associated with that malady, which afflicted some two million patients in the United States alone.

Another drug, for relieving gastrointestinal woes, was *PCE*, a polymer-coated form of erythromycin introduced in 1986. Erythromycin maintained its position in the 1980s as the biggest-selling antibiotic in the world.

Wearing an antiseptic "clean suit" to maintain maximum purity, a production technician carefully and precisely made *Abbokinase*, a drug for dissolving blood clots.

Promalin, a growth
regulator developed by
Abbott's Chemical and
Agricultural Products
Division, improved the
shape and skin of Red
Delicious apples.

In 1987, Abbott launched a major new drug to fight hypertension, or high blood pressure: the chemical compound terazosin, marketed as *Hytrin*. This was an alpha blocker, a class of medicines that block the nerve impulses constricting the arteries and veins, allowing them to relax and expand, thus lowering blood pressure.

Hytrin was powerful: Patients only had to take it once a day. This allowed *Hytrin to* address an issue typical of patients with high blood pressure, who are noted for not taking their prescribed dosages:

"The once-a-day dosage and low side effects of *Hytrin* promote optimal patient compliance," noted Robert S. Janicki, Abbott's vice president for pharmaceutical R&D. The drug also minimized the common side effects, such as sexual dysfunction, depression, or effect on heart rate or cholesterol, seen with other blood-pressure drugs.

The drug did not come quickly or cheaply. "It took about 12-1/2 years to get *Hytrin* to market," stated Schoellhorn, "from the discovery of the molecule to FDA approval." To develop it, Abbott over the years rang up R&D costs about double the entire research budget for 1970.

Noted Schoellhorn of the highly competitive hypertension field: "This is not a market for the timid." But it was a potentially lucrative one — consumer spending on blood pressure treatments was $2.5 billion a year and rising.

Abbott was putting together a strong array of cardio-vascular drugs. *Hytrin* joined fellow antihypertensives *Enduron* and *Enduronyl*, and *Abbokinase*, the blood-clot dissolving agent.

Not all the R&D effort went into the search for commercially lucrative pharmaceuticals. Indeed, Abbott had long produced drugs, such as *Diasone,* for leprosy, which made little money, but which were effective against rare diseases that presented great patient need, but no opportunity for an innovator to recoup its R&D investment due to the small size of the patient population.

It was in that spirit, in fact, that Congress passed the Orphan Drug Act of 1983. The Act supplied tax credits, filing fee waivers, and other incentives for firms to research and develop drugs and biologics to treat rare diseases.

Abbott had the privilege of making the first such "orphan drug." It was *Panhematin*, approved in 1983, an enzyme inhibitor derived from red blood cells. *Panhematin* relieved symptoms of acute porphyria, an enzyme

deficiency that can cause severe abdominal and back pains, and even respiratory paralysis. Acute porphyria afflicted just 3,000 patients in the United States. "We are pleased," noted Schoellhorn, "to be able to bring this vital agent to market to benefit those few patients whose health — and lives — may depend on it."

As Abbott developed new pharmaceutical and diagnostic products, the agricultural research center, first set up in the 1950s, rolled out innovations of its own. A growth regulator, *Promalin*, improved the shape of the lobes and skin of the well-known Red Delicious variety of apples. And work continued on a bacillus that 30 years prior had produced a natural insecticide. A new product, *Vectobac*, a different strain of the same microbe, yielded a substance to check the population of notorious summer pests: blackflies and mosquitoes.

A New Management Team

The middle and late 1980s, into the start of the 1990s, saw a number of shifts in top management.

Major changes occurred in January 1985. Kirk Raab, Abbott's president since 1981, joined Genentech, the leading biotechnology firm, as its president and CEO. Chairman Schoellhorn took on the additional role of company president.

Three young leaders then joined Charles J. Aschauer, Jr. as executive vice presidents. Aschauer still headed up the hospital products business, which by now included the Sorenson products and medical lasers.

One of the three promoted was Jack W. Schuler, who was responsible for the diagnostics, pharmaceutical, chemical, and agricultural products divisions.

The second was Thomas R. Hodgson, president of Abbott's international group, and formerly head of the hospital products division.

The third was Duane L. Burnham, the company's chief financial officer. Burnham took on additional duties with corporate engineering and materials management and with the nutritional products business.

In early 1987, Chairman Schoellhorn again revised the management team. Jack Schuler was made Abbott president and chief operating officer. Executive vice president and CFO Duane Burnham became vice chairman.

More big changes took place in 1989 and 1990. In August 1989, Jack Schuler left Abbott, joining the venture capital firm Crabtree Partners. Schuler would later be chairman of the board of the medical waste management company Stericycle, as well as Ventana Medical Systems, a maker of clinical diagnostic devices.

In January 1990, Bob Schoellhorn retired as CEO, and was succeeded by Duane Burnham. Schoellhorn later became owner and CEO of Marathon Coach, Inc.

In March, Burnham was named chairman of the board. Also that year, Tom Hodgson took on the role of company president and chief operating officer.

Jack W. Schuler was instrumental in the rise of Abbott's diagnostics division. He went on to serve as the company's president and chief operating officer.

TOP

An aerial view from the 1980s of Abbott Park, the company's burgeoning world headquarters. Over the next decade the 480-acre campus would fill in with new buildings to the south (bottom) and north (top), of this core.

BELOW
From its earliest days, when staff was almost entirely female, Abbott has been a force for women's presence and advancement in the workplace. In 1988, Abbott's plant in Barceloneta, Puerto Rico, which by then employed 16 female engineers, welcomed the Society of Women's Engineers for a tour of the facilities.

Into the Fortune 100

In 1987, sales had surpassed $4 billion, placing Abbott, for the first time, into the rarefied realm of the Fortune 100, *Fortune* magazine's list of the largest U.S.-based firms, by sales. Since just 1974 Abbott's market worth had grown 1,900 percent as the number of its shares had risen 16-fold.

Commercial success crested to the end of the decade. In 1989, earnings totaled approximately three-quarters of a billion dollars, at $3.85 a share, ranking 37th among the Fortune 500.

The company's total return to investors grew for the 18th consecutive year, to 33.1 percent in 1989, a remarkable rise from the IV recall year of 1971. Also in 1989, the lofty goal of 15 percent or more growth in earnings per share was again fulfilled — for the 18th straight year.

Since the 1920s, Abbott had paid 264 consecutive quarters of dividends to its shareholders, a record that has continued uninterrupted through the present day.

Decade at a Glance

1980–1990

1980 ▲

Abbott continues to develop and market innovative agricultural products, like the plant-growth regulator, *Promalin*.

Company revenues top $2 billion.

Abbott purchases the medical device firm Sorenson Research of Salt Lake City, Utah, founded by James LeVoy Sorenson, creator of the computerized heart monitor, among many other innovative medical devices. The acquisition provides Abbott with the first catheters that can remain in the body for extended periods, bolstering the company's critical-care business.

1981

The *TDx* therapeutic drug monitoring system is introduced, allowing physicians to adjust the doses of medicine in patients' bloodstreams, avoiding adverse reactions and expensive hospital stays.

▼

Chairman Edward J. Ledder, top, retires after 42 years at Abbott, and President and CEO Robert A. Schoellhorn, bottom, attains the post of chairman of the board. The new company president, Abbott's tenth, is G. Kirk Raab.

▼

Since just 1974, the market value of a share of Abbott stock has increased 800 percent.

1982 ▲

An aerial view of Abbott Park, the company's fast-growing world headquarters.

A pharmaceutical resurgence hits high gear: Seven new drugs are introduced that will account for 17 percent of sales in 1985.

1983

The U.S. FDA approves *Chlamydiazyme*, an enzyme immunoassay to detect Chlamydia.

Abbott consolidates three of its Japanese units into one unified healthcare firm, called Dainabot, K.K., strengthening its foothold in the world's second-largest economy.

The company manufactures the first "orphan drug," *Panhematin*. It treats acute porphyria, a rare enzyme deficiency that can cause severe back and stomach pains.

1984

From 1979 to 1984, Abbott hires 15 percent more employees, while sales per employee rise 57 percent.

Aided by a recovered national economy, total sales hit $3 billion. A company mantra is "an average compounded growth rate of 15 percent over any five-year period."

Depakote, a drug for treating epilepsy, is introduced. A successor to *Depakene*, its coating permits slow release of the drug.

▼

1985

Abbott's TAP joint venture with Takeda Chemical Industries introduces the drug *Lupron* for prostate cancer. The drug and the joint venture go on to become blockbuster successes.

▼

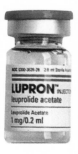

U.S. Health and Human Services Secretary Margaret Heckler and FDA Commissioner Frank Young call a press conference to hail approval of an Abbott breakthrough: the first licensed test to identify the AIDS virus. A team of Abbott employees working around the clock for eight months produces the test, called *HTLV-III EIA*, the first major medical victory in the fight against HIV/AIDS.

Abbott introduces *Vision*, an automated whole-blood analyzer. *Vision* lets physicians test blood on the spot instead of waiting 24–72 hours to get back blood work results.

Abbott's *ADD-Vantage* intravenous drug delivery system allows hospitals to store medications more effectively in powdered form, mixing them into solution only at the time of use. The product was adopted by many pharmaceutical companies.

President Raab resigns to lead Genentech. Chairman Schoellhorn takes on the additional role of company president.

1986
Abbott enters the growing market for blood tests for illegal or abused drugs, introducing tests that are accurate and inexpensive. The *TDx* system detects substances such as cocaine and PCP.

Abbott introduces 70 new diagnostics, including *TestPack*, a tool for the doctor's office that can rapidly test for conditions like strep throat, Chlamydia, and viral infection. *TestPack* also reliably detects pregnancy and introduces the now standard "+/−" method of reporting test results.

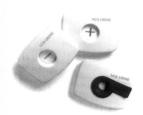

PCE, a polymer-coated form of erythromycin that relieves gastrointestinal woes, is introduced.

1987
Duane L. Burnham becomes Abbott's vice chairman and Jack W. Schuler becomes its president.

Sales surpass $4 billion, placing Abbott for the first time in the Fortune 100.

Abbott launches *Hytrin*, an alpha blocker drug that fights hypertension.

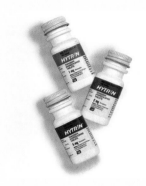

The *IMx*, a blood chemistry analyzer for medium-sized laboratories, is introduced, and tests for cancer, heart conditions, anemia, hepatitis, and other conditions. It will become the world's leading automated immunoassay system.

Technician examining the sample-holding carousel of the *IMx* immunoassay system.

1988
Hospital and laboratory products, driven by diagnostics, amount to 47 percent of Abbott's total revenues, and 58 percent of its international sales. The company is by far the world's leader in testing for HIV and in testing of blood donated to blood banks.

Abbott celebrates its centennial. A highlight of the festivities is a gathering for 22,000 on the Lake County, Illinois, fairgrounds, where music legend Johnny Cash played and presented a guitar to Chairman and CEO Bob Schoellhorn.

Abbott enters into an agreement to set up a China-based biotechnology joint-venture. Called Ningbo Abbott Biotechnology Ltd., it is Abbott's first modern experience in doing business in China.

1989
The FDA approves TAP's *Lupron Depot*, a reformulation of *Lupron* that can be taken just once a month. The new dosing makes it a blockbuster.

1990–2000
Steady Growth Through a Turbulent Time

More than a decade after HIV, the virus that causes AIDS, had been identified and characterized, there were still no viable treatments for the disease that had become the greatest medical challenge of its time. Abbott had been responsible for one of the first true breakthroughs in AIDS medicine, the first licensed test to detect HIV in blood, in 1985. In the '90s, Abbott was again a leader in the next great success in the fight against AIDS: the development of the first effective medications to treat the deadly and elusive disease.

PREVIOUS SPREAD
Building at Abbott Park, the company's global headquarters, reaches its peak, as the south campus (upper-left corner) is completed with the construction of building AP34. The 480-acre location includes research, manufacturing, and administrative facilities, staffed by more than 8,000 employees.

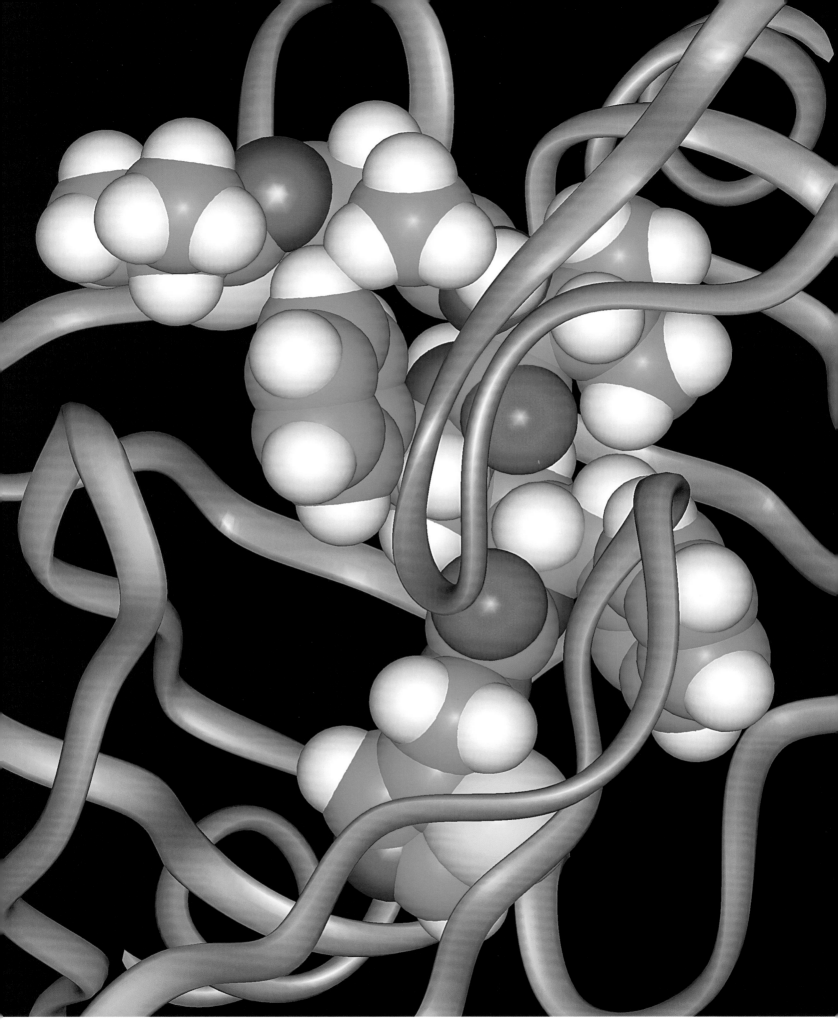

Computer rendering of Abbott's first HIV protease inhibitor drug *Norvir* (ritonavir), showing the molecule's atoms with the following color scheme: carbon (green), oxygen (red), nitrogen (blue), hydrogen (white), and sulfur (yellow). The protein of the HIV virus, with which *Norvir* interacts, is shown as an orange-colored ribbon, which represents the protein "backbone."

Biaxin, chemical name clarithromycin, was the latest in the long Abbott line of effective and profitable antibiotics. Abbott promoted *Biaxin*'s success in fighting bacteriological infections with an award-winning ad campaign built around Bix the bulldog, who reflected the drug's strengths and the company's.

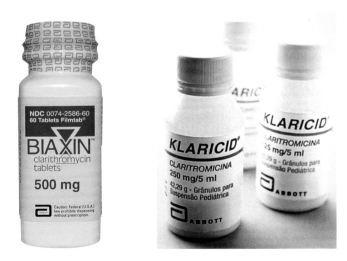

Biaxin was marketed as *Klacid* and *Klaricid* outside the United States, and became Abbott's first billion-dollar product.

The 1990s were a period of significant change and turmoil in the healthcare industry, characterized by the Clinton administration's healthcare reform effort in the United States, large-scale consolidation of the industry through a number of mega-mergers, and tens of thousands of industry layoffs. Still, Abbott remained undistracted by the events roiling around it and, by carefully managing its business, enjoyed another decade of steady growth and success.

Pharmaceutical Breakthroughs

The primary driver of the company's growth throughout the decade was its reinvigorated pharmaceutical business, as the pharma renaissance begun by Abbott in the 1980s came to fruition in dramatic fashion. A series of major new drug launches throughout the decade established the company as once again a major player in what had been its original business. These new products drew on both Abbott's own research prowess and on strategic alliances with firms around the world.

In 1990, Abbott introduced the antibiotic clarithromycin, a long-awaited successor to its decades-old mainstay, erythromycin. The drug was known as *Biaxin* in the United States, and *Klacid* or *Klaricid* in other countries. The Japanese drug company Taisho Pharmaceutical developed the compound and partnered with Abbott — because of its marketing strength and its manufacturing expertise in fermentation — to commercialize *Biaxin* outside Japan. The novel drug avoided the stomach pains and nausea caused by some other anti-infectives, and found particular use in treating middle-ear and other infections common in children. It was later found to be highly effective against the bacterium *H. pylori*, thus becoming a popular cure for ulcers.

Biaxin proved a spectacular success. By only its second year on the U.S. market, it became the United States' number-one adult respiratory antibiotic. In 1993, it passed erythromycin as Abbott's best-selling drug,

Duane L. Burnham, left,
was named the company's new
chairman and chief executive
officer, while Thomas R.
Hodgson, right, took on the
role of company president,
and chief operating officer.

island's $18 billion in wages, $3.6 billion from the pharmaceutical sector alone. Meanwhile, Puerto Rico had been transformed from being one of the poorest places in the Caribbean to having the area's highest per-capita income.

In 1995, a 10-year phase-out of Section 936's tax advantages began. Nonetheless, Abbott continued to build up its production in Puerto Rico, as the island offered strong infrastructure, proximity to the United States, a long-established working relationship with Abbott, a skilled workforce, and other operating advantages.

The company continued providing orphan drugs for rare conditions with the introduction, in 1991, of *Survanta*. The drug treated respiratory distress syndrome, or RDS, in newborn infants. RDS is a condition in which an infant lacks natural wetting agents to coat and lubricate the air sacs of the lungs, making them stiff and leading to their collapse. Breathing becomes difficult, and death can result. RDS typically occurs among premature babies, whose bodies aren't yet able to produce the wetting agents, known as surfactants.

Continues on page 292 ▶

with annual sales around $400 million. For years, *Biaxin* would be Abbott's single biggest-selling product, and was its first to reach one billion dollars in annual sales.

Remarkably, erythromycin continued to sell briskly. The old standby had been introduced during the postwar antibiotics boom. Its patent had expired in 1970. Nonetheless, Abbott's continuing innovations in formulation and presentation kept the franchise strong and gave it expertise in the marketing of "branded generics," which would become a major strategic business for the company in the years ahead.

To keep up with demand for *Biaxin*, Abbott built its largest manufacturing plant to that date, the Abbott Chemical Plant, or ACP, at the company's major manufacturing site in Barceloneta, Puerto Rico.

Abbott's expansion on that Caribbean island had been spurred by Section 936, a long-standing provision of the U.S. Internal Revenue Service code. Section 936 was devised as an incentive for economic development on Puerto Rico, offering a tax exemption for U.S.-based multinational firms on income generated from manufacturing plants there. As a result, hundreds of U.S. companies set up production in Puerto Rico. By the mid-1990s, such companies accounted for almost two-thirds of the

To meet worldwide demand for its blockbuster antibiotic clarithromycin, Abbott constructed the Abbott Chemical Plant (ACP) at its site in Barceloneta, Puerto Rico. ACP was the company's largest-ever capital investment to that time.

Abbott's Norvir Breaks Through Against AIDS

Abbott came late to the race to develop an effective HIV protease inhibitor to fight HIV. But, through a remarkable effort, the company achieved one of its greatest scientific triumphs, changing the course of the HIV epidemic and saving innumerable lives.

Abbott was a leader in the decade's greatest medical story: The long-sought development of a successful medication to fight AIDS. Abbott's breakthrough work, represented by Antiviral Venture head John M. Leonard, M.D., later senior vice president for Pharmaceuticals, Research and Development, was highlighted on the cover of *The Washington Post Magazine*.

In 1987, Abbott had slowly begun, almost by accident, to put together an HIV research team. Dale Kempf, an organic chemist from the University of Illinois, had started out at the firm by working on blood pressure drugs. His task was to find chemicals that inhibited the action of a "protease" called renin. A protease is an enzyme that helps dissolve proteins. Other researchers, meanwhile, suspected that protease inhibitors might throw a wrench into the works of HIV. Jake Plattner, Abbott's head of infectious diseases research, paid him a visit.

"Dale," he said, "we think HIV makes a protease. We'd like to borrow some of your compounds to see if they can inhibit that protease."

"Of course you can," replied Kempf, "but I think I can make better ones for you." Kempf began to moonlight — "submarine" he called it — laboring on HIV protease inhibitors in his spare time while doing blood pressure research during normal hours. Enthralled by his new work, he quickly transferred to the infectious disease unit. "The HIV epidemic had become front-page news," he noted, "and if there was a way that I could somehow contribute to stopping it, that's what I wanted."

Over the next year and a half, Kempf and two other chemists got down to work. They applied sophisticated means to determine the molecular structure of the virus. One was to shoot X-rays at the crystals of the HIV protease. By analyzing mathematically how the X-rays scattered, they used computer graphics programs to build a model of the protease. The enzyme looked rather like two right hands clasping each other.

To block the protease, they turned to a second tool: nuclear magnetic resonance, or NMR. Many molecules are too small to be seen with microscopes. But NMR allowed even the atoms of a compound to be deduced. With this knowledge, Kempf and his colleagues made hundreds of these would-be inhibitors by methodically heating, cooling, and purifying off-the-shelf chemicals in the lab.

Meanwhile, the team gained a new member, Dan Norbeck, later Abbott's head of pharmaceutical discovery. A literature major at Wheaton College, Norbeck was drawn to what he termed the "romance of science" and went on to earn a Ph.D. in organic chemistry from Cal Tech. "When I was in graduate school," he recalled, "I started reading about this new disease. It grabbed everyone's attention. People kept asking, 'What's the cause?' 'Is there a cure?' It was exciting to come and work on something so important."

At length, the scientists created a compound that appeared to inhibit the HIV protease, and stopped the virus from growing *in vitro* ("in glass," as opposed to *"in vivo,"* in a living being). Abbott added resources to the effort, and 11 scientists tackled the first tests of the inhibitor on laboratory rats. Here they hit a major roadblock. The animals' bloodstreams readily absorbed the substance, but their livers just as quickly removed it, before the molecule could do its job.

The researchers went back to the drawing board, creating and trying out hundreds of variants of the molecule. "There were times when we'd ask ourselves," remembered Norbeck, "do we really have the skills to be competitive in this area?"

But in 1991, came a "Eureka" moment. "As soon as we put it into rats for the first time," remembered Kempf, "we knew we had something special. Instead of rapidly disappearing, it stayed in the blood for more than eight hours!" The substance was dubbed ritonavir.

The next year, another key player joined the HIV team, to lead it through its clinical trial phase. This was Dr. John M. Leonard, later Abbott's senior vice president, Pharmaceuticals, Research and Development. He had fought the disease before, in San Francisco near the beginning of the AIDS epidemic in the early 1980s. "It was an exciting period because the biotech industry was getting started," Leonard remembered. "I decided I could best serve others by figuring out how to make new medicines."

A molecular virologist who had studied at Johns Hopkins and Stanford, Leonard recalled the day, not long after joining Abbott as head of its Antiviral Venture Team, when a co-worker had visited his new office. She told him, "Where I used to work, we always looked for something to celebrate, to liven things up. We should do that here."

Leonard answered: "You know how football players celebrate a touchdown by spiking the ball? Maybe we should do that!" Days later, his friend handed Leonard a wrapped box. Inside was a Nerf football. "Okay," he laughed, "it goes on my windowsill. We'll use it on special occasions."

Over the course of the effort the Nerf ball would gather dust, seeming to mock Leonard and his team's Herculean efforts, involving the creation and testing of hundreds of promising compounds.

During this period of early testing, costs were high, and progress uncertain and slow. At first, ritonavir cost $500,000 a kilogram to produce. At that price, a patient would go through about $200,000 of the drug in a year.

As a company, Abbott had to balance the chance of a successful new drug versus the uncertainty and cost of drug development. On average, only one compound in ten thousand makes it all the way through development to the patient. Thousands of pages of data had to be gathered and sent to the United States Food and Drug Administration (FDA), which, after all the effort and expense, could decide against approval for a variety of reasons. Development costs were steep, and would soon average $1 billion for a new drug.

Leonard began to attend regular meetings with Chief Operating Officer Thomas R. Hodgson on his team's progress, or lack thereof.

In 1999, Abbott received the Prix Galien, considered the pharmaceutical industry's highest honor, for the groundbreaking, and life-saving, development of *Norvir*.

Hodgson told him, "'I want us to succeed with this. I don't know how we're going to get there,'" Leonard remembered. "So meet with me monthly and show me your progress. We'll decide together what we should do.'" Of the get-togethers, Leonard noted: "I can say there were times when this program hung by the thinnest of threads. I can recall Hodgson when he seemed to be asking for a reason to believe.

"You read about a breakthrough medicine," Leonard continued, "and people on the outside think all of this is automatic. But on the inside, sometimes the destiny of a new drug depends on the outcome of a conversation between two people."

The next challenge was to test the promising compound on human subjects. A group of HIV patients received doses of ritonavir over several months. "What we saw," stated Leonard, "was something we did not expect.

"The virus had fallen to levels that were less than 1 percent of what had been in their blood!"

After each hard-won product victory, the Norvir/Kaletra team would spike this Nerf football in manager John Leonard's office. Today the ball, somewhat the worse for wear, occupies a position of honor in Abbott's archives.

With the potential for the first effective treatment for AIDS in sight, Abbott moved fast. It had to — it was in a race. The pharmaceutical houses Merck and Hoffmann La Roche (Roche) had their own protease inhibitors in development, had begun earlier, and were further along in the process.

The next hurdle was a large-scale, Phase III clinical trial involving many hundreds of patients. Such a trial normally takes 24 months; Hodgson wanted it done in eight. In 1995, the company leased an office building near its headquarters and filled it with a hundred photocopiers and fax machines to send and receive data on the trials. Hundreds of employees were hired or reassigned to work on the rush project. That summer, pharmaceutical R&D chief Andre Pernet gathered a swarm of scientists in the firm's expansive, Lake County, Illinois, cafeteria.

Pernet told the assembled troops: "Okay, guys, we have a fantastic new drug on our hands. We need to sprint to the finish line. We need all hands on deck."

As Abbott cranked up, a competitor surged ahead. In fall 1995, the U.S. FDA approved Roche's protease inhibitor, called saquinavir. All the efforts of Abbott's HIV team, Norbeck noted, could have been "for naught from a medical and a commercial viewpoint." However, it was soon found that the human liver rapidly purged saquinavir from the bloodstream, limiting its efficacy.

Meantime, the large-scale trial of ritonavir, which would be given the brand name *Norvir*, plunged forward. In late 1995, the results were revealed. The drug reduced HIV symptoms and lessened mortality. As important, *Norvir* remained in the bloodstream much longer than other protease inhibitors. Kempf's constant tweaking of its molecule was about to produce a major payback.

On February 29, 1996, during a 12-hour session in Washington, D.C., Abbott presented its New Drug Application (NDA) to the agency's advisory committee, with FDA commissioner David Kessler on hand. The Abbott crew was ready, having trucked in files of supporting documents from headquarters; some 3,000 slides had been prepared to answer any questions. The next day, March 1, *Norvir* was approved. The drug had cleared all regulatory hurdles in record time.

Along with Merck's compound indinavir, *Norvir* was one of the first protease inhibitors approved for use. In 1999, the Prix Galien, considered the equivalent of a Nobel Prize for the pharmaceutical industry, was awarded to Abbott for its work on *Norvir*.

In Abbott Park, on the day of Norvir's FDA approval, Kempf strode into Leonard's office, and grabbed the dusty Nerf ball. He told his boss and friend: "I've been waiting a long time for this moment" — and spiked the ball.

"Nine years had passed since we started working on an HIV medicine," he later reflected. "But I knew our work still wasn't over." The team would go on to make an even greater breakthrough against HIV/AIDS in the years ahead. ∎

Adapted from best-selling author Robert Shook's book Miracle Medicines: Seven Life-Saving Drugs and the People Who Created Them.

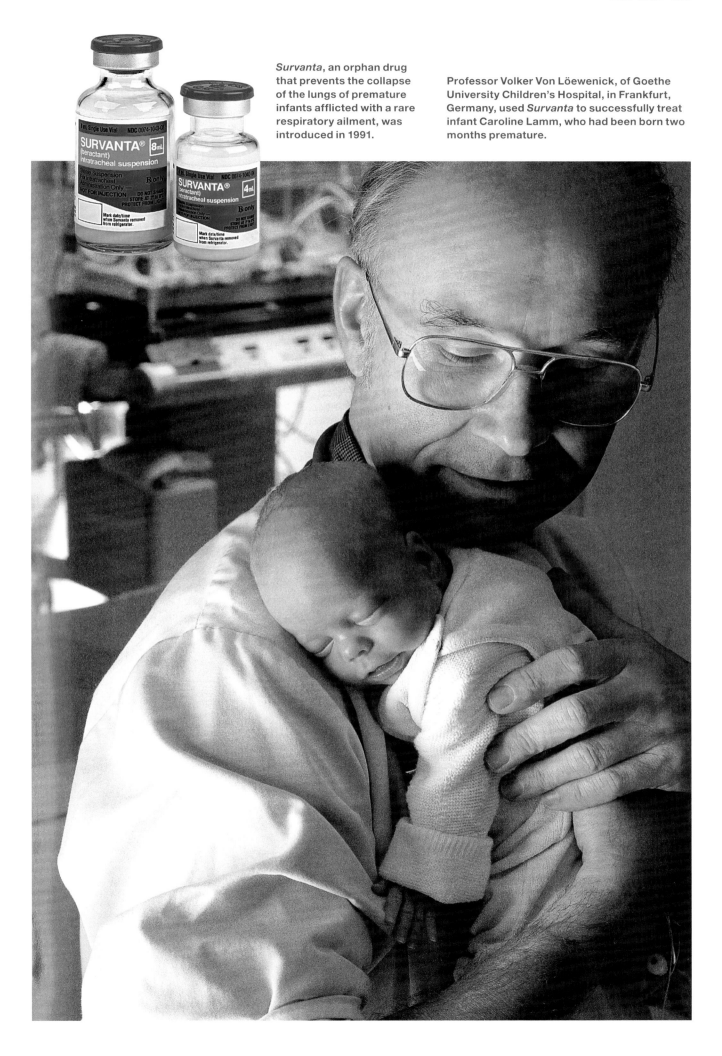

Survanta, an orphan drug that prevents the collapse of the lungs of premature infants afflicted with a rare respiratory ailment, was introduced in 1991.

Professor Volker Von Löewenick, of Goethe University Children's Hospital, in Frankfurt, Germany, used *Survanta* to successfully treat infant Caroline Lamm, who had been born two months premature.

Ultane, marketed outside the United States as *Sevorane*, is a universal anesthetic, notable for its paucity of side effects.

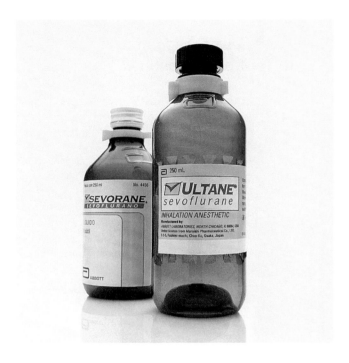

Survanta was made up of a substance called beractant, containing lipids, fatty acids, and proteins. It coated the surface of the air sacs, allowing them to inflate. A doctor applied *Survanta* through a flexible tube directly to the lungs of an infant soon after birth. The physician used a scope to direct the tube down the infant's air passages. *Survanta* saved the lives of many premature infants.

The company also added to its storied history in anesthetics, and its track record of marketing effective new drugs developed by Japanese partners, with sevoflurane. Called *Ultane* in the United States and *Sevorane* in many international markets, Abbott acquired the rights to the compound in 1992 from Maruishi Pharmaceutical Co., Ltd.

Like its distant predecessor *Pentothal*, the colorless liquid had excellent properties for anesthesia. Sevoflurane was stable, even when exposed to acids or high temperatures, and could be mixed with other anesthetics like ether. The drug induced patients quickly and smoothly. It could also be used for effective maintenance of anesthesia throughout a procedure, and it had very few side effects, making it a "universal" anesthetic, especially useful for pediatric and outpatient care.

In the decade, several new applications were approved for *Lupron*, the drug first launched for prostate cancer in 1985 by TAP.

In 1990, *Lupron Depot 3.75 mg* was approved to treat endometriosis, an extra-uterine growth that can trigger severe pelvic pain and impede fertility. The drug was later found effective in fighting uterine fibroid tumors, growths in the smooth muscle of the walls of the uterus. They can lead to pelvic pain, heavy menstrual flow, and infertility in roughly half of the women afflicted. In concert with iron therapy, *Lupron Depot 3.75 mg* also could treat related anemia.

In 1993, *Lupron Depot PED* was introduced for the treatment of central precocious puberty, or premature sexual development in boys and girls. This condition is characterized, before age nine, by the development of facial hair and enlargement of the testes in boys, and the development of breasts and of menstruation in girls. Central precocious puberty also triggers a premature growth spurt in the early years, but results in much shorter-than-average height in maturity. To address the disorder, *Lupron Depot PED* continually stimulates the pituitary gland, responsible for production of the sex hormones, thus returning growth and sexual development to normal.

Continues on page 294 ▸

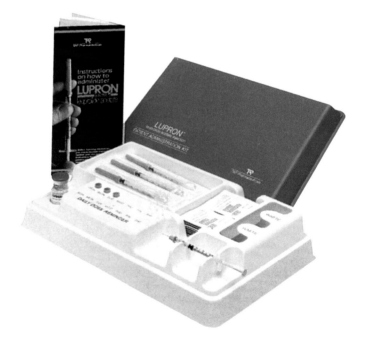

Lupron, the first blockbuster drug from Abbott's TAP Pharmaceuticals joint venture, was a remarkably versatile hormone therapy, used in the treatment of prostate cancer in men, endometriosis in women, and precocious puberty in children.

A Novel Drug to Help the Newly Born

As a professor of pediatrics at a Boulder, Colorado, hospital in the 1980s, Dr. Jessie Groothuis especially noticed the wheezing. From November through April, many prematurely born babies and children under age two would come down with respiratory syncytial virus, or RSV, a chronic lung affliction with cold-like symptoms.

"They would wheeze all day, as if they were asthmatics," Groothuis recalled. "They wouldn't be able to drink because they were so busy trying to breathe."

By age two, most children have come down with RSV. In some, it can lead to serious complications. Perhaps 60 million are afflicted worldwide; about 160,000 die annually.

Groothuis watched some of the infants catch pneumonia, be placed on a ventilator, or even die. The existing asthmatic and antiviral therapies were ineffective.

She knew that when RSV afflicts an infant, the body's antibodies respond, increasing in number to attack the virus. Unlike some illnesses, however, the antibodies drop off, allowing the disease to grow stronger.

For her RSV work, Groothuis teamed up with Carole Heilman, a microbiologist at the National Institute for Allergy and Infectious Diseases of the National Institutes of Health.

"We produced research," Groothuis noted, "showing that if you could keep antibodies up, RSV doesn't go deep into the lungs, which means doctors are able to treat it more easily."

Their study called for developing a drug to maintain patients' antibodies. They were awarded federal funding for a vaccine developed from the antibodies of nurses whose work with RSV-afflicted infants made them resistant to the disease.

Enter Abbott. Along with the biotech firm Medimmune, it developed the vaccine, called palivizumab, and marketed it under the brand name *Synagis*. Groothuis herself joined the Abbott team, and managed the clinical trials for *Synagis*, which demonstrated a 55 percent reduction in RSV-caused hospitalization of premature infants.

Synagis elicited the first federal approval of a breakthrough therapeutic technology: monoclonal antibodies. Monoclonal antibodies are highly specific, binding to a particular part of an antigen, that is, the invading organism causing the disease, making them highly effective and yielding few side effects.

The novel medicine rapidly became the standard treatment for RSV. In 2000, according to the National Institutes of Health, 100,000 patients received the drug.

At birth, twins Kasandra and Alondra each weighed no more than 3-1/2 pounds. They were given *Synagis* to help them through the challenge of their premature birth.

Stated an NIH analysis: "*Synagis* reduced the number of days an infant must spend in the hospital, the severity of the infection, the need for oxygen treatments, as well as the incidence of admitting the children to the intensive care unit."

The drug, therefore, not only made a major medical impact — it extended Abbott's role in pediatric medicine and began its experience in therapeutic monoclonal antibodies, which would play a major role in the years ahead. ∎

"Tummy" was the mascot for *Prevacid*, the blockbuster medication for gastroesophageal reflux disease (GERD). Marketed by Abbott's TAP joint venture, it was a top-five U.S. drug.

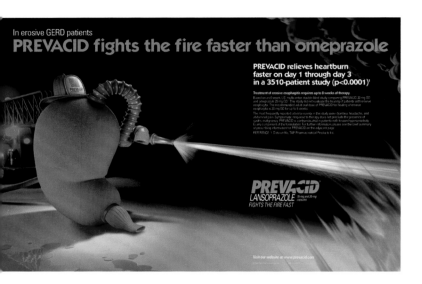

In erosive GERD patients

PREVACID fights the fire faster than omeprazole

PREVACID relieves heartburn faster on day 1 through day 3 in a 3510-patient study (p<0.0001)¹

PREVACID
LANSOPRAZOLE
FIGHTS THE FIRE FAST

Approved in 1995 was TAP's second blockbuster drug in a row: *Prevacid*. A proton pump inhibitor to treat acid reflux, *Prevacid* was an even greater success than *Lupron*, becoming a top-five drug in the United States.

A medicine straddling the line between pharmaceuticals and vitamins, both long-standing Abbott strengths, was introduced in 1998, when Abbott was granted U.S. FDA approval for *Zemplar*. The key ingredient in *Zemplar* was paricalcitol, a substance similar to the active form of vitamin D. It reduces the amount of parathyroid hormone, found in high levels among persons with long-term kidney disease. *Zemplar* helped ward off bone ailments stemming from that condition. It also treated the related ailment of hyperparathyroidism, or overactivity of the thyroid glands — organs that control the body's level of calcium.

The AIDS drug *Norvir*, after an arduous eight-year research effort, proved, in 1996, a true breakthrough therapy for HIV sufferers. And the Abbott HIV team of scientists kept working throughout the 1990s to achieve other significant advancements for patients. Following *Norvir* at the end of the decade was the improved, second-generation protease inhibitor *Kaletra*, which became the most-used treatment in its class. Together, *Norvir* and *Kaletra* were important components of the "AIDS cocktails" that transformed HIV from a veritable death sentence to a chronic, yet manageable, malady (see "Capsules" pages 288 and 314 for details).

Other new drugs, or new formulations, reached market with considerable success. The alpha blocker *Hytrin*, developed in the 1980s for high blood pressure, found a new application. It was used to treat symptoms of benign

prostatic hyperplasia, or BPH, the enlarged prostate gland common among men over age 50. Clinical tests showed it improved urinary flow problems for more than half of those tested. This new use of *Hytrin* was marketed in a novel way, through free 21-day doses of the drug. BPH quickly became *Hytrin's* most widespread use, and Hytrin the leader in the category.

Abbott further bolstered its cardiovascular line in 1998 with *TriCor*, a drug manufactured by the French firm Fournier and marketed by Abbott. A fibrate, or derivative of fibric acid, *TriCor* was a "triple threat" to heart ailments. First, it lowered triglyceride levels, which are linked to inflamed arteries. Second, it increased levels of high-density lipoprotein (HDL), or "good cholesterol." Third, it decreased low-density lipoprotein (LDL), or "bad cholesterol." Fibrates cut the liver's production of triglyceride-carrying particles, and increase the removal of triglycerides from the bloodstream. Abbott would build on this base as it expanded its cardiovascular drug franchise in the years to come.

Navigating a Time of Change

In ascending to the post of chief executive officer, in January 1990, Duane L. Burnham offered a sure hand to a successful enterprise. Burnham provided stability and assurance throughout an often turbulent decade.

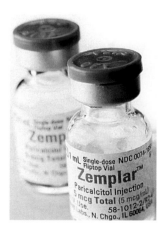

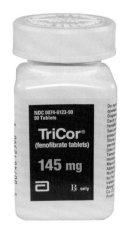

Zemplar helps with kidney-related bone ailments through a substance akin to the active form of vitamin D.

The aptly named drug **TriCor** treated lipid disorders in three distinct ways: lowering triglycerides and LDL (the "bad" cholesterol), and raising HDL (the "good" cholesterol).

This Is How BPH Feels

The 1990s were a time of steady growth for Abbott, during which the company concentrated primarily on organic growth of existing businesses.

"Our success," stated Burnham, "has been in selecting our markets and in sticking to healthcare as our business." Noted one analyst of Abbott: "They don't try to be all things to all people."

Burnham saw the bottom-line approach as a good match for the industry environment: "Our established strategy of reducing the total cost of healthcare and helping our customers operate more efficiently leaves us well prepared for the cost-conscious future," he said.

One instance of the effort toward greater efficiency was the formation in January 1990 of the new Corporate Hospital Marketing Division, or CHMD. CHMD was aimed at strengthening relationships and sales with key clients such as large hospital groups. Unique among Abbott's commercial divisions, CHMD placed in one organization the responsibilities for distribution, marketing, customer consulting, and customer service across the company's range of businesses. The new organization was headed by Robert L. Parkinson, later Abbott's president and chief operating officer.

CHMD's 500 employees were soon lining up long-term contracts with providers such as Lutheran General Health Care System. This was an Illinois-based healthcare network consisting of 15 senior living centers, 10 nursing homes, hospitals, and more than 90 substance abuse treatment centers in the United States and Sweden. Sales teams for relationships with such large, integrated health-system customers included representatives of all Abbott commercial divisions — diagnostics, pharmaceuticals, nutritionals, and hospital products — representing the breadth and synergy of Abbott's offerings, and simplifying the process of dealing with Abbott's varied businesses for the customer. In the years ahead, CHMD would evolve into Abbott's Corporate Marketing group, responsible for the stewardship of the corporate brand.

Burnham adroitly handled the company's successful response to the decade's biggest healthcare issue, the 1993–94 national healthcare plan proposal by United States President Bill Clinton, and spearheaded by First Lady Hillary Rodham Clinton.

The early and mid-1990s were a time of significant cost cutting in the industry, as governments worldwide strove to rein in the rising cost of healthcare. The Clinton plan, offered in fall 1993 after months of politicking and internal bargaining, called for a system of universal coverage. To achieve coverage for all Americans, the plan called for government subsidies to low-income individuals and small firms, some tax levies, and also certain government mandates, such as a requirement for all employers to contribute to the expense of their workers' health insurance premiums. Preventive care was stressed. The plan also would have imposed ceilings on insurance premiums.

The controversial proposal added to the uncertainty and turmoil affecting the healthcare industry. Indeed, many healthcare firms saw their market value fall off significantly during this era. In early 1992, the 10 largest publicly traded U.S. health products companies had a combined market capitalization of $289 billion. By fall 1994, that figure had plunged to $164 billion in anticipation of changes to come.

Some companies responded to this business environment by trying to cut costs through acquisitions and mergers — and through layoffs. In 1993 alone, large pharmaceutical, hospital supply, and medical device firms shed more than 35,000 jobs.

The *AxSYM* device, Abbott's next great advance in diagnostic instrumentation, could conduct more than 100 tests involving more than 85 immunoassays in an hour.

Thankfully Abbott, as it had in other difficult times for the industry, withstood the storm better than most. The company, which now had some 50,000 employees, undertook no broad-based layoffs, and avoided the temptation to merge for the sake of synergies. And, at a time of financial threat for the industry, Abbott's bottom line was strong, with sales and earnings rising steadily during the fierce U.S. debate over healthcare policy.

Abbott was supportive of the general notion of managed competition, whereby health-care consumers would organize into large purchasing groups to drive down costs. The idea was that consumers would comparison-shop for plans, services, and products of the best price and quality. However, Abbott and the rest of the industry questioned other parts of the Clinton plan that, it was feared, would stifle the innovation on which both patients and the industry depended.

Burnham's public statements recalled those President Cain had made in the 1960s during the Senate Kefauver hearings. Burnham noted: "Abbott supports the goals of healthcare reform — access to care for all Americans and reduction in the rate of cost growth … We believe a market-based approach is the best way to reform the U.S. healthcare system … Reform must encourage innovation in products, processes, and practices in order to improve care and reduce the rate of cost growth. Abbott opposes price controls and increased government regulations as a means of accomplishing these goals."

After a lengthy nationwide debate, the Clinton health-care proposal was voted down in the United States Senate in summer 1994, due to concerns similar to those cited by Abbott.

Keeping the Lead in Diagnostics

The diagnostics division, which had led the company's growth in the 1970s and 1980s, continued to be number one in its field through further innovation, as well as expansion into new markets and technologies.

In 1991, Abbott made an important step into the field of hematology testing, a rare segment of the diagnostics market in which it was not already a leader, with its acquisition of Sequoia-Turner Corp. That same year, Abbott developed the first automated test for monitoring prostate-specific antigen, or PSA. A protein, PSA is produced by the prostate gland, and can be used to screen for prostate cancer and to monitor the effectiveness of therapies to fight it.

A major new product was introduced in 1994, *AxSYM*, an immunoassay diagnostic system for hospitals and high-volume labs. The watchword for *AxSYM* was "throughput." Managed by an intelligent workstation, it conducted more than 100 tests of various types per hour, a major advance. The system handled more than 85 immunoassays, performing cardiovascular, cancer, fertility, thyroid, infectious disease, metabolic, hepatitis, HIV, and toxicology testing, among other uses. Results for each test were generated in as little as eight minutes.

Commented new diagnostics chief Miles D. White about the value *AxSYM* would provide: "In the era of healthcare reform, laboratories are faced with increasing pressure to produce accurate test results with faster turnaround time and lower overall laboratory costs."

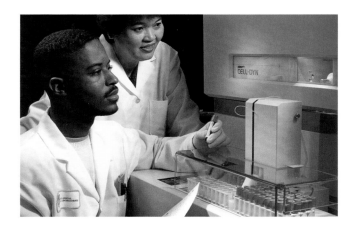

The acquisition of California-based Sequoia-Turner enhanced Abbott Diagnostics' position in hematology. It was also the first deal spearheaded by Miles White, who would go on to build the company with major acquisitions as its chairman and CEO.

Like his predecessors, CEO Duane L. Burnham was a builder. Three major new edifices, worth $100 million, were added to the Lake County world headquarters on his watch. Building began in 1992 for these 600,000-square-feet of facilities, which housed 1,400 researchers, technicians, and office workers. Another 1,100 workers were added at other area sites; these employees were in addition to the 3,300 Abbott employees who had joined the Lake County workforce in the previous five years. "Our growth rate has been accelerated," Burnham stated simply.

Illinois Governor Jim Edgar (second from left) attends the opening of a new research building at Abbott Park with Chairman and CEO Duane L. Burnham (right). Abbott was the state's largest investor in research and development.

The 1996 acquisition of Massachusetts-based MediSense marked Abbott's entry into the field of glucose monitoring for people with diabetes. This would lead, in the decade to come, to the creation of a major new division, Abbott Diabetes Care, based in Alameda, California.

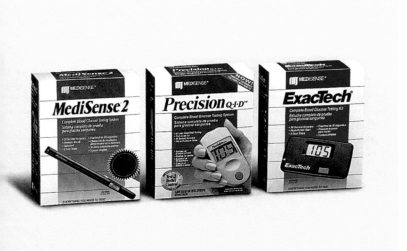

In time, *AxSYM* would be the vehicle for the first completely automated immunoassay for the hepatitis A virus, as well as testing for cardiac troponin, a protein important in the diagnosis of heart attacks. It also detected and measured the presence of antibodies that were indicators of thyroid disorders such as Addison's disease and Cushing's syndrome.

When White spearheaded the acquisition of Sequoia-Turner, early in the '90s, it was a sign of things to come. As head of ADD he would lead another important strategic move in the diagnostics arena, Abbott's largest deal of the decade. This was the $876 million acquisition, in 1996, of

MediSense Inc. An innovator in blood glucose monitoring, MediSense developed devices that allowed people with diabetes to test their own blood sugar levels. Monitoring diabetes early on is vital to avoiding serious, subsequent health problems such as kidney disorders, blindness, and amputation of extremities.

MediSense products reflected the growing trend toward the convenient and inexpensive self-monitoring of medical conditions. Its kits were "minimally invasive," an approach that Abbott's diagnostics business had long promoted. Only a small finger-prick's worth of blood was required for testing and analysis.

The acquisition also provided a foundation for synergy between different Abbott divisions with expertise in the same disease state. For instance, following this entry into diabetes care, Abbott would also begin making nutritionals aimed at the special dietary needs of people with diabetes. In a similar way, it would complement its HIV tests and medications with specially formulated nutritional products for HIV patients, to help them regain and maintain weight and strength. Burnham encouraged this kind of synergy, noting that the company "must capture … opportunities that exist across product lines, across markets, and across organizational structure."

By the end of the decade, Abbott cemented its position in the high-volume testing and blood-screening markets with the launch of two innovative diagnostic systems.

First, in 1997, Abbott announced plans to develop an advanced family of analyzers called *ARCHITECT*. Across the industry, laboratories were consolidating, creating the

A Proud Tradition of Antibiotics

1910s
Chlorazene

One of Abbott's early prominent antibacterials was *Chlorazene*, a chlorine-based antiseptic manufactured during the First World War.

1920s
Metaphen

The topical antiseptic *Metaphen* was introduced in the 1920s.

Edward A. Ogunro, left, reviews software integration testing details for the ARCHITECT i2000. Dr. Ogunro would later become head of Hospital Products Research and Development, Medical and Regulatory Affairs.

Abbott's *PRISM* became the world's leading blood screening system. *PRISM* would later be used to test 100 percent of the U.S. blood supply.

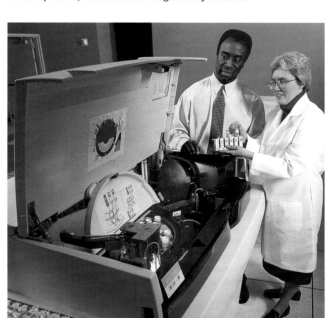

need for systems that could process hundreds of tests per hour. The *ARCHITECT* family was designed to be modular and scalable, to meet the requirements of even the largest testing facilities.

The line was officially launched in early 1999, with the introduction of the i2000 SB, a high-speed system capable of performing up to 200 tests per hour. True to its name, *ARCHITECT* allowed laboratories to build a system customized to their particular needs. By linking a series of

up to four i2000 modules together, a laboratory could process as many as 800 tests per hour. Early in the next decade, *ARCHITECT* expanded its utility by offering the c8000, a module that, when linked with an i2000SR, let laboratories combine immunoassay and clinical chemistry testing in a single workstation.

Another important diagnostic system was *AbbottPRISM*, which quickly became the number-one blood screening system in most European countries.

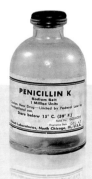

1940s

Penicillin

In the 1940s, Abbott became one of the first and largest producers of penicillin.

1950s

Erythrocin

A decade later came *Erythrocin* (erythromycin), a drug practically free of side effects.

1990s

Clarithromycin

In 1990, clarithromycin, (marketed as *Biaxin* in the U.S. and *Klacid* and *Klaricid* elsewhere) an antibiotic easy on the stomach, was introduced; it became Abbott's best-selling product to that time.

PRISM is a high-volume, fully automated analyzer with unprecedented process controls, designed to run blood bank virology immunoassays in a rapid and error-checked manner to ensure that transfused blood is as safe as possible. By removing the manual steps and consolidating the testing into a single system, *PRISM* provides testing that is both accurate and highly reliable.

In the 1990s, Abbott also introduced the first rapid tests — simple diagnostics that could be used at home for quick initial diagnoses without the help of a professional — for HIV, pregnancy, and other conditions.

By the end of the decade, only one U.S. FDA-approved rapid HIV test was commercially available in the United States. This was the Abbott Murex Single Use Diagnostic System (SUDS) HIV-1 test. According to the U.S. Government's Centers for Disease Control, "This test can provide definitive negative and preliminary positive test results at the time of testing, and identify women who might need antiretroviral treatment and whose infants might benefit from [medication]." In the following decade, Abbott would ship tens of millions of rapid HIV tests to Africa, for free or at no profit, to help battle that continent's AIDS pandemic.

Nutrition for Every Need

To supplement its long leadership in infant formula Abbott expanded its scientific approach to nutrition into new areas to meet new needs. *Grow* brand pre-school milk was aimed at children three years and older, picking up where traditional

Grow was first developed to meet demand, primarily in Asia, for "follow-on" formulas for children aged three and older.

infant formula feeding left off. And, in a sign of things to come for Abbott, its development was led outside the United States, in Asia, where such "follow-on" formulas were popular. And a series of variations of *Similac* were developed, including, in 1994, *Similac Neocare* and, later, *Similac NeoSure*, with a formula to help spur weight gain in premature infants. *Similac Advance*, introduced in 1997, contained nucleotides akin to those in breast milk, helping develop an infant's immune system. Other nutrients added were fatty acids and iron to aid in a baby's visual and brain development.

Another success story was *Ensure*, the line of mineral- and vitamin-rich nutritional beverages and snack bars for people seeking a healthy supplement to their diets, or even as a sole source of nutrition for those unable to consume solids. First introduced in the 1970s, *Ensure* took off in the '90s as the leading all-purpose adult nutritional in a fast-growing market.

Given such success, *Ensure* naturally attracted competitors: by the mid-'90s it faced off against some 14 rival products. Abbott responded strongly to keep its top spot, leveraging its formidable sales group, extensive distribution, and R&D expertise.

Abbott rolled out distinctive flavors of *Ensure* tailored to regional markets. For example, while U.S. consumers favored milk shake-like flavors such as chocolate and vanilla, the European market leaned toward savory flavors, including asparagus and mushroom.

New formulations were regularly rolled out — including those for healthy adults seeking a dietary supplement. An example was *Ensure High Protein*, introduced in 1994 for more active consumers.

Building on the success of its *Ensure* line of adult nutritional products, Abbott pioneered a new category: disease-specific nutritionals, products formulated to address the unique dietary needs associated with particular disease states.

One such product was *Pulmocare*, for lung disease patients. *Pulmocare* was a high-calorie, low-carbohydrate formula to help reduce the body's production of carbon dioxide. The formula was aimed at helping patients with chronic obstructive pulmonary disease, cystic fibrosis, or respiratory failure.

Another disease-specific nutritional was *Advera*, for the dietary management of patients infected with HIV. High in calories and protein to help maintain body weight and muscle, *Advera* was introduced in 1993.

The most successful of Abbott's disease-specific nutritionals was *Glucerna*, a product formulated specifically for people with diabetes and others with dietary restrictions.

The disease-specific nutritional *Pulmocare* was introduced to help patients with respiratory ailments, by cutting the body's generation of carbon dioxide.

milk products such as infant formula and food supplements were stored largely in metal cans. This was due to the need for thoroughly sterilizing the contents of the cans, which were subjected to extreme pressure and heat that plastic containers could not withstand. However, metal cans, once opened, presented problems of safe and easy storage.

Abbott technicians solved these problems for infant formulas like *Similac* by separating the processes for sterilizing plastic bottles and their contents, and then filling the bottles under sterile conditions as well.

A metal foil was used to hermetically and aseptically seal the bottle. A new optical testing system was created to scrutinize each seal for missing or misplaced foil.

Production engineers also devised a magnetic resonance imaging system that could make a final inspection of nutritionals after their placement in shipping crates.

Continues on page 304 ▶

Glucerna's low saturated fatty acids and high mono-unsaturated fatty acids were aimed at promoting lower lipid levels, an important factor in cardiac health. *Glucerna* also contained slowly digested carbohydrates, which clinical studies showed led to lower levels of blood glucose.

First introduced in 1998, *Glucerna* is a group of cereals, health shakes, and snack bars to aid in the management of glucose levels, lipids, and weight. The products were fortified with a combination of vitamins and other nutrients that showed promise in addressing the effects of diabetes. *Glucerna* was meant as a supplement to healthy diet and exercise.

This array of nutritional offerings also included enteral products, which are fed to a patient by tube when food cannot be taken orally. *Jevity* was a calorically dense, high-in-fiber enteral offering. A second such product was *Osmolite*, a liquid food rich in nitrogen. Another was *Oxepa*, for the dietary management of acute respiratory distress syndrome. *Oxepa* reduced the time patients had to spend on ventilators and in intensive care.

The seemingly mundane world of packaging saw technical innovations that generated safety, convenience, and considerable cost savings for consumers, and competitive advantage for Abbott. Previously, low-acid

Duane L. Burnham

Duane Burnham joined Abbott as its chief financial officer after already having served as CEO of another company. He used Abbott's well-known financial discipline and built upon the company's strengths and traditions, fostering breakthrough science and steering Abbott through a turbulent environment while delivering robust growth.

Duane L. Burnham was Abbott's Chairman and CEO for most of the 1990s, a time of growing profitability, infrastructure, and financial and organizational complexity for the company.

Even before joining Abbott, in 1982, Duane Burnham had a reputation as a shrewd manager with a focus on the bottom line. A CPA and an MBA graduate of the University of Minnesota, in 1980 he became president and CEO of Bunker Ramo, a large, Chicago-based electronic cable manufacturer. Burnham was just 37 years old. His company had growing profits and little debt, making it an attractive takeover target. Its new chief pursued a strategy some might view as counterintuitive: He started acquiring other companies. This tactic significantly boosted Bunker Ramo's value, leading to its acquisition by chemical maker Allied Corp.

Burnham then joined Abbott as its chief financial officer. In 1986, he was promoted to vice chairman with responsibility for an array of functions that prepared him to run the company as a whole: corporate administration and planning, information technology, corporate engineering, treasury, taxes, controllership. In 1989, he was named Abbott's CEO and, in 1990, chairman of the board.

Burnham's tenure focused primarily on growing the company's existing businesses and on maximizing return to shareholders.

In his first year as CEO, Abbott's revenues were $4.8 billion, its earnings $752 million. In 1998, Burnham's final year as CEO, revenues had more than doubled to $11.9 billion, and profits had almost tripled, to $2.1 billion. David A. Jones, chairman of health insurance giant Humana, Inc., and a long time member of Abbott's board, said of Burnham's time at the helm: "During nearly a decade … the total annual return to shareholders has exceeded 20 percent per year."

Perhaps the greatest challenge of Burnham's era was the Clinton administration's U.S. healthcare reform effort from 1993 to 1994. Anticipating massive change to its business model, the healthcare industry reacted strongly, cutting costs through a series of mega-mergers and workforce reductions that resulted in tens of thousands of jobs lost — but not at Abbott.

Despite these extreme reactions across the industry, Burnham kept Abbott independent, profitable, and rock-solid financially. There was belt-tightening at Abbott, but no drastic measures. Burnham was firmly against mega-mergers, believing they burdened companies with unjustifiable debt. "The acquiring companies often pay too much, counting on anticipated synergies and saving," Burnham stated.

He geared Abbott toward growth through new, cost-effective products developed internally. But he was, by no means, averse to looking outward. "We retain a small-to-medium-deal orientation that maximizes value to Abbott," he told the Annual Meeting of shareholders in 1995, "which minimizes the cultural clashes that often accompany major corporate mergers."

In considering an outside transaction, Burnham was known for "doing his homework." Recalled future Abbott CEO Miles D. White, then head of diagnostics: "Any time you were working to complete a deal with another company … the internal negotiation was much tougher than the one with the other side. I think the term 'due diligence' is a tribute to Duane, because no one could be more thorough."

In 1991, Burnham moved Abbott into the field of hematology diagnostics with the purchase of Sequoia-Turner Corp. The structure for vetting deals and the cash reserve that Burnham established gave Abbott the wherewithal, in the following decade, for a series of significant strategic acquisitions.

In 1997, Burnham, made a bigger move when he approved the $876 million acquisition of MediSense Inc., a maker of blood tests for people with diabetes. It was by far Abbott's largest acquisition since 1964, when it had bought M & R Dietetic Laboratories, the foundation of its nutritional products business. Abbott saw the MediSense glucose meters, which only required a patient to prick a finger to measure blood glucose levels, as a path to making non-invasive tests in the future. This acquisition served as the foundation of what would become a new division, Abbott Diabetes Care.

Burnham greatly boosted the company's R&D and investments in physical plant. In his term, Abbott stayed atop the world of high tech, and entered the new world of the Internet. He also presided over major construction at the Abbott Park headquarters and at many other locations around the world. During Burnham's tenure, Abbott added thousands of employees

around the world. Scores of buildings in a dozen countries were erected, including a major expansion of the Zwolle manufacturing plant for infant nutrition in the Netherlands. "Duane is a builder," noted White. "Growth was his mantra."

Through his tenure, Abbott's stock market value grew from $11.7 billion to $59 billion, a fivefold increase.

In January 1998, after almost a decade as Abbott's leader, Burnham announced his retirement. President Thomas R. Hodgson also retired, making way for a new management team. Humana's Jones, who had led the Abbott selection committee for a new CEO, said Burnham and Hodgson had "developed internally the exceptional team of senior leadership that will lead Abbott in the future."

Burnham arranged an admirable parting gesture. He and his wife Susan made the largest single donation that the United Way of Lake County, Illinois, had ever received — $1 million. The endowment was aimed at such work as parenting courses and the training of young leaders. "I've placed great emphasis on Abbott's responsibility to the communities in which our company operates," Burnham said. "I've urged our people to give back … with both time and money. This gift is simply an extension of that principle."

Abbott honored Burnham's leadership with the establishment of the Duane and Sue Burnham Scholarship Fund at Northwestern University's medical school to continue his commitment by helping develop new medical talent to keep improving lives through better care. ∎

Packaging technicians solved another problem — that of sunlight penetrating plastic bottles to spoil their contents — by employing a substance applied by every sunbather. Low-acid products such as *Similac with Iron* and *Ensure* adult nutritionals were especially susceptible to degradation through exposure to light and to the resulting higher temperatures. So material specialists made the containers of layered material, and plied some layers with titanium dioxide — a common ingredient in sun block. And mothers much preferred the easily re-sealable bottles over cans, which, once opened, had to be stored in messy plastic bags or wastefully tossed away.

By the late 1990s, the medical products industry was studying another innovation important to modern packaging, and especially helpful in tracking healthcare goods. This was bar codes, which promised to reduce many errors in administering medication. Already common in other business sectors, their use was hampered in the medical field, where it was difficult to inscribe the codes on items such as pills, glass vials, and plastic IV containers. Abbott's action preceded requirements from the U.S. FDA to adopt such measures to ensure patient safety.

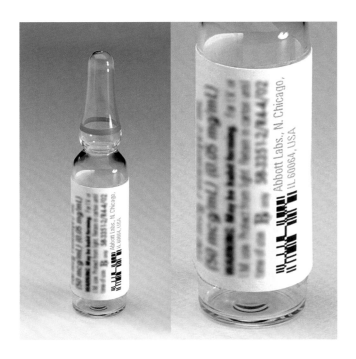

Abbott took the initiative to institute bar codes on its pharmaceutical and IV products to reduce medication errors and ensure patient safety. The federal government later mandated the same measures for U.S. industry.

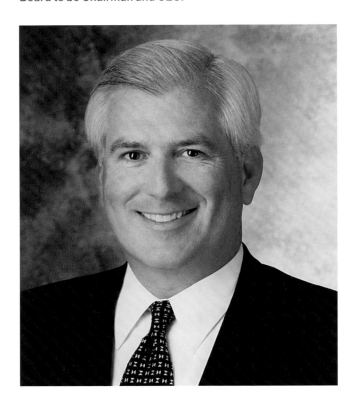

After rising to head Abbott's world-leading diagnostics business, in 1998 Miles D. White was chosen by Abbott's Board to be Chairman and CEO.

Transition: New Challenges, New Leadership

While Abbott weathered the external challenges of the 1990s with relative calm and ease, as the decade drew to a close the company found itself facing an array of significant hurdles.

After rapidly growing shareholder value for many years, annual growth slowed. In 1998, sales of pediatric nutritionals, long a company mainstay, fell. Some industry analysts even suggested that Abbott should leave the field.

In pharmaceuticals, the sales of Abbott's flagship product *Biaxin* were beginning to slow compared to new competition. The patent for *Hytrin*, its drug to treat prostate enlargement and high blood pressure, expired. Generic versions were challenging it and other company offerings. The company's pipeline of new drugs had slowed. Few pharmaceuticals with major sales potential were near market.

Further, the capsule form of *Norvir*, Abbott's important HIV drug, had to be pulled off the market for several months due to a rare change in the molecule that affected how it dissolved in the body. It was available only in liquid form until Abbott scientists determined how to reformulate it successfully.

In late 1998, the FDA, due to concerns over Abbott's manufacturing process, had ordered the company to suspend marketing of the blood clot-dissolving drug *Abbokinase*, although no fault was ever found with the product itself.

Meanwhile, beginning in 1997, Burnham had initiated a process by which the Board of Directors would choose successors to himself and president and chief operating officer Tom Hodgson.

Abbott had long been a breeding ground for top healthcare industry leaders. This depth of talent provided the company a rich pool of candidates to succeed Burnham and Hodgson when they announced, in 1997, that they would step down at the end of the following year. One candidate was U.S. pharmaceuticals head Paul N. Clark, who would later become CEO and president of the biotechnology firm ICOS. Another was international operating chief Robert L. Parkinson, Jr. who would become Abbott's president and chief operating officer, then chairman and CEO of the diversified health products company Baxter International.

The third candidate was Miles D. White, who had successfully headed up the diagnostics division since 1994. In a vetting session in New York, board members pressed White with tough questions — and liked the way he took control of the dialogue with his strategic vision for Abbott's future.

On the first day of 1999, at 43 years of age, White became Abbott's youngest CEO since Dr. Abbott himself. From the start, he would have his hands full.

In fact, a major challenge emerged that year, when the FDA found what it termed deficiencies in the manufacturing processes for many of Abbott's diagnostic products.

While signing a consent decree with the U.S. Government to resolve the issue, Abbott admitted no wrong-doing, and affirmed that its diagnostic tests worked properly. In fact, the FDA stated it found no evidence that Abbott's tests caused patient harm. The agency did not require retesting or recall of any kits.

Meanwhile, other companies continued to engage in a flurry of acquisitions to strengthen their product lines, cut costs, and establish economies of scale. It was rumored that Abbott, always an acquirer, might itself become a target for take-over.

Despite these challenges, the strong stewardship of CEO Duane Burnham and COO Tom Hodgson had left the company with healthy cash balances. Abbott was profitable, returned a steady dividend, maintained strong market positions across its range of businesses, and had significant cash reserves that would allow it to invest in new research or to make strategic acquisitions. Miles White, the new CEO, had fresh ideas on refocusing and reinvigorating Abbott's business. The stage was set for a major resurgence in the new century.

Decade at a Glance

1990–2000

1990

Robert A. Schoellhorn retires as CEO, and is succeeded by Duane L. Burnham. Thomas R. Hodgson takes on the role of company president, and chief operating officer.

Lupron Depot 3.75 mg is approved to treat endometriosis, an extra-uterine growth that can trigger severe pelvic pain and impede fertility.

Abbott's Corporate Hospital Marketing Division (CHMD) is formed to consolidate distribution, marketing, customer consulting, and customer service into one organization, to strengthen sales to key clients such as large hospital groups.

Abbott introduces the antibiotic clarithromycin, a long-awaited successor to erythromycin. The drug is known as *Biaxin* in the United States, and *Klacid* and *Klaricid* in other countries. For years, the drug would be Abbott's single biggest-selling product.

1991

Abbott develops the first automated test for monitoring prostate-specific antigen, PSA, used to screen for prostate cancer.

Abbott acquires Sequoia-Turner Corp., an important player in hematology testing.

The company introduces the orphan drug *Survanta*, to treat respiratory distress syndrome, or RDS, in newborn infants.

1992

The 1990s see a building boom under CEO Duane Burnham, including major new edifices at the world headquarters in Lake County, Illinois, worth $100 million. These made room for hundreds of new researchers, technicians, and office workers.

Abbott acquires the rights for the anesthetic sevoflurane, from Maruishi Pharmaceutical Co., Ltd. of Japan. The compound, called *Ultane* in the United States and *Sevorane* in many international markets, is known as a "universal anesthetic" due to its versatility and few side effects.

1993

Abbott's TAP joint venture introduces *Lupron Depot PED* for the treatment of central precocious puberty, or premature sexual development in boys and girls.

The Clinton administration attempts to pass a national healthcare plan in the United States, touching off a two-year national debate. Abbott supports key goals of healthcare reform, such as greater access to care and reduced costs, while preferring a market-based approach that improves care while discouraging red tape and encouraging medical innovation.

1994

The Clinton healthcare plan is voted down in the U.S. Senate.

Abbott introduces *Ensure High Protein,* a nutritional product for more active consumers.

AxSYM, an immunoassay diagnostic system for hospitals and high-volume labs, is introduced. It can handle more than 85 different immunoassays.

1995

The drug *Depakote* is approved for treatment of the manic phase of bipolar disorder, or manic depression, which becomes its primary use.

The *PRISM* system for automated, high-volume testing of blood plasma is introduced outside the United States. Abbott products like *PRISM* are used to test much of the world's blood supply.

1996

Abbott acquires MediSense Inc., an innovator in blood glucose monitoring. This lays the foundation for a future Abbott division: Abbott Diabetes Care.

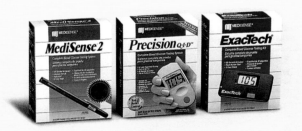

The U.S. FDA approves *Norvir*, a protease inhibitor drug that is a major breakthrough in the treatment of HIV/AIDS. For this achievement, Abbott is later awarded the Prix Galien, the pharmaceutical industry's highest scientific honor.

1997

Similac Advance is introduced. It contains nucleotides, fatty acids, and minerals that help to develop an infant's immune system and visual and brain development.

1998

Depakote surpasses lithium, long the leading treatment for bipolar disorder, in addressing the manic episodes associated with that malady.

Ensure snack bars and drinks are introduced.

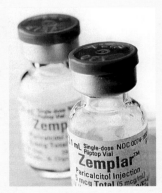

Abbott introduces *Glucerna*, a group of cereals, health shakes, and snack bars formulated specifically for people with diabetes and others with dietary restrictions.

The FDA approves *Zemplar*, a drug that helps ward off bone ailments stemming from long-term kidney disease. *Zemplar* also treats hyperparathyroidism, or overactivity of the thyroid glands.

The FDA orders Abbott, due to concerns over its manufacturing process, to suspend marketing of the blood clot-dissolving drug *Abbokinase*.

Abbott markets *TriCor*, a drug manufactured by the French firm Fournier. *TriCor* lowers triglyceride levels, linked to inflamed arteries, while increasing "good cholesterol" and decreasing "bad cholesterol."

After rising through Abbott's world-leading diagnostics business, Miles D. White is chosen by Abbott's board as CEO.

Abbott veteran Bob Parkinson is named to support White as president and chief operating officer.

1999

As part of a consent decree between Abbott and the U.S. Government, Abbott agrees to take many of its diagnostic test kits off the market until it revamps its manufacturing processes to meet FDA guidelines.

Abbott acquires Perclose, Inc., a maker of closure devices that ease the sealing of punctures in catheter insertion or coronary bypass surgery.

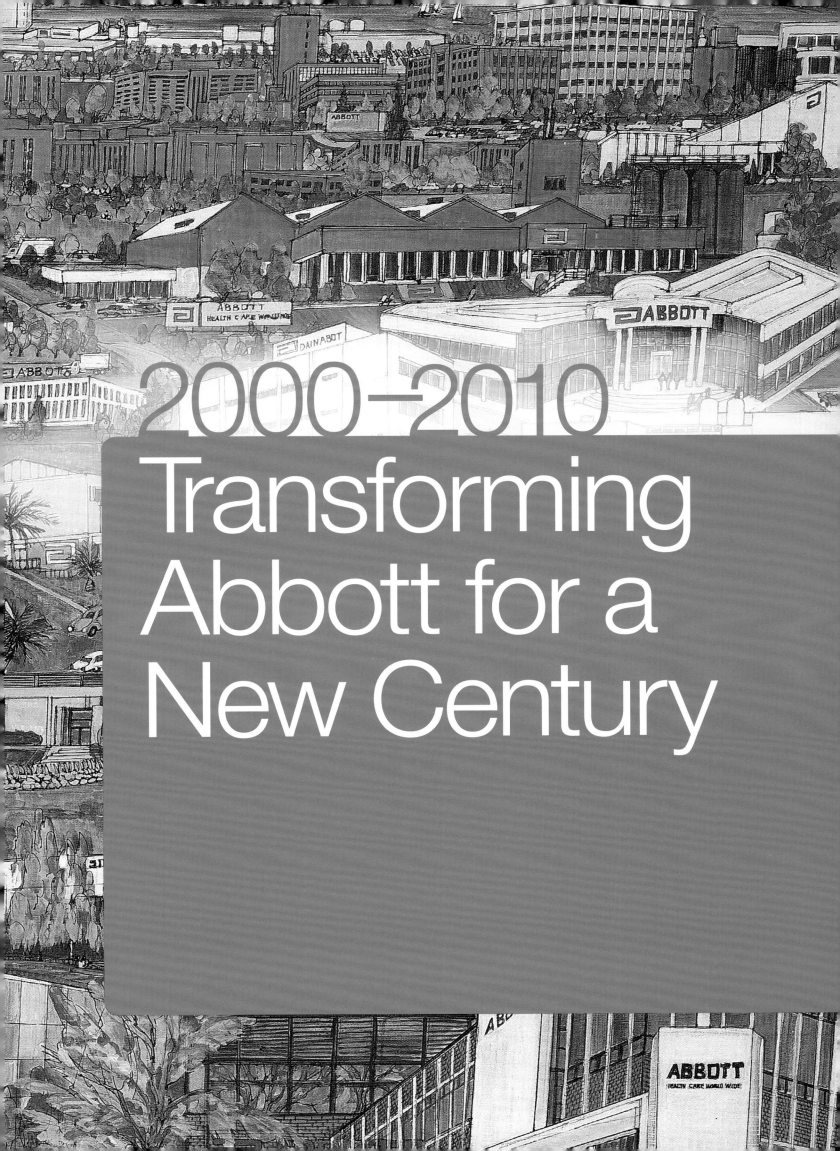

2000–2010
Transforming Abbott for a New Century

Abbott entered the new millennium facing great challenges, but with significant strengths to take them on and to seize emerging opportunities. With new leadership and new strategy and priorities, the beginning of the 2000s was a time of extraordinary activity and achievement for Abbott. Under new Chairman and CEO Miles D. White, Abbott not only successfully addressed the host of issues that had arisen at the close of the 1990s, but undertook the process of shaping the company for a new era of sustainable, high-quality growth in an increasingly global, ever-more-competitive business environment.

PREVIOUS SPREAD
To reflect the company's tremendous growth and change, Abbott commissioned "Abbott City 2000," an updating of the 1960 cityscape that first captured the company's increasing scope and globalism.

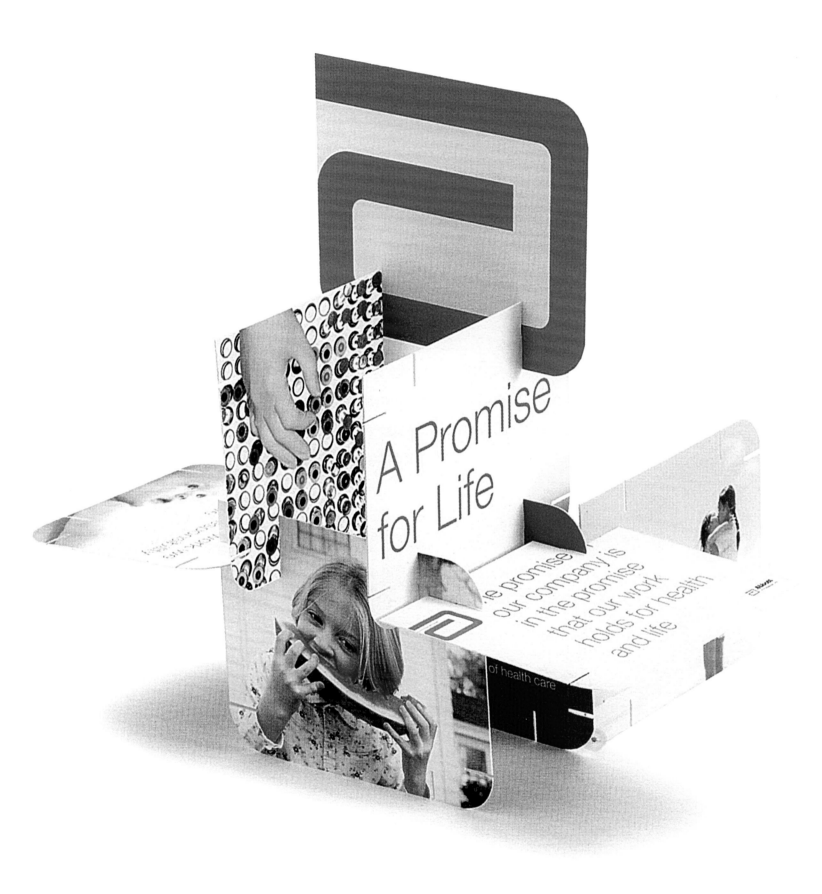

To provide a foundation and framework for the transformation it was engineering, Abbott rebranded itself in 2005, retaining its venerable, and still distinctive, "A" logo, but updating its visual identity and, more importantly, creating its "Promise for Life," (see pages viii–ix) a statement of purpose that placed the company's work in the context of its four core values: Pioneering, Achieving, Caring, and Enduring.

In January 1999, Miles D. White had become Abbott's new CEO. In April of that year he also assumed the post of Chairman of the Board. Like his predecessors in difficult times — such as Dr. Abbott, S. DeWitt Clough, and Edward J. Ledder — he faced significant challenges and responded to them forcefully, leading the company to new levels of success.

A New Strategy for the New Millennium

And those challenges were many, and significant. As Abbott's new leadership took the reins, it faced a healthcare environment that was different from, and vastly more difficult than, any the company had known before — and changing at an unprecedented pace.

Cost pressures were an old theme in the industry, but had reached new heights as budgets around the world strained and the issue of how to care for millions of uninsured and underserved people came to the fore. This required more than ever that companies like Abbott deliver powerful innovation that improved care while reducing its total cost.

At the same time, innovation was slowing across the pharmaceutical industry. New-product pipelines were struggling at all the major pharma companies, as pharmaceutical research simply became more difficult than ever before. Over the decades since Dr. Abbott and his peers created it, the industry had, essentially, collected all of the low-hanging fruit, and much in the upper branches, as well; all that remained were the most difficult therapeutic targets, in the very highest reaches — and they were more elusive and expensive to capture than ever before.

Further complicating the process of bringing new technologies to market was an increasingly rigorous global regulatory environment. The United States Food and Drug Administration (FDA), and its peer agencies around the world, were demanding a higher level of both safety and innovation than ever before, often rejecting products that would earlier have been approved.

Many global dynamics were changing fast, with the rise of the Internet and its revolutionary implications. And political and socio-economic changes were bringing large nations with populations representing half the world's people into the global economy for the first time, creating tremendous new challenges and opportunities.

Abbott, meanwhile, had its own particular issues to address, including slowing growth in some businesses. The question before White and his new administration: how to again accelerate the company's growth and sustain it for superior performance over the long term?

Fixing Pharma

The leadership team would quickly go to work on an aggressive new strategy to achieve these goals. The core of the strategy would be to rebuild the company on its diversified foundation with an enhanced portfolio of businesses

In a long-established "tradition" of new Abbott chief executives, Miles White was confronted, on taking the reins, with an array of tough challenges. Over the years to come he would not only address them successfully, but transform the company for the new century.

that could deliver that sustained, high-quality growth. The strategy was consistent with Abbott's long-term commitment to a balanced and diverse portfolio of businesses.

And White was ready to dramatically remake the composition of the company to achieve this goal. The strategy was for all of Abbott's businesses to compete in fast-growing, higher-end markets aligned with the world's leading healthcare needs, most of them driven by a rapid pace of technological innovation. This would require a rigorous, unsentimental analysis of Abbott's business portfolio, as well as the opportunities surrounding it. All of Abbott's businesses would be transformed by the changes to come.

A top priority was restarting the pharmaceutical engine that had been the company's strongest driver through the '90s. This required strengthening Abbott's scientific capability, filling its new-product pipeline, and expanding its global commercial presence. "We had a lot of products that were going generic, and there wasn't much in the pipeline behind them," remembered White. "That had to be priority Number One" on the growth agenda. "Internal research and development alone," he noted pointedly, "cannot provide all the growth that Abbott or any modern pharmaceutical company needs."

What swiftly followed was a series of acquisitions made according to a well-defined set of strategic criteria. To be considered for addition to Abbott, businesses had to be aligned with areas of significant medical need, driven by new technology that could offer breakthrough patient benefits, and capable of delivering high growth and profitability.

After exhaustive preparation, White set his sights on Knoll Pharmaceutical Co., which was a perfect fit for his strategy. Based in Ludwigshafen, Germany, and almost 11,000 employees strong, Knoll was a division of BASF, the world's largest chemical company. Founded in New York City in 1904, and later relocated to Orange, New Jersey, Knoll had long been known for work in cardiovascular disease and convulsive therapy. In 1976, BASF had purchased it, and later built a major new research center in Worcester, Massachusetts.

Continues on page 316 ▶

Kaletra Hits AIDS with Combination Punches

With the HIV drug *Norvir* approved, Abbott's next step in fighting AIDS was to refine its work into a second-generation drug that would take the protease inhibitor breakthrough to the next level for patients around the world.

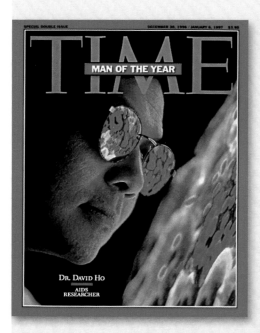

The worldwide effort against HIV was one of the world's leading news stories. *Time* magazine reflected the magnitude of the achievements being made in AIDS medicine when, in 1996, it chose Dr. David Ho, an AIDS scientist who worked with Abbott's research team, as its "Man of the Year."

Previously, experts had thought HIV lay dormant in the body for several years before attacking a patient in force. But Dr. David Ho, a leading independent AIDS researcher and Abbott collaborator, and colleagues showed that, from the start, the virus daily spewed out millions of copies of itself into the bloodstream from the lymph nodes. Over time, this constant assault overwhelmed the patient's overtaxed immune system. "It's like a person running on a treadmill," noted Ho. "It doesn't matter how fast the person runs."

Ho reasoned you had to hit HIV fast and hard, with multiple drugs right at the start of the infection. "You could use one drug at a time," he said, "but the virus is inevitably going to win because it has such a propensity to mutate." He suggested employing a combination of drugs including protease inhibitors.

He published his findings in *Nature*, and they triggered a sensation, receiving the most citations of any article in the prestigious journal's history to that time. Ho was named *Time* magazine's Man of the Year for 1996, the year in which, thanks to the development of HIV protease inhibitors like Abbott's *Norvir*, meaningful progress was first made in the treatment of AIDS.

Abbott's team had followed his ideas and put them to the test. It decided to combine *Norvir* with saquinavir, the drug made by Hoffmann La Roche. The researchers now included Dr. Eugene Sun, a Harvard-trained physician who had experience treating AIDS at the University of California San Francisco Medical Center in the early days of the epidemic. Abbott's scientists figured that pairing saquinavir with *Norvir* would boost the potency of saquinavir a hundredfold.

Sun obtained samples of the Roche drug for testing with *Norvir*. "It was like a nuclear explosion," he said of the experiments. The new combination turned out to be just as potent as hoped. As a result, combining two or more drugs to fight HIV, a so-called "AIDS cocktail," became more common and, soon, the standard of care. The cocktail was a daily menu of up to 50 pills, including drugs to fight side effects and ancillary infections.

But Abbott scientists still faced two big roadblocks: the virus's evasive tendency to mutate, and the need to keep antiviral drugs in the bloodstream even longer. Sun and Kempf knew that, as HIV mutated and the protease inhibitors became less effective when the virus developed resistance to it, some patients would grow sicker.

The lead discovery scientists on the *Kaletra* project were, left to right, organic chemists Drs. Dale Kempf, Hing Leung Sham, and Dan Norbeck, then Abbott's head of pharmaceutical discovery. For their work in HIV, the three researchers were named Heroes of Chemistry by the American Chemical Society, the world's largest scientific organization.

"We must come up with a way," said Sun, "to maintain an effective dose of HIV drugs inside the body 24 hours a day. Current drugs are too weak."

In 1995, the team again turned to the help of high-tech imaging, making 3-D models of the HIV protease to pinpoint the site of its mutation. Abbott's Dr. Hing Sham devised a compound called ABT-378 (ABT for "Abbott"), or lopinavir. It bound to the HIV protease in a different spot than *Norvir.* Thus the mutations had no effect on it. Lopinavir killed HIV strains that were resistant to *Norvir.*

Again drawing on Ho's theory, the scientists went on to combine *Norvir* (ritonavir) and lopinavir, into a new drug called *Kaletra.* This formulation boosted the staying-power of lopinavir in the bloodstream by an astonishing 7,700 percent.

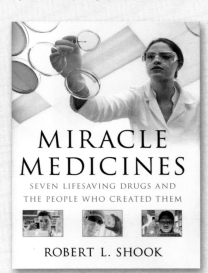

MIRACLE MEDICINES

SEVEN LIFESAVING DRUGS AND THE PEOPLE WHO CREATED THEM

ROBERT L. SHOOK

In 2007, best-selling author Bob Shook released *Miracle Medicines*, a collection of tales of breakthroughs in pharmaceutical science and the people who made them. Abbott's development of *Norvir* and *Kaletra* open the book.

In fall 1996, Abbott kicked off the clinical trials for *Kaletra*, with Dr. Sun heading the effort. "There was no placebo," Sun explained. "We had no intention of using a sugar pill on an AIDS patient, who would die without real medication."

Dr. Robert Murphy of Northwestern University in Chicago conducted the trials. After a few weeks, Murphy contacted Sun with an unusual predicament.

"I have some interesting news to tell you," Murphy said. "I'm getting calls from patients in these trials who are concerned because they think we're giving them a placebo."

"We're testing several different doses of *Kaletra*," replied Sun, "but everyone is getting *Kaletra*. There is no placebo, Rob," he remarked. "You know that."

"Yes," answered Murphy, "but they're convinced they must be getting placebos because there are no side effects from the new drug."

"Back then," Sun explained, "HIV drugs were like poison and made patients sick, much as chemotherapy does. They'd have diarrhea, vomit, and lose weight. That's because HIV drugs were poorly absorbed.

"So when we heard this news," Sun concluded, "we knew this medication was going all the way." In fact, for almost every patient who finished the seven-year trial, HIV practically disappeared from their bloodstreams, as did many side effects. Patients would have to stay on the drugs indefinitely, but they were freed from most symptoms, and able to live their lives.

After the long process of trials, on September 15, 2000, the U.S. FDA stamped its approval on *Kaletra.*

In John Leonard's office, surrounded by his fellow researchers, Sun picked up Leonard's now aged and tattered Nerf ball, long a totem of success, and spiked it, followed by a well-earned round of high fives.

Thirteen years of overcoming obstacles had led to smashing successes in the greatest medical challenge of the era. ■

Adapted from the best-selling author Robert Shook's book Miracle Medicines: Seven Life-Saving Drugs and the People Who Created Them.

The German firm had drugs in such fields as heart disease, pain therapy, thyroid deficiency, and weight management. Most important, it had world-leading antibody technology, developed at its Massachusetts R&D Center, and an experimental medication, called D2E7, which applied that know-how to fight autoimmune disorders, such as rheumatoid arthritis. As such, Knoll was a very valuable commodity. And, because BASF was refocusing on its core chemical business, Knoll had become available.

BASF, in effect, put its pharmaceutical business, Knoll, up for auction. In late November 2000, Eli Lilly offered to co-market D2E7; rumors of an outright purchase swirled. In mid-December, top Abbott officers, under a company initiative code-named "Color," engaged in secret negotiations with Knoll executives. White flew to Germany to speak with Knoll's vice chairman, winning his agreement to hear out Abbott's offer. In the end Abbott won, as it had in earlier times with its persuasive wooing of The Dermatological Research Laboratories and with M&R Dietetics. On December 14, it purchased Knoll for $6.9 billion in cash, its largest acquisition ever.

Major acquisitions "aren't one-man deals," White stressed. "They take a team of people" to pull off. Among the key executives evaluating potential acquisitions like Knoll were Richard A. Gonzalez, later the company's president and chief operating officer; Thomas C. Freyman, executive vice president and chief financial officer; Richard W. Ashley, executive vice president, Corporate Development; senior vice president, International Operations, William G. Dempsey, later executive vice president, Pharmaceutical Products Group; vice president of Business Development James L. Tyree, later executive vice president, Pharmaceutical Products Group; and vice president of Business Development Sean E. Murphy. This core group, and many others across the company, would be very busy in the years to come, as Abbott aggressively reengineered itself.

Careful preparation and teamwork lay behind any fast-paced move. A 20-person business development unit scrutinized acquisition targets. "We're up to date on our homework," said White, "so that if we want to get into a new segment, we can."

In the years to come, as Abbott executed a series of highly successful acquisitions, it developed a particular expertise in this arena, leading it to be named consistently

Abbott brought in a trove of research knowledge and technical personnel through its acquisition of Knoll Pharmaceutical.

by *The Deal* magazine as the best deal maker in the healthcare industry. Over time the company moved from forming special teams to integrate acquired companies, to a full-time department focused on this increasingly crucial task.

By acquiring Knoll's research expertise Abbott overnight boosted its pharmaceutical R&D budget by 50 percent, to about $1 billion a year. Roughly 500 skilled scientists and managers came on board. "We needed to make sure the R&D engine that was going to develop new medicines was a good engine," recalled White. The deal also built Abbott's commercial infrastructure, doubling its salesforce in Europe to about 2,500. And it brought Abbott a large stake in, and eventual full ownership of, the Japanese drug company Hokuriku Seiyaku, which Knoll had partly owned. This significantly heightened Abbott's presence in Japan. Knoll "increased our international [pharmaceutical] operations and presence by about 40 percent," said White.

Knoll's drugs became part of Abbott's pharmaceutical line. They included *Synthroid*, the leading hormone replacement to treat hypothyroidism and goiter, as well as the weight loss drug *Meridia* (also known as *Reductil*). Above all, it brought in D2E7, a biologic drug in development for immunological conditions. Under the trade name *Humira*, it would become Abbott's biggest product ever and the world's top-selling pharmaceutical.

With the *Humira* success in hand, scientists at the Worcester R&D Center, now known as the Abbott Bioresearch Center, or ABC, continued to focus on the cutting edge of autoimmune research. Another advance made at ABC was Dual Variable Domain Immunoglobulins, or DVD-Ig. These combine the function of two antibodies into a single molecule, creating the potential for a single drug that zeroes in on two different targets, fighting disease in two different ways, simultaneously.

Improving the Business Mix: the Medical Products Strategy

Strengthening its pharmaceutical position transformed a long-existing Abbott business. While doing so, the Abbott team simultaneously advanced its strategy of moving into businesses that were new to Abbott — rapidly growing, more profitable areas of medical technology. White and Richard A. Gonzalez, then the company's medical products chief, led the Abbott management team in examining the market to see what innovations and organizations would best fit with Abbott's growth strategy.

Vascular Devices

An area of particular interest was vascular devices to help strengthen the heart or assist in cardiac procedures. This was a rapidly growing healthcare market driven by much technological innovation. Though its long-term plans were ambitious, Abbott entered the market in a relatively small way with the 1999 acquisition of Perclose, Inc., for $680 million. Head-

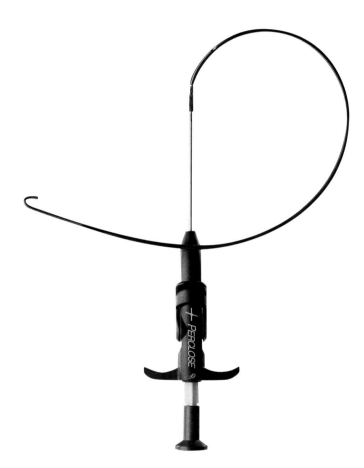

quartered in Redwood City, California, Perclose was a maker of closure devices, such as *Prostar*, *Techstar,* and *The Closer*. Perclose technology eased the sealing of punctures caused by catheter insertion or coronary bypass surgery. Perclose devices made it possible to heal access sites in a patient's body in a matter of hours rather than the days previously required. This meant quicker patient recovery, and reduced the total cost of procedures by shortening hospital stays. The acquisition proved "a cornerstone of our vascular strategy," noted White. "It got us in touch with a lot of the key scientists and engineers" in that field.

In 2002, Abbott took a second step into the vascular market with its acquisition of the cardiovascular stent business of UK-based Biocompatibles International. Stents are small metal scaffoldings that heal clogged arteries by holding them open to allow greater blood flow. Biocompatibles was prized for its stents coated with phosphorylcholine, or PC, a polymer that mimics the exterior surface of red blood cells. In so doing, it lessens the immune system's response to the foreign object that is the stent. Blood clots or tissue growths can result from the insertion of a stent, or a balloon during angioplasty. Abbott followed the Biocompatibles move with the 2003 purchase of the Dutch firm Jomed N.V., which specialized in stents, angioplasty balloons, and guiding catheters.

Remarked Rick Gonzalez, "Innovative opportunities were emerging out of a lot of the smaller companies." Such firms had "the kind of failure rate that most companies wouldn't be willing to accept." But Abbott had the cash and the willingness to take risks — and had done its homework on the prospective acquisitions.

Through these multiple, smaller-sized acquisitions, the company built its Abbott Vascular Devices division, or AVD, and learned the vascular market. AVD was developing its first internally designed drug-eluting, or drug-coated, stent, when a game-changing opportunity arose.

> "Luck favors the prepared. And we were really prepared."
>
> — MILES WHITE

In 2006, Abbott joined forces with Boston Scientific to help it acquire Guidant Corp., an Indianapolis-based maker of cardiovascular devices, in one of the business world's biggest deals of the year. The rival suitor, giant Johnson & Johnson, was outmaneuvered. As part of this transaction, Guidant's California-based vascular and endovascular businesses came to Abbott. Boston Scientific paid $26 billion for the total Guidant organization. Abbott subsequently paid Boston Scientific approximately $4 billion for the Guidant vascular and endovascular businesses, which Boston Scientific had to divest due to its strong existing position in those markets.

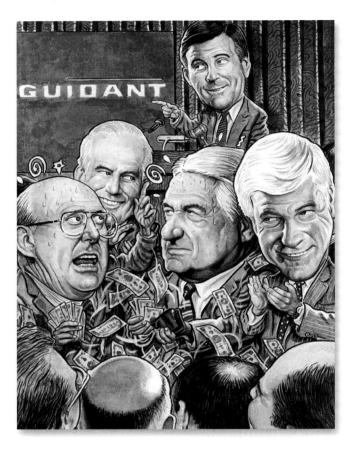

Forbes magazine dubbed Abbott the big winner in the Guidant acquisition, one of the year's biggest business stories. This illustration from the magazine's coverage portrays Abbott CEO Miles White (second from left) flashing the winner's smile.

"The Federal Trade Commission required someone to acquire Guidant's stent business," recalled Gonzalez. "We were one of only a handful of companies that fit that profile because of all the work we had done to create and build our own cardiovascular presence … It gave us a significant opportunity to quickly become number one or two in that marketplace." Added White: "Luck favors the prepared. And we were really prepared."

These assets proved to be the jewels in the Guidant crown, which led *Forbes* magazine to dub Abbott the big winner in what was one of the year's biggest business stories.

Abbott brought on board the business's 6,000 employees, $1 billion in annual revenues, an extensive product portfolio, and a rich pipeline of industry-leading technologies, including a new drug-eluting stent with best-in-class potential. The deal was one of the year's most talked about, and was hailed as one of its best — particularly for Abbott.

Abbott's *Xience V* is a "drug-eluting" stent, meaning it is coated with a medication that helps ward off the clotting and vessel renarrowing that can occur in an artery over time after insertion of a stent. *Xience* quickly became the world leader in this category.

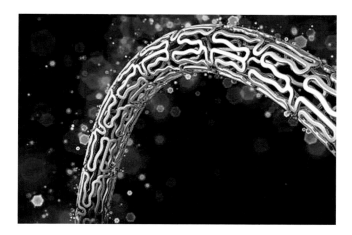

The Guidant acquisition effectively fulfilled the vascular strategy Abbott had pursued for seven years, instantly propelling the company to the number-three position in the global vascular care market, and positioning it to become the market leader in the years ahead. Armed with Guidant's soon-integrated technology, Abbott launched its own cutting-edge drug-eluting stent (DES), *Xience V*. In short order, the *Xience* platform became the world's leading DES. Abbott went on to develop, among other innovations in this field, *Absorb*, a bioresorbable vascular scaffold that, after reopening vessels, slowly disappears, like sutures, as it is metabolized by the body.

Optimizing the Portfolio

But strengthening Abbott's business mix wasn't only about acquisitions. Abbott's goal was to concentrate solely on opportunities that fit its strategic profile: technology-driven businesses that offered superior growth and margins. Achieving this goal required finding new owners for some existing Abbott businesses that, while still profitable, no longer met this profile and, consequently, would not receive the attention and funding they would need to succeed as Abbott moved ahead.

In 2000, Abbott sold its sizeable agricultural products business, which had evolved from byproducts like animal feed additives derived from its early pharmaceuticals, and from the 1956 purchase of the Long Grove, Illinois, farm. The purchaser, Sumitomo Chemical Co., Ltd., acquired the line of naturally occurring biopesticides, plant growth regulators, and other products for farming and forestry. Commented White: "The sale is another strategic step that will allow us to focus on the growth of our core healthcare businesses."

Agricultural products and animal health products had, for many years, been seen essentially as peripheral businesses that were largely byproducts of Abbott's other operations. However, as Abbott re-evaluated its operations and opportunities, it recognized that the outlook for the veterinary care market had changed significantly. To capture the potential created by the growing dedication of owners to their pets' needs, the company formed Abbott Animal Health, and began adapting more of its products for animal-specific uses. Offerings included the *CliniCare* liquid diet for canines or felines recovering from surgery or dental procedures, and a set of anesthetics — *SevoFlo* and *PropoFlo* for dogs, and *IsoFlo* for dogs and horses. Further, the *AlphaTRAK* blood glucose device for dogs and cats permitted an on-the-spot diagnosis through a hand-held, easily readable monitor for pets with diabetes.

Continues on page 323 ▶

Abbott sold its agricultural products line in 2000, but retained its long-standing group of products for veterinary medicine, while adding innovations such as glucose monitoring for companion animals with diabetes.

Humira: A "Pipeline in a Product" to Fight Immune System Disorders

The breakthrough biologic drug *Humira* was discovered and developed at the 35-acre Abbott Bioresearch Center (ABC) in Worcester, Massachusetts, overlooking the University of Massachusetts Medical Center.

In the 1980s scientists there, then working for BASF's Knoll division, were researching antibodies to treat cancer. An antibody is a protein used by the immune system to attack foreign objects such as viruses and bacteria. The scientists were specifically looking at "monocolonal" antibodies.

These are antibodies that are all identical, being copies ("clones") from one ("mono") parent cell of a particular immune cell. Monoclonal antibodies can be made in large numbers in the lab. Because they are identical, they all act the same way against a particular antigen. In great numbers, they can act quickly and effectively against disease.

Over time, the Worcester scientists learned such antibodies had promise in fighting autoimmune diseases. At first, they worked with antibodies called "chimeras," from the mythical Greek animal that is part lion, snake, and goat. A chimera antibody typically is one made up of mouse and human elements.

However, the human immune system rejects such artificially made antibodies. In 1995, the Worcester scientists succeeded in creating a fully human monoclonal

antibody. Because these are practically identical to antibodies produced naturally by the human body, the immune system does not reject them, thus they do not require other drugs to dampen immune response. They have half lives more on the order of human antibodies — weeks rather than hours or days — so they can be given by infrequent injection, about once a week. In trials beginning in 1997, the Knoll-developed antibody proved effective against rheumatoid arthritis.

That disease afflicted more than 5 million people around the world, often under 40 years of age. By wearing away a joint's interior and the surrounding bone, it can lead to severe joint pain and swelling, fatigue, depression, disability, even deformity.

Rheumatoid arthritis is one of several "autoimmune diseases," in which the body's immune system overreacts and assaults healthy tissue. A protein called tumor necrosis factor-alpha, or TNF-a, helps trigger such disorders.

Scientists at the Abbott Bioresearch Center (ABC) in Massachusetts developed *Humira*, the first fully human monoclonal antibody. Abbott acquired the Center as part of its purchase of Knoll Pharmaceutical Co.

For ease of use by people with rheumatoid arthritis, *Humira* came contained in pre-filled syringes.

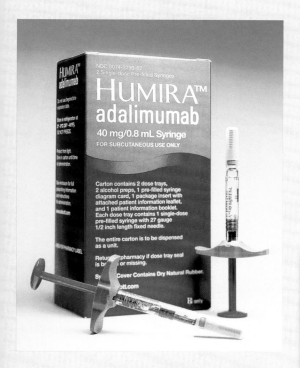

Blocking TNF helps treat them. The *Humira* antibody, like a guided missile, specifically targets TNF-a.

In 2000, as Humira entered final clinical trials, Abbott purchased BASF's pharmaceutical business, including Knoll. The company made the Worcester plant, with its unsurpassed biologics capability, its Bioresearch Center.

Abbott rushed to expand the Center, adding several hundred employees and spending $50 million on a 63,000-square-foot expansion of its manufacturing plant.

The antibody proteins were mass-produced in large steel containers that workers filled with nutrients. Chemists found that, as in fermenting beer, an important substance for making *Humira* was yeast. Yeast allowed researchers to more easily find the antibodies that bind to an antigen. "Instead of putting the antibodies on the surface of viruses," explained one expert, "you put them on yeast. It allows you

to immediately pick out the highest-affinity antibodies. It shortens antibody development by months to years."

On December 31, 2002, the U.S. FDA approved *Humira* for the treatment of moderate-to-severe rheumatoid arthritis. The approval was in near-record time, just nine months after Abbott's submission for the drug. *Humira* was the first fully human monoclonal antibody approved as a medicine.

Abbott's strategy paid off. In 2003, *Humira* quickly became the most successful product launch in Abbott's history.

"Before starting *Humira*, some patients couldn't dress themselves or hold their children or grandchildren," stated Dr. Charles A. Birbara of the University of Massachusetts. "*Humira* has given them their lives back." Further, *Humira* came in a pre-filled syringe that people with arthritis, even

December 31, 2009

Dear Sirs,

I am writing you in reference to my experience with the drug HUMIRA. Since starting this drug to treat my rheumatoid arthritis I have been freed of my symptoms of disabling pain and restrictions that RA put on my lifestyle. I'd like to share with you a short story of this experience.

I was diagnosed with RA in 2005 at the age of 37. At that time, I was rated moderate to severe. I had arthritis in most of my joints, and had lost the ability to do simple tasks such as button my jeans. Being a warehouse laborer for a large U.S. paint manufacturer, my job required me to lift heavy paint products. Of course you can see the dilemma this created. Naturally, I missed a lot of time from work and my job and my future were in jeopardy. Thanks to federal laws regarding disabilities, I was protected from termination temporarily.

Upon meeting my Rheumatologist, he quickly saw the need for aggressive treatment and started me on several drugs. It wasn't until after a few months of other medicines without success that he started me on HUMIRA. I saw instant results. It took a while for full effects to start but after a period my symptoms quickly dissipated. I was able to return to work at 100% capacity and ensure that I would continue on with the company.

It gets better. Having a strong background in extreme sports and craftsmanship, I felt the need to continue my lifestyle and do the things I love. Some of those activities that had been taken away by RA include, Downhill mountain bike racing, rock climbing, backpacking, snowboarding, working on cars, tasks with hand tools, and most important, two young children. My biggest fear is that I wouldn't be able to pick my children up to hold them ever again because of the pain RA caused me.

I was able to return to doing everything I loved because of this drug. I started working on cars again as a hobby, and finished building my house. Last summer, I spent six days hiking the Appalachian Trail with my eight and ten year old children and started mountain biking again. And in 2010, I plan on making a return to Downhill mountain bike racing!

So to sum it all up, you drug has given me my life back. I have a new outlook on life and have positively accepted my disease and refuse to let it stop me from achieving any goals. In 2009, I decided to leave the life of a laborer and enrolled in nursing school and pursue a RN degree. My passion and life's calling to help people with medical problems became evident through my own suffering.

HUMIRA is a truly a miracle drug and has released me from the bondage of RA. I cannot thank you enough for the freedom you have given me.

A letter from an arthritis patient testified to *Humira*'s life-changing effect on her condition.

To ramp up production of *Humira*, Abbott made its largest capital investment to date in construction of a biologics manufacturing plant at Barceloneta, Puerto Rico.

Abbott scientists who created *Humira* garnered the prestigious Prix Galien USA for the pharmaceutical industry's Best Biotechnology Product.

"O ser humano só é completo quando tem um filho, escreve um livro e planta uma árvore"

Provérbio chinês

Venha plantar
uma árvore neste
domingo e comece assim
a escrever mais um capítulo da história de sua vida.

HUMIRA™
adalimumabe
Humano em todos os sentidos

Word of *Humira*'s ability to let patients live more normal lives was found in advertisements published in many languages, as well as in a steady stream of testimonial letters to Abbott from grateful patients from around the world.

those with hands compromised by the disease, found easy to use. And the medicine was powerful: It only had to be administered once a week. Abbott gave *Humira* away free to Medicare patients until the drug fell under Medicare's prescription drug benefit, lowering the cost to users.

The tumor necrosis factor that *Humira* attacks is involved in a number of autoimmune diseases other than rheumatoid arthritis, such as psoriasis, ankylosing spondylitis, and Crohn's disease. Thus, White, envisioning additional therapies, termed *Humira* a "pipeline in a product." His characterization proved prophetic.

In 2005, the FDA cleared *Humira* to fight psoriatic arthritis. Its symptoms are severe pain in the joints, tendons, or spine. It is also linked to psoriasis, in which the skin forms scaly, inflamed lesions called plaques. Psoriasis afflicts about 125 million people worldwide.

In 2007, the FDA and the European Commission first approved *Humira* as a treatment for Crohn's disease. This malady is a chronic inflammation of the gastrointestinal tract that can lead to cramping, weight loss, ulcers, and bleeding. Said clinical trial patient Rocio Lopez: "The unpredictable symptoms made working and relationships difficult. I was afraid to leave the house." After she began taking *Humira*, Lopez reported, "My Crohn's symptoms are under control and I have more freedom to live my life."

In 2008, *Humira* was approved to treat juvenile idiopathic arthritis, from which "pain and inflammation can be debilitating," noted Dr. Daniel J. Lovell of Cincinnati Children's Hospital Medical Center, "making it

hard for sufferers to run, jump, play, or participate in other activities with children their age." *Humira* also treats ankylosing spondylitis, commonly called arthritis of the spine, as well as chronic plaque psoriasis, with its itchy and painful skin lesions, and ulcerative colitis, for a total of nine uses thus far.

To increase production of *Humira* and other drugs, Abbott opened, in 2007, a 330,000-square-foot plant in Barceloneta, Puerto Rico. Costing $450 million, it was, in dollar terms, Abbott's largest capital investment to that time. The plant was designed to tackle biologics demanding advanced manufacturing techniques.

That same year, Abbott received the prestigious Galen Prize (today known as the Prix Galien USA), considered the "Nobel Prize" of the pharmaceutical industry, for the breakthrough it had achieved with *Humira*.

To cap its success, *Humira* became the world's top-selling pharmaceutical in 2012 with sales of approximately $9 billion — more than Abbott's total sales as recently as 1993. ∎

A stock is born. Hospira CEO Christopher B. Begley (center), Board Chairman David A. Jones (fourth from right), and senior staffers ring the bell at the New York Stock Exchange on the day "HSP," formerly Abbott's Hospital Products Division, is first listed as an independent, publicly held company.

BOTTOM
Hospira's global headquarters, in Lake Forest, Illinois.

Creating a New Company

In 2004, Abbott spun off its long-standing Hospital Products Division, with its largely commoditized product lines of IV kits and fluids, and supplies such as syringes. The new firm was dubbed Hospira, from the words "hospital," "spirit," and "*spero*," Latin for hope, after a naming contest among its employees.

By divesting its hospital products group, Abbott was able to focus on higher-growth, higher-technology businesses. Its shareholders immediately benefited, gaining a special dividend and a share of Hospira stock for every 10 shares of Abbott stock held. White commented, "The new hospital products company will enable Abbott … to sustain a technologically advanced, higher-growth medical and pharmaceutical products portfolio."

At the same time, Hospira was granted financial and strategic flexibility. Hospira also benefited from the size and wealth of contacts that the business had built up since Abbott's 1930s entry into hospital IVs. With 14,000 employees, 14 manufacturing plants worldwide, and $2.5 billion in sales, Hospira at its founding ranked 660th in the Fortune 1000 listing of the world's largest firms.

Hospira had strong leadership, well versed in the hospital industry. Its CEO was Christopher B. Begley, formerly president of Abbott's Hospital Products Division. Chairman of Hospira's board was David A. Jones, a long time Abbott board member, and co-founder and chairman of Humana Inc. Hospira would quickly prove the soundness of Abbott's strategy, as it thrived in independence, with its stock price doubling in its first six years of independent operation.

Diabetes Care

Another area of particular interest to Abbott was diabetes care. Diabetes had reached epidemic proportions worldwide, and technology was advancing to meet this growing healthcare need. Abbott had entered the market with its 1996 purchase of MediSense. In 2004, it expanded its position and capabilities, completing the acquisition of another, larger glucose-monitoring innovator, Therasense, of Alameda, California, for $1.2 billion.

Therasense was a pioneer in the trend toward self-monitoring glucose testers requiring smaller, less painful blood samples and yielding faster results than competitors. In 2000, it had brought to market the *FreeStyle* monitor, which let people with diabetes test glucose by using just 0.3 microliters of blood from their hand or forearm. Results were generated within seven seconds. Under Abbott, steady improvements would continue, resulting in continually smaller and faster monitors for greater patient convenience.

People with diabetes were able to easily check their glucose levels pain-free with Abbott's *FreeStyle* monitors.

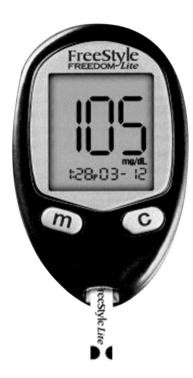

Abbott later introduced the pager-sized *FreeStyle Navigator*, which wirelessly provided minute-by-minute data and alerted users when glucose levels got out of balance. The device worked through a hair-thin sensor, patched painlessly under the skin.

Abbott then combined its Therasense and MediSense units to create its Abbott Diabetes Care division, a top-three global competitor.

Across the Medical Products Spectrum

Business diversity was the central plank in Abbott's growth platform, and the company was open to a range of businesses that fit its strategic criteria.

In 2003, Abbott acquired Austin, Texas-based medical device maker, Spinal Concepts for $170 million. A year later Abbott added to it Spine Next, S.A., of Bordeaux, France, a manufacturer of orthopedic spinal implant devices used during spinal fusion surgery. Spine Next was known for

a dynamic stabilization device called the Wallis System, that treats early degenerative disc disease without fusion of the vertebrae, helping patients preserve motion. Together these companies formed a new division, known as Abbott Spine.

Abbott Spine was aimed at penetrating another fast-growing, high-technology market, in this case back surgeries, hundreds of thousands of which were performed yearly in the United States alone.

However, as opposed to its experience in constructing a leading vascular care business through a series of acquisitions, Abbott concluded that the orthopedic market was not a good fit for its strategy. To focus its business lines and to concentrate on more profitable opportunities, in late 2008 Abbott Spine was sold off for approximately $360 million to Zimmer Holdings, Inc., a maker of orthopedic devices.

Abbott also began exploring medical optics, and found it to be a highly attractive market that fit its criteria perfectly. This research would lead to new opportunities later in the decade.

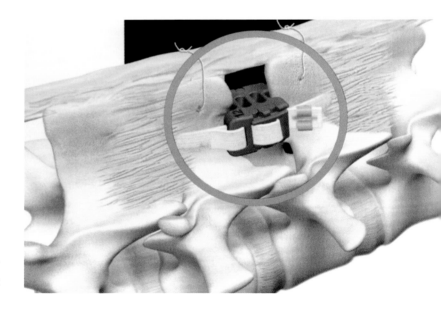

The illustration above shows the Wallis stabilization device from Abbott Spine, after implantation.

With its 2006 acquisition of Kos Pharmaceuticals, Abbott put together a full array of medicines to address cardiovascular disease by managing lipids, and to enhance its position in the world's largest pharmaceutical market.

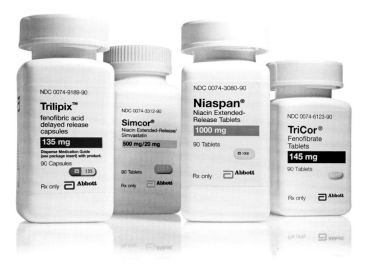

Leading in Lipid Management

Following up on the grand-slam success of the Knoll purchase, Abbott made another major move in the pharmaceutical realm in December 2006, when it completed the acquisition of New Jersey-based Kos Pharmaceuticals for $3.7 billion.

Kos was developing an asthma drug and an inhaled insulin product. The latter complemented Abbott's array of diagnostics and nutritional offerings for diabetes. But the strategic core of the transaction was Kos' strength in the management of lipids, or blood fats, the world's largest pharmaceutical market. Kos' *Niaspan* was a long-acting formulation of niacin, vitamin B3, which raises high-density lipoprotein, or HDL, the "good cholesterol." *Advicor* combined *Niaspan* and lovastatin, a natural statin shown by large-scale trials to reduce low-density cholesterol, or LDL, the "bad cholesterol."

A Kos-developed drug approved in 2008 by the U.S. FDA was *Simcor*. It was a combination of *Niaspan* and simvastatin, another LDL-reducing substance synthesized from the fungus *Aspergillus terreus*.

The Kos purchase "complements our existing commercial and research and development expertise," noted White. Its products formed a formidable franchise along with Abbott's *TriCor* — a fibrate drug for reducing LDL and triglycerides and for increasing HDL. In fact, Abbott had established a strong presence across the spectrum of cardiac health: cholesterol drugs, stents to relieve acute arterial and vascular conditions, and nutritionals to enhance cardiovascular health.

Underscoring this synergy, in 2008 Abbott received approval of *Trilipix*, an advanced fenofibrate drug that could be used in combination with statins, the most-used family of cholesterol treatments. And extensive cardiovascular research continued.

Regaining Leadership in Nutrition

Abbott's nutrition business had also faced its share of challenges entering the 2000s. Growth had slowed in its once-dominant U.S. business. Again, aggressive steps were needed to return the business to its traditional strength.

Abbott's answer was to enter the fastest-growing segment of the nutrition market: healthy-living nutritionals for people on the go. In 2003, Abbott acquired the ZonePerfect Nutrition Company, a maker of nutrition bars. The following year, it added the science-based sports nutrition firm EAS. With its *Myoplex* protein shakes for bodybuilders and other athletes, EAS had garnered celebrity customers such as actor Sylvester Stallone and supermodel Cindy Crawford. Bill Philips, author of the 1990s bestseller *Body-for-LIFE*, had founded the Golden, Colorado-based company. Its acquisition complemented Abbott's *Ensure* line of healthy shakes.

Abbott entered the fast-growing healthy-living nutritional market with its 2003 acquisition of ZonePerfect Nutrition Company.

The *Ensure* reclosable bottle was named a winner at the 2004 DuPont Awards competition for innovation in packaging. The threaded, reclosable cap and hand-friendly grip gained the Gold Award.

Dear Mr. White,

after just completing the Ironman California on May 19th 2001 with the nutritional help of your product, Ensure Lights, I just wanted to let you know how much I appreciate that your company makes this supplement for active and fit individuals.

During this endurance event, which features a 2.4 mile swim, a 112 mile bike ride, and a 26.2 mile run within a 17 hour day and deadline, I drank 8 Ensure Lights, which gave my 65 year old engine the fuel necessary to not only complete, but place third in my age group. As I am continuing triathlons, as well as participating in future Ironman events, I am certain to continue my supplementation with Ensure.

A 65-year-old finisher of an ironman competition, who drank eight bottles of *Ensure Light* during the 17-hour ordeal, thanked CEO Miles White for the energy-boosting product.

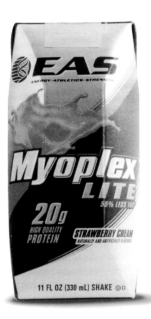

The company quickly built its position in the healthy-living market with the acquisition of the science-based sports nutrition firm EAS.

Another strong driver of growth in the nutrition business was rapid international expansion in developing markets around the world, especially in Asia. There, Abbott's long-time flagship nutritional, *Similac*, was a standout product, highly desired in growing economies like China. To ensure it made the most of this opportunity, Abbott formed a new division, Abbott Nutrition International (ANI). ANI separated nutrition marketing from Abbott International, which then became solely the company's international pharmaceuticals business. This allowed each organization to concentrate entirely, and more effectively, on a single business.

To meet the region's growing demand, and to better meet the specific dietary needs and preferences of its consumers, in 2009 Abbott completed its largest Asian investment to date, and its largest-ever capital investment in the nutrition business, when it opened a $300 million nutrition products manufacturing plant in Singapore. Abbott also opened in that island city its first pharmaceutical R&D center in Asia, as well as a nutrition science R&D facility. As global demand continued to grow, Abbott would also add new nutrition manufacturing facilities in Jiaxing, China, Gujarat, India, and Tipp City, Ohio.

Abbott had continued to market its nutritionals, such as *Similac,* under the respected Ross brand — the name of the business's founding family — since its acquisition in 1964. As part of the company's global branding initiative, and to bolster further expansion abroad, the business was renamed Abbott Nutrition in 2007.

Along with expanding sales of *Similac* in Asia, Abbott's engineers and nutrition scientists continued to make enhancements to the *Similac* brand that tracked scientific discoveries in infant development and nutrition. This took form in *Similac Advance EarlyShield*, the first infant formula that uniquely blended prebiotics, nucleotides, and antioxidants — nutrients naturally found in breast milk, and which are important in the formation of a baby's immune system.

An infant relies on millions of "good" bacteria in the digestive tract to support immune system development. Prebiotics are carbohydrates found in breast milk, and in *Similac Advance Earlyshield*, which help stimulate the growth of such beneficial bacteria. Nucleotides are immune-building nutrients that help an infant make important antibodies. Abbott researchers designed the nucleotide blend and level in *Similac Advance EarlyShield* to match the nucleotides in breast milk. Finally, this new formulation of *Similac Advance* contained antioxidants found in breast milk, including: lutein, found in spinach; lycopene, found in tomatoes; and beta-carotene, found in carrots. These antioxidants can help protect certain cells in the eyes and skin.

In order to get closer to its growing customer base in emerging markets, Abbott made its largest-ever capital investment in both its nutrition business and Asia, when it built this state-of-the-art manufacturing facility in Singapore, opened in 2009.

Abbott advances in infant formula were represented by *SimplePac*, an easy-to-use packaging innovation, and *Similac Advance EarlyShield*, a blend of antioxidants, omega fatty acids, nucleotides, and prebiotics for bolstering a baby's immune system and brain development.

The McGhee sextuplets — Elijah, Isaac, Josiah, Madison, Olivia, and Rozonno, Jr. — at six months of age, happy and healthy on *Similac* infant formula.

Similac Advance EarlyShield also contained two omega fatty acids: docosahexaenoic acid (DHA), and arachidonic acid (ARA), which research indicated assists the development of infants' mental and visual faculties.

The container for *EarlyShield* was also innovative, and relied on the advice of those who know best — moms. In its product design research, Abbott talked with more than 1,600 mothers about improving the container, packaging, and formula preparation for *Similac* products. A common complaint from mothers with infants was that they "didn't have enough hands" in making formula. The result was the *SimplePac* container. With the new, one-hand grip and scoop in a hinged lid, *SimplePac* made for faster and less messy baby bottle preparation.

Thanks largely to these innovations, by the end of the decade, *Similac* was, again, the market leader, by the largest share it had enjoyed in years.

Diagnostics' Dramatic Comeback

Abbott's diagnostics business faced two challenges: to return to strong growth and profitability and to address the consent decree it had entered into. Abbott responded strongly throughout the century's first decade, not only by transforming its production processes into an industry standard, but through a series of adept business moves and internal R&D measures to acquire and develop diagnostic products and novel approaches. The diagnostics line was restored to profitability, innovation, and growth.

Abbott continued to focus on internally developed innovations as well. One example was its multifaceted *ARCHITECT* system, originally introduced in 1999, and growing by the year in sophistication, speed, and breadth of tests offered. *ARCHITECT* was enhanced by the continual addition of new components to expand the system, allowing it to perform up to 1,800 clinical chemistry tests and up to 200 immunoassays an hour.

Some of the cutting-edge research behind the new products explored the very molecular and genetic basis of disease. In fall 2001, Abbott agreed to acquire, for $355 million, Illinois-based Vysis Inc., which had leading genomic tests for chromosome changes linked to congenital disorders and cancer. Prominent among these was the *PathVysion* HER-2 DNA Probe kit, which helped identify women who possessed a particular gene indicating the

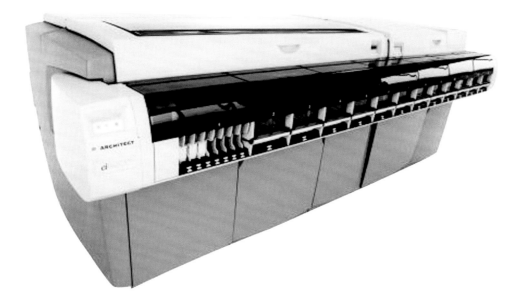

The *ARCHITECT* integrated diagnostics system used advanced software and robotic technology to perform high-speed diagnostic tests.

likelihood that they could benefit from treatment with the Genentech drug Herceptin. "This acquisition further strengthens our position in molecular diagnostics," said Thomas D. Brown, senior vice president, Diagnostics Operations. "It provides an excellent fit with our long-term strategy of expanding our capabilities in diagnostics while targeting unmet needs, particularly in the area of cancer."

Also noteworthy was the *UroVysion* test, which detected genetic changes in bladder cells to aid in diagnosing bladder cancer or its recurrence. *UroVysion* was the first U.S. FDA-approved test to use DNA probes for identifying up to four chromosomal abnormalities associated with bladder cancer.

Both *PathVysion* and *UroVysion* employed a probe technology called DNA Fluorescence In Situ Hybridization, or FISH. FISH was a powerful means to detect genetic aberrations in malignant tissues, and to more efficiently treat a wide range of cancers. These single- and multi-colored probe sets offered researchers and clinicians various ways to identify deletion or translocation of portions of chromosomes and genes that occur in cancers.

Independent research backed up the effectiveness of these approaches. For instance, a 2006 *Journal of Urology* study showed that *UroVysion* had about twice the sensitivity of conventional urine cell tests in the initial diagnosis of bladder cancer in patients with blood in their urine. The results showed that *UroVysion* detected 69 percent of bladder tumors, while traditional cytology detected just 38 percent.

Abbott continued to work with the most advanced research organizations in molecular and genetic diagnostics. In 2002, Abbott formed an alliance with Celera Diagnostics, an arm of the company that sequenced the human genome, which aimed to develop an array of next-generation molecular diagnostics.

Continues on page 332 ▶

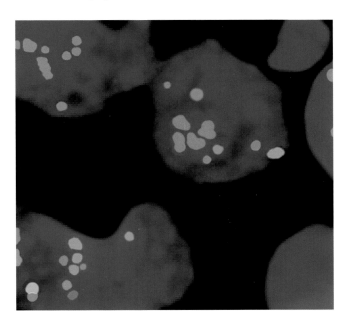

This image of cancerous breast tissue tested with Abbott's *PathVysion* HER-2 DNA Probe kit revealed reddish dots representing multiple copies of the HER-2 gene, an indicator of whether a patient will respond well to treatment with the drug Herceptin.

Abbott House: Living Symbol of a Great Tradition

In 2005, Abbott opened and dedicated Abbott House, a replica of Dr. Abbott's 1891 home in the Ravenswood neighborhood of Chicago. Abbott House embodies the whole of our legacy and shows how generation after generation of Abbott people have taken up the challenges of their time to keep fulfilling the promise of our company.

Dr. Abbott's 1891 Chicago home.

Abbott House is a physical link to Abbott's past, connecting us directly to our founder. To strengthen that link, a number of architectural highlights from Dr. Abbott's home were moved to Abbott House, including the weather vanes atop the cupola and the coach house.

Left to right: Abbott's last four CEOs, Bob Schoellhorn, Miles White, Ted Ledder, and Duane Burnham, prepare to officially open Abbott House in 2005.

BELOW LEFT
Abbott's story is told through self-guided exhibits that trace the company's evolution from its creation through its growth as a business, in pictures, words, interactive video, and artifacts that are displayed throughout the house.

BELOW
The pharmacy in Abbott House re-creates an early 1900s drugstore, complete with authentic cabinetry to showcase hundreds of Abbott products from across its history.

In Claude Monet's famous water garden in Giverny, France, there is a Japanese bridge made of beechwood, surrounded by a variety of plantings by Monet himself. In 1999, the Clara Abbott Foundation chose this bridge to represent its purpose and mission — providing a bridge of help and hope to Abbott families in their times of greatest need. This replica bridge stands on the Abbott House grounds and serves as a symbol of the gift Clara Abbott gave more than 70 years ago to honor her husband's memory.

In September 2003, Abbott dedicated a new facility in Des Plaines, Illinois, to serve as headquarters for its worldwide molecular diagnostics business.

The i-STAT 1 hand-held analyzer offered test results in minutes using as little as two drops of blood. Testing was performed for blood gases, coagulation, hematology, glucose, and cardiac markers, among other medical indices.

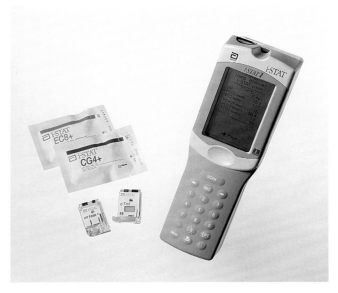

The Celera, Vysis, and other initiatives were organized into a new division of the company, called Abbott Molecular. This business included instruments and reagents to conduct sophisticated analysis of patients' DNA and RNA. It was geared to offer physicians critical information on early detection of pathogens, and on subtle changes in patients' genes and chromosomes. The objective was to spur earlier diagnosis, selection of appropriate therapies, and monitoring of a disease's progress or regression.

Abbott's long-time and growing strength in hand-held, rapid-testing devices was strengthened with the 2003 acquisition, for $392 million, of East Windsor, New Jersey-based i-STAT, a manufacturer of fast, point-of-care blood analyzers. The purchase led to the establishment of Abbott's Point of Care division, whose devices enabled physicians to make more rapid diagnoses and decisions on conditions like chest pain experienced by a patient.

A Proud Tradition of Cardiovascular Treatments

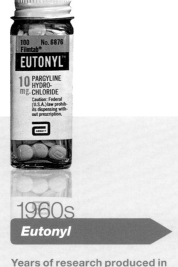

1960s
Eutonyl

Years of research produced in 1963 the hypertension drug *Eutonyl*.

1970s
Abbokinase

Tested aboard the Apollo spacecraft in 1975 was *Abbokinase*, for breaking up blood clots.

Abbott teams up to market test for SARS

By Bruce Japsen
Tribune staff reporter

Abbott Laboratories is finalizing an agreement with an undisclosed firm to distribute a medical test to detect the deadly SARS virus, the company said.

The North Chicago-based medical-product giant said its partner company has a test in use to detect a coronavirus in the same family. Now, the partner is working to gain regulatory approval in the U.S. and elsewhere so that the test can be used to detect SARS, a strain of pneumonia known as severe

Abbott co-introduced, with the German firm artus GmbH, a test for identifying severe acute respiratory syndrome, or SARS, in 2003. The disease had touched off a near pandemic, and panic, in the early 2000s, while killing more than 700 people. Abbott and artus introduced the PCR, or polymerase chain reaction, test for SARS, along with similar tests for tuberculosis and Chlamydia. PCR is a gene-amplification technique used to create multiple copies of a target genetic sequence, allowing for easier detection. The tests were developed with Celera Diagnostics. In 2007, Abbott and Celera also developed a PCR test for the precise measurement of levels of the hepatitis B virus.

As reported in the *Chicago Tribune*, Abbott collaborated with a German partner to devise a test for identifying SARS, a respiratory illness that killed hundreds of people in 2003, raising fears of pandemic that made it one of the year's biggest healthcare stories.

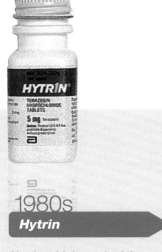

1980s
Hytrin

Hytrin, which reached the market in 1987, was a once-a-day drug to fight high blood pressure.

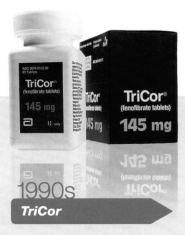

1990s
TriCor

The versatile *TriCor*, launched in 1998, altered levels of cholesterol while reducing levels of triglycerides.

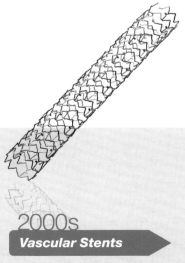

2000s
Vascular Stents

Abbott enters a new business. Its *Xience V* drug-eluting stent quickly became the global leader.

Chairman and CEO Miles White visits a remote village in Tanzania that had been hit hard by HIV, leaving a large population of AIDS orphans and vulnerable children. Abbott's response is its Step Forward program, which marks the beginning of the transformation of the company's approach to global citizenship.

Abbott established a modern outpatient department at Tanzania's Muhimbili National Hospital for patients with chronic conditions such as HIV.

Superior Performance, Sustainable Growth

The positive results from Abbott's aggressive strategic moves were evidenced by the company's results. In just the five years from 2002 to 2007, sales soared from $15.3 billion to $25.9 billion, an increase of 69 percent. Under White's leadership, profits rose to $3.6 billion.

A year later, in fall 2008, came a worldwide financial crisis marked by the implosion of the United States mortgage and banking industries, and a sharp sell-off on Wall Street. Abbott was, however, on firm financial ground and, as in the aftermath of the Panic of 1907 and the Crash of 1929, fared far better than most. The Standard & Poor's stock index fell 38 percent for the year, and pharmaceutical stocks dropped 21 percent; Abbott, on the other hand, dipped only 5 percent.

Indeed, in December 2008 Abbott declared its 340th consecutive quarterly dividend, a remarkable streak stretching back some 84 years. It also boosted the amount of its dividend for the 36th straight year, returning more than $2 billion in cash to shareholders. From 1986 through 2008, the total return to shareholders of Abbott stock was nearly 1,800 percent. In fact, from the debut in 1957 of the Standard & Poors index of 500 large publicly traded U.S. companies, Abbott had compiled the second-highest average annual return of all the originally listed S&P firms.

Meanwhile, its record cash flow, about $7 billion for 2008, placed it in the enviable, if accustomed, position of having the means for R&D, potential acquisitions, employee investment, and other purposes.

In the 2000s, Abbott had again met challenge with response. The result was a greatly strengthened company — more global, more diverse, and better able to deliver superior performance on a sustainable basis.

As Miles White put it in 2008, "We want to manage so that we're around for another 120 years."

A Citizen of the World

Abbott's transformation in the 2000s did not apply only to its business structure and results. White's team also led far-reaching change in the company's culture and the way it related to the world around it. This amounted, in addition to the new strategic approach to reviving and growing its businesses, to an innovative and wide-ranging strategy for Abbott's efforts in corporate sustainability.

In the wake of the catastrophic 2004 Indian Ocean tsunami, Abbott employees delivered clothes, blankets, and Abbott nutritionals to those stricken by flooding and lack of food and clean water.

For several decades, society's expectations of companies and their role had been rapidly evolving — and rising. White determined to make Abbott a leader in all aspects of its operations, including areas that spoke to the company's social responsibility. This meant not just in philanthropy, which also accelerated significantly, but in the way it ran its business, its environmental stewardship, its sourcing of supplies around the world and the practices of its suppliers, and in addressing social needs in its area of expertise — such as access to medicines — as well as in its compact with the employees who made the company work.

Under this approach, Abbott made a major commitment to "global citizenship," an evolving concept that informed how the company advanced its business objectives, applied its social investment and philanthropy, and exercised its influence as a major, worldwide corporation to make a productive, positive contribution to society through all of its actions as an organization.

Emblematic of such efforts were Abbott's far-reaching initiatives to combat HIV/AIDS. Since the 1980s, Abbott had made a significant contribution to the fight against this disease through the development of innovative tests and medicines. Building on this history, Abbott and the Abbott Fund established an international initiative known as Step Forward, a program to improve the lives of orphans and vulnerable children affected or infected by HIV/AIDS in developing countries.

Central to this worldwide caring effort was the Abbott Fund, a non-profit charity first established in 1951. The Fund supported and partnered with a broad range of organizations, including community-based charities, academic institutions, medical and health professional associations, international relief agencies, and not-for-profit

organizations. Its aim was to support new approaches in such areas as healthcare access and scientific and medical innovation. Among its many partner organizations were CARE International, Partners in Health, and the American Heart Association.

In time, Step Forward developed into Abbott's family of Global Care Initiatives, through which Abbott and the Abbott Fund have invested more than $250 million in four key areas: strengthening healthcare systems, helping children affected by HIV/AIDS, preventing mother-to-child transmission of HIV, and expanding access to testing and treatment.

To help pregnant women find out their HIV status, Abbott donated more than 20 million HIV rapid tests free of charge to qualifying programs in 69 developing countries, including all of Africa. Rapid testing allowed women to learn their status in just 15 minutes. Local programs could then offer HIV-positive mothers counseling and free and convenient therapy to prevent their children from being infected.

In 2012 alone, Abbott and the Abbott Fund contributed more than $730 million in grants and products, the majority of which were directed toward providing patients access to medicine and healthcare through capacity-building partnerships, product donations, and patient assistance programs.

Around the globe, Abbott engaged in fast emergency response as well as long-term charitable programs. A prime example took place after the great Indian Ocean tsunami of December 26, 2004, resulting from an earthquake off the coast of Indonesia.

Ocean surges inundated coastal communities in 11 countries, killing more than 150,000 people, and depriving millions of people of housing, food, or drinkable water. Abbott sprang into action. It donated more than $7.5 million in goods and monies. Working with relief agencies, the company and area affiliates such as Abbott India and Abbott Indonesia sent and helped distribute needed Abbott products, like the pediatric nutritional *Gain SmartChoice*, *Similac* infant formula, and the antibiotic *Biaxin*.

Abbott's policy is to aid in acute emergency situations like this worldwide, leading the company to mount quick responses of aid and technical assistance to victims of the September 11, 2001, terror attacks, the destruction wreaked by Hurricane Katrina, and the Chinese, Japanese, and Haitian earthquakes, among other emergency situations around the world.

Abbott turned its ArchiTour promotional trucks into mobile diagnostics centers and sent them to the U.S. Gulf Coast to help victims of Hurricane Katrina.

A singular act of environmental charity took place in early 2005, when a group of dolphins were stranded off the Florida Keys. The sea mammals beached themselves, became dehydrated, and faced death. Abbott rushed boxes of *Pedialyte* to volunteers from the Marine Mammal Conservancy and the Florida Keys Marine Mammal Rescue Team. The *Pedialyte* oral solution was normally for dehydrated children, but worked just fine in this unusual rescue.

But, in the 2000s, Abbott moved beyond traditional philanthropy, into strategic corporate citizenship, in concert with the evolving and expanding view of the role of companies in society. The company increasingly evaluated — and modified — its business practices to ensure that its effects on society and the environment were thoughtful and beneficial, in order to maintain the sustainability of the company and the community.

A notable example was Abbott's participation, starting in 2005, in the Partnership for Prescription Assistance, or PPA. Undertaken during Miles White's term as chairman of PhRMA (the Pharmaceutical Research and Manufacturers of America, the industry's leading trade organization), the PPA helped persons without health insurance or coverage receive discounted pharmaceuticals and other medical care products. In a related effort, Abbott's Patient Assistance Programs provided hundreds of millions of dollars' worth of free medications to hundreds of thousands of financially challenged patients.

A similar initiative to broaden patient access to medicines was Abbott's involvement, with nine other major medical care firms and more than 40,000 pharmacies, in the Together Rx Access Card. It provided steep savings on hundreds of brand-name and generic prescription drugs to lower-income persons lacking health insurance. By 2007, more than a million Americans had enrolled in the Together Rx plan.

Similarly, the company adapted its pricing practices in developing countries to broaden access, reducing prices based on local economies' ability to afford them. This included distributing some products at or below cost in the world's poorest nations.

Abbott increasingly employs clean energy technologies, such as solar power and co-generation.

Abbott's highest honor, the Chairman's Award, is presented to employees who have demonstrated extraordinary workplace leadership, performance, and innovation. Senior executives make recommendations to the chairman and CEO, who reviews and selects the winners. "These honorees represent the very finest at Abbott," noted Miles White, "and their innovative approach and collaborative teamwork on critical projects help ensure the company's future success." Each year the winners and their work are celebrated with a dinner hosted by the chairman at Abbott House.

Progressive environmental policies and practices were also a continually rising priority in Abbott's operations. A particular focus was an effort to reduce water use and waste. In 2008, Abbott adopted a new water policy that set a goal of reducing corporate water use, indexed to sales, by 40 percent by 2011. To help achieve this, the company targeted for action four of its major worldwide manufacturing sites: Campoverde, Italy; Temecula, California; Singapore; and Casa Grande, Arizona. Over two years, the plant in Campoverde alone reduced water consumption by more than 20 percent, some 51 million gallons per year, while increasing overall production. Previously, in 2000, the U.S. Environmental Protection Agency made the Casa Grande facility a charter member of the National Environmental Performance Track program. Due to changes in its manufacturing processes, the plant had achieved annual reductions of 635,000 pounds of product packaging and 240,000 pounds of biochemical waste.

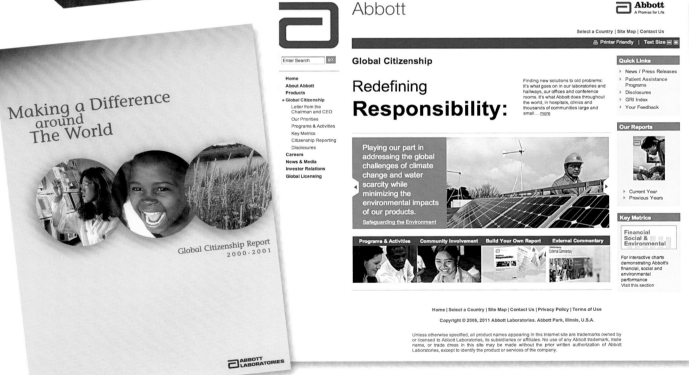

Abbott began producing a formal annual Global Citizenship Report beginning in 2001. This report summarized not just such elements as philanthropic giving, but, increasingly, the many ways in which the company was adapting its business to meet evolving standards of practice as an employer, a manufacturer, a purchaser of services, as well as in corporate governance — that is to say, in all of its actions that affect its various stakeholder groups and the environment. Above is the company's first citizenship report (left). Today the bulk of its reporting is done online (right) to reduce paper usage.

Early Discoveries, the child care center at Abbott's corporate headquarters, has facilities befitting a technology company, immersing its young charges in science, computers and, in the case of its aquarium, an introduction to marine bioscience.

As a result of its efforts in enhancing access to health-care, assisting the needy, providing opportunities, security and growth for its employees, protecting patients and consumers, and safeguarding the environment, Abbott repeatedly earned inclusion on the Dow Jones Sustainability Index, the world's top recognition for leadership in responsible economic, environmental, and social performance.

"Sustainability is a critical part of our approach to business," said Miles White. "Operating in a way that creates long-term value for our investors and stakeholders is an expectation of leaders across Abbott, from research and development, to marketing and sales, to human resources and environmental management."

A Premier Employer

To meet the ambitious performance goals he had set, White recognized the need to also take Abbott to the next level as an employer. The company had always been a highly desirable workplace, but, between increasing global competition for talent and rising expectations of employer behavior, it would have to strategically enhance this aspect of its operations, as well. Under human resources executive vice president Stephen R. Fussell, it tackled this work with the

same zeal it had brought to the rebuilding of its business and product portfolios, as the company rethought the nature of the employment experience it offered, and of the compact between the company and the people who made it work.

A highly visible area of advancement was in employee benefits. The Abbott employee benefits program, impressive since the days of "Sunny Jim" Stiles, was now extended with new approaches for employees of different ages. To retain veteran talent, the company initiated its innovative Emeritus Program to keep valuable retirement-eligible employees in their roles. A much-admired benefit for working parents with young children was the development of an extensive and innovative child-care solutions program, including a state-of-the-art child-care center at Abbott Park.

The 46,000-square-foot facility, named Early Discoveries, was one of the five largest in the United States, and offered computer learning stations, an art and science studio, and a 210-gallon aquarium. The center can accommodate more than 400 children, from infants to those of elementary-school age.

Continues on page 344 ▶

Supporting and Strengthening Women Leaders

Abbott's growth in the new millennium came at a time when the company, long devoted to equal opportunity, reemphasized that commitment by strongly supporting the inclusion, development, and leadership of women across the company. By ensuring that the composition of its management team more closely mirrors that of the markets it serves, Abbott made itself even better able to respond to the needs of its customers.

From 2000 to 2012, Abbott increased its percentage of women at every level of management.

▶ The number of women in management roles increased by 53 percent.
▶ The number of women in director-level positions increased by 81 percent.
▶ The number of women in divisional vice president positions rose 154 percent.
▶ The percentage of corporate officers who are women rose by 58 percent. In 2011, 22 percent of Abbott corporate officers were women, compared with an average of less than 15 percent across the Fortune 500.

Laura J. Schumacher, executive vice president, general counsel and secretary, represented Abbott at the 2009 Working Mother Work Life Congress, where the company was recognized as one of the Top Ten Companies for Working Mothers. In the 2000s, Abbott was recognized as one of *Working Mother* Magazine's 100 Best Companies for Working Mothers for 10 consecutive years.

GREAT PLACE TO WORK®

Abbott was named a "Great Place to Work" in the United States and in countries across Europe and Asia.

During this time, as well, a number of organizations around the world have recognized Abbott's advancement of women leaders. The company was named a "Great Place to Work" in the United States and in countries across Europe and Asia. It was lauded as a top company for executive women and for its best-in-class initiatives to advance and enhance the careers of women. In addition, for 10 consecutive years Abbott has been recognized in the United States as one of the "100 Best Companies for Working Mothers."

Abbott Families: Stewards of Our Company from Generation to Generation

Since its beginning, Abbott has been a company of families. For 125 years multiple generations have made their livelihoods, and fulfilled their dreams, here.

It began with Dr. Abbott himself. In 1890, when he was 32, Dr. Abbott had his parents and his sister, Lucy, working for his fast-growing company. In fact, he used the home they lived in — just two blocks north of his drugstore in Chicago's Ravenswood neighborhood — as an extension of the pharmacy. The parlor stored spare cans of granules; the kitchen was an extra laboratory.

Dr. Abbott's father, Luther, helps with the bottling of granules.

Abbott family: (from left) Eileen, Robert Sr., and Bob Anderson.

"My Great Aunt Worked for Dr. Abbott in 1908."
The family of Bob Anderson has worked at Abbott for more than a century. His great aunt, Ester Anderson, began working for Dr. Abbott in 1908 as a pill maker at the Ravenswood, Chicago, location. She retired in 1957, just four months before her 50th anniversary with the company. Bob's grandmother, Florence Anderson, worked here in the 1930s; an aunt, Nancy Anderson, worked here in the 1950s; Bob's father, Robert Anderson Sr., began his 37-year Abbott engineering career in 1955; Bob's wife, Eileen Anderson, began at Abbott in 1995; and Bob, himself, added his link to the chain when he joined Abbott in 2001.

A match made at Abbott.
Gary Young has been an Abbott employee since 1974.

If not for the Abbott cafeteria, Gary might not be here at all. That's where his parents, Patrick and Nadine Young, first met in 1951. Gary's grandfather, Al Garrett, also worked at Abbott, as did an uncle, Billy Garrett, cousins Richard and Robert Garrett, and Gary's daughter, Rachael Young. Gary is married to Christine Young, who has been with Abbott since 1979.

Gary Young appeared, along with his father, Patrick, in an *Abbott Topics* employee newsletter article promoting company benefits. "I like to tell people this was my first job with Abbott," jokes Gary.

A few of the many Abbott people from the Gallegos family tree: (from left) Gilbert, Vicki, Joseph (retired), Cyndi Nolder-Ruiz, and Richard.

"We have Abbott in our Blood."
The Gallegos family includes 22 Abbott employees spanning three generations. This long line of employment began with Joseph F. Gallegos, now retired, and continues today with 21 others, including Gilbert Gallegos, who says, "This company has provided for our family all of my life. We have Abbott in our blood."

A legacy lives on.
Joe Nemmers shares a name with his father. But he wasn't Joe Nemmers, Jr.; at least not until he started working full-time at Abbott. That was when the Abbott operator decided that it was too confusing having two Joe Nemmers at the company and added the "junior" and "senior" to their names. The Nemmers' family connection to Abbott began in 1944, when Irvin

Joseph (Joe) M. Nemmers, "Sr." (left) and "Jr.," seen here in Abbott's Centennial Year, 1988, represent two of the four generations of their family to work at Abbott continuously since 1944.

Nemmers — father of the elder Joe — came to work for the company. Joe, "senior" joined his dad in 1946, retiring 45 years later. Joe, "junior" — who spent his high school summers working at the Hospital Products facility in North Chicago, Illinois, as part of a jobs program for children of employees — began his professional career at Abbott in 1980, and rose to the level of executive vice president, with responsibility for the diagnostics and animal health businesses. Today, the Nemmers-Abbott tradition continues with Joe's son, Max, who works in human resources.

Bruce Horrom worked at Abbott for more than 50 years, met his wife at the company, and welcomed several of his children as fellow Abbott employees.

"Everyone contributes to making this company a success."
As a promising young associate research chemist in 1946, Bruce Horrom was hired by Ernest Volwiler, former Abbott chairman and distinguished scientist. In a career that spanned more than a half century at Abbott, Bruce amassed a body of work that includes the synthesis or invention of 23 compounds that reached

the chronic toxicity or clinical trial stage — three of which became commercial products — and the authorship of 58 articles and 630 patents. "Back then, we chemists thought everything at Abbott revolved around us," Bruce said. "Since then, I've learned the value that everyone contributes to making this company a success." That "everyone" includes the family Bruce raised with his wife, Mickey, whom he met when she was working in the Abbott library. Their sons John, Bob, and Preston all worked at Abbott, as did daughter Cheryl and daughter-in-law Janice. In all, the family has given more than 100 years of total service to the company.

And what of Dr. Abbott's family?
Well, it's still represented today by Bryan Ford, a great grandson of Dr. Abbott. Bryan currently works in Abbott's nutrition business. ∎

In 2005, a group of Wallace C. Abbott's descendants visited Abbott House. At left is Bryan Ford, great grandson of Dr. Abbott and, to the far right, is Bryan's father, Roland (Rolly) Ford, both of whom built careers at the company.

Refreshing Abbott's Brand and Renewing Its Promise

Abbott had used its iconic "A" logo since 1959, by far the longest time the company had employed the same mark. As the company was moving mountains to change its business for strong and sustainable growth, as well as becoming a best-practice leader in multiple aspects of its operations, CEO Miles White decided it was time to re-examine the corporate brand as well.

After considering many alternatives, Abbott chose to keep its venerable logo, which it found to be well recognized and respected. But it enhanced the symbol with the addition of a new "brandline," "A Promise for Life." This phrase captured the company's many commitments to the diverse stakeholders it served. It also connected to Abbott's newly adopted statement of purpose, which used the phrase as its title.

In 2005, the refreshed and reconceived Abbott brand was launched — first to Abbott employees — through this booklet, "Our Brand Promise." Employees were introduced to the company's new graphic identity and, more importantly, to the ideas behind the brand, as captured in the new brand promise.

A Promise for Life
Turning Science into Caring

Our Values:

PIONEERING
ACHIEVING
CARING
ENDURING

We are here for the people we serve in their pursuit of healthy lives. This has been the way of Abbott for more than a century—passionately and thoughtfully translating science into lasting contributions to health.

Our products encircle life, from newborns to aging adults, from nutrition and diagnostics through medical care and pharmaceutical therapy.

Caring is central to the work we do and defines our responsibility to those we serve:

We advance leading-edge science and technologies that hold the potential for significant improvements to health and to the practice of health care.

We value our diversity—that of our products, technologies, markets and people—and believe that diverse perspectives combined with shared goals inspire new ideas and better ways of addressing changing health needs.

We focus on exceptional performance—a hallmark of Abbott people worldwide—demanding of ourselves and each other because our work impacts people's lives.

We strive to earn the trust of those we serve by committing to the highest standards of quality, excellence in personal relationships, and behavior characterized by honesty, fairness and integrity.

We sustain success—for our business and the people we serve—by staying true to key tenets upon which our company was founded over a century ago: innovative care and a desire to make a meaningful difference in all that we do.

The promise of our company is in the promise that our work holds for health and life.

Abbott
A Promise for Life

BELOW
***Abbott World*, the company's long-standing employee magazine, both embodied the new brand in its design, and educated employees about what it meant for them, their company, and the people they served.**

May 2005

Abbott World

2 Upfront
3 Our values
4 Who we are, what we stand for
   Our visual identity
7 **Pioneering** Leading the way in targeted medicine
8 **Achieving** Driving change to achieve excellence
10 **Caring** Our caring response helps tsunami victims
   Reaching out to caregivers, patients and consumers
12 **Enduring** Pediatric nutritionals enjoy generations of growth
15 Our brand
16 A Promise for Life

Connecting our values, identity and business goals

Abbott
A Promise for Life

TOP
"A Promise for Life" is Abbott's statement of purpose, capturing the essence of what the company is here to do, and laying out its four core values: Pioneering, Achieving, Caring, and Enduring. Together our values and our Promise provide employees a framework and a guide in their daily work for helping make choices that will best serve stakeholders and fulfill the company's mission.

Profiles in **Diversity Journal**
Volume 4, Number 2 • March/April 2002
$12.95 U.S.

IBM Corporation
An Interview with Ted Childs, Part

JPMorgan Chase
The Diversity Education
Center of Excellence:
Bringing the Learning Together

SBC Communications
The Evolution of a Successful
Diversity Program

National Security Agency
Think Ability

Ford Motor Compan
Keeping the Momentum

Stairway To Success
Experienced and diverse leadership backs
Abbott Laboratories' CEO Miles White
thanks to an aggressive "pipeline"
program of education and support

As a result of its innovative efforts to build a continually better workplace and work experience for its employees, Abbott came to be consistently recognized as a top employer, including specifically for minorities, women, working mothers, and scientists; as one of the best companies for internships, or at which to begin a career; and, in many countries around the world, as one of the few best employers, period.

50 Best Companies for Minorities

In an ideal world the leading companies for minority employees would be tops for everyone. But this is not an ideal world, and some companies are still more successful at fostering diversity in their workplace than others. The good news: Corporate America is raising the bar, and the best keep on getting better. FORTUNE's list shows which 50 companies rank at the very top. **By Cora Daniels**

A Company Transformed

By decade's end, the business press was recognizing the achievements of Abbott and its leadership. The financial magazine *Barron's*, for instance, lauded Abbott as one of its most respected companies in the world.

Noted *Barron's* of Abbott: "Management has done a superb job in shedding slow-growing divisions, refocusing the portfolio and building intrinsic value." The editors praised Abbott and White for having "delivered the best stock performance among all of its Big Pharma peers" over the previous three- and five-year periods. *Barron's* also repeatedly placed Abbott's chief, Miles White, in its list of the world's 30 best CEOs.

And, for the first time, *Fortune* magazine, whose annual ranking of the World's Most Admired Companies is arguably the top gauge of corporate reputation, ranked Abbott the most admired company in its industry.

Continues on page 348 ▶

Abbott's efforts in global citizenship were also recognized, with the company being named repeatedly to the Dow Jones Sustainability Indexes, the world's top recognition for leadership in responsible economic, environmental, and social performance.

In recognition of the transformation achieved at Abbott, Miles White has been named five consecutive times to *Barron's* magazine's list of the world's 30 best CEOs. This clipping is from the first time, in 2009.

BARRON'S — World's Best CEOs

Miles **White**
Abbott Laboratories, CEO since '99

Why: Producing just what the doctor ordered.

When Miles White took charge of Abbott in 1999, he found a company in search of an identity. While industry peers were diversifying, Abbott largely stayed true to its origins—or was stuck in them, slow-moving and dull. White changed all that.

In a decade, mainly through acquisitions and R&D, he broadened the base of Abbott into fast-growing health-care mar- kets—medical devices, diagnostics and nutritional products—and new drugs. Abbott's common paid investors an annual average of 4% from 1999 through 2008,

Annualized Price Change

One Year	-12.7%
While CEO	3.1%
S&P 500	-3.7%
2009 P/E	12.9
5-Yr. Profit Growth	8.0%

ABT / NYSE — $48 — $70 / 60 / 50 / 40 — 2008 2009

compared with a negative 1% return for the S&P 500 and a negative 0.29% return for the S&P 500 Healthcare Index. In 2008, the company outperformed the S&P 500 Healthcare Index by 20 percentage points. In the past three- and five-year periods, White's Abbott has delivered the best stock performance among all of its Big Pharma peers.

—Neil A. Martin

FORTUNE WORLD'S MOST ADMIRED COMPANIES® 2010
#1- PHARMACEUTICALS

In 2010, *Fortune* magazine named Abbott the most admired company in its industry.

Three generations of Abbott chief financial officers, (left to right) Thomas C. Freyman, Bernard H. Semler, and Duane L. Burnham (who, after serving as CFO, would become the company's CEO). Abbott's strong financial systems and the discipline they created throughout the company were among the keys to the long-term success that made Abbott the second-best performing member of the S&P 500 over the Index's first 50 years.

Miles D. White

For Miles White, it was always about building. Building up companies, communities, capabilities, and results. It would come as no surprise, therefore, that his tenure as CEO — the second-longest in the company's history, after Dr. Abbott himself — would see Abbott transformed in virtually every aspect of its operations. The goal: building the company to achieve sustainable, high-quality growth in an ever-more competitive global business environment.

Miles D. White, Abbott's second-youngest and second-longest-serving CEO, after Dr. Abbott himself, would transform the company for a new century.

Miles White began his career in the Chicago office of consulting giant McKinsey & Company in 1980. An inspiration there was Marvin Bower, one of the fathers of professional management consulting. "Every year, even in retirement, Marvin would have a session with the young people who were new to the firm," recalled White.

"Marvin's mantra to us was to 'be a builder ...' About doing what's right for the client. About thinking and working and building for the long term ... It was all about building: building the company, the community, the family, and, always, the people they comprise."

The McKinsey icon was a "servant leader," noted White. "He knew that by helping to build those around him — by raising and strengthening their abilities, their understanding, their confidence, their principles — they would help him build the outstanding firm that he envisioned." These core ideas, also inculcated by his preparatory school, Culver Academy, in Indiana, of which he would also become chairman, formed the foundation for White's leadership approach.

White earned his bachelor's degree in engineering from Stanford University, as well as a Master's in Business Administration. After school it was on to McKinsey, where he picked up the firm's "toolkit" for analyzing problems and devising solutions: "how to communicate ideas, sharpen and support a point of view, approach a problem, and come at things from a lot of different angles."

With his engineering bent, White expected his next destination would be Silicon Valley. But he was persuaded to interview at Abbott. His first position with the company was national sales manager for Abbott Diagnostics, which was then the company's fastest-growing and highest-profile business.

Yet White was in for some culture shock. The "real world" of Abbott differed from the theoretical setting of graduate school or even consulting. It "was a very tactical environment," he remembered. "The people who succeeded had to fit the norm of having come into an entry-level position and stayed a long time." White added, "Complex and elegant solutions don't help unless they can actually be executed inside the company."

Not that White, a hands-on type, minded much. "I never wanted to be a strategic-planning guy, I wanted to be an operations guy." He got his wish. At Abbott, he gained experience as a supervisor in diagnostics marketing, sales, and operations. He oversaw the development and launch of Abbott's blockbuster *AxSym* diagnostic instrument in 1993, and was made president of ADD, then the company's largest business, in 1994 at the age of just 38. He showed signs of things to come by orchestrating Abbott's largest acquisitions of the decade: Sequoia-Turner and MediSense. The Sequoia-Turner deal, noted White, "gave me a taste of what you can do through acquisitions." By 1998, his division's sales were growing at four times the industry's rate.

At 43 years of age, White was named Abbott's second-youngest CEO ever, after Dr. Abbott himself. He took the reins on the first day of 1999.

The job's demands were intense from the outset. He had to deal with the U.S. Government consent decree mandating reorganization of the company's diagnostics manufacturing practices. For three years he rode

herd over painstaking changes to a vast production process. White commented: "I wouldn't wish the experience on anyone." But the silver lining was that he wound up addressing not just diagnostics, but all of Abbott's quality systems.

By the late 1990s, growth was lagging and new engines were scarce. White needed to take steps that could pay off quickly while he also accelerated the longer-term process of filling the new-product pipeline through research and development. For the near term, he would build the company through acquisitions. He engineered an aggressive series of transactions, across the company's business portfolio — and beyond it, into entirely new businesses for the company, such as vascular care and medical optics — all according to a highly defined set of criteria designed to build the Abbott of the future and deliver superior results on a sustainable basis. At the end of a decade of constant activity, this strategy was richly rewarded, as Abbott was named both the top deal maker and most admired company in its industry. White, meanwhile, was repeatedly hailed by *Barron's* magazine as one of the world's 30 best CEOs.

Optimizing Abbott's business portfolio required divesting, as well as acquiring. White spun off the firm's hospital products division, which no longer fit the company's growth strategy. In doing so, he created Hospira, a Fortune 600 corporation, allowing the hospital products business to thrive in independence.

These decisive building efforts paid major dividends. Under White Abbott's revenues soared well past previous highs, growing from $12 billion to $40 billion. And, as with predecessors such as George Cain, White pushed global growth. In 2008, Abbott's international revenues exceeded those in the United States for the first time, and would accelerate in that direction — where the greatest potential for growth lay.

But White did not restrict his interest and energies to building Abbott's business portfolio. He remade every aspect of the

company's operations, challenging Abbott people to be the best in everything the company did. As a result, Abbott soon became a recognized leader in functions as diverse and wide-ranging as quality and human resources, environmental practice and corporate governance. And he changed the company's view of, and approach to, the world around it, by committing Abbott to leadership in global citizenship.

In his "off" hours, White sought to build up other institutions. He served on the boards of other corporations including Caterpillar, Motorola, The Tribune Company, and McDonald's Corporation, as well as Northwestern Memorial Hospital. He served as the chairman of the Federal Reserve Bank of Chicago, and of the Pharmaceutical Research and Manufacturers of America (PhRMA), the industry's leading trade association. Closer to home he served as chairman of the Civic Committee of the Commercial Club of Chicago, and Northwestern University's Kellogg School of Management. He also served on the board of trustees of Northwestern University, the Lyric Opera, the Joffrey Ballet, the Museum of Science and Industry, The Field Museum, where he also served as chairman, and as a Fellow of the American Academy of Arts and Sciences.

As Abbott approached its quasquicentennial (125th) year, White took his vision for the company and his penchant for building to a new level, with the single largest strategic decision in Abbott's long history: separating the business into two leading healthcare companies of roughly equal size: a diversified medical products company that retained the Abbott name and identity, and a research-based pharmaceutical company, called AbbVie (see pages 352–369).

"The life of a successful company is one of constant transformation," said White. "As Benjamin Franklin put it, 'When you're finished changing, you're finished.' And, at 125, Abbott's best years are still ahead of us." ∎

And Transformed Again

And at this peak moment of success, while enjoying a crescendo of recognition for the successful transformation the company had achieved over a decade of constant strategic effort, White started over again — or, more to the point, continued the ongoing process, adapting the company yet again to meet the changes taking place in its always dynamic business environment.

"We can't rest on our laurels," said White. "The world we do business in is constantly changing — we have to do the same."

The time to prepare for the future was when things were at their best. White and his management team set about finding the next set of growth drivers to keep the company's great momentum going in the years ahead. The years 2009 and 2010 would prove to be a new watershed in charting the company's course forward, including, perhaps, Abbott's most active period ever of building by acquisition—which was saying much, given the activity of the previous decade.

The keys: new businesses, new technologies, and new markets.

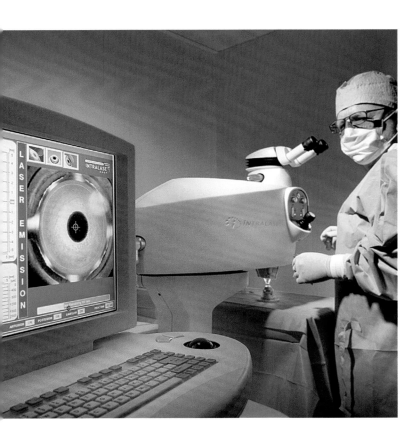

Abbott's acquisition of Advanced Medical Optics, the leader in Lasik surgery instruments, brought in that firm's products, such as the *Excimer Laser System*, for conducting vision correction.

New Business: Medical Optics

Since it began preparing its medical products strategy, Abbott had been interested in the vision care business, which exemplified its diversification strategy. The market was large and growing, was technology driven, and offered the potential for superior return on investment. Abbott bided its time, but entered the business in a significant way when the right opportunity arose.

Abbott added this new plank to its business diversity platform in early 2009 with the $1.36 billion acquisition of Advanced Medical Optics, Inc. (AMO). Renamed Abbott Medical Optics, AMO was the world's leading manufacturer of devices for the well-known Lasik surgery to correct nearsightedness, farsightedness, and astigmatism, millions of which procedures were performed annually. It was the number-two maker of instruments for cataract surgery, and was the third-largest maker of such eye-care products as contact lens solutions.

With the rising number of aging baby boomers needing cataract surgery — the most performed surgery in the world — and with the growing popularity of corrective surgery among all age groups, the acquisition of AMO promised a major return. "The demographics" for the business, noted White, "are all in our favor worldwide." Abbott quickly consolidated its new position in vision care by adding to AMO with the acquisition of Visiogen, Inc., an innovator of accommodating intraocular lenses for people with cataracts.

New Technologies: Across Businesses

Abbott Vascular had been built into a market leader and a top-three global player. In 2009, Abbott added a new branch to the business with the acquisition of eValve, a California-based technology innovator with an exciting new product known as *MitraClip*, used to perform minimally invasive heart repair.

Abbott then enhanced its laboratory diagnostics business with the addition of STARLIMS, a leader in laboratory informatics to help customers manage their increasing data volume.

And the acquisition of IBIS Technologies expanded the Abbott Molecular business with an innovative testing technology that succeeded in identifying the first cases of the swine flu in the United States in 2009, one of the year's major medical stories. The *Wall Street Journal* recognized the power of this product with that year's Technology Innovation Award.

With the addition of IBIS and its T5000 system, Abbott gained access to biosensor technology that diagnosed the first U.S. cases of swine flu in 2009, earning the company the *Wall Street Journal's* Gold award for Technology Innovation.

New Markets: Growing Globalization

Earlier in its transformation process, Abbott had begun to adjust its organizational structure to reflect the growing globalism of the company and its business. For decades, Abbott's revenues had stood at basically two-thirds from the United States, one-third from the rest of the world. In the 2000s this ratio began to change, dramatically. In 2008, for the first time ever, Abbott sales were greater outside the United States than within, by just a fraction of a percent. But the trend continued, and the gap grew until, by 2011, the proportion of U.S. to ex-U.S. sales had essentially reversed.

Following the Knoll acquisition, White had "globalized" the company's pharmaceutical business, bringing its formerly separate divisions for pharmaceutical research, manufacturing, U.S. marketing, and international marketing into one integrated, worldwide organization known as the Pharmaceutical Products Group (PPG). This would serve as the model for Abbott's nutrition business, as well, which also had an increasingly large international component.

Emerging Markets

One of the chief drivers of the shift in the company's revenue sources was the explosive growth of so-called "emerging markets" — large countries with significant economic potential that, due to internal cultural and political changes, were entering the global economy, with significant implications. The most prominent of these countries were Brazil, China, India, Mexico, Russia, South Korea, and Turkey. This group of countries was growing its markets at a multiple of the slowing rate of developed economies.

Abbott took an early step toward capturing the potential of this new dynamic by forming its "RIC" region — for Russia, India, and China — recognizing that the business characteristics of these markets were distinct and more similar to one another than to geographical neighbors. This organization would serve as the incubator of a major corporate direction to come.

After more than a decade of extraordinary efforts to rebuild the company, Abbott had reached a new peak — larger, more diverse, more global, and better recognized for its achievements than ever before. But the world around it, the global business environment, and the nature of healthcare had all evolved significantly over this period. As Abbott looked to its future, it saw very different paths ahead for its varying businesses, and critical choices to be made. As a result, the greatest change in Abbott's long history was soon to come.

Abbott's acquisition of technology innovator eValve brought it the *MitraClip* device for non-invasive structural heart repair.

Decade at a Glance

2000–2010

Humira, Abbott's fully-human monoclonal antibody drug, is approved by the U.S. FDA. It will go on to become the world's leading pharmaceutical and the company's most successful product to date.

▼

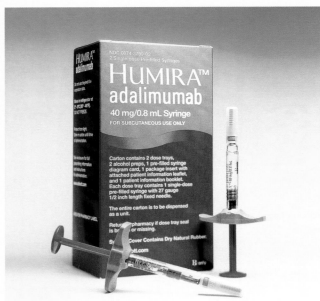

▲ 2000

Abbott announces its intention to purchase Knoll Pharmaceutical Co., a division of BASF, for $6.9 billion. With the acquisition, its largest ever, Abbott's international presence is immediately expanded by 40 percent and its scientific capability significantly enhanced.

Abbott sells its agricultural products business to Sumitomo, Inc., allowing the company to focus more effectively on its core healthcare businesses.

Abbott Animal Health is formed as a separate division, devising veterinary applications for a variety of the company's products.

Abbott launches Step Forward, a program to support AIDS orphans and vulnerable children in the developing world, which will transform the company's approach to global citizenship.

2001

Abbott acquires Vysis, Inc., laying the foundation for the creation of a new division, Abbott Molecular Diagnostics.

▼

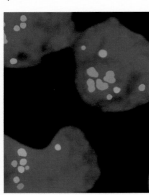

2002

Abbott enters the cardiovascular stent field with the acquisition of BioCompatibles, Inc.

2003

Abbott enters the healthy-living nutrition market when it adds ZonePerfect to its nutrition portfolio.

▼

Abbott's Point-of-Care Diagnostics business is founded with the acquisition of i-STAT.

▼

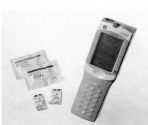

Abbott's vascular business continues to expand with the addition of Jomed N.V.

The acquisition of TheraSense, a leader in glucose monitoring technology that requires smaller blood samples, leads to the formation of Abbott Diabetes Care.

▼

2004

EAS joins the Abbott Nutrition family, bringing with it science-based sports nutrition products.

The spin-off of Abbott's Hospital Products Division creates Hospira, today a strong, independent Fortune 600 company.

▼

2005

Abbott helps found the Partnership for Prescription Assistance to help ensure that people in the U.S. without health coverage can still receive their prescriptions.

The company opens Abbott House, a living symbol of its tradition, its culture, and its brand.

▼

2006

Abbott acquires the vascular and endovascular businesses of Guidant, Inc., making the company a leader in the global vascular market.

▼

The purchase of Kos Pharmaceuticals, with its portfolio of marketed and investigational lipid management therapies, builds Abbott's presence in the largest segment of the pharmaceutical market.

▼

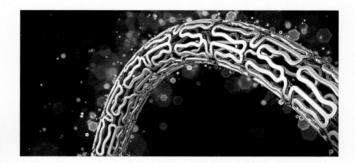

▲

The *Xience V* drug-eluting stent is launched. It goes on to become the market leader.

2007

As part of Abbott's ongoing corporate branding initiative, the Ross Products Division is renamed Abbott Nutrition.

2008

Similac Advance Early Shield brings infant formula closer to breast milk, helping Abbott regain leadership in this important market.

▼

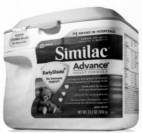

The launch of *Trilipix*, an advanced fenofibrate drug that can be used in combination with statins, solidifies Abbott's position in the lipid management market.

2009

Abbott completes its largest-ever investment in Asia with the construction of a $300 million nutrition products manufacturing facility in Singapore.

Abbott Vascular broadens its portfolio, adding eValve, and its innovative *MitraClip* technology.

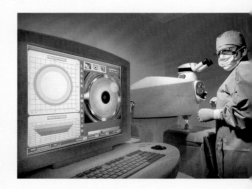

▲

Abbott enters an entirely new business with the purchase of Advanced Medical Optics. It subsequently enhances its new Abbott Medical Optics division with the acquisition of Visiogen and its accommodating intraocular lens technology.

The Next Chapter

One Vision, Two New Companies

As it approached its 125th anniversary, Abbott remained true to its long tradition of continual, focused evolution. Rather than looking back, its eyes were on the future and the best way to sustain the success of its diverse healthcare businesses. The result was the boldest transformation in the company's history: the creation of two new, leading healthcare companies — AbbVie and the new Abbott.

In the face of a changing world economy and the evolving business of healthcare, Miles White drew upon Abbott's 125-year legacy of continuous reinvention to lead the single biggest change in the company's history. By executing this fundamental transformation, Abbott positioned itself, and its new sister company, AbbVie, to better meet the needs of patients and consumers around the world.

By the end of 2010, it had become clear that the strategic actions Abbott had undertaken over the previous decade had been extremely successful, dramatically reshaping and strengthening the company. Abbott had expanded its global presence and aggressively rebuilt its pharmaceutical pipeline.

This period also saw significant change in the company's operating environment, including the rise of emerging markets and their growing impact on global business. At the same time, rising regulatory standards had changed the landscape for new healthcare products.

These changes in the environment essentially led each of Abbott's businesses to pursue distinctly different operating models. And it was clear to White and his team that the research-based pharmaceutical products business differed — in fundamental and important ways — from the rest of Abbott.

White's team had previously realized that the pharmaceutical business in developing and emerging markets had a unique profile as well. This insight led to the

formation of a new organization known as the Established Pharmaceuticals Division, or EPD.

The creation of EPD was driven by two major acquisitions. The first was Solvay Pharmaceuticals, formerly part of the Belgium-based Solvay Group, which became Abbott's second-largest acquisition ever, after Knoll. Second was a game-changing expansion into India with the acquisition of Piramal Healthcare Solutions.

Solvay brought Abbott both a significantly expanded presence in emerging markets — Solvay's business in certain developing countries was larger than Abbott's — and a large portfolio of what were known in the industry as "established products," also known as "branded generics." These were decidedly not conventional generic drugs, which are copies of branded, innovative medications. Branded generics are products that are not on patent, but that have strong brand identity and customer loyalty, and premium pricing. The earlier Knoll acquisition had also brought Abbott a number of these products, including medicines like *Synthroid*, for hypothyroidism, which continued to lead its market more than 40 years after launch.

These products were particularly appealing in emerging markets, where their brand equity was appreciated — consumers would rather use the established, original product than a generic copy. Solvay's product portfolio consisted primarily of branded generics. Abbott used this new aspect of its portfolio to forge a major position in this now highly attractive market.

Then, the company announced an agreement to acquire Piramal Healthcare Solutions, a leading marketer of established pharmaceuticals, based in Mumbai, India. This move made Abbott India's largest pharmaceutical company in the very year that the company celebrated its 100th anniversary of doing business on the subcontinent.

Solvay Pharmaceuticals

Chairman and CEO Miles D. White (left) capped 14 years of transformational change with his biggest strategic decision yet: the creation of a new company, AbbVie, from Abbott's proprietary pharmaceutical business. Abbott veteran Richard A. Gonzalez (right), head of Abbott's global pharmaceutical business and the company's former COO, was chosen to be AbbVie's Chairman and CEO.

In other words, as a result of changes in its business environment, Abbott had, in essence, become two separate companies under one roof. While the company was built on a diversity of businesses, it was not seeking diversity of business models. And it was finding this dichotomy to be counterproductive in some regards — particularly in relation to its stock valuation. The differences in these models created a lack of clear identity for each business. To White, this distinction was decisive and called for an equally decisive change.

Two Leading Companies

In October of 2011, seeking to differentiate its distinct businesses and unlock shareholder value, Abbott announced one of the most visionary and transformative moves in its long history — it would separate into two leading healthcare companies: a diversified medical products company and a research-based pharmaceutical company. It was a challenging decision, and one that spoke to Abbott's long history of embracing productive change.

In the same stroke, Abbott announced a partnership agreement with India-based Zydus Cadila to market a broad range of its branded-generic products across a large group of emerging markets.

This reorganization provided Abbott with, in essence, two distinct pharmaceutical businesses: one built on research-based, proprietary drugs, the other on branded generics. It became clear to Abbott that this distinction existed not only within pharmaceuticals, but between what had become two divergent business models within the company.

Fundamentally, R&D in the research-based pharmaceutical business had become focused on specialty therapeutic areas — such as immunology, chronic kidney disease, and multiple sclerosis — while Abbott's other new-product pipelines continued to have a broader mix.

Research-based pharmaceuticals were largely a business of developed markets. Abbott's diversified medical products businesses, on the other hand, had a higher growth rate because more of their business was in developing and emerging markets, which were growing faster. And, finally, research-based pharmaceuticals had different product-approval and life cycles, R&D profiles, and regulatory environments than Abbott's other businesses.

"At AbbVie, the 125-year history we share with Abbott roots us in a set of deeply held values. These guide our way, driving how we treat our patients and each other, and how we design our strategies and operate our business. And they keep us focused on what matters most – our patients and our people."

— RICHARD A. GONZALEZ

AbbVie's senior management team, led by Chairman and CEO Richard A. Gonzalez (center), celebrates the new company's listing on the NYSE under the ticker symbol ABBV.

On January 2, 2013, an AbbVie banner on the New York Stock Exchange announced the launch of the new biopharmaceutical company created from Abbott's proprietary pharmaceutical business.

The new pharmaceutical company would comprise all the elements of Abbott's global pharmaceutical business with the exception of EPD, whose emphasis on branded generics and developing markets made it less like its sister pharmaceutical business and more like the businesses in the diversified medical products portfolio: nutritionals, diagnostics, and devices.

AbbVie would be a new kind of enterprise – a biopharmaceutical company — blending the stability, global scale, resources, and commercial capabilities of a pharmaceutical company with the focus and culture of a biotech. In branding this new company, White and his team chose a name that established its enduring connection to Abbott (Abb), while suggesting the Latin root for "life" (Vie), underscoring the company's mission.

To lead this new business, Abbott turned to one of the key architects of its transformation, Miles White's trusted former right hand, Rick Gonzalez. Gonzalez had returned to part-time duty after a brief early retirement in the role of president of Abbott Ventures, Inc., a new venture capital group the company formed to pursue promising new technology in the medical products space. It was soon mirrored by Abbott Biotech Ventures, Inc., a similar group working in pharmaceuticals under the leadership of James Tyree, former head of PPG. When Olivier Bohuon, Tyree's successor as head of global pharmaceuticals, left Abbott to return to France as CEO of Pierre Fabre Group, Gonzalez returned full-time as head of Abbott's global pharmaceutical business. So, when the decision was made to create the new company, he was the clear choice to be its CEO. Joining Gonzalez on the new company's senior management team were Laura J. Schumacher as general counsel; William J. Chase as chief financial officer; Carlos Alban as head of commercial operations; Dr. John M. Leonard as chief scientific officer; and Timothy J. Richmond as chief human resources officer.

Separating into two companies was as complex a task as any Abbott had undertaken in its entire history, but the company tackled the process with its usual discipline and vigor, smoothly transitioning over the course of 2012, and launching two strong new businesses on January 1, 2013.

The Next Chapter

As Abbott began its 125th year in operation, then, it undertook one of the boldest and most forward-looking actions in its long history: the launch of a new company and the re-launch of Abbott as a very different one than it had long been.

> "You're never finished building a company. That's how we've thrived for 125 years, so far. We're here to carry on that great legacy — at both Abbott and AbbVie — to take it higher and farther, and to hand it on to the next generation of our companies to do the same. We intend for our next 125 years to be as great as the last — for the sake of all the people, around the world, our companies are here to serve."
>
> — MILES D. WHITE

From the Abbott that had grown up over a century and a quarter, there would now be two leading healthcare companies — both Fortune 200-level global enterprises; both top-10 companies in their respective industry segments; both carrying forward the same tradition; and both ready to compete and succeed in the healthcare environment of the 21st century. Abbott was, once again, transforming itself to meet its ever-changing future.

"It's a constant process," said Miles White. "You're never finished building a company. That's how we've thrived for 125 years, so far. We're here to carry on that great legacy — at both Abbott and AbbVie — to take it higher and farther, and to hand it on to the next generation of our companies to do the same. We intend for our next 125 years to be as great as the last — for the sake of all the people, around the world, our companies are here to serve."

Continues on page 366 ▶

A Tale of Two Companies

With their separation complete, Abbott and AbbVie became independent companies that share a common legacy and strong prospects for future success. However, while both companies have broad, sustainable portfolios, extensive global presence, and strong, innovative new product pipelines, it was their differences that promised to allow Abbott and AbbVie to achieve even greater success as separate businesses.

	Stock Ticker Symbol	Company Profile	Strategic Focus
Abbott A Promise for Life	ABT	A unique mix of diversified healthcare businesses, including Nutrition, Established Pharmaceuticals, Diagnostics and Medical Devices. A growth-focused, large-cap medical device company with a broad and balanced durable growth portfolio, significant emerging-market presence, and accelerating margins and cash flow.	▸ Expanding geographically ▸ Developing new technologies ▸ Accelerating margins/ cash flow
abbvie	ABBV	A specialty-focused, research-based biopharmaceutical company, combining the focus, culture, and agility required to achieve breakthrough science with the stability and resources to effectively commercialize scientific discoveries.	▸ Continuing growth of leading brands ▸ Advancing specialty-focused pharma pipeline ▸ Strong margins and robust cash flow

"Abbott City 125," a new version, by artist Mark McMahon, of the "cityscape" paintings made up of Abbott — and, now, AbbVie — locations around the world. This update captures the extraordinary growth and change the company achieved in the short time since "Abbott City 2000," marking a watershed period in its long history.

Sales in 2012	Sales by Product Type	Market Leadership	Number of Employees
$21.5 Billion	26% Medical Devices 30% Nutrition 24% Established Pharma 20% Diagnostics	▸ #1 in global nutrition ▸ #1 in U.S. pediatric nutrition products ▸ #1 in worldwide adult nutrition products ▸ #1 in immunoassay diagnostics ▸ #1 in blood screening ▸ #1 drug-eluting stent globally; first bioresorbable vascular scaffold ▸ #1 pharmaceutical company in India	70,000
$18.4 Billion	25% Primary Care 75% Specialty	▸ #1 anti-TNF biologic worldwide ▸ #1 market share in testosterone replacement ▸ #1 hormone therapy for the palliative treatment of advanced prostate cancer ▸ #1 prescribed brand for treating thyroid disease ▸ Leading antiviral therapies for HIV ▸ Leading pancreatic enzyme replacement therapy ▸ Only approved product for the prevention of RSV	21,500

Abbott Products

Abbott's strong portfolio of diversified healthcare technologies includes a range of products that hold strong leadership positions in the markets they serve.

Core Laboratory Diagnostics

Abbott's broad range of innovative instrument systems and tests for hospitals, reference labs, blood banks, physician offices, and clinics provides early, accurate detection and management of medical conditions.

Point-of-Care Diagnostics

Abbott point-of-care products provide healthcare professionals immediate access to accurate, critical diagnostic test results at the point of patient care.

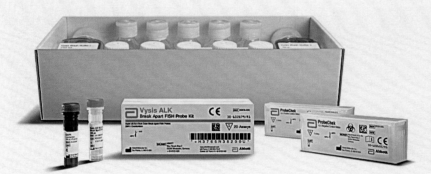

Molecular Diagnostics

Abbott is a leader in the rapidly growing area of molecular diagnostics — the analysis of DNA, RNA, and proteins at the molecular level — with instruments and tests that are used to detect pathogens and subtle changes in patients' genes and chromosomes. These tests enable physicians to detect diseases earlier and more accurately, select the appropriate therapies, and improve the monitoring of disease.

Established Pharmaceuticals

Abbott's extensive portfolio of established pharmaceuticals varies from market to market, targeted to the specific needs of each region.

Vascular Care

Abbott's vascular portfolio is focused on leading-edge, minimally invasive devices that help people impacted by heart disease, stroke, carotid artery disease, critical limb ischemia, and other serious vascular conditions.

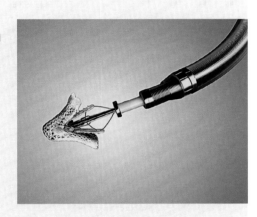

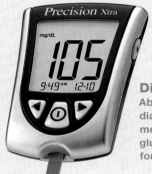

Diabetes Care

Abbott's focus in diabetes care is to help people with diabetes effectively monitor and manage this serious metabolic condition. The company offers innovative glucose-monitoring systems, test strips, and services for both in-home and hospital settings.

Vision Care

Abbott provides a full range of advanced vision technologies and support focused on delivering optimal vision and lifestyle experiences to patients of all ages. For cataracts, Abbott offers lens removal systems, viscoelastics, and intraocular lenses. Abbott is also the world's leading provider of laser vision correction (LASIK) technologies; and the company offers a broad selection of corneal care products — such as contact lens cleaning systems and lubricating eye drops.

Nutritional Products

Abbott's nutritional products are designed to promote health and well-being for people of all ages. The company's diverse product portfolio includes some of the world's most trusted brands, including *Similac*, *Ensure,* and *Glucerna*.

AbbVie Products

AbbVie's portfolio of biologics and other compounds addresses some of the world's most complex medical needs.

AndroGel
AndroGel is the leading testosterone-replacement therapy, with more than 60 percent category market share.

Humira
Since it was launched as a treatment for rheumatoid arthritis in 2003, *Humira* has steadily added indications and is currently the leading pharmaceutical in the world.

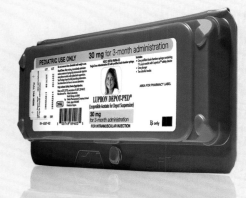

Lupron
Lupron is the leading hormone therapy for the palliative treatment of advanced prostate cancer and also is indicated for a variety of other conditions, including endometriosis, uterine fibroids, and precocious puberty.

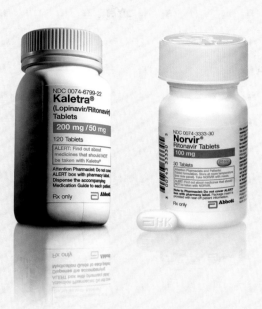

Kaletra and Norvir

Kaletra and *Norvir* are the leading protease inhibitors for the treatment of HIV.

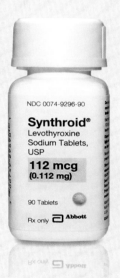

Synthroid

Synthroid is the leading branded synthetic hormone therapy for thyroid disease. It is also one of the most widely prescribed medicines in the United States.

Synagis

Synagis is the only approved product for the prevention of respiratory syncytial virus (RSV), a disease that can be life-threatening for infants.

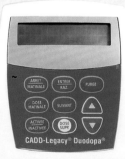

Duodopa

Duodopa is an intestinal gel used to treat advanced Parkinson's disease.

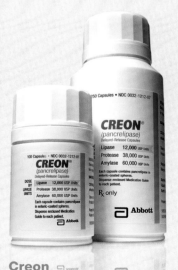

Creon

Creon is the leading pancreatic enzyme therapy for conditions associated with cystic fibrosis and chronic pancreatitis.

Their separation complete, Abbott and AbbVie are well positioned to address the healthcare challenges of the 21st century.

Into the Future

AbbVie looks to the future from a position of significant strength. It has a strong base of sustainable leadership positions across its specialty-focused commercial portfolio and a compelling late-stage pipeline, with a number of treatments in development that are designed to make a life-changing difference in people's lives. Everything the company does moves it toward that end goal of addressing today's health issues — from life-threatening illnesses to chronic conditions.

Key to its mission as an independent biopharmaceutical company is advancing its pipeline. AbbVie is focused on delivering transformational medicines; therapies that offer significant patient benefits and clinical value propositions. They are dedicated to collaborating with peers, academics, government, and advocacy groups to find the solutions to the most pressing areas of unmet clinical need.

In short, Abbvie is dedicated to delivering truly innovative medications that will make a difference in people's lives in a remarkable way.

The new **Abbott** is one of the largest, and most truly globalized, diversified healthcare products companies in the world. The company boasts a new-product pipeline that includes game-changing medical technologies, next-generation diagnostic systems, new formulations, new packaging, new flavors, and other brand enhancements. And the new Abbott is aligned with important trends for the future of healthcare.

Abbott's strong presence around the world positions the company well to capitalize on the continuing growth in emerging economies; growth that is increasing demand for better healthcare and nutrition and accelerating the development of healthcare systems.

Abbott is also well positioned to meet the needs of an aging world population. Its product portfolio directly addresses the needs of older people at a time when the number of those over the age of 70 is expected to triple — to one billion — by the middle of the century.

As people around the world call for more cost-effective, customer-focused innovation, Abbott is dedicated — in each of its businesses — to creating products that not only improve people's quality of life, but also create value by improving the efficiency and effectiveness of healthcare systems.

As Abbott and AbbVie begin their next 125 years, both companies are highly conscious of the remarkable legacy they share, and are committed to expanding on that long history of success. They look to the future fully confident that they are creating two of the best healthcare companies of the 21st century. In the years to come, Abbott and AbbVie people are committed to ensuring that their new companies will help more people, and do more to make the world a better place, than ever before.

A History of Continual Transformation
The First 125 Years

Abbott's long history is one of continual growth and focused change as the company adapts itself to changing circumstances in its business and the world. Abbott and AbbVie — the sister company it created in 2013 — carry forward that tradition of successful transformation, some of the most notable of which in their shared history are captured here.

1888
Dr. Wallace Calvin Abbott begins making granules of alkaloidal medicine in his People's Drug Store in Chicago.

1907
The company begins doing business in the United Kingdom, its first foray outside the United States, beginning an international expansion that is still accelerating today.

1914
Abbott switches its focus from alkaloidal to synthetic medicines. One year later, in recognition of this evolution, the company changes its name from the Abbott Alkaloidal Company to Abbott Laboratories.

1920
Abbott acquires growing room for the future, purchasing a 26-acre site in North Chicago that will become its headquarters for 40 years.

1935
Abbott begins to manufacture intravenous (IV) fluids. In time, Abbott will become the largest supplier of IV solutions in the United States.

1942
Abbott's wartime effort to ramp up production of penicillin begins a decades-long period of leadership in the development of life-saving antibiotics.

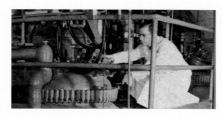

1955
Abbott's radio-iodine is the first atomic medicine listed by the U.S. Pharmacopoeia. Its foray into nuclear medicine lays the groundwork for a major new Abbott business of the future: diagnostics.

1964
Abbott acquires M&R Dietetic Laboratories, spearheading the company's growing role in nutrition.

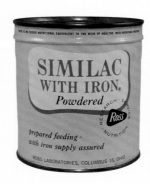

1973

The Abbott Diagnostics Division is formed, cementing the company's position as a leader in modern medical diagnostics. In the same year, Abbott introduces its first adult medical nutritional, *Ensure*.

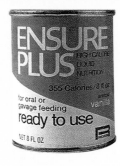

1996

Abbott enters the diabetes testing arena with the acquisition of MediSense, Inc.

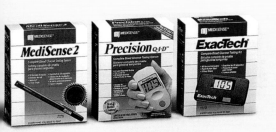

1999

Abbott enters the vascular care business with the acquisition of Perclose.

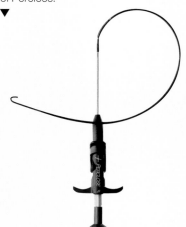

2000

Abbott acquires Knoll, the pharmaceutical business of BASF, adding expertise in biologic pharmaceuticals to its already impressive scientific portfolio.

2004

Abbott spins-off its hospital products division to create Hospira, today a strong, independent Fortune 600 company.

2006

The acquisitions of the vascular and endovascular businesses of the Guidant Corporation propel Abbott to the number three position in the global vascular market.

2010

Abbott acquires the Solvay and Piramal pharmaceutical businesses, expanding its presence in emerging markets around the world. Later this year, the company creates a new business, the Established Pharmaceuticals Division, to better capture the opportunities these markets present.

2013

In the company's 125th year, Abbott's businesses become two leading healthcare companies: AbbVie and the new Abbott, both well positioned to meet the challenges of an ever-evolving world and to carry their shared legacy of success into the future.

Afterword

Abbott Board of Directors

Abbott's earliest board consisted entirely of family members and close friends, when the company was a closely held concern. Outside directors were first added in 1957. Today the company is a recognized leader in corporate governance. The following list names all directors to sit on Abbott's board since its formation.

Wallace C. Abbott, M.D.
1900–1921

Clara A. Abbott
1900–1908, 1911–1924

James W. Ranson
1900–1930

Louis P. Scoville
1900–1907

William F. Waugh, M.D.
1900–1908

Henry B. Shattuck
1906–1910, 1915–1930

George F. Toenges
1908–1909

Edward E. Gore
1908–1909

Samuel R. Jenkins
1908–1911

Edward H. Ravenscroft
1908–1952

Frank G. Murray
1909–1911

Edward Ridgely
1909–1911

Julian C. Ryer
1910–1919

Claude O. Brown
1911–1930

Alfred S. Burdick, M.D.
1913–1933

Simeon DeWitt Clough
1915–1950

Emilie D. Falk
1920–1921

Ralph E. Heilman
1920

Alfred W. Bays
1924–1951

Jay Dunne
1929–1937

William C. Freeman
1929–1932

S.W. White
1929

Rolly M. Cain
1930–1947

Edmund L. Drach
1930–1953

Fred W. Scheigert
1930–1937

James F. Stiles, Jr.
1930–1958

Ernest H. Volwiler, Ph.D.
1930–1959

George W. Raiziss, Ph.D.
1933–1945

Ferdinand H. Young
1933–1954

Joseph F. Biehn, M.D.
1934–1950

Carl Nielsen
1934–1946

Edgar B. Carter
1935–1952

Raymond E. Horn
1935–1952

Claud A. Thornburg
1937–1954

Floyd K. Thayer
1938–1962

Charles S. Downs
1944–1963

Edward A. Ravenscroft
1944–1971

Hugh D. Robinson
1946–1961

Elmer B. Vliet
1946–1962

George R. Cain
1947–1972

Norman A. Hansen
1950–1962

George R. Hazel, M.D.
1950–1967

Herbert S. Wilkinson
1951–1971

Roger Adams, Ph.D.
1952–1959

Harold D. Arneson
1952–1961

Robert D. Coghill, Ph.D.
1952–1956

David M. Kennedy
1957–1968

Frederick J. Kirchmeyer
1957–1968

Charles S. Brown, Ph.D.
1959–1981

Willis Gale
1959–1966

Arthur W. Weston, Ph.D.
1959–1968

James L. Allen
1960–1973

Lowell T. Coggeshall, M.D.
1961–1969

John F. Fennelly
1962–1968

Paul Gerden
1962–1971

Albert R. Wayne
1963–1971

Richard M. Ross
1964–1984

Abbott Corporate Officers

The key to Abbott's success has always been the people who make the company work. Key contributors have changed the company's course, leading to new opportunities and greater success. Abbott's corporate officers are the people chiefly responsible for its operations, the successful execution of its strategies, and the leadership of its people around the world. The following lists service dates of corporate officer-level positions, and the last officer-level title held.

Edward H. Ravenscroft
Chairman of the Board
1913–1950

Alfred W. Bays
Secretary and Counselor
1929–1954

C.O. Brown
Treasurer
1929

Alfred S. Burdick, M.D.
President
1929–1931

Simeon DeWitt Clough
Chairman of the Board
1929–1951

James W. Ranson
Vice President
1929

Henry B. Shattuck
Vice President
1929

Rolly M. Cain
*President and
General Manager*
1930–1947

F.W. Scheigert
Secretary
1930–1931

James F. Stiles, Jr.
Chairman of the Board
1930–1957

Ernest H. Volwiler, Ph.D.
Chairman of the Board
1932–1959

Raymond E. Horn
President
1937–1951

Edward A. Ravenscroft
Executive Vice President
1944–1970

Ferdinand H. Young
*Vice President in Charge
of Production*
1944–1955

Edgar B. Carter
*Assistant Secretary;
Executive Director of
Research*
1946–1952

Charles S. Downs
*Vice President,
Public Relations*
1946–1963

Edmund L. Drach
*Vice President in
Charge of Purchases*
1947–1953

George R. Cain
*Chairman of the Board and
Chief Executive Officer*
1950–1972

Paul Gerden
*Executive Vice President,
Administration*
1951–1971

Claud A. Thornburg
*Assistant Treasurer
and Comptroller*
1951–1955

Elmer B. Vliet
Chairman of the Board
1952–1962

Hugh D. Robinson
*Vice President,
in Charge of Production*
1953–1960

Floyd K. Thayer
*Vice President,
Chemical Division*
1953–1962

Herbert S. Wilkinson
*Vice President,
Office of the President*
1953–1971

Robert V. Jaros
*Vice President and
Treasurer*
1957–1970

Norman A. Hansen
Vice President, Personnel
1958–1962

Charles S. Brown, Ph.D.
*Executive Vice President,
Administration*
1960–1981

Frederick J. Kirchmeyer
*Vice President,
Agricultural Products*
1960–1968

Peter J. Marschall
Vice President, Engineering
1960–1966

Edward G. Beyer
*Vice President,
Financial Services*
1961–1972

David M. Crawford
*Secretary and
General Counsel*
1961–1963

George R. Hazel, M.D.
*Vice President,
Medical Affairs*
1961–1967

Edward R. Luter
*Vice President,
Fiscal Affairs*
1961–1962

Arthur W. Weston, Ph.D.
*Vice President, Corporate
Scientific Affairs*
1961–1971

James W. Milne
*Vice President, Corporate
Quality Assurance*
1962–1972

Robert W. Nichols
*Vice President,
Chemical Division*
1962–1966

Albert R. Wayne
*Executive Vice President,
International Operations*
1962–1968

Edward J. Ledder
Chairman of the Board
1963–1981

Laurence R. Lee
*Senior Vice President,
Administration, and
Secretary*
1963–1988

Charles H. Montgomery
Controller
1964–1967

Richard M. Ross
*Vice President,
Office of the President*
1964–1975

Tilden Batchelder
*Vice President,
Special Projects*
1965–1977

Lucien J. Sichel
Vice President, Washington
1965–1976

Michael J. Balma
Vice President, Personnel
1966–1982

Granger F. Kenly
*Vice President,
Corporate Public Affairs*
1966–1971

Glenn S. Utt, Jr.
Executive Vice President
1966–1983

Erwin von Allmen
Vice President,
Corporate Planning
1966–1967

Donald L. Kasdorf
Controller
1967–1970

Melvin Birnbaum
Vice President, and
President, Consumer
Products Division
1968–1971

David O. Cox
Vice President
1968–1982

Herbert M. Gross, Ph.D.
Vice President, and
President, Hospital
Products Division
1968–1971

James M. Price, M.D.
Vice President,
Scientific Development
1968–1978

George W. Young
Vice President, International
Administration and Senior
Vice President, International
Division
1968–1976

Robert C. Barnes
Vice President,
Corporate Engineering
1969–1987

Bernard H. Semler
Executive Vice President,
Finance
1969–1982

James A. Hanley
Vice President
and Treasurer
1970–1991

Richard W. Kasperson
Vice President, Corporate
Regulatory Affairs
1970–1987

Charles J. Aschauer, Jr.
Executive Vice President
1971–1989

William D. Pratt
Vice President,
Public Affairs
1971–1981

Gordon X. Reed
Vice President, Corporate
Manufacturing and
Industrial Engineering
1971–1973

John B. Weium
Vice President and
Controller
1971–1972

John E. Condon, Ph.D.
Vice President, Corporate
Quality Assurance
1972–1988

Lester E. Hammar
Vice President and
Controller
1972–1988

Milton J. Henrichs
Vice President,
Pharmaceutical Operations
1972–1985

David W. Ortlieb
Executive Vice President
and President,
International Division
1972–1983

Roland W. Puder
Vice President,
Materials Management
1972–1979

Walter Roberts, Jr.
Vice President, Consumer
Products, and President,
Consumer Division
1972–1975

Robert A. Schoellorn
Chairman of the Board
1973–1990

Harry F. Upton
Vice President,
Consumer Products
1974–1978

James L. Vincent
Executive Vice President
and Chief Operating Officer
1974–1979

G. Kirk Raab
President and Chief
Operating Officer
1975–1985

Ira Ringler
Vice President,
Pharmaceutical Products
Research and Development
1975–1983

Daniel E. Gill
Vice President,
Hospital Products
1977–1978

Joseph S. Jenckes
Vice President,
Washington, D.C.
1977–1994

Joseph A. Sasenick
Vice President,
Consumer Products
1979–1983

William M. Hillborn
Vice President, Chemical
and Agricultural Products
1980–1981

Thomas R. Hodgson
President and Chief
Operating Officer
1980–1998

William D. Smart
Vice President,
Ross Products
1980–1987

James L. Sorenson
Vice President,
Sorenson Products
1980–1981

James G. Andress
Vice President, HomeCare
1981–1984

Charles A. Baker
Vice President,
International Operations
1981–1984

Lael F. Johnson
Senior Vice President,
Secretary and General
Counsel
1981–1994

John C. Kane
Senior Vice President,
Ross Products
1981–1993

John G. Kringel
Senior Vice President,
Hospital Products
1981–1998

Duane L. Burnham
Chairman and Chief
Executive Officer
1982–1999

Abbott Corporate Officers

Continued

David C. Jones
Vice President,
Public Affairs
1982–1986

David A. Thompson
Senior Vice President,
Strategic Improvement
Processes
1982–1995

Garrison E. Bielen
Vice President,
Sorenson Products
1983–1984

O. Ralph Edwards, Jr.
Vice President,
Human Resources
1983–1992

Robert S. Janicki, M.D.
Senior Vice President,
Scientific and Medical
Affairs
1983–1990

David V. Milligan, Ph.D.
Senior Vice President,
Chief Scientific Officer
1984–1996

Paul N. Clark
Executive Vice President
1985–1998

James L. Farlander
Vice President,
Corporate Purchasing
1985–1989

Kenneth W. Farmer
Vice President,
Management Information
Services and
Administration
1985–2000

John F. Lussen
Vice President, Taxes
1985–2004

Richard H. Morehead
Vice President, Corporate
Planning and Development
1985–1996

Richard B. Hamilton
Vice President,
Public Affairs
1986–1991

Richard W. Gast
Vice President,
Ross Products
1987–1989

J. Duncan McIntyre
Senior Vice President,
International Operations
1987–1995

Daniel O. Struble
Vice President,
Corporate Engineering
1987–1995

Theodore A. Olson
Vice President and
Controller
1988–1999

Don G. Wright
Vice President, Corporate
Quality Assurance and
Regulatory Affairs
1988–1996

Arthur D. Collins, Jr.
Vice President,
Diagnostics Business
Unit Operations
1989–1992

Thomas M. McNally
Senior Vice President,
Ross Products
1989–1998

Robert L. Parkinson, Jr.
President and Chief
Operating Officer
1989–2001

Joy A. Amundson
Senior Vice President,
Ross Products
1990–2001

Gary P. Coughlan
Senior Vice President,
Finance and Chief
Financial Officer
1990–2001

Ferid Murad, M.D., Ph.D.
Vice President,
Pharmaceutical Products
Research and Development
1990–1993

Thomas C. Freyman
Executive Vice President,
Finance and Chief Financial
Officer
1991–Present

Ellen M. Walvoord
Senior Vice President,
Human Resources
1991–1999

Robert N. Beck
Senior Vice President,
Human Resources
1992–1995

Hank T. Pietraszek
President, TAP
Pharmaceuticals Inc.
1992–1993

Christopher B. Begley
Senior Vice President,
Hospital Products
1993–2004

Thomas D. Brown
Senior Vice President,
Diagnostic Operations
1993–2002

Gary R. Byers
Vice President, Audit
1993–2003

Yasuchika Hasegawa
President, TAP Holdings Inc.
1993–1998

Jay B. Johnston
Vice President, Diagnostic
Assays and Systems
1993–1999

James J. Koziarz, Ph.D.
Vice President, Hep/Retro
R&D and Assay Technical
Support, Diagnostics
1993–2004

Christopher A. Kuebler
Vice President,
European Operations
1993–1994

Carl A. Spalding
Vice President, Ross
Pediatric Products
1993–1998

William H. Stadtlander, Jr.
Vice President, Ross
Medical Nutritional
Products
1993–2001

Josef Wendler
Senior Vice President,
International Operations
1993–1999

Miles D. White
Chairman of the Board and
Chief Executive Officer
1993–Present

Jose M. de Lasa
Executive Vice President
and General Counsel
1994–2005

Andre G. Pernet, Ph.D.
Vice President,
Pharmaceutical Products
Research and Development
1994–1999

Catherine V. Babington
Vice President, Public Affairs
1995–2010

Mark E. Barmak
Vice President, Government Affairs
1995–2002

David B. Goffredo
Senior Vice President, Pharmaceutical Operations
1995–2003

Richard A. Gonzalez
President and Chief Operating Officer
1995–2007
Executive Vice President, Pharmaceutical Products Group
2009–2012

Lance B. Wyatt
Senior Vice President, Global Pharmaceutical Manufacturing
1995–2004

Patrick J. Balthrop
Vice President, Vascular Devices
1996–2001

William G. Dempsey
Executive Vice President, Pharmaceutical Products Group
1996–2007

Guillermo A. Herrera
Senior Vice President, International Operations
1996–2004

Arthur J. Higgins
Senior Vice President, Pharmaceutical Operations
1996–2001

Marcia A. Thomas
Vice President, Diagnostic Quality Assurance, Regulatory Affairs and Compliance
1996–2002

H. Thomas Watkins
President, TAP Pharmaceutical Products Inc.
1996–2004

Steven J. Weger, Jr.
Vice President, Corporate Planning and Development
1996–2004

Edward L. Michael
Executive Vice President Diagnostics Products
1997–2012

Douglas C. Bryant
Vice President, Abbott Vascular, Asia and Japan
1998–2007

Thomas F. Chen
Senior Vice President, International Nutrition
1998–2011

Edward J. Fiorentino
Exec. Vice President, TAP Pharmaceutical Products, Inc.
1998–2009

Susan M. Widner
Vice President, Corporate Marketing
1998–2011

Michael G. Beatrice
Vice President, Compliance and Regulatory Liaison and Advisor
1999–2012

Christopher A. Bleck
Vice President, Pediatrics, Ross Products
1999–2001

Gary L. Flynn
Senior Vice President, Ross Products
1999–2004

Stephen R. Fussell
Executive Vice President, Human Resources
1999–Present

Robert B. Hance
Senior Vice President, Vascular
1999–2012

Elaine R. Leavenworth
Vice President, Government Affairs
1999–Present

John M. Leonard, M.D.
Senior Vice President, Pharmaceuticals, Research and Development
1999–2012

Greg W. Linder
Vice President, Controller
1999–2013

Daniel W. Norbeck, Ph.D.
Vice President, Global Pharmaceutical Discovery
1999–2008

Edward A. Ogunro, Ph.D.
Vice President, Hospital Products R&D, Medical and Regulatory Affairs
1999–2004

Thomas M. Wascoe
Senior Vice President, Human Resources
1999–2005

John C. Landgraf
Executive Vice President, Nutritional Products
2000–2013

Jeffrey M. Leiden, M.D., Ph.D.
President and Chief Operating Officer, Pharmaceutical Products Group, Chief Scientific Officer
2000–2006

Karen L. Miller
Vice President, Information Technology
2000–2005

Michael J. Collins
Vice President, Medical Products Group, HealthSystems
2001–2007

Terrence C. Kearney
Vice President and Treasurer
2001–2004

Holger A. Liepmann
Executive Vice President, Nutritional Products
2001–2011

Richard J. Marasco
Vice President, Nutrition International, Europe and Canada
2001–2007

Heather L. Mason
Senior Vice President, Diabetes Care
2001–Present

P. Loreen Mershimer
Vice President, Pharmaceutical Products, Integrated Healthcare Marketing and Policy
2001–2009

Joseph M. Nemmers, Jr.
Executive Vice President, Diagnostics and Animal Health
2001–2007

Abbott Corporate Officers

Continued

Roberto Reyes
Vice President,
Latin America and Canada
2001–2002

Mary T. Szela
Senior Vice President,
Global Strategic Marketing
and Services,
Pharmaceutical Products
Group
2001–2012

James L. Tyree
Executive Vice President
Pharmaceutical Products
Group
2001–2012

John Arnott
Vice President, Hospital
Products Business Sector
2002–2004

William E. Brown III, Ph.D.
Vice President,
Diagnostic Assays and
Systems Development
2002–2007

Thomas J. Dee
Vice President,
Finance Operations
2002–2013

Mark F. Gorman
Vice President, Ross
Products, Medical
Nutritionals
2002–2004

Gerald Lema
Vice President, Diagnostic
Commercial Operations,
Asia and Pacific
2002–2004

Sean E. Murphy
Vice President, Licensing/
New Business
Development
2002–2010

Olivier Bohuon
Executive Vice President,
Pharmaceutical Products
2003–2010

Charles M. Brock
Vice President and
Chief Ethics and
Compliance Officer
2003–2008

Jaime Contreras
Senior Vice President,
Core Laboratory
Diagnostics, Commercial
Operations
2003–Present

Gary E. McCullough
Senior Vice President,
Ross Products
2003–2007

Laura J. Schumacher
Executive Vice President,
General Counsel and
Secretary
2003–2012

AJ J. Shoultz
Vice President, Taxes
2003–Present

Alejandro A. Aruffo, Ph.D.
Vice President,
Pharmaceuticals
Development
2004–2008

Richard W. Ashley
Executive Vice President,
Corporate Development
2004–Present

Jeffrey R. Binder
Senior Vice President,
Diagnostic Operations
2004–2007

Zahirali (Zahir) A. Lavji
Vice President,
Pharmaceuticals,
International Marketing
2004–2010

D. Stafford O'Kelly
Vice President, Molecular
Diagnostics
2004–2012

Donald V. Patton Jr.
Senior Vice President,
U.S. Pharmaceuticals
2004–2011

Greg E. Arnsdorff
Vice President, Point of
Care Diagnostics
2005–2013

Robert E. Funck
Vice President,
Controller
2005–Present

Lawrence E. Kraus
Vice President,
Manufacturing Global
Pharmaceutical Operations
2005–2007

Mark Masterson
Vice President, Pacific,
Asia and Africa Operations,
Abbott International
2005–2008

Preston T. Simons
Vice President, Information
Technology
2005–Present

Eugene Sun, M.D.
Vice President,
Pharmaceuticals Clinical
Development
2005–2011

Carlos Alban
Senior Vice President,
Proprietary Pharmaceutical
Products, Global
Commercial Operations
2006–2012

John M. Capek, Ph.D.
Executive Vice President,
Medical Devices
2006–Present

Charles D. Foltz
Senior Vice President,
Abbott Vascular
2006–Present

Kevin P. Rhatigan
Vice President and
President, U.S.
Cardiovascular Commercial
Operations
2006–2007

Ronald N. Spaulding
Vice President,
Vascular, Commercial
Operations
2006–2008

John B. Thomas
Vice President, Investor
Relations and Public Affairs
2006–2012

Glenn S. Warner
Vice President,
Strategic Initiatives,
Pharmaceutical Products
Group
2006–2012

William J. Chase
Vice President, Licensing
and Acquisitions
2007–2012

Honey Lynn Goldberg
Vice President, Associate
General Counsel,
Corporate Transactions
2007–2013

**Cecilia L. Kimberlin,
Ph.D.**
Vice President, Abbott
Quality and Regulatory
2007–2012

Steven J. Lichter
Vice President
Established
Pharmaceuticals,
Operations
2007–Present

Michael J. Warmuth
Executive Vice President,
Established
Pharmaceuticals
2007–Present

Brian J. Blaser
Executive Vice President,
Diagnostic Products
2008–Present

Robert B. Ford
Vice President, Diabetes
Care, Commercial
Operations
2008–Present

John F. Ginascol
Vice President,
Nutrition, Supply Chain
2008–Present

Santiago Luque
Vice President,
Pharmaceuticals,
Latin America
2008–2012

Corlis D. Murray
Senior Vice President,
Quality Assurance,
Regulatory and Engineering
Services
2008–Present

Ramachandran
Rajamanickam
Vice President, Nutrition,
Asia Pacific
2008–Present

John R. Schilling, M.D.
Vice President,
Sales and Marketing,
Pharmaceutical Operations
2008–2011

James P. Sullivan, Ph.D.
Vice President,
Pharmaceuticals Discovery
2008–2012

David E. Wheadon, M.D.
Vice President, Global
Pharmaceutical Regulatory
and Medical Sciences
2008–2009

Thomas A. Hurwich
Vice President,
Internal Audit
2009–2012

James V. Mazzo
Senior Vice President,
Abbott Medical Optics
2009–2012

Gary M. Winer
Vice President,
Pharmaceuticals, Japan
2009–2012

David Forrest
Executive Vice President
Nutritional Products
2010–Present

Brendan McAtamney
Vice President,
Established
Pharmaceuticals,
Commercial
2010–2013

Pascale Richetta
Vice President,
Pharmaceuticals, Western
Europe and Canada
2010–2012

Ronald O. Robison
Vice President,
Regulatory Affairs
Pharmaceutical Products
Group
2010–2012

J. Scott White
Senior Vice President,
International Nutrition
2010–Present

Valentine Yien
Vice President, Treasurer
2010–Present

Jose Calle
Vice President,
Absorb and Structural
Heart Commercial
Development
2011–2013

Katherine C. Doyle
Senior Vice President,
U.S. Nutrition
2011–Present

Catherine Mazzacco
Vice President, Abbott
Medical Optics,
Commercial
2011–Present

Azita Saleki-Gerhardt
Vice President,
Pharmaceuticals,
Manufacturing and Supply
2011–2012

Jeffrey R. Stewart
Vice President, Proprietary
Pharmaceuticals, U.S.
2011–2012

John D. Coulter
Vice President,
Molecular Diagnostics
2012–Present

Paul K. Magill
Senior Vice President,
Chief Marketing Officer
2012–Present

Hubert L. Allen
Executive Vice President,
General Counsel and
Secretary
2013–Present

Jeffery G. Barton
Vice President,
Licensing and Acquisitions
2013–Present

Nancy Berce
Vice President, Business
Process and Financial
Operations
2013–Present

Sharon J. Bracken
Vice President,
Point of Care Diagnostics
2013–Present

Michael J. Buck
Vice President,
Vascular, Global Market
Development
2013–Present

Kathryn S. Collins
Vice President,
Chief Ethics and
Compliance Officer
2013–Present

Georges H. De Vos
Senior Vice President,
Established
Pharmaceuticals,
Emerging Markets
2013–Present

Gene Huang
Vice President,
Chief Economist
2013–Present

David P. Mark
Vice President,
Internal Audit
2013–Present

Jean-Yves Pavee
Senior Vice President,
Established
Pharmaceuticals,
Developed Markets
2013–Present

Murthy V. Simhambhatla
Senior Vice President,
Abbott Medical Optics
2013–Present

Gregory A. Tazalla
Vice President,
Strategic Initiatives
2013–Present

Brian B. Yoor
Vice President,
Investor Relations
2013–Present

AbbVie Board of Directors

To ensure AbbVie's success as an independent company, Abbott carefully apportioned senior talent to provide leadership depth and quality. Its Board of Directors includes several members who know the business from previous service on Abbott's Board, as well as important perspective and expertise from other leaders new to it. AbbVie's management corps includes the team that had already made the business a leader in its markets, as well as top talent from Abbott's corporate functions.

Robert J. Alpern, M.D.
2013–Present

Edward J. Rapp
2013–Present

Roxanne S. Austin
2013–Present

Roy S. Roberts
2013–Present

William H.L. Burnside
2013–Present

Glenn F. Tilton
2013–Present

Richard A. Gonzalez
2013–Present

Frederick H. Waddell
2013–Present

Edward M. Liddy
2013–Present

AbbVie Executive Leadership Team

Carlos Alban
Executive Vice President,
Commercial Operations
2013–Present

William J. Chase
Executive Vice President,
Chief Financial Officer
2013–Present

Richard A. Gonzalez
Chairman of the Board and
Chief Executive Officer
2013–Present

Thomas A. Hurwich
Vice President, Controller
2013–Present

Timothy J. Richmond
Senior Vice President,
Human Resources
2013–Present

Azita Saleki-Gerhardt, Ph.D.
Senior Vice President,
Operations
2013–Present

Laura J. Schumacher
Executive Vice President,
Business Development,
External Affairs and
General Counsel
2013–Present

Abbott Sales by Year

(in U.S. dollars)

Per Annual Report

Year	Sales	Year	Sales
1888	2,000	1913	587,000
1889	4,500	1914	617,000
1890	8,000	1915	594,000
1891	11,000	1916	664,000
1892	14,000	1917	904,000
1893	21,000	1918	1,259,000
1894	29,000	1919	1,486,000
1895	43,000	1920	1,663,000
1896	64,000	1921	1,453,000
1897	86,000	1922	1,651,000
1898	100,000	1923	2,154,000
1899	120,000	1924	2,164,000
1900	125,000	1925	2,226,000
1901	133,000	1926	2,379,000
1902	146,000	1927	2,531,000
1903	162,000	1928	3,357,000
1904	185,000	1929	3,502,000
1905	200,000	1930	4,309,000
1906	240,000	1931	4,054,000
1907	290,000	1932	3,622,000
1908	360,000	1933	4,066,000
1909	445,000	1934	5,193,000
1910	546,000	1935	6,118,000
1911	600,000	1936	7,768,000
1912	538,000	1937	9,510,000

Year	Sales	Year	Sales	Year	Sales
1938	9,727,000	1963	158,648,000	1988	4,936,991,000
1939	11,485,000	1964	212,586,000	1989	5,379,751,000
1940	12,981,000	1965	236,802,000	1990	6,158,682,000
1941	16,744,000	1966	265,804,000	1991	6,876,588,000
1942	20,005,000	1967	303,341,000	1992	7,851,912,000
1943	33,265,000	1968	350,955,000	1993	8,407,843,000
1944	38,428,000	1969	403,877,000	1994	9,156,009,000
1945	37,930,000	1970	457,503,000	1995	10,012,194,000
1946	54,210,000	1971	458,105,000	1996	11,013,460,000
1947	59,621,000	1972	521,818,000	1997	11,883,462,000
1948	66,931,000	1973	620,398,000	1998	12,477,845,000
1949	67,552,000	1974	765,415,000	1999	13,177,625,000
1950	73,506,000	1975	940,660,000	*2000	11,520,600,000
1951	84,366,000	1976	1,084,856,000	2001	13,918,500,000
1952	85,528,000	1977	1,244,976,000	2002	15,279,537,000
1953	88,142,000	1978	1,445,017,000	2003	17,280,333,000
1954	88,106,000	1979	1,683,168,000	2004	19,680,016,000
1955	91,707,000	1980	2,038,155,000	2005	22,337,808,000
1956	96,789,000	1981	2,342,524,000	2006	22,476,322,000
1957	111,271,000	1982	2,602,447,000	2007	25,914,238,000
1958	116,598,000	1983	2,927,873,000	2008	29,527,552,000
1959	122,602,000	1984	3,103,962,000	2009	30,764,707,000
1960	125,968,000	1985	3,360,273,000	2010	38,167,000,000
1961	129,850,000	1986	3,807,634,000	2011	38,851,300,000
1962	144,127,000	1987	4,387,876,000	2012	39,873,900,000

*2000 and forward adjusted for Hospira spin-off

Bibliography

A

Abbott, Dr. W.C. "'Cactin,' What Are Its Therapeutic Properties?" *Texas State Journal of Medicine* 3 (February 1908): 268.

Abbott, Dr. W.C. "Dosimetric Chips." *The Medical World* IX (December 1891): 291.

Abbott, Dr. W.C. "For Ourselves and Others." *The Medical World* IX (December 1891): 472.

"Abbott, Wallace Calvin." *Who's Who in American History, Volume 1, 1897–1942.* Chicago: A.A. Marquis Co., 1943.

Abbott, W.C. "Class Ode-'82." *The Academy Student IV*, no. 5 (June 1882): 35.

Abbott, W.C. "Hyoscine Morphine and Cactin Anesthesia." *The Chicago Medical Recorder* 29 (January-December 1907): 557–561.

"Abbott Alkaloidal Company Ad." *Southern California Practitioner* 24 (January 1909): 53.

"Abbott anticancer drug Ok'd." *Chicago Tribune*, January 31, 1989.

"Abbott Dedicates New Research Laboratories." *Druggist's Circular* 82 (November 1938): 22–23, 60.

"Abbott: Its Role in the Cyclamate Ban." *Chicago Tribune*, November 2, 1969.

"Abbott Jubilant over FDA Award." *Chicago Tribune*, March 4, 1985.

"Abbott Laboratories and Swan-Myers Company Combine." *Midwestern Druggist* (November 1930): 76–8.

"Abbott Laboratories and Swan-Myers Company Join Forces." *International Journal of Medicine and Surgery* (November 1930): 609–10.

"Abbott Laboratories and Swan-Myers Company Join Forces." *Radiology* 16 (January 1931): 74–75. Accessed January 17, 2013. doi: 10.1148/16.1.74b.

"Abbott Laboratories Invests in Boston Scientific Corp." *Medical Advertising News*, August 15, 1983.

"Abbott Laboratories Marks Fiftieth Year." *Oil, Paint, and Drug Reporter* 134 (October 1938): 27.

"Abbott Laboratories' New Research Building." *Proofs* (December 1937).

"Abbott Laboratories, Swan-Myers Combine; Managements United." *Drug Trade News* 5, no. 2 (November 1930): 1.

"Abbott Laboratories to Buy Medisense for $876 Million." *The New York Times*, March 30, 1996.

"Abbott Laboratories." *Wall Street Journal*, October 23, 1945.

"Abbott Labs Acquire New Research Building." *Drug Trade News* 12, no. 20 (September 1937): 40.

"Abbott Labs: Adding Hospital Supplies to Bolster Drug Operations." *Business Week*, July 23, 1979.

"Abbott Labs adopts orphan drug Panhematin." *Drug Topics* 21, no. 127 (November 1983): 15–16.

"Abbott Labs Sells Similac Recipe to the Soviets." *New York Times*, December 9, 1976.

"Abbott Labs to Buy BASF Unit for $6.9 Billion." *Wall Street Journal*, December 15, 2000.

"Abbott Remedy for Dandruff Now on Market." *Waukegan News-Sun*, September 19, 1951.

"Abbott Adopts Insurance Plan." *Waukegan News-Sun*, October 22, 1945.

"Abbott's Humira wins OK to treat juvenile arthritis." *Bloomberg News*, February 23, 2008.

"Abbott's new division gains accounts." *Health Industry Today*, May 1, 2011.

"Abbott Shows Fast Progress in Past Decade." *Waukegan News-Sun*, May 4, 1950.

"About a Man Who Gave a Million Dollar No!" *The Rotarian*, January 1940.

"'Accident Bringing Chemical Plant Here." *Wichita Eagle Magazine*, December 13, 1959.

"A Dream Match That Didn't Come Off – and Why." *Health Industry*, November 1963.

"Advertisement." *Journal of the American Medical Association* XLIX no. 25 (1907): 2103–06.

"A Highly Qualified Observer." *LIFE Magazine*, January 4, 1954.

Albertini, Luigi. *The Origins of the War of 1914*. London; New York: Oxford University Press, 1952–57.

American Association of Colleges of Pharmacy. "Volwiler Research Achievement Award." Accessed January 14, 2013.

American Chemical Society. "Glenn T. Seaborg Award for Nuclear Chemistry." Accessed January 11, 2013.

American Chemical Society. "Priestley Medal." Accessed January 14, 2013.

American Chemical Society. "Selman Waksman and Antibiotics." Accessed January 14, 2013.

American Chemical Society. "The Discovery of Organic Free Radicals by Moses Gomberg." Accessed January 14, 2013.

American Institute of Chemists. "Gold Medal Award Winners." Accessed January 14, 2013.

American Medical Association. "Full List of Annual Meetings and Presidents." Accessed January 11, 2013.

American Medical Association. *Nostrums and Quackery*. Chicago: Press of American Medical Association, 1912–36.

American Steel and Wire Company. "Taming the Wild Prairie: A History of DeKalb County." Accessed January 14, 2013.

"An Interesting Example of the Subordination of Science to Commercialism." *Journal of the American Medical Association* XLIX, no. 25 (1907): 2103–06.

"Anti-Diphtheric Serum." *The Medical Times* 34 (December 1907): v.

Aoki, Naomi. "A Dose of Hope, Worcester, Abbott bank on Humira for a needed lift." *Boston Globe*, January 8, 2003.

"Applied Chemistry Medal..." *The Condenser* 8 (September 1954): 95–6.

"Art Advertising is Subject of League Speaker." *Waukegan News-Sun*, October 9, 1946.

Art Institute of Chicago. "About This Artwork: Henri de Toulouse-Lautrec, 'At the Moulin Rouge'." Accessed January 14, 2013.

"As They Appear to Me." *Ad Sense* 12 (December 1901): 310.

"Audubon Outlook, The." *Newsletter of the Lake County Audubon Society* 34, no. 3 (2009).

B

Backus, M.P. and J.F. Stauffer. "The Production and Selection of a Family of Strains in Penicillium Chrysogenum." *Mycologia* 47, no. 4 (July-August 1955): 429–463.

Bailar, John C. *Moses Gomberg: February 8, 1866–February 12, 1947*. National Academy of Sciences (U.S.); Biographical Memoirs. New York: Columbia University Press, 1970.

"Bandits Seize and Rule $3,000,0000 Plant for 7 Hours." *Harold Examiner*, June 13, 1927.

Becker, Gabriel. *"A Study of the History and Development of Abbott Laboratories."* MBA Thesis, University of Louisville, 1956.

"Big Pill Bill to Swallow." *Life Magazine*, February 15, 1960.

"Bind Your Loose Sheets in a Tengwall File". *The Magazine of Business*, December 1901.

Black, John T. "Rubber." *Annual Survey of American Chemistry* VI (1931): 529–543.

Blair, William. "Lowell Coggeshall is Dead at 86; Authority on Diseases of Tropics." *The New York Times*, November 13, 1987.

Bloomberg Businessweek. "Boone Powell Jr. Profile." Accessed January 14, 2013.

Bloomberg Businessweek. "Edward J. Ledder Profile." Accessed January 11, 2013.

Bloomberg Businessweek. "Executive Profile: Jack W. Schuler."

Bloomberg Businessweek. "Executive Profile: James L. Tyree." Accessed January 11, 2013.

Bloomberg Businessweek. "Executive Profile: James L. Vincent." Accessed January 11, 2013.

Bloomberg Businessweek. "Tech That's Still Ticking." Accessed January 14, 2013.

Bok, Edward. "Works and Not Words. An Appeal from Mr. Bok to the Medical Profession." *Journal of the American Medical Association* XLIV, no. 20 (May 1905): 1628–1629.

Boston Scientific. "Standard Occlusion Balloon Catheter." Accessed January 14, 2013.

"Break Ground for Abbott Edition." *Waukegan News-Sun*, December 22, 1936.

Buckley, W.C. "Rational Aphrodisiac Treatment by the Use of the Alkaloids." *The Medical Summary Journal* 25 (March 1903): 195–96.

Burdick, Alfred S. "The Manufacture of Synthetic Medicinal Chemicals in America." *Journal of the American Pharmaceutical Association* 11, no. 2 (1922): 98–108.

Burdick, Alfred S. "Wallace Calvin Abbott – A Physician Who Increased the Efficiency of his Colleagues." *Journal of the American Medical Editors' Association* (June 1925): 11.

Burggraeve, Adoph. *The Essentials of Dosimetric Pharmacy and Pharmacodynamia*. New York: W.J. Morrison, 1891.

Burggraeve, Adoph. *The New Handbook of Dosimetric Therapeutics*. Translated by Henry Arthur Allbutt. London: Standring, 1884.

C

"Calcidin Advertisement," *Vermont Medical Monthly* 13, no. 2 (1907): p.iii.

The Canadian Medical Association Journal. "Abbott Laboratories Ad." Accessed January 14, 2013.

Celera. "Abbott's RealTime Hepatitis B Viral Load Test Receives CE Marking in Europe." Last modified June 21, 2007.

Centers for Disease Control and Prevention. "Epidemiologic Notes and Reports Nosocomial Bacteremias Associated with Intravenous Fluid Therapy — USA." Last modified May 2, 2001.

Centers for Disease Control and Prevention. "Patient Facts: Learn More about Legionnaires' disease." Last modified June 1, 2011.

Centers for Disease Control and Prevention. "Vital Statistics of the United States 1961 Volume 1-Natality."

Chace, Arthur F., M.D. and Morris S. Fine, Ph.D. "The Use of Atophan and Radium Emanation in the Treatment of Gout and the Arthritides." *Journal of the American Medical Association* LXIII, no. 11 (1914): 945–46.

"Chairman Cain Looks into the Abbott Future." *Investor's Reader*, November 20, 1968.

Chatterjee, S. N. "Injection of sulphetrone and diasone in leprosy." *Antiseptic* 46, no. 4 (April 1949): 282.

Chemical and Engineering News. "The Priestley Medalists, 1923–2008." Last modified April 7, 2008.

"Chemists Create 'Life' in Lab Tests." *Chicago Tribune*, Friday, June 14, 1963.

Chicago Tribune. "Sharing technologies: Abbott Laboratories and Perkin-Elmer..." Last modified April 11, 1994.

Chinese Academy of Medical Sciences. Accessed January 14, 2013. "Peking Union Medical College."

"Cited By Chemists' Institute." *North Western Druggist* 60, no. 3 (March 1952): 61–2.

Bibliography

ClinicalTrials.gov. "Dose Ranging Study Comparing the Efficacy, Safety and Pharmacokinetics of Intravenous Infusions of ABT-874 vs. Placebo in Subjects with Active Crohn's Disease." Last modified August 18, 2011.

ClinicalTrials.gov. "Efficacy and Safety of ABT-874 in Subjects with Moderate to Severe Chronic Plaque Psoriasis." Last modified August 22, 2100.

Clinton, Patrick. "From Good to Great, Act Two." *Pharmaceutical Executive*, December 1, 2003.

"Clough Made President of Abbott Laboratories." *The Professional Bulletin* 1, no. 3 (March 1933): 6.

CNBC. "US to Experience Stagflation Worse Than 1970s: Jim Rogers." Last modified October 14, 2011.

CNN Justice. "Lipstick Killer" behind bars since 1946." Last modified October 24, 2009.

CNN Money. "Fortune 500: 1987 Full List." Accessed January 11, 2013.

CNN Money. "Fortune 500: 1989 Profits." Accessed January 11, 2013.

CNN Money. "Lilly, BASF mull deal?" Last modified November 17, 2000.

Cohen, J. B. "Research in Antiseptics." *British Medical Journal* (August 1915): 261–62, doi: 10.1136/bmj.2.2851.312-c.

Coleman, W. L., M.D. "Dosimetry." *The Medical World* VIII (July 1890): 273.

Collins, James. Good to Great: *Why Some Companies Make the Leap... and Others Don't.* New York: HarperBusiness, 2001.

Cornell University. "Bacillus Thuringiensis." Accessed January 14, 2013.

"Council on Pharmacy and Chemistry." *Journal of the American Medical Association* 93, no. 9 (1929): 693. Accessed January 14, 2013. doi: 10.1001/jama.1929.02710090033011.

"Credit Given to Advertising for Abbott's Record." *Advertising Age* 5, no. 23 (June 1934): 16.

"Current Comment." *Journal of the American Medical Association* 131, no. 12 (1946): 977.

"Current Comment." *Journal of the American Medical Association* LXVIII, no. 16 (1917): 1185–87.

Dakin, H. D. and E. K. Dunham. "Relative Germicidal Efficiency of Antiseptics of Chlorin Group and Acriflavine and Other Dyes." *British Medical Journal* 2, no. 2968 (November 1917): 641, doi: 10.1136/bmj.2.2968.641.

Dakin, Henry. "A Report on the Use of Dichloramin T Toluene Parasite Phondichloramin in the Treatment of Infected Wounds." *Transactions of the meeting of the American Surgical Association* 35 (1917): 392–93.

Dakin, H. D. "The Treatment of Infected Wounds." *Journal of the American Medical Association* LXIX, no. 23 (1917): 1994–95.

"Death of J.W. Ranson At Home in Illinois." *St. Johnsbury Academy News: The Republican Weekly* (1937).

"Deaths." *Journal of the American Medical Association* 109, no. 10 (1937): 807–08.

"Dedicated N.U.'s New Abbott Hall." *Chicago Daily Tribune*, October 21, 1940.

Demkovich, L. E. "Drug Industry Trying to Change FDA's Slow but Sure Policy." *The National Journal* 11, no. 29 (July 1979): 1211–5.

"'Direct Sell' Key to Abbott Fortune." *Crain's Chicago Business*, February 19, 1979.

Discover Medicine. "Drug Profile: Humira." Last modified May 21, 2009.

"Doctors' War Grows Bitter." *Chicago Daily Tribune*, March 10, 1909.

Dormandy, Thomas. *The Worst of Evils: The Fight Against Pain*. New Haven: Yale University Press, 2006.

Dow Jones. "2009 Technology Innovation Winners and Runners-Up." Accessed January 14, 2013.

"Dr. Abbott Pills and Principles." *American Professional Pharmacist* 25, no. 1 (January 1959): 40–4.

"Dr. A.S. Burdick, Ravinia, Dies of Pneumonia at 66." *Chicago Tribune*, February 12, 1933.

"Dr. Burdick of Abbott Dies." *Waukegan News-Sun*, February 13, 1933.

"Dr. Richard K. Richards." *San Jose Mercury*, February 1, 1983.

"Dr. Roger Adams, 82, Dies." *The Washington Post*, July 8, 1971.

Drugs.com. "Simcor Approval History." Accessed January 14, 2013.

Durant, Thomas M. "Drugs and the Washington Climate." Accessed January 15, 2013.

Ebert, Henry G., M.D. "Amputation of the Thigh under Hyoscine-Morphine-Cactin Anesthesia." *The Medical Sentinel* 15 (January 1907): 283.

"Echoes and News." *Medical News* 75, no. 18 (October 1899): 562.

"Ernest H. Volwiler Succeeds Pauling as ACS President." *Chemical and Engineering News* 28, no. 1 (January 1950): 47.

"Ex-Abbott Chairman, Lake Bluff Leader Dies." *Waukegan News-Sun*, January 18, 1994.

"FDA Approves Abbott's Ultane." *Wall Street Journal*, June 9, 1995.

"FDA approves AIDS drug in 72 days." *FDA Consumer* 30, no. 4 (May 1996): 3.

"FDA Approves Anti-Seizure Drug for Manic-Depression." *Chicago Tribune*, June 7, 1995.

"FDA Approves Epilepsy Drug." *World News Digest*, March 31, 1978.

"FDA Finds Cyclamate Doesn't Cause Cancer." *Chicago Tribune*, June 27, 1984.

"Financial News." *Chemical and Engineering News* 11, no. 5 (1933): 73.

Fishbein, Morris, M.D. "History of the American Medical Association." *Journal of the American Medical Association* 133, no. 7 (February 1947): 464–75

Food and Drug Administration. "Letter to Miles D. White and Robert L. Parkinson, Jr. from DEPARTMENT OF HEALTH AND HUMAN SERVICES," July 14, 1999.

Foote, Henry W. "Analytical Chemistry of the Common Metals." *A Survey of American Chemistry* 2 (1927): 130–135.

Forbes.com. "The 400 Richest Americans." Last modified September 20, 2007.

"Former Abbott Head, J.F. Stiles, Dead." *Waukegan News-Sun*, October 27, 1965.

"Former Head of Abbott is Genetech President." *New York Times*, February 15, 1985.

"France Production and Planning." *Chemical and Engineering News* 29, no. 24 (June 1951): 2362–68, doi: 10.1021/cen-v029n024. p2362.

Free Library, The. "Abbott Launches AxSYM System in the U.S." Accessed January 14, 2013.

Funk, Casmir. *The Vitamins*. Translated by Harry E. Dtjbin. Baltimore: Williams & Wilkins Co., 1922.

G

Gill, Thomas J., M.D., and Peter A. Ward, M.D. "Immunopathology: Hypersensitivity or Tolerance?" *Journal of the American Medical Association* 238, no. 18 (1977): p. 1921–23.

Glauberman, Scott P. "The Real Thalidomide Baby: The Evolution of The FDA In The Shadow of Thalidomide, 1960–1997." *Food and Drug Law* (Winter 1997): 1–17.

"Going for a Medical Combat." *Chicago Daily Tribune*, March 9, 1909.

Gomberg, M. "Organic Radicals." *Chemical Reviews* 1 (1924): 91–97.

Goodyear. "Historic Overview." Accessed January 11, 2013.

Google. "U.S. Patent Number 5,750,226: Light excluding multi-layer plastic barrier bottle." Accessed January 14, 2013.

"Great Thebes Bridge Opens." *Popular Mechanics*, July 1905.

Grinker, Roy R., and John P. Spiegel. *Men Under Stress*. New York: McGraw-Hill, 1963.

"Growth & Income: Abbott Laboratories." *Zacks Equity Research*, November 6, 2008.

H

Halasey, Steve. "Next-Generation Diagnostics: Big, Small, and Fast." *Medical Device & Diagnostic Industry Magazine*, April 1, 1999.

"Hard Fires Exhaust Men." *Chicago Daily Tribune*, November 10, 1905.

Harvard University. "Harvard University Quinquennial catalogue of the officers and graduates 1636–1930." Accessed January 11, 2013.

"Hay Fever and How to Escape It." *Popular Mechanics*, July 1938.

Haynes, W. *Who's Who in the Chemical and Drug Industries*. England: Haynes Publishing, 1928.

"Heart Throbs in Prose and Verse." *National Magazine*, 1904–1905.

Heller, Steven. "Graphic Content | A Logo Legend." The New York Times Style Magazine, May 5, 2010.

"How Dr. Ledder Cured Abbott Labs." Forbes Magazine, August 1, 1975.

I

"Identification Guide for Solid Dosage Forms." *Journal of the American Medical Association* 182, no. 12 (1962). Accessed January 14, 2012. doi: 10.1001/ jama.1962.03050510001001.

Internal Revenue "Industry Director Directive on Section 936 Exit Strategies." February 2, 2007.

Invent Now. "Hall of Fame: Donalee Tabern." Accessed January 11, 2013.

Invent Now. "Hall of Fame: Ernest Volwiler." Accessed January 11, 2013.

"Inventors Hall of Fame Taps Former Abbott Labs Chief." *The Sun*, February, 15, 1986.

J

Japsen, Bruce. "Abbott spinoff in works: New company to sell hospital products parent to retain most lucrative lines." *Chicago Tribune*, August 23, 2003.

John Jakes Website. "About John Jakes." Accessed January 14, 2013.

Journal of the American Medical Association. "JAMA Home." Accessed January 11, 2013. http://jama.ama-assn.org/.

J.P. Morgan. "History." Accessed January 11, 2013.

K

Kaplowitz, Paul B. "Precocious Puberty: Making the distinction between common normal variants and more serious problems." *Contemporary Pediatrics* 23, no. 8 (2006): 55–58, 61.

Kirchmeyer, Frederick J., and Marjorie B. Moore. Bisulphite Derivatives of Z-Methyl. US Patent 2,367,302, filed March 25, 1940, and issued January 16, 1945.

Klumpp, Theodore G. "Penicillin and Streptomycin." *American Journal of Public Health* 36, no. 7 (July 1946): 711.

Bibliography

Knowles, Francine. "Abbott plays its hand." *Chicago Sun-Times*, August 12, 2002.

Knowles, Francine. "Largest child care center in state opens at Abbott." *Chicago Sun-Times*, June 15, 2001.

L

LaFee, Scott. "Infants who might have once died from respiratory syncytial virus now survive, thanks to a breakthrough vaccine and Jessie Groothuis." *The San Diego Union-Tribune*, June 1, 2005.

Lake County Forest Preserves. "Raven Glen Forest Preserve." Accessed January 15, 2013.

Lanker, Brian, and Nicole Newnham. *They Drew Fire: Combat Artists of World War II*. New York: TV Books, 2000.

"Lanwermeyer Plans Busy Leisure Time." *News-Sun*, December 11, 1959.

Lawrence Livermore National Laboratory. "History." Accessed January 11, 2013.

Lee, Captain Walter E. "The Treatment of Infection and Infected Wounds with the Chlorine Antiseptics." *North Carolina Medical Society Journal* (April 1918): 311–12.

Lee, James A. "Planning Equipment and Layout in a Fine Chemical Plant." *Chemical and Metallurgical Engineering* 36, no. 3 (March 1929): 132–136.

Leech, Paul Nicholas, Ph.D., William Rabak, Ph.G., Sc.B., A. H. Clark, Ph.G., Sc.B. "American-Made Synthetic Drugs—II." *Journal of the American Medical Association* 73, no. 10 (1919): 754–59.

Li, Jie Jack. *Laughing Gas, Viagra, and Lipitor: the human stories behind the drugs we use*. Oxford: Oxford University Press, 2006.

"List of Exhibitors." *Journal of the American Medical Association* LXVIII, no. 18 (1917): 1375.

"List Securities up on Chicago Stock Exchange." *Chicago Daily Tribune*, March 21, 1929.

"Lithium effective against suicides, researchers say." *Houston Chronicle*, September 21, 2003.

"Loose Leaf Ledgers and Improved Binders for Bankers' Use." *The Bankers Magazine*, 1905.

Lowes Hotels. "Don CeSar Beach Hotel." Accessed January 15, 2013.

Lucas, Sarah. "The Philly Killer: 1976's Legionnaires' Disease." Accessed January 15, 2013.

M

MacLellan Kirsty, Colin Loney, R. Paul Yeo, and David Bhella. "The 24-Angstrom Structure of Respiratory Syncytial Virus Nucleocapsid Protein-RNA Decameric Rings." *Journal of Virology* 81, no. 17 (September 2007): 9519–24, doi: 10.1128/JVI.00526–07.

Mahoney, Tom. *The Merchants of Life; An Account of the American Pharmacutical Industry*. New York: Harper, 1959.

Marvin, Dr. C.F. "Service of the Weather Bureau to Aviation." *Science* (December 1928): 561. doi: 10.1126/science.68.1771.561.

Matson, Edward J. "Selenium Sulfide as an Antidandruff Agent." *Journal of Cosmetic Science* 7, no. 5 (1956): 459–466.

Mayo Clinic. "Mayo Clinic History." Accessed January 11, 2013.

McKee, E. S. "Pilula Laxativa Composita." *The Columbus Medical Journal* 30 (May 1906): 213.

"Medicare Helps Push Drug Spending Up; With New Benefit, Prescription Purchases Increased in 2006, Study Shows." *The Washington Post*, January 8, 2008.

"Medicine and the War." *Journal of the American Medical Association* 126, no. 3 (1944): 175–177. doi: 10.1001/jama.1944.02850380037016.

"Men of Medicine Meet In Chicago." *Chicago Daily Tribune*, May 30, 1908.

"Merger of M&R Dietetic Laboratories, Inc. and Abbott Laboratories." *Journal of Dairy Science* 47, no. 4 (1964): 18.

Microsoft Corporation. "Digital Equipment Corporation Nineteen Fifty-Seven to the Present." Accessed January 11, 2013.

"Midwest Stock Exchange." *Chicago Tribune*, December 31, 1963.

"Miles White of Abbott Laboratories: On the Mend." *Institutional Investor*, March 14, 2005.

"Miscellany." *Journal of the American Medical Association* L, no. 11 (1908): 894–900.

"M.J. Romansky, 95; Modified Penicillin." *The New York Times*, August 17, 2006.

Monterey Institute of International Studies. "David A. Jones Profile." Accessed January 14, 2013.

"Movements of Mining Men." *Mining American*, July to December, 1905.

"M&R Dietetic Votes Merger with Abbott." *Chicago Tribune*, February 18, 1964.

N

NASA Technical Report Server. "Feasibility of Commercial Space Engineering: Production of Pharmaceuticals." Last modified November 9, 1978.

National Aeronautics and Space Administration. "The Flight of Apollo-Soyuz." Last modified October 22, 2004."

National Archives. "Executive Order 12564 — Drug-free Federal workplace." Last modified September 16, 1986.

National Cancer Institute. "Prostate-Specific Antigen (PSA) Test." Last modified July 24, 2012.

National Center for Biotechnology Information. "Endocarditis." Last modified July 16, 2012.

National Institute of Standards and Technology. "Radionuclide Half-Life Measurements." Last modified October 5, 2010.

National Institutes of Health, "Dr. Carole Heilman Named Director of NIAID's Division of Microbiology and Infectious Diseases," news release, July 26, 1999.

National Institutes of Health Office of Technology Transfer, "Synagis: Helping Infants and Parents Breathe Easier: A Case Study," Website of the National Institutes of Health.

National Science Foundation. "National Science Board, Staff, Committees, and Advisory Panels." Accessed January 14, 2013.

"New Research Building Marks Abbott's 50th Anniversary." *The Meyer Druggist* 61, no. 10 (October 1938): 18–38.

"New York Session: American Medical Association, Sixty-Eighth Annual Session, New York City, June 4–8, 1917." *Journal of the American Medical Association* LXVIII, no. 18 (May 1917): 1354.

"New Study in Journal of Urology Shows UroVysion(TM) DNA Test Superior to Standard Cytology In Diagnosing Bladder Cancer In At-Risk Patients." *Medical News Today*, July 21, 2006.

"News & Notes." *California Medicine* 97, no. 3 (September 1962): 197–98.

The New York Times. "Michael Sveda, the Inventor Of Cyclamates, Dies at 87." Last modified August 21, 1999.

Nichols, Jeannette Paddock, and Roy Franklin Nichols. *The Growth of American Democracy*. New York; London: D. Appleton-Century, Co. 1939.

Nobelprize.org. "David Baltimore-Autobiography." Accessed January 14, 2013.

Nobelprize.org. "The Nobel Prize and the Discovery of Vitamins." Accessed January 14, 2013.

Nobelprize.org. "The Nobel Prize in Physics 1939: Ernest Lawrence." Accessed January 14, 2013.

Nobelprize.org. "The Nobel Prize in Physiology or Medicine 1998." Accessed January 14, 2013.

Northwestern University. "Abbott Hall." Accessed January 14, 2013.

"Note by the Publishers." *The Medical Standard* 23 (January 1900): 6.

"Now-An Atomic Drugstore." *Collier's Weekly*, January 21, 1955.

"Obituaries-Stiles." *The News-Sun*, September 19, 1984.

"Obituary." *Chicago Sun-Times*, September 1, 1960.

"Obituary-Alfred S. Burdick, M.D." *International Journal of Medicine and Surgery* 46 (March 1933): 145.

"Obituary: James LeVoy Sorenson." *Deseret News*, Tuesday, January 22, 2008.

Ody, Elizabeth. "Unrecognized Potential at Abbott Labs." *The Kiplinger Washington*, August 7, 2008.

Office of Inspector General, "The Orphan Drug Act Implementation and Impact." Website of the Department of Health and Human Services.

Official Jack Dempsey Website. "Biography," Accessed January 11, 2013.

Ohio History Central. "American Steel and Wire Company." Accessed January 14, 2013.

Ohio History Central. "M & R Dietetic Laboratories." Last modified July 1, 2005.

"Organization Section." *Journal of the American Medical Association* 138, no. 4 (1948): 299–300.

PBS. "A Detailed Timeline of the Healthcare Debate portrayed in 'The System': Events leading up to Clinton's Healthcare Address to Congress." Accessed January 14, 2013.

PBS. "Mexican Revolution and Immigration." Accessed January 14, 2013.

PBS. "The Army Art Program." Accessed January 14, 2013.

PBS. "Worldwide Flu Pandemic Strikes: 1918–1919." Accessed January 14, 2013.

PBS. "WWI Timeline: 1914." Accessed January 14, 2013.

"Pentothal Used at Mayo for 50 Years." *The Mayo Alumnus* 22, no. 4 (Winter 1986): 37.

PerkinElmer Inc. "History." Accessed January 11, 2013.

"The Personal Attacks upon Dr. Simmons." *Texas State Journal of Medicine* 5, no. 2 (June 1909): 45–46.

Pfeiffer, Naomi. "Lipid-lowering drug tames soaring triglyceride levels." *Drug Topics* 142, no. 6 (March 1998): 28.

"Pharmacology." *Journal of the American Medical Association* LI, no. 20 (1908): 1710–13.

PhRMA. "About PhRMA." Accessed January 14, 2013.

PhRMA. "Drug Development Costs Have Increased." Accessed January 15, 2013.

Piott, Steven, and Ballard Campbell. "American Reformers, 1870–1920: Progressives in Word and Deed." *The Historian* 70 (Summer 2008): 344–46.

"Post History." Accessed January 14, 2013.

Postom Company, Inc. *This Journey Through the Pure Food Factories That Make Postum and Grape-Nuts Takes You Up-Stairs, Down-Stairs and All Over the Place: There is Considerable to See, and "There's a Reason."* Battle Creek, Michigan: The Company, 1906.

PR Newswire. "Abbott Laboratories and Artus Introduce Automated Diagnostic Tests for SARS and Other Infectious Diseases." Last modified October 28, 2003.

PR Newswire. "Abbott Laboratories Enters Agreement with Artus GmbH for SARS Diagnostic Test." Last modified May 15, 2003.

Bibliography

PR Newswire. "Dow Jones Sustainability Index Again Recognizes Abbott for Continued Leadership in Business, Environmental and Social Performance." Last modified September 14, 2007.

"Promotions at Abbott Listed." *News-Sun*, May 17, 1947.

Pruyser, Paul W. "Psychological Testing In Epilepsy: II. Personality". *Epilepsia* B1, no. 1 (February 1937): 23–36.

"Pulse: The Medical Student Section of JAMA." *Journal of the American Medical Association* 271, no. 5 (February 1994): 397–403.

R

Rabbitts, Jennifer A., Douglas R. Bacon, Gregory A. Nuttall, and S. Breanndan Moore. "Mayo Clinic and the Origins of Blood Banking," *Mayo Clinic Proceedings* 89, no. 9 (September 2007): p. 1117–18.

Raber, Linda. "1946: Roger Adams (1889–1971)." *Chemical and Engineering News* 86, no. 14 (April 2008): 55–67, doi: 10.1021/cen-v086n014.p055.

"Report to the Nation's Doctors on a 'Big Pill Bill to Swallow'." *Life Magazine*, March 21, 1960.

RICE University. "Principles of Spectrophotometry." Last modified August 10, 2012. s/methods/protein/spectrophotometer.html.

Riley, Robert W. "A Century of Editors." *Journal of the American Medical Association* 250, no. 2 (1983): 230–35.

Ringler, Ira. "RPhs Help Patients Self-Administer Injectable Prostate Cancer Drug." *American Druggist* 192 (July 1985): 39.

"Roger Adams, dean of U.S. chemists, 1889–1971." *Chemical and Engineering News* 49, no. 28 (July 12): 9, doi: 10.1021/cen-v049n028.p009.

"Roger Adams." *The Detroit Chemist* 5, no. 2 (February 1933): 3–4.

Rogers, Michael, Patricia Sellers, H. John Steinbreder, Daniel P. Wiener, and Ford S. Worthy. "War on Drugs." *Fortune Magazine*, September 29, 1986.

Romansky, Monroe J., Charles W. Foulke, Ray A. Olsson, and J. Robert Holmes. "Ristocetin in Bacterial Endocarditis: An Evaluation of Short-Term Therapy." *Arch Intern Med.* 107, no. 41 (1961): 480–493.

Romansky, Monroe J., Robert J. Murphy, and George E. Rittman. "Single Injection Treatment of Gonorrhea with Penicillin in Beeswax-Peanut Oil: Results in 175 Cases." *Journal of the American Medical Association* 128, no. 6 (1945): 404–407. doi: 10.1001/jama.1945.02860230008002.

Romer, Christina D. "The Hope That Flows From History." *New York Times*, August 13, 2011.

Roosevelt, Theodore. *Theodore Roosevelt: An Autobiography.* New York: Charles Scribner's Sons, 1913.

S

"S. De Witt Clough: He Personifies Enlightened Leadership." *The Drug and Cosmetic Industry* 58, no. 1 (January 1946): 43.

Santoli, Michael. "Kudos to You." *Barron's*, February 16, 2009.

Saxon, Wolfgang. "Ernest Volwiler, 99, Medicinal Chemistry Leader." *The New York Times*. Accessed January 11, 2013.

Schmahl, D. "Fehlen einer kanzerogenen Wirkung von Cyclamat, Cyclohexylamin und Saccharin bei Ratten." *Arzneimittelforschung* 23, no. 10 (1973): 1466–70.

Schmidt-Nielsen, Signe and Sigval Schmidt-Nielsen. "Some Liver Oils Yielding a Strong Colour Reaction with Antimony Trichloride." *Biochemistry Journal* 23, no. 6 (1929): 1153–57.

Sham, H. "ABT-378, a highly potent inhibitor of the human immunodeficiency virus protease." *Antimicrobial Agents and Chemotherapy* 42, no. 12 (December 1998): 3218–24.

Shelling, D.H., and K.B. Hopper. "Calcium and Phosphorus Studies." *Bulletin of the John Hopkins Hospital* 58 (1936): 137.

Shook, Robert. *Miracle Medicines: Seven Lifesaving Drugs and the People Who Created Them.* New York: Portfolio, 2007.

Simmons, George H. "Reply of Dr. Simmons to Charges Preferred Against Him in the Chicago Medical Society." *Texas State Journal of Medicine* 5, no. 3 (July 1909): 130–131.

"Sixteen Years at the University of Illinois." Accessed January 14, 2013.

Smithsonian Institute. "Smithsonian Institution Archives: Science Service Records." Accessed January 14, 2013.

Soumerai, Stephen B., Dennis Ross-Degnan, Eric E. Fortess, and Bryan L. Walser. "Determinants of Change in Medicaid Pharmaceutical Cost Sharing: Does Evidence Affect Policy?" *The Milbank Quarterly* 75, no. 1 (1997): 11–34, doi: 10.1111/1468–0009.00043.

Standard & Poor's. "A History of Standard & Poor's." Accessed January 14, 2013.

Stieglitz, Julius. "Procain and Novacain Identical." *Journal of the American Medical Association* 70, no. 25 (June 1918): 1969.

"Study Indicates Abbott epilepsy drug can ease effects of manic depression." *The Wall Street Journal*, March 23, 1994.

Summers, S. Lewis, T. H. Carmichael, Henry Beates, Walter R. Rentschler, and John A. Sherger. *Rheumatism, Uratic Deposits, & Arthritis and an Effective Remedy.* Ambler, Penn: Dr. S. Lewis Summers, 1926.

Swann, Patrick. *Academic Scientists and the Pharmaceutical Industry: Cooperative Research in Twentieth-Century America.* Baltimore: Johns Hopkins University Press, 1988

T

"Takeda Abbott Pharmaceuticals (TAP) in 2002." *Duke School of Business*, November 2003.

Takeda. "History: 1985–1999." Accessed January 11, 2013.

"Tengwall Co." *The Trow Directory* 54 (March 1906): 713.

Tengwall Talk. "Are You a Back Number?" *Practical Druggist and Pharmaceutical Review of Reviews* 14 (October 1903): 151.

Together RX Access, LLC. "Member Companies." Accessed January 14, 2013.

Tolman, Richard C., and Elmer B. Vliet. "A Tyndallmeter for the Examination of Disperse Systems." *The Journal of the American Chemical Society* 41, no. 3 (March 1919): 297–300.

"Transcription of Interview with Edward J. Ledder and Nick Poulos." *Chicago Tribune*, January 11, 1973.

"'Twas Nice Robbery; Not a Thing Missing." *Chicago Daily News*, June 13, 1927.

"Two Safes are Blown by Gunmen." *The Waukegan Daily News*, June 13, 1927.

"Two's Company." *Financial Times*, July 7, 1995.

U

United States Patent and Trademark Office. "Patent Number: US002039345." Accessed January 14, 2013.

University of Connecticut. "The Economic Impact of Prevention." Accessed January 14, 2013.

"University of Illinois Annual Register: 1911–1912." Accessed January 14, 2013.

University of Illinois. "Roger Adams: An Inventory of the Papers of Roger Adams at the University of Illinois Archives." Accessed January 14, 2013.

University of Illinois. "The Department of Chemistry at the University of Illinois: The Roger Adams Fund." Accessed January 14, 2013.

University of Miami. "Dr. E. M. Papper." Accessed January 15, 2013.

University of Minnesota. "Cyclohexylsulfamate Pathway Map." Last modified March 16, 2012.

University of Wisconsin Board of Regents Collection. "Minutes of the Meeting of the Executive Committee of the Board of Regents of the University of Wisconsin: October 7, 1935." Accessed January 14, 2013.

University of Wisconsin. "Harry Steenbock." Last modified September 7, 2011.

United States Nuclear Regulatory Commission. "Atomic Energy Commission." Last modified December 10, 2012.

University of Wisconsin, Madison. "Chancellors and Presidents of the University of Wisconsin-Madison." Last modified February 21, 2011.

USDA. "Additives in Meat and Poultry Products." Last modified November 2008.

U.S. Department of Defense. "Pentagon History." Last modified December 14, 2012.

U.S. Department of Health & Human Services. "What Is a Stent?" Last modified November 8, 2011.

U.S. Department of State Office of the Historian. "OPEC Oil Embargo, 1973–1974." Accessed January 14, 2013.

U.S. Food and Drug Administration. "FDA Approval of New Formulation of Kaletra." Last modified March 27, 2009.

U.S. Food and Drug Administration. "FDA's Approval of the First Oral Contraceptive, Enovid." Last modified April 15, 2009.

U.S. Food and Drug Administration. "History." Last modified July 29, 2010.

U.S. Food and Drug Administration. "Results for Orphan Drug Product Designations Search." Accessed January 14, 2013.

U.S. Food and Drug Administration. "Significant Dates in U.S. Food and Drug Law History." Last modified November 6, 2012.

U.S. National Library of Medicine. "Photograph: Major General Norman T. Kirk, the Surgeon General, at Rear Echelon Headquarters, USASOS U.S. Army Signal Corps." Accessed January 14, 2013.

V

"Vincent, 40, Resigns His Abbott Labs Post." *The Wall Street Journal*, July 22, 1980.

"Vincent resigns post at Abbott." *Chicago Tribune*, July 22, 1980.

Vliet, Elmer. "Brief History of Abbott Laboratories." *American Chemical Industry* 6 (1949): 8.

W

Walters, C. A., M.D. "Enlarged Prostate." *The Medical World* VII (May 1889): 244.

White, James Terry, ed. "Abbott, Wallace Calvin." *National Cyclopedia of American Biography*. New York: The J. T. White Company, 1967.

White, James Terry, ed. "Ravenscroft, Edward Hawks." *National Cyclopedia of American Biography*. New York: The J. T. White Company, 1951.

Wilde, Arthur Herbert. *Northwestern University History: 1855–1905*. New York: The University Pub. Co., 1905.

Willette, Robert E. "Drug Testing Programs." *NIDA Research Monograph* 73 (1986): 6.

Wisconsin Alumni Research Foundation. "Steenbock and WARF's Founding." Accessed January 14, 2013.

Z

Zimmer, Inc. "Zimmer Holdings, Inc. Announces Agreement to Acquire Abbott Spine, an Innovator in Spinal Technology." Last modified September 4, 2008.

Index

Index

Continued

Index

Continued

Index

Continued

Index

Continued

Credits

Abbott
All photographs are from the archives of Abbott.

1888–1900
A Hustling Start to a Grand Medical Enterprise
6 Reproduced from *The Academy Student*, St. Johnsbury Academy (St. Johnsbury, VT, 1882), cover.

1900–1910
Overcoming Early Challenges
32 Copyright © 1907 American Medical Association. All rights reserved; **33** Reproduced by permission from Collier's Magazine, *"Death's Laboratory," Colliers: The National Weekly* (New York: P.F. Collier & Son Company, 1905), cover; **34** Reproduced from *"Doctors' War Grows Bitter,"* Chicago Daily Tribune (Chicago, 1909), 5.

1920–1930
Soaring Growth in the Roaring Twenties
77 The Manufacture of Synthetic Medicinal Chemicals in America, by Alfred Burdick. Copyright © 1922 Journal of the American Pharmaceutical Association. Reproduced with permission of John Wiley & Sons, Inc.; **79** Reproduced from *"New Drug Lured Chicago Gunmen,"* New York Sun (New York, 1927); **83, 84, 85** Reproduced by permission from James Lee, *"Planning Equipment," Chemical and Metallurgical Engineering* (New York: McGraw-Hill Company Inc., 1929), 132–136.

1930–1940
Growing Through the Great Depression
95 Reprinted with permission from E.H. Volwiler et al. "5,5-Substituted Barbituric Acids." Journal of the American Chemical Society 52 (1930): 1676–1679. Copyright 1930 American Chemical Society; **110** © Bowness, Hepworth Estate; © Estate of Raphael Soyer, courtesy of Forum Gallery, New York, NY; **111** Reproduction, including downloading of Basaldella works, is prohibited by copyright laws and international conventions without the express written permission of Artists Rights Society (ARS), New York; **120** From TIME, October 31 © 1949 Time Inc. Used under license. TIME and Time Inc. are not affiliated with, and do not endorse products or services of, Licensee.

1940–1950
Meeting the Challenges of World War II and the World it Made
133, 134 Reproduced by permission from Brian Lanker Archives; **144** Image used with permission of the American Chemical Society; **156** Reproduced from *They Drew Fire* (New York, 2000), 153.

1950–1960
Abbott in the Age of Atoms and Antibiotics
189 Reprinted by Permission of Forbes Media LLC © 2012.

1960–1970
From Good to Great
203 Reproduced by permission from Jim Collins, *From Good to Great* (New York: HarperCollins Publishers Inc., 2001), cover; **206** © 2012 The Associated Press; **206** Copyright 1960. The Picture Collection Inc. used with Permission. All rights reserved; **211** From Chicago Tribune, June 14 © 1963 Chicago Tribune. All rights reserved. Used by permission and protected by the Copyright Laws of the United States. The printing copying redistribution, or retransmission of this Content without express written permission is prohibited; **211** Reproduced by permission from Wright's Media, *"Enzyme May Yield Virus Clue," Medical World News* (Maxwell M. Geffen, 1964), 41; **217** Reproduced from *S.S. Boston Floating Hospital Postcard,* The Leighton & Valentine Co. (New York, 1918). **236** Image courtesy of Chemical and Engineering News.

1970–1980
Challenge and Response
238 © Rocky Mount Telegram; **242** From TIME, August 16 © 1976 Time Inc. Used under license. TIME and Time Inc. are not affiliated with, and do not endorse products or services of, Licensee; **242** Reproduced by permission from Wright's Media, *"'Killer Bug That Puzzled Scientists," U.S. News and World Report* (U.S. News and World Report Licensing, 1976), cover; **244** Reproduced by permission from Copyright Clearance Center, *"Girl, 6, Has Rare Epilepsy,"* The Columbus Dispatch (CCC Republication, 1977).

1980–1990
Reaching New Scientific and Commercial Heights
263 From Chicago Tribune, March 4 © 1985 Chicago Tribune. All rights reserved. Used by permission and protected by the Copyright Laws of the United States. The printing copying redistribution, or retransmission of this Content without express written permission is prohibited.

1990–2000
Steady Growth Through a Turbulent Time
288 From The Washington Post, © May 18, 1997 The Washington Post. All Rights Reserved. Used by permission and protected by the Copyright Laws of the United States. The printing, copying, redistribution, or retransmission of the Material without express written permission is prohibited; **289** Reproduced by permission from The Galien Foundation, *Prix Galien Award* (1999); **297** From Chicago Tribune, June 3 © 1994 Chicago Tribune. All rights reserved. Used by permission and protected by the Copyright Laws of the United States. The printing copying, redistribution, or retransmission of this Content without express written permission is prohibited.

2000–2013
Transforming Abbott for a New Century
314 From TIME, December 30 © 1996 Time Inc. Used under license. TIME and Time Inc. are not affiliated with, and do not endorse products or services of, Licensee; **315** Reproduced by permission from Robert L. Shook, *Miracle Medicines: Seven Lifesaving Drugs and the People Who Created Them* (New York: Portfolio, 2007), cover; **318** Reproduced by permission by The Deal Magazine, *Guidant Deal Caricature, The Deal* (New York: The Deal LLC., 2006); **322** Reproduced by permission from The Galien Foundation, *Prix Galien Award* (2007); **333** From Chicago Tribune, April 25 © 2003 Chicago Tribune. All rights reserved. Used by permission and protected by the Copyright Laws of the United States. The printing copying redistribution, or retransmission of this Content without express written permission is prohibited; **339** From Working Mother, October © 2002 Working Mother. All rights reserved. Used by permission and protected by the Copyright Laws of the United States. The printing, copying, redistribution, or retransmission of this Content without express written permission is prohibited; **339** Reproduced by permission from Working Mother Media, *WorkLife Congress Photograph* (New York: Bonnier Corporation, 2009); **344** From Fortune Magazine, June 28 © 2004 Time Inc. Used Under License. Fortune Magazine and Time Inc. are not affiliated with, and do not endorse products or services of, Licensee; **344** Reproduced by permission from DiversityInc., *Top 50 Companies for Diversity Logo* (Princeton, NJ: DiversityInc., 2010); **344** Reproduced by permission from Great Place to Work Institute, 2011 *Great Place to Work, Best Multinational Workplaces Europe Logo* (2011); **344** Reproduced by permission from LabX Media Group, 2012 *Best Place to Work: Industry Logo, The Scientist* (New York: LabX Media, 2012); **344** Reproduced by permission from Profiles in Diversity Journal, *"Stairway to Success," Profiles in Diversity Journal* (Cleveland, OH: Profiles in Diversity Journal, 2002), cover; **344** Reproduced with permission from SAM Indexes, *2011/2012 Dow Jones Sustainability Indexes Logo* (Zurich, Switzerland: Sam Indexes, 2011); **344** Reproduced by permission from Profiles in Diversity Journal, *"Stairway to Success," Profiles in Diversity Journal* (Cleveland, OH: Profiles in Diversity Journal, 2002), cover; **345** From Fortune Magazine, March 22 © 2010 Time Inc. Used Under License. Fortune Magazine and Time Inc. are not affiliated with, and do not endorse products or services of, Licensee; **345** Reprinted with permission of Barron's, Copyright © 2009 Dow Jones & Company, Inc. All Rights Reserved Worldwide.

Acknowledgements

Abbott's history is both long and full; the process of capturing its story was as well. Many people contributed to the making of this book. Abbott extends its thanks to all those whose skills, recollections and personal archives made this volume, and all our efforts to preserve our company's history, possible. We would particularly like to thank several people whose efforts over a number of years brought this book to life: Sheryl Ault, Joe Daab, Jenna Daugherty, Don Emery, Brock Haldeman, Michael Leland, Rachel Lewandowski, Marija Markovic, Patrick Maxton, David H. McDonald, Ed Moser, Pat Newell, JoAnna Roman, Jennifer Searcy, Emily Simkin, and Bruce Weindruch.

And, of course, the thousands of Abbott people, around the world, whose constant commitment to our mission made the history captured in these pages.

A Promise For Life: The Story of Abbott was produced using sustainable printing techniques and materials.

The paper used for this book was made using an Elemental Chlorine Free Process.

This entire book and carton was printed using soy based inks.

This entire book and carton can be recycled.